Arms and Foreign Policy in the Nuclear Age

Arms
and Foreign Policy
in the Nuclear Age

edited by **MILTON L. RAKOVE**

for the American Foundation for Continuing Education

New York
OXFORD UNIVERSITY PRESS
London   1972   Toronto

For Jack, Helen, and Roberta

Foreword

One of the basic obstacles which stands in the way of a theoretical understanding of international relations is the fact that the empirical raw material is composed of what is perennial in the nature of international relations and what is novel. Each historic event is in one sense unique, having appeared in this particular configuration never before and not likely to appear again. Yet in another sense, that historic event is a typical emanation of human nature which will reveal itself under similar conditions in a similar way. How does what is novel impinge upon what is perennial and vice versa? How to do justice to the perennial and the novel, the unique and the typical alike is the never-ending and always hazardous task of political understanding.

The burden of that task has been dramatically increased by the availability of nuclear weapons as instruments of foreign policy. The availability of nuclear weapons, together with the other technological revolutions of transportation and communications, has ushered in a novel period of history, as distinct from the age that preceded it as the Middle Ages have been from antiquity, and the Modern Age has been from the Middle Ages.

iii

In discharging the intellectual task of integrating the novelty of the Nuclear Age into our political understanding we have gone from one extreme to the other. On the one hand, we have tended to minimize that novelty and have attempted to assimilate the novel technological facts to our conventional political categories. Instead, we should have created new political categories commensurate with the novelty of the empirical facts. On the other hand, we have tended to go to the other extreme by assuming that the political experience of the ages and the political categories and principles derived therefrom are altogether no longer relevant to our contemporary problems and must be replaced by entirely new categories and principles. More particularly, in view of the vast uncertainties with which all politics, and especially contemporary politics, confronts the observer and actor, many of us have endeavored to seek refuge in the deceptive appearance of certainty which a quantitative approach to foreign policy provides.

It is the great merit of the collection of readings, which Professor Rakove has put together that it gives us a comprehensive and systematic view of the different positions that have been taken in regard to international relations throughout history and in modern times. The reader is not drawn into a particular school of thought, and no particular position is suggested to him. Rather, he is acquainted with all the basic positions that have been taken throughout history. In consequence, he is forced to think for himself, which is the first and most important step in the educational enterprise.

New York
September 1971

HANS J. MORGENTHAU

The AFCE is a not-for-profit educational organization, currently based at Syracuse University, devoted to the development of reading material in many fields. We should be happy to have your comments and criticism on *Arms and Foreign Policy in the Nuclear Age*, as such evaluations will help determine the direction of public policy programs adopted by our Board of Directors and staff.

ALEXANDER N. CHARTERS,
President, AFCE

Address all correspondence to:
Mrs. Doris S. Chertow, Editor
American Foundation for Continuing Education
105 Roney Lane
Syracuse, New York 13210

Contents

INTRODUCTION

The Blowing Up
of the Parthenon

SALVADOR DE MADARIAGA

ON SEPTEMBER 26, 1687, A VENETIAN BOMB, FALLING ON A TURKISH POWDER MAGAZINE, BLEW THE PARTHENON TO PIECES. Men had risen to that height where such beauty is conceived and brought forth. Men had fallen to that depth where such beauty is destroyed. But while the building of the Parthenon was thought out and willed, its destruction was neither willed nor thought out. It just happened. The first was an act of man; the second just a fact of social nature.

Our civilization is for a considerable part a willed and thought-out creation of man. Under this vast and, on the whole, beautiful Parthenon, which men have erected through the ages, a powder magazine of atomic and hydrogen bombs is being stored. Any day, the dreaded explosion may be touched off. No one will have willed it. And the long chain of human acts which we call history will end and be destroyed by a mere fact that will just happen.

From *The Blowing Up of the Parthenon*. Reprinted by permission of Frederick A. Praeger, New York.

How can we prevent this disaster? Let us keep in mind the fundamental difference between the chain of acts which we call history and that fact we dread that might be their destroyer. How can we tell an act from a fact? In this; that for a fact to be an act it must first have been an idea. If a thing just happens it is only a fact; if it takes place because it was willed and thought out it is an act. Morosini did not mean to blow the Parthenon to pieces; nor did the Turks who had hidden their powder magazine there mean the Parthenon to be blown to pieces. The thing just happened as a combination of incoherent circumstances and thoughtless or not well thought out action pointing in different directions. And any day the dreaded explosion of our world-wide Parthenon may happen in the same not thought-out, unwilled way.

The liberal world is drifting blindly, as it is always bound to do under an empirical leadership. When its material solidarity has already become a byword and a commonplace, its leaders, far from sounding loud the call to that moral solidarity which is its only salvation, remain fondly attached to the rule of thumb of Palmerston. This cynical gentleman's dictum "we have no friends; we only have interests" is quoted with praise in Great Britain, and may be considered as the quintessence of American policy if we are to believe one of its brilliant exponents, Mr. George Kennan.

Hence that empty call to union so often repeated on both sides of the English speaking world: "Let us unite." As if union were a policy. Men do not unite just in order to unite, and calls to union are idle. Men unite in the process of and as a means to achieving something. "Let us have dinner"; "let us climb the Jungfrau"; "let us set up a Bank"; "let us go hunting big game"—these are calls to common action which will incidentally bring about the union of the men concerned for the time the common action lasts. But "let us unite" will never bring about any union, for union in itself is no aim.

It is this aimlessness of the liberal world that is so frightening, for it brings to the situation that incoherence, that mesh of unwilled and unthought-out purposes from which such a disaster as the blowing up of the Parthenon can easily spring. If all that the West is thinking of is self-defence, then we are the more exposed to the knot of unfortunate circumstances which under a sudden fear may release the dreaded explosion. Don't we know the phrase that covers it? "Attack is the best defence." And the destruction of our World Parthenon will follow.

The situation, nevertheless, is quite simple. The progress of science has made the world one in its material and even in its moral life. All it lacked was a due awareness of this oneness. The invention of the atomic and hydrogen bombs has now deepened this oneness by threatening the world with oneness in death. The time has come therefore to handle world affairs with a due sense of their oneness. The Soviet Union leaders see this. Unfortunately, they are dogmatically blind as to how to get there; so that, though they are right in wanting to lead the world as one, they are wrong to lead it towards hell. But the Anglo-Saxon leaders of the West do not see it at all. They still react towards the world as if it were a pack of foreigners who will never have the sense or the power to be English or American, as the case may be. These foreigners must, of course, be given advice, money, technical assistance; they must be helped to their feet, encouraged and talked to nicely; everything but admitted to an equal status in a truly co-operative organization of the world. For that, the Anglo-Saxon leaders are not yet ready. They still trot on, riding Palmerston's blind mare, until some day she puts her foot on the hydrogen bomb switch, and then perhaps they will wake up, too late, and quote Shake speare:

Oh, Iago, the pity of it!

I THE NATURE OF
INTERNATIONAL POLITICS

The Nature of Politics

EDWARD H. CARR

MAN HAS ALWAYS LIVED IN GROUPS. The smallest kind of human group, the family, has clearly been necessary for the maintenance of the species. But so far as is known, men have always from the most primitive times formed semi-permanent groups larger than the single family; and one of the functions of such a group has been to regulate relations between its members. Politics deals with the behavior of men in such organised permanent or semi-permanent groups. All attempts to deduce the nature of society from the supposed behavior of man in isolation are purely theoretical, since there is no reason to assume that such a man ever existed. Aristotle laid the foundation of all sound thinking about politics when he declared that man was by nature a political animal.

Man in society reacts to his fellow men in two opposite ways. Sometimes he displays egoism, or the will to assert himself at the expense of others. At other times he displays sociability, or the desire to co-operate with others, to enter into reciprocal relations of goodwill and friendship with them, and even to subordinate himself to them. In every society, these two qualities can be seen at work. No society can exist unless a substantial proportion of its members exhibits in some degree the desire for co-operation and mutual goodwill. But in every society some sanction is required to produce the measure of solidarity requisite for its maintenance; and this sanction is applied by a controlling group or individual acting in the name of the society. Membership of most societies is voluntary, and the only ultimate sanction which can be applied is expulsion. But the peculiarity of political society, which in the modern world takes the form of the state, is that membership is compulsory. The state, like other societies, must be based on some sense of common interests and obligations among its members. But coercion is regularly exercised by a governing group to enforce loyalty and obedience; and this coercion inevitably means that the governors control the governed and "exploit" them for their own purposes.

The dual character of political society is therefore strongly marked. Professor Laski tells us that "every state is built upon the consciences of men." On the other hand, anthropology, as well as much recent history, teaches that "war seems to be the main agency in producing the state"; and Professor Laski himself, in another passage, declares that "our civilisation is held together by fear rather than by good-will." There is no contradiction between these apparently opposite views. When Tom Paine, in the *Rights of Man*, tries to confront Burke with the dilemma that "governments arise either *out* of the people or *over* the people," the answer is that they do both. Coercion and conscience, enmity and good-will, self-assertion and self-subordination, are present in every political society. The state is built up out of these two conflicting aspects of human nature. Utopia and reality, the ideal and the institution, morality and power, are from the outset inextricably blended in it. In the making of the United States, as a modern American writer has said, "Hamilton stood for strength, wealth and power, Jefferson for the American dream"; and both the power and the dream were necessary ingredients.

If this be correct, we can draw one important conclusion. The utopian who dreams that it is possible to eliminate self-assertion from politics and to base a political system on morality alone is just as wide of the mark as the realist who believes that altruism is an illusion and that all political action is based on self-seeking. These errors have both left their mark on popular terminology. The phrase "power politics" is often used in an invidious sense, as if the element of power or self-assertion in politics were something abnormal and susceptible of elimination from a healthy political life. Conversely, there is a disposition, even among some writers who are not strictly speaking realists, to treat politics as the science of power and self-assertion and exclude from it by definition actions inspired by the moral consciousness. Professor Catlin describes the *homo politicus* as one who "seeks to bring into conformity with his own will the wills of others, so that he may the better attain his own ends." Such terminological implications are misleading. Politics cannot be divorced from power. But the *homo politicus* who pursues nothing but power is as unreal a myth as the *homo economicus* who pursues nothing but gain. Political action must be based on a co-ordination of morality and power.

This truth is of practical as well as theoretical importance. It is as fatal in politics to ignore power as it is to ignore morality. The fate of China in the nineteenth century is an illustration of what happens to a country which is content to believe in the moral superiority of its own civilisation and to despise the ways of power. The Liberal Government of Great Britain nearly came to grief in the spring of 1914 because it sought to pursue an Irish policy based on moral authority unsupported (or rather, directly opposed) by effective military power. In Germany, the Frankfort Assembly of 1848 is the classic example of the impotence of ideas divorced from power; and the Weimar Republic broke down because many of the policies it pursued—in fact, nearly all of them except its opposition to the communists—were unsupported, or actively opposed, by effective military power. The utopian, who believes that democracy is not based on force, refuses to look these unwelcome facts in the face.

On the other hand, the realist, who believes that, if you look after the power, the moral authority will look after itself, is equally in error. The most recent form of this doctrine is embodied in the much-quoted phrase: "The function of force is to give moral ideas time to take root." Internationally, this argument was used in 1919 by those who, unable to defend the Versailles Treaty on moral grounds, maintained that this initial act of power would pave the way for subsequent moral appeasement. Experience has done little to confirm this comfortable belief. The same fallacy is implicit in the now commonly held view that the aim of our policy should be "to rebuild the League of Nations, to make it capable of holding a political aggressor in restraint by armed power, and thereafter to labour faithfully for the mitigation of just and real grievances." Once the enemy has been crushed or the "aggressor" restrained by force, the "thereafter" fails to arrive. The illusion that priority can be given to power and that morality will follow, is just as dangerous as the illusion that priority can be given to moral authority and that power will follow.

Before proceeding, however, to consider the respective roles of power and morality in politics, we must take some note of the views of those who, though far from being realists, identify politics with power and believe that moral concepts must be altogether excluded from its scope. There is, according to this view, an essential antinomy between politics and morality; and the moral man as such will therefore have nothing to do with politics. This thesis has many attractions, and reappears at different periods of history and in different contexts. It takes at least three forms.

(i) Its simplest form is the doctrine of non-resistance. The moral man recognises the existence of political power as an evil, but regards the use of power to resist power as a still greater evil.

This is the basis of such doctrines of non-resistance as those of Jesus or of Gandhi, or of modern pacifism. It amounts, in brief, to a boycott of politics.

(ii) The second form of the antithesis between politics and morality is anarchism. The state, as the principal organ of political power, is "the most flagrant, most cynical and most complete negation of humanity." The anarchist will use power to overthrow the state. This revolutionary power is, however, not thought of as political power, but as the spontaneous revolt of the outraged individual conscience. It does not seek to create a new political society to take the place of the old one, but a moral society from which power, and consequently politics, are completely eliminated. "The principles of the Sermon on the Mount," an English divine recently remarked, would mean "sudden death to civilised society." The anarchist sets out to destroy "civilised society" in the name of the Sermon on the Mount.

(iii) A third school of thought starts from the same premise of the essential antithesis between morality and politics, but arrives at a totally different conclusion. The injunction of Jesus to "render unto Caesar the things that are Caesar's and unto God the things that are God's" implies the coexistence of two separate spheres: the political and the moral. But the moral man is under an obligation to assist—or at any rate not to obstruct—the politician in the discharge of his non-moral functions. "Let every soul be subject to the higher powers. The powers that be are ordained of God." We thus recognise politics as necessary but non-moral. This tradition, which remained dormant throughout the Middle Ages, when the ecclesiastical and the secular authority was theoretically one, was revived by Luther in order to effect his compromise between reformed church and state. Luther "turned on the peasants of his day in holy horror when they attempted to transmute the 'spiritual' kingdom into an 'earthly' one by suggesting that the principles of the gospel had social significance." The division of functions between Caesar and God is implicit in the very conception of an "established" church. But the tradition has been more persistent and more effective in Lutheran Germany than anywhere else. "We do not consult Jesus," wrote a German liberal nineteenth-century pastor, "when we are concerned with things which belong to the domain of the construction of the state and political economy," and Bernhardi declared that "Christian morality is personal and social, and in its nature cannot be political." The same attitude is inherent in the modern theology of Karl Barth, which insists that political and social evils are the necessary product of man's sinful nature and that human effort to eradicate them is therefore futile; and the doctrine that Christian morality has nothing to do with politics [was] vigorously upheld by the Nazi regime. This view is basically different from that of the realist who makes morality a function of politics. But in the field of politics it tends to become indistinguishable from realism.

The theory of the divorce between the spheres of politics and morality is superficially attractive, if only because it evades the insoluble problem of finding a moral justification for the use of force. But it is not ultimately satisfying. Both non-resistance and anarchism are counsels of despair, which appear to find widespread acceptance only where men feel hopeless of achieving anything of political action; and the attempt to keep God and Caesar in watertight compartments runs too much athwart the deep-seated desire of the human mind to reduce its view of the world to some kind of moral order. We are not in the long run satisfied to believe that what is politically good is morally bad; and since we can neither moralise power nor expel power from politics, we are faced with a dilemma which cannot be completely resolved. The planes of utopia and of reality never coincide. The ideal cannot be institutionalised, nor the institution idealised. "Politics," writes Dr. Niebuhr, "will, to the end of history, be an area where conscience and power meet, where the ethical and coercive factors of human life will interpenetrate and work out their tentative and uneasy compromises." The compromises, like solutions of other human problems, will remain uneasy and tentative. But it is an essential part of any compromise that both factors shall be taken into account.

A Realist Theory of International Politics

HANS J. MORGENTHAU

. . . THE HISTORY OF MODERN POLITICAL THOUGHT IS THE STORY OF A CONTEST BETWEEN TWO SCHOOLS THAT DIFFER FUNDAMENTALLY IN THEIR CONCEPTIONS OF THE NATURE OF MAN, SOCIETY, AND POLITICS. One believes that a rational and moral political order, derived from universally valid abstract principles, can be achieved here and now. It assumes the essential goodness and infinite malleability of human nature, and blames the failure of the social order to measure up to the rational standards on lack of knowledge and understanding, obsolescent social institutions, or the depravity of certain isolated individuals or groups. It trusts in education, reform, and the sporadic use of force to remedy these defects.

The other school believes that the world, imperfect as it is from the rational point of view, is the result of forces inherent in human nature. To improve the world one must work with those forces, not against them. This being inherently a world of opposing interests and of conflict among them, moral principles can never be fully realized, but must at best be approximated through the ever temporary balancing of interests and the ever precarious settlement of conflicts. This school, then, sees in a system of checks and balances a universal principle for all pluralist societies. It appeals to historic precedent rather than to abstract principles, and aims at the realization of the lesser evil rather than of the absolute good.

This theoretical concern with human nature as it actually is, and with the historic processes as they actually take place, has earned for the theory presented here the name of realism. What are the tenets of political realism? No systematic exposition of the philosophy of political realism can be attempted here; it will suffice to single out six fundamental principles, which have frequently been misunderstood.

Six Principles of Political Realism

1. Political realism believes that politics, like society in general, is governed by objective laws that have their roots in human nature. In order to improve society it is first necessary to understand the laws by which society lives. The operation of these laws being impervious to our preferences, men will challenge them only at the risk of failure.

Realism, believing as it does in the objectivity of the laws of politics, must also believe in the possibility of developing a rational theory that reflects, however imperfectly and onesidedly, these objective laws. It believes also, then, in the possibility of distinguishing in politics between truth and opinion—between what is true objectively and rationally, supported by evidence and illuminated by reason, and what is only a subjective judgment, divorced from the facts as they are and informed by prejudice and wishful thinking.

* * *

For realism, theory consists in ascertaining facts and giving them meaning through reason. It assumes that the character of a foreign policy can be ascertained only through the examination of the political acts performed and of the foreseeable consequences of these acts. Thus, we can find out what statesmen have actually done, and from the foreseeable consequences of their acts we can surmise what their objectives might have been.

Yet examination of the facts is not enough. To give meaning

to the factual raw material of foreign policy, we must approach political reality with a kind of rational outline, a map that suggests to us the possible meanings of foreign policy. In other words, we put ourselves in the position of a statesman who must meet a certain problem of foreign policy under certain circumstances, and we ask ourselves what the rational alternatives are from which a statesman may choose who must meet this problem under these circumstances (presuming always that he acts in a rational manner), and which of these rational alternatives this particular statesman, acting under these circumstances, is likely to choose. It is the testing of this rational hypothesis against the actual facts and their consequences that gives meaning to the facts of international politics and makes a theory of politics possible.

2. The main signpost that helps political realism to find its way through the landscape of international politics is the concept of interest defined in terms of power. This concept provides the link between reason trying to understand international politics and the facts to be understood. It sets politics as an independent sphere of action and understanding apart from other spheres, such as economics, ethics, aesthetics, or religion. Without such a concept a theory of politics, international or domestic, would be altogether impossible, for without it we could not distinguish between political and nonpolitical facts, nor could we bring at least a measure of systematic order to the political sphere.

We assume that statesmen think and act in terms of interest defined as power, and the evidence of history bears that assumption out. That assumption allows us to retrace and anticipate, as it were, the steps a statesman—past, present, or future—has taken or will take on the political scene. We look over his shoulder when he writes his dispatches; we listen in on his conversation with other statesmen; we read and anticipate his very thoughts. Thinking in terms of interest defined as power, we think as he does, and as disinterested observers we understand his thoughts and actions perhaps better than he, the actor on the political scene, does himself.

The concept of interest defined as power imposes intellectual discipline upon the observer, infuses rational order into the subject matter of politics, and thus makes the theoretical understanding of politics possible. On the side of the actor, it provides for rational discipline in action and creates that astounding continuity in foreign policy which makes American, British, or Russian foreign policy appear as an intelligible, rational continuum, by and large consistent within itself, regardless of the different motives, preferences, and intellectual and moral qualities of successive statesmen. A realist theory of international politics, then, will guard against two popular fallacies: the concern with motives and the concern with ideological preferences.

To search for the clue to foreign policy exclusively in the motives of statesmen is both futile and deceptive. It is futile because motives are the most illusive of psychological data, distorted as they are, frequently beyond recognition, by the interests, and emotions of actor and observer alike. Do we really know what our own motives are? And what do we know of the motives of others?

Yet even if we had access to the real motives of statesmen, that knowledge would help us little in understanding foreign policies and might well lead us astray. It is true that the knowledge of the statesman's motives may give us one among many clues as to what the direction of his foreign policy might be. It cannot give us, however, the one clue by which to predict his foreign policies. History shows no exact and necessary correlation between the quality of motives and the quality of foreign policy. This is true both of moral and of political qualities.

We cannot conclude from the good intentions of a statesman that his foreign policies will be either morally praiseworthy or politically successful. Judging his motives, we can say that he will not intentionally pursue policies that are morally wrong, but we can say nothing about the probability of their success. If we want to know the moral and political qualities of his actions, we must know them, not his motives. How often have statesmen been motivated by the desire to improve the world, and ended by making it worse? And how often have they sought one goal, and ended by achieving something they neither expected nor desired?

* * *

Good motives give assurance against deliberately bad policies; they do not guarantee that the policies they inspire will be in fact morally good and politically successful. What it is important to know, if one wants to understand foreign policy, is not primarily the motives of a statesman, but his intellectual ability to comprehend the essentials of foreign policy, as well as his political ability to translate what he has comprehended into successful political action. It follows that while ethics in the abstract judges the moral qualities of motives, political theory must judge the political qualities of intellect, will, and action.

A realist theory of international politics will also avoid the other popular fallacy of equating the foreign policies of a statesman with his philosophic or political sympathies, and of deducing the former from the latter. Statesmen, especially under contemporary conditions, may well make it a habit of presenting their foreign policies in terms of their philosophic and political sympathies in order to gain popular support for them. Yet they will distinguish with Lincoln between their "*official* duty," which is to think and act in terms of the national interest, and their "*personal* wish," which is to see their own moral values and political principles realized throughout the world. Political realism does not require, nor does it condone, indifference to political ideals and moral principles, but it requires indeed a sharp distinction between the desirable and the possible, between what is desirable everywhere and at all times and what is possible under the concrete circumstances of time and place.

It stands to reason that not all foreign policies have always followed so rational, objective, and unemotional a course. The contingent elements of personality, prejudice, and subjective preference, and of all the weaknesses of intellect and will which flesh is heir to, are bound to deflect foreign policies from their rational course. Especially where foreign policy is conducted under the conditions of democratic control, the need to marshal popular emotions to the support of foreign policy cannot fail to impair the rationality of foreign policy itself. Yet a theory of foreign policy which aims at rationality must for the time being, as it were, abstract from these irrational elements and seek to paint a picture of foreign policy which presents the rational essence to be found in experience, without the contingent deviations from rationality which are also found in experience.

The difference between international politics as it actually is and a rational theory derived from it is like the difference between a photograph and a painted portrait. The photograph shows everything that can be seen by the naked eye; the painted portrait does not show everything that can be seen by the naked eye, but it shows, or at least seeks to show, one thing that the naked eye cannot see: the human essence of the person portrayed.

Political realism contains not only a theoretical but also a normative element. It knows that political reality is replete with contingencies and points to the typical influences they exert upon foreign policy. Yet it shares with all social theory the need, for the sake of theoretical understanding, to stress the rational elements of political reality; for it is these rational elements that make reality intelligible for theory. Political realism presents the theoretical construct of a rational foreign policy which experience can never completely achieve.

At the same time political realism considers a rational foreign policy to be good foreign policy; for only a rational foreign policy minimizes risks and maximizes benefits and, hence, complies both with the moral precept of prudence and the political requirement of success. Political realism wants the photographic picture of the political world to resemble as much as possible its painted portrait. Aware of the inevitable gap between good—that is, rational—foreign policy and foreign policy as it actually is, political realism maintains not only that theory must focus upon the rational elements of political reality, but also that foreign policy ought to be rational in view of its own moral and practical purposes.

Hence, it is no argument against the theory here presented that actual foreign policy does not or cannot live up to it. The argument misunderstands the intention of this [article], which is to present not an indiscriminate description of political reality, but a rational theory of international politics. As such it cannot help being selective. Far from being invalidated by the fact that, for instance, a perfect balance of power policy will scarcely be found in reality, it starts with the assumption that reality is deficient in this respect.

3. Realism does not endow its key concept of interest defined as power with a meaning that is fixed once and for all. The idea of interest is indeed of the essence of politics and is unaffected by the circumstances of time and place. Thucydides' statement, born of the experiences of ancient Greece, that "identity of interest is the surest of bonds whether between states or individuals" was taken up in the nineteenth century by Lord Salisbury's remark that "the only bond of union that endures" among nations is "the absence of all clashing interests." It was echoed and enlarged upon in our century by Max Weber's observation:

> Interests (material and ideal), not ideas, dominate directly the actions of men. Yet the "images of the world" created by these ideas have very often served as switches determining the tracks on which the dynamism of interests kept the actions moving.

Yet the kind of interest determining political action in a particular period of history depends upon the political and cultural context within which foreign policy is formulated. The goals that might be pursued by nations in their foreign policy can run the whole gamut of objectives any nation has ever pursued or might possibly pursue.

The same observations apply to the concept of power. Its content and the manner of its use are determined by the political and cultural environment. Power may comprise anything that establishes and maintains the control of man over man. Thus power covers all social relationships which serve that end, from physical violence to the most subtle psychological ties by which one mind controls another. Power covers the domination of man by man, both when it is disciplined by moral ends and controlled by constitutional safeguards as in Western democracies, and when it is untamed and barbaric force which finds its laws in nothing but its own strength and its sole justification in its aggrandizement.

Political realism does not assume that the contemporary conditions under which foreign policy operates, with their extreme instability and the ever present threat of large-scale violence, cannot be changed. The balance of power, for instance, is indeed a perennial element of all pluralistic societies, as the authors of *The Federalist* papers well knew; yet it is capable of operating, as it does in the United States, under conditions of relative stability and peaceful conflict. If the factors that have given rise to these conditions can be duplicated on the international scene, similar conditions of stability and peace will then prevail there, as they have over long stretches of history among certain nations.

What is true of the general character of international relations is also true of the nation state as the ultimate point of reference of foreign policy at the present time. While the realist indeed believes that interest is the perennial standard by which political action must be judged and directed, the contemporary connection between interest and the national state is a product of history, and is therefore bound to disappear in the course of history. Nothing in the realist position militates against the assumption that the present division of the political world into nation states will be replaced by large units of a quite different character, more in keeping with the technical circumstances and the moral requirements of the contemporary world.

The realist parts company with other schools of thought before the all-important question of how the contemporary world is to be transformed. The realist is persuaded that this transformation can be achieved only through the workmanlike manipulation of the perennial forces that have shaped the past as they will the future. The realist cannot be persuaded that we can bring about that transformation by confronting a political reality that has its own laws with an abstract ideal that refuses to take those laws into account.

4. Political realism is aware of the moral significance of political action. It is also aware of the ineluctable tension between the moral command and the requirements of successful political action. And it is unwilling to gloss over and obliterate that tension and thus to obfuscate both the moral and the political issue by making it appear as though the stark facts of politics were morally more satisfying than they actually are, and the moral law less exacting than it actually is.

Realism maintains that universal moral principles cannot be applied to the actions of states in their abstract universal formulation, but that they must be filtered through the concrete circumstances of time and place. The individual may say for himself: *Fiat justitia, pereat mundus* ("Let justice be done, even if the world perish"), but the state has no right to say so in the name of those who are in its care. Both individual and state must judge political action by universal moral principles, such as that of liberty. Yet while the individual has a moral right to sacrifice himself in defense of such a moral principle, the state has no right to let its moral disapprobation of the infringement of liberty get in the way of successful political action, itself inspired by the moral principle of national survival. There can be no political morality without prudence; that is, without consideration of the political consequences of seemingly moral action. Realism, then, considers prudence—the weighing of the consequences of alternative political actions—to be the supreme virtue in politics. Ethics in the abstract judges action by its conformity with the moral law; political ethics judges action by its political consequences. Classical and medieval philosophy knew this and so did Lincoln when he said:

> I do the very best I know how, the very best I can, and I mean to keep doing so until the end. If the end brings me out all right, what is said against me won't amount to anything. If the end brings me out wrong, ten angels swearing I was right would make no difference.

5. Political realism refuses to identify the moral aspirations of a particular nation with the moral laws that govern the universe.

As it distinguishes between truth and opinion, so it distinguishes between truth and idolatry. All nations are tempted—and few have been able to resist the temptation for long—to clothe their own particular aspirations and actions in the moral purpose of the universe. To know that nations are subject to the moral law is one thing, while to pretend to know with certainty what is good and evil in the relations among nations is quite another. There is a world of difference between the belief that all nations stand under the judgment of God, inscrutable to the human mind, and the blasphemous conviction that God is always on one's side and that what one wills oneself cannot fail to be willed by God also.

The light-hearted equation between a particular nationalism and the counsels of Providence is morally indefensible, for it is that very sin of pride against which the Greek tragedians and the Biblical prophets have warned rulers and ruled. That equation is also politically pernicious; for it is liable to engender the distortion in judgment which, in the blindness of crusading frenzy, destroys nations and civilizations—in the name of moral principle, ideal, or God himself.

On the other hand, it is exactly the concept of interest defined in terms of power that saves us from both that moral excess and that political folly. For if we look at all nations, our own included, as political entities pursuing their respective interests defined in terms of power, we are able to do justice to all of them. And we are able to do justice to all of them in a dual sense: We are able to judge other nations as we judge our own and, having judged them in this fashion, we are then capable of pursuing policies that respect the interests of other nations, while protecting and promoting those of our own. Moderation in policy cannot fail to reflect the moderation of moral judgment.

6. The difference, then, between political realism and other schools of thought is real and it is profound. However much the theory of political realism may have been misunderstood and misinterpreted, there is no gainsaying its distinctive intellectual and moral attitude to matters political.

Intellectually, the political realist maintains the autonomy of the political sphere, as the economist, the lawyer, the moralist maintain theirs. He thinks in terms of interest defined as power, as the economist thinks in terms of unity; the lawyer, of the conformity of action with legal rules; the moralist, of the conformity of action with moral principles. The economist asks: "How does this policy affect the welfare of society, or a segment of it?" The lawyer asks: "Is this policy in accord with the rules of law?" The moralist asks: "Is this policy in accord with moral principles?" And the political realist asks: "How does this policy affect the power of the nation?" (Or of the federal government, of Congress, of the party, of agriculture, as the case may be.)

The political realist is not unaware of the existence and relevance of standards of thought other than the political one. As political realist, he cannot but subordinate these other standards to the political one. And he parts company with other schools when they impose standards of thought appropriate to other spheres upon the political one. It is here that political realism takes issue with the "legalistic-moralistic approach" to international politics. That this issue is not, as has been contended, a mere figment of the imagination, but goes to the very core of the controversy, can be shown from many historical examples. Two will suffice to make the point.

In 1939 the Soviet Union attacked Finland. This action confronted France and Great Britain with two issues, one legal, the other political. Did that action violate the Covenant of the League of Nations and, if it did, what counter measures should France and Great Britain take? The legal question could easily be answered in the affirmative, for obviously the Soviet Union had done what was prohibited by the Covenant. The answer to the political question depended, first, upon the manner in which the Russian action affected the interests of France and Great Britain; second, upon the existing distribution of power between France and Great Britain, on the one hand, and the Soviet Union and other potentially hostile nations, especially Germany, on the other; and, third, upon the influence that the counter measures were likely to have upon the interests of France and Great Britain and the future distribution of power. France and Great

Britain, as the leading members of the League of Nations, saw to it that the Soviet Union was expelled from the League, and they were prevented from joining Finland in the war against the Soviet Union only by Sweden's refusal to allow their troops to pass through Swedish territory on their way to Finland. If this refusal by Sweden had not saved them, France and Great Britain would shortly have found themselves at war with the Soviet Union and Germany at the same time.

The policy of France and Great Britain was a classic example of legalism in that they allowed the answer to the legal question, legitimate within its sphere, to determine their political actions. Instead of asking both questions, that of law and that of power, they asked only the question of law; and the answer they received could have no bearing on the issue that their very existence might have depended upon.

The other example illustrates the "moralistic approach" to international politics. It concerns the international status of the Communist government of China. The rise of that government confronted the Western world with two issues; one moral, the other political. Were the nature and policies of that government in accord with the moral principles of the Western world? Should the Western world deal with such a government? The answer to the first question could not fail to be in the negative. Yet it did not follow with necessity that the answer to the second question should also be in the negative. The standard of thought applied to the first—the moral—question was simply to test the nature and the policies of the Communist government of China by the principles of Western morality. On the other hand, the second—the political—question had to be subjected to the complicated test of the interests involved and the power available on either side, and of the bearing of one or the other course of action upon these interests and power. The application of this test could well have led to the conclusion that it would be wiser not to deal with the Communist government of China. To arrive at this conclusion by neglecting this test altogether and answering the political question in terms of the moral issue was indeed a classic example of the "moralistic approach" to international politics.

This realist defense of the autonomy of the political sphere against its subversion by other modes of thought does not imply disregard for the existence and importance of these other modes of thought. It rather implies that each be assigned their proper sphere and function. Political realism is based upon a pluralistic conception of human nature. Real man is a composite of "economic man," "political man," "moral man," "religious man," etc. A man who was nothing but "political man" would be a beast, for he would be completely lacking in moral restraints. A man who was nothing but "moral man" would be a fool, for he would be completely lacking in prudence. A man who was nothing but "religious man" would be a saint, for he would be completely lacking in worldly desires.

Recognizing that these different facets of human nature exist, political realism also recognizes that in order to understand one of them one has to deal with it on its own terms. That is to say, if I want to understand "religious man" I must for the time being abstract from the other aspects of human nature and deal with its religious aspect as if it were the only one. Furthermore, I must apply to the religious sphere the standards of thought appropriate to it, always remaining aware of the existence of other standards and their actual influence upon the religious qualities of man. What is true of this facet of human nature is true of all the others. No modern economist, for instance, would conceive of his science and its relations to other sciences of man in any other way. It is exactly through such a process of emancipation from other standards of thought, and the development of one appropriate to its subject matter, that economics has developed as an autonomous theory of the economic activities of man. To contribute to a similar development in the field of politics is indeed the purpose of political realism.

It is in the nature of things that a theory of politics which is based upon such principles will not meet with unanimous approval—nor does, for that matter, such a foreign policy. For theory and policy alike run counter to two trends in our culture which are not able to reconcile themselves to the assumptions and results of a rational, objective theory of politics. One of these trends disparages the role of power in society on philosophic grounds that stem from the experience and philosophy of the nineteenth century; . . . The other trend, opposed to the realist theory and practice of politics, stems from the very relationship that exists, and must exist, between the human mind and the political sphere. . . . the human mind in its day-to-day operations cannot bear to look the truth of politics straight in the face. It must disguise, distort, belittle, and embellish the truth—the more so, the more the individual is involved actively in the processes of politics, and particularly in those of international politics. For only by deceiving himself about the nature of politics and the role he plays on the political scene is man able to live contentedly as a political animal with himself and his fellow men.

* * *

The Depreciation of Political Power

The aspiration for power being the distinguishing element of international politics, as of all politics, international politics is of necessity power politics. While this fact is generally recognized in the practice of international affairs, it is frequently denied in the pronouncements of scholars, publicists, and even statesmen. Since the end of the Napoleonic Wars, ever larger groups in the Western world have been persuaded that the struggle for power on the international scene is a temporary phenomenon, a historical accident that is bound to disappear once the peculiar historic conditions that have given rise to it have been eliminated. Thus Jeremy Bentham believed that the competition for colonies was at the root of all international conflicts. "Emancipate your colonies!" was his advice to the governments, and international conflict and war would of necessity disappear. Adherents of free trade, such as Cobden and Proudhon, were convinced that the removal of trade barriers was the only condition for the establishment of permanent harmony among nations, and might even lead to the disappearance of international politics altogether. "At some future election," said Cobden, "we may probably see the test 'no foreign politics' applied to those who offer to become the representatives of free constituencies." For Marx and his followers, capitalism is at the root of international discord and war. They maintain that international socialism will do away with the struggle for power on the international scene and will bring about permanent peace. During the nineteenth century, liberals everywhere shared the conviction that power politics and war were residues of an obsolete system of government, and that with the victory of democracy and constitutional government over absolutism and autocracy international harmony and permanent peace would win out over power politics and war. Of this liberal school of thought, Woodrow Wilson was the most eloquent and most influential spokesman.

In recent times, the conviction that the struggle for power can be eliminated from the international scene has been connected with the great attempts at organizing the world, such as the League of Nations and the United Nations. Thus Cordell Hull, then U.S. Secretary of State, declared in 1943 on his return from the Moscow Conference, which laid the groundwork for the United Nations, that the new international organization would mean the end of power politics and usher in a new era of international collaboration. Mr. Philip Noel-Baker, then British Minister of State, declared in 1946 in the House of Commons that the British government was "determined to use the institutions of the United Nations to kill power politics, in order that, by the methods of democracy, the will of the people shall prevail."

. . . the struggle for power is universal in time and space and is an undeniable fact of experience. It cannot be denied that throughout historic time, regardless of social, economic, and political conditions, states have met each other in contests for power. Even though anthropologists have shown that certain primitive peoples seem to be free from the desire for power, nobody has yet shown how their state of mind and the conditions under which they live can be recreated on a worldwide scale so as to eliminate the struggle for power from the international scene. It would be useless and even self-destructive to free one or the other of the peoples of the earth from the desire for power while leaving it extant in others. If the desire for power cannot be abolished everywhere in the world, those who might be cured would simply fall victims to the power of others.

The position taken here might be criticized on the ground that conclusions drawn from the past are unconvincing, and that to draw such conclusions has always been the main stock in trade of the enemies of progress and reform. Though it is true that certain social arrangements and institutions have always existed in the past, it does not necessarily follow that they must always exist in the future. The situation is, however, different when we deal not with social arrangements and institutions created by man but with those elemental biopsychological drives by which in turn society is created. The drives to live, to propagate, and to dominate are common to all men. Their relative strength is dependent upon social conditions that may favor one drive and tend to repress another, or that may withhold social approval from certain manifestations of these drives, while they encourage others. Thus, to take examples only from the sphere of power, most societies condemn killing as a means of attaining power within the society, but all societies encourage the killing of enemies in that struggle for power which is called war. Dictators look askance at the aspirations for political power among their fellow citizens, but democracies consider active participation in the competition for political power a civic duty. Where a monopolistic organization of economic activities exists, competition for economic power is absent, and in competitive economic systems certain manifestations of the struggle for economic power are outlawed, while others are encouraged.

Regardless of particular social conditions, the decisive argument against the opinion that the struggle for power on the international scene is a mere historic accident must be derived from the nature of domestic politics. The essence of international politics is identical with its domestic counterpart. Both domestic and international politics are a struggle for power, modified only by the different conditions under which this struggle takes place in the domestic and in the international spheres.

The tendency to dominate, in particular, is an element of all human associations, from the family through fraternal and professional associations and local political organizations, to the state. On the family level, the typical conflict between the mother-in-law and her child's spouse is in its essence a struggle for power, the defense of an established power position against the attempt to establish a new one. As such it foreshadows the conflict on the international scene between the policies of the status quo and the policies of imperialism. Social clubs, fraternities, faculties, and business organizations are scenes of continuous struggles for power between groups that either want to keep what power they already have or seek to attain greater power. Competitive contests between business enterprises as well as labor disputes between employers and employees are frequently fought not only, and sometimes not even primarily, for economic advantages, but for influence over each other and over others; that is, for power. Finally, the whole political life of a nation, particularly of a democratic nation, from the local to the national level, is a continuous struggle for power. In periodic elections, in voting in legislative assemblies, in lawsuits before courts, in administrative decisions and executive measures—in all these activities men try to maintain or to establish their power over other men. The processes by which legislative, judicial, executive, and administrative decisions are reached are subject to pressures and counterpressures by "pressure groups" trying to defend and expand their positions of power. In the words of John of Salisbury:

> Though it is not given to all men to seize princely or royal power, yet the man who is wholly untainted by tyranny is rare or nonexistent. In common speech the tyrant is one who oppresses a whole people by a rulership based on force; and yet it is not over a people as a whole that a man can play the tyrant, but he can do so if he will even in the meanest station. For if not over the whole body of the people, still each man will lord it as far as his power extends.

In view of this ubiquity of the struggle for power in all social relations and on all levels of social organization, is it surprising that international politics is of necessity power politics? And would it not be rather surprising if the struggle for power were but an accidental and ephemeral attribute of international politics when it is a permanent and necessary element of all branches of domestic politics?

The Morality of Nations

REINHOLD NIEBUHR

NATIONS ARE TERRITORIAL SOCIETIES, THE COHESIVE POWER OF WHICH IS SUPPLIED BY THE SENTIMENT OF NATIONALITY AND THE AUTHORITY OF THE STATE. The fact that state and nation are not synonymous and that states frequently incorporate several nationalities, indicates that the authority of government is the ultimate force of national cohesion. The fact that state and nation are roughly synonymous proves that, without the sentiment of nationality with its common language and traditions, the authority of government is usually unable to maintain national unity. The unity of Scotland and England within a single British state and the failure to maintain the same unity between England and Ireland, suggest both the possibilities and the limitations of transcending nationality in the formation of states. For our purposes we may think of state and nation as interchangeable terms, since our interest is in the moral attitudes of nations which have the apparatus of a state at their disposal, and through it are able to consolidate their social power and define their political attitudes and policies.

The selfishness of nations is proverbial. It was a dictum of

From *Moral Man and Immoral Society*. Copyright 1932 by Charles Scribner's Sons; renewal copyright © 1960 by Reinhold Niebuhr. Reprinted by permission of Charles Scribner's Sons and SCM Press Ltd, London.

George Washington that nations were not to be trusted beyond their own interest. "No state," declares a German author, "has ever entered a treaty for any other reason than self interest," and adds: "A statesman who has any other motive would deserve to be hung." "In every part of the world," said Professor Edward Dicey, "where British interests are at stake, I am in favor of advancing these interests even at the cost of war. The only qualification I admit is that the country we desire to annex or take under our protection should be calculated to confer a tangible advantage upon the British Empire." National ambitions are not always avowed as honestly as this, as we shall see later, but that is a fair statement of the actual facts, which need hardly to be elaborated for any student of history.

What is the basis and reason for the selfishness of nations? If we begin with what is least important or least distinctive of national attitudes, it must be noted that nations do not have direct contact with other national communities, with which they must form some kind of international community. They know the problems of other peoples only indirectly and at second hand. Since both sympathy and justice depend to a large degree upon the perception of need, which makes sympathy flow, and upon the understanding of competing interests, which must be resolved, it is obvious that human communities have greater difficulty than individuals in achieving ethical relationships. While rapid means of communication have increased the breadth of knowledge about world affairs among citizens of various nations, and the general advance of education has ostensibly promoted the capacity to think rationally and justly upon the inevitable conflicts of interest between nations, there is nevertheless little hope of arriving at a perceptible increase of international morality through the growth of intelligence and the perfection of means of communication. The development of international commerce, the increased economic interdependence among the nations, and the whole apparatus of a technological civilisation, increase the problems and issues between nations much more rapidly than the intelligence to solve them can be created. . . . Such is the social ignorance of peoples, that, far from doing justice to a foe or neighbor, they are as yet unable to conserve their own interests wisely. Since their ultimate interests are always protected best, by at least a measure of fairness toward their neighbors, the desire to gain an immediate selfish advantage always imperils their ultimate interests. If they recognise this fact, they usually recognise it too late. . . .

* * *

There is always, in every nation, a body of citizens more intelligent than the average, who see the issues between their own and other nations more clearly than the ignorant patriot, and more disinterestedly than the dominant classes who seek special advantages in international relations. The size of this group varies in different nations. Although it may at times place a check upon the more extreme types of national self-seeking, it is usually not powerful enough to affect national attitudes in a crisis. . . . It is of course possible that the rational interest in international justice may become, on occasion, so widespread and influential that it will affect the diplomacy of states. But this is not usual. In other words the mind, which places a restraint upon impulses in individual life, exists only in a very inchoate form in the nation. It is, moreover, much more remote from the will of the nation than in private individuals; for the government expresses the national will, and that will is moved by the emotions of the populace and the prudential self-interest of dominant economic classes. Theoretically it is possible to have a national electorate so intelligent, that the popular impulses and the ulterior interests of special groups are brought under the control of a national mind. But practically the rational understanding of political issues remains such a minimum force that national unity of action can be achieved only upon such projects as are either initiated by the self-interest of the dominant groups, in control of the government, or supported by the popular emotions and hysterias which from time to time run through a nation. In other words the nation is a corporate unity, held together much more by force and emotion, than by mind. Since there can be no ethical action without self-criticism, and no self-criticism without the rational capacity of self-transcendence, it is natural that national attitudes can hardly approximate the ethical. Even those tendencies toward self-criticism in a nation which do express themselves are usually thwarted by the governing classes and by a certain instinct for unity in society itself. For self-criticism is a kind of inner disunity, which the feeble mind of a nation finds difficulty in distinguishing from dangerous forms of inner conflict. So nations crucify their moral rebels with their criminals upon the same Golgotha, not being able to distinguish between the moral idealism which surpasses, and the anti-social conduct which falls below that moral mediocrity, on the level of which every society unifies its life. While critical loyalty toward a community is not impossible, it is not easily achieved. It is therefore probably inevitable that every society should regard criticism as a proof of a want of loyalty. This lack of criticism, as Tyrrell the Catholic modernist observed, makes the social will more egotistic than the individual will. "So far as society has a self," he wrote, "it must be self-assertive, proud, self-complacent and egotistical."

* * *

The social ignorance of the private citizen of the nation has thus far been assumed. It may be reasonable to hope that the general level of intelligence will greatly increase in the next decades and centuries and that growing social intelligence will modify national attitudes. It is doubtful whether it will ever increase sufficiently to eliminate all the moral hazards of international relations. There is an ethical paradox in patriotism which defies every but the most astute and sophisticated analysis. The paradox is that patriotism transmutes individual unselfishness into national egoism. Loyalty to the nation is a high form of altruism when compared with lesser loyalties and more parochial interests. It therefore becomes the vehicle of all the altruistic impulses and expresses itself, on occasion, with such fervor that the critical attitude of the individual toward the nation and its enterprises is almost completely destroyed. The unqualified character of this devotion is the very basis of the nation's power and of the freedom to use the power without moral restraint. Thus the unselfishness of individuals makes for the selfishness of nations. That is why the hope of solving the larger social problems of mankind, merely by extending the social sympathies of individuals, is so vain. Altruistic passion is sluiced into the reservoirs of nationalism with great ease, and is made to flow beyond them with great difficulty. What lies beyond the nation, the community of mankind, is too vague to inspire devotion. The lesser communities within the nation, religious, economic, racial and cultural, have equal difficulty in competing with the nation for the loyalty of its citizens. The church was able to do so when it had the prestige of a universality it no longer possesses. Future developments may make the class rather than the nation the community of primary loyalty. But for the present the nation is still supreme. It not only possesses a police power, which other communities lack, but it is able to avail itself of the most potent and vivid symbols to impress its claims upon the consciousness of the individual. Since it is impossible to become conscious of a large social group without adequate symbolism this factor is extremely important. The nation possesses in its organs of government, in the panoply and ritual of the state, in the impressive display of its fighting services, and, very frequently, in the splendors of a royal house, the symbols of unity and greatness, which inspire awe and reverence in the citizen. Furthermore the love and pious attachment of a man to his countryside, to familiar scenes, sights, and experiences, around which the memories of youth have cast a halo of sanctity, all flows into the sentiment of patriotism; for a simple imagination transmutes the universal beneficences of nature into symbols of the peculiar blessings which a benevolent nation bestows upon its citizens. Thus the sentiment of patriotism achieves a potency in the modern soul, so unqualified, that the nation is given *carte blanche* to use the power, compounded of the devotion of individuals, for any purpose it desires. Thus, to choose an example among hundreds, Mr. Lloyd George during the famous Agadir Crisis in 1911 in which a European war became imminent, because marauding nations would not allow a new robber to touch their spoils in Africa, could declare in his Mansion House speech: "If a situation were to be forced upon us in which peace could only be preserved by the surrender of the great and beneficent position Britain has won by centuries of heroism and achievement, by allowing Britain to be treated, when her interests were vitally affected, as if she were of no account in the cabinet of nations, then I say emphatically that peace at that price would be a humiliation intolerable for a great country like ours to endure."

The very sensitive "honor" of nations can always be appeased by the blood of its citizens and no national ambition seems too base or petty to claim and to receive the support of a majority of its patriots.

Unquestionably there is alloy of projected self-interest in patriotic altruism. The man in the street, with his lust for power and prestige thwarted by his own limitations and the necessities of social life, projects his *ego* upon his nation and indulges his anarchic lusts vicariously. So the nation is at one and the same time a check upon, and a final vent for, the expression of individual egoism. Sometimes it is economic interest, and sometimes mere vanity, which thus expresses itself in the individual patriot. Writing of his friend, Winston Churchill, Wilfrid Scawen Blunt said: "Like most of them, it is the vanity of empire that affects him more than the supposed profits or the necessities of trade, which he repudiates." The cultural imperialism which disavows economic advantages, but gains a selfish satisfaction in the aggrandisement of a national culture through imperialistic power, may reveal itself in the most refined and generous souls. Men like Ruskin and Tennyson were not free from it, and it is not absent even from religious missionary enterprises. Paul Pfeffer reports that some Russians hope not only to bestow their form of government upon the whole world but expect that Russian will become the universal language. While economic advantages of national aggression usually accrue to privileged economic groups rather than to a total population, there are nevertheless possibilities of gain in imperialism for the average citizen; and he does not fail to count upon them. . . .

A combination of unselfishness and vicarious selfishness in the individual thus gives a tremendous force to national egoism, which neither religious nor rational idealism can ever completely check. The idealists, whose patriotism has been qualified by more universal loyalties, must always remain a minority group. In the past they have not been strong enough to affect the actions of nations and have had to content themselves with a policy of disassociation from the nation in times of crisis, when national ambitions were in sharpest conflict with their moral ideals. Whether conscientious pacifism on the part of two per cent of a national population could actually prevent future wars, as Professor Einstein maintains, is a question which cannot be answered affirmatively with any great degree of certainty. It is much more likely that the power of modern nationalism will remain essentially unchecked, until class loyalty offers it effective competition.

Perhaps the most significant moral characteristic of a nation is its hypocrisy. We have noted that self-deception and hypocrisy is an unvarying element in the moral life of all human beings. It is the tribute which morality pays to immortality; or rather the device by which the lesser self gains the consent of the larger self to indulge in impulses and ventures which the rational self can approve only when they are disguised. One can never be quite certain whether the disguise is meant only for the eye of the external observer or whether, as may be usually the case, it deceives the self. Naturally this defect in individuals becomes more apparent in the less moral life of nations. Yet it might be supposed that nations, of whom so much less is expected, would not be under the necessity of making moral pretensions for their actions. There was probably a time when they were under no such necessity. Their hypocrisy is both a tribute to the growing rationality of man and a proof of the ease with which rational demands may be circumvented.

The dishonesty of nations is a necessity of political policy if the nation is to gain the full benefit of its double claim upon the loyalty and devotion of the individual, as his own special and unique community and as a community which embodies universal values and ideals. The two claims, the one touching the individual's emotions and the other appealing to his mind, are incompatible with each other, and can be resolved only through dishonesty. This is particularly evident in war-time. Nations do not really arrive at full self-consciousness until they stand in vivid, usually bellicose, juxtaposition to other nations. The social reality, comprehended in the existence of a nation, is too large to make a vivid impression upon the imagination of the citizen. He vaguely identifies it with his own little community and fireside and usually accepts the mythos which attributes personality to his national group. But the impression is not so vivid as to arouse him to any particular fervor of devotion. This fervor is the unique product of the times of crisis, when his nation is in conflict with other nations. It springs from the new vividness with which the reality and the unity of his nation's discreet existence is comprehended. In other words, it is just in the moments when the nation is engaged in aggression or defense (and it is always able to interpret the former in terms of the latter) that the reality of the nation's existence becomes so sharply outlined as to arouse the citizen to the most passionate and uncritical devotion toward it. But at such a time the nation's claim to uniqueness also comes in sharpest conflict with the generally accepted impression that the nation is the incarnation of universal values. This conflict can be resolved only by deception. In the imagination of the simple patriot the nation is not a society but Society. Though its values are relative they appear, from his naive perspective, to be absolute. The religious instinct for the absolute is no less potent in patriotic religion than in any other. The nation is always endowed with an aura of the sacred, which is one reason why religions, which claim universality, are so easily captured and tamed by national sentiment, religion and patriotism merging in the process. The spirit of the nationally established churches and the cult of "Christentum und Deutschtum" of pre-war Germany are interesting examples. The best means of harmonising the claim to universality with the unique and relative life of the nation, as revealed in moments of crisis, is to claim general and universally valid objectives for the nation. It is alleged to be fighting for civilisation and for culture; and the whole enterprise of humanity is supposedly involved in its struggles. In the life of the simple citizen this hypocrisy exists as a naive and unstudied self-deception. The politician practices it consciously (though he may become the victim of his own arts), in order to secure the highest devotion from the citizen for his enterprises. The men of culture give themselves to it with less conscious design than the statesmen because their own inner necessities demand the deceptions, even more than do those of the simple citizens. The religious or the rational culture to which they are devoted helps them to realise that moral values must be universal, if they are to be real; and they cannot therefore give themselves to national aspirations, unless they clothe them in the attributes of universality. A few of them recognise the impossibility of such a procedure. Among most, the force of reason operates only to give the hysterias of war and the imbecilities of national politics more plausible excuses than an average man is capable of inventing. So they become the worst liars of war-time. . . .

* * *

Perhaps the best that can be expected of nations is that they should justify their hypocrisies by a slight measure of real international achievement, and learn how to do justice to wider interests than their own, while they pursue their own. . . .

* * *

If it is true that the nations are too selfish and morally too obtuse and self-righteous to make the attainment of international justice without the use of force possible, the question arises whether there is a possibility of escape from the endless round of force avenging ancient wrongs and creating new ones, of victorious Germany creating a vindictive France and victorious France poisoning Germany with a sense of outraged justice. The morality of nations is such that, if there be a way out, it is not as easy as the moralists of both the pre-war and post-war period have assumed.

Obviously one method of making force morally redemptive is to place it in the hands of a community, which transcends the conflicts of interest between individual nations and has an impartial perspective upon them. That method resolves many conflicts within national communities. . . . But if powerful classes in national societies corrupt the impartiality of national courts, it may be taken for granted that a community of nations, in which very powerful and very weak nations are bound together, has even less hope of achieving impartiality. Furthermore the prestige of the international community is not great enough, and it does not sufficiently qualify the will-to-power of individual nations, to achieve a communal spirit sufficiently unified, to discipline recalcitrant nations. . . . Even if it should be possible to maintain peace on the basis of the international *status quo*, there is no evidence that an unjust peace can be adjusted by pacific means. A society of nations has not really proved itself until it is able to grant justice to those who have been worsted in battle without requiring them to engage in new wars to redress their wrongs.

Since the class character of national governments is a primary, though not the only cause of their greed, present international anarchy may continue until the fear of catastrophe amends, or catastrophe itself destroys, the present social system and builds more co-operative national societies. There may not be enough intelligence in modern society to prevent catastrophe. There is certainly not enough intelligence to prompt our generation to a voluntary reorganisation of society, unless the fear of imminent catastrophe quickens the tempo of social change.

Foreign Policy:
The Realism of Idealism

THOMAS COOK and MALCOLM MOOS

Utilizing Power

Much of the difficulty both in defining and in implementing the idea of the national self-interest has arisen from ambiguities in the concept of power. Since today power is usually, though not uniformly, accepted as the very substance, the key idea and concern, of politics, the difficulty tends to grow rather than decrease. In discussions of the international or world order, confusion has been particularly great. For there "power politics," a facile but largely meaningless phrase with overtones of healthy realism or sinister immoralism, has rather generally been taken to denote the essence of the matter, as well as in some mysterious way to provide a key to the analysis and solution of all problems.

* * *

Politics . . . does mean power generated and used, with force and constraint as techniques to channelize and limit activities, although consent is needed to make the power effective by leading to the positive fruition of policy and eliminating friction. Certainly it would be idiotic in internal or in international affairs to talk of powerless politics. The issues are always how to generate and to use power; what is the interest which power is to serve; what conception of interest, duly accepted, will be most effective as a generator of power; and, especially in the international field,

From *The American Political Science Review*, Vol. XLVI, No. 2, June, 1952. Reprinted by permission of The American Political Science Association.

what is the relation of force and persuasion to the diminution of conflict and the creation of harmony.

The international order is composed of many powers which differ in their particular interests, yet whose members all share common humanity. Although particular national policies are in competition here, the competition is not simply a struggle between the particular powers at the moment involved in a specific issue. It is also directed toward getting the allegiance or support of third parties, singly or in groups. Since these also have their interests and aspirations which are supported by various degrees of will and strength, power has a limited, though not precisely defined, force at its command. In the resultant competition, the relative effectiveness of any two opposed parties in winning the support of a third, prior to war and short of conquest, is the outcome of a parallelogram of force and principle.

The probable rationale of the otherwise misleading and confusing term "power politics" arises from an essential difference between internal and international politics. In the internal sphere the political institution known as the state is accepted at once as the locus of contention between interest groups and persons and as the necessary order for their better fulfillment. Struggles can normally be solved by essentially diplomatic means, with an accepted enforcement agency endowed with force as a reserve in the background. Such solutions are possible just because of acknowledged common purpose and shared interest. In the world order, however, common purpose is often unrecognized and is rarely dominant, despite acknowledgments of an ultimate common humanity. Similarly, organs of settlement and enforcement of the rules of a common order, when adjustment by politic compromise fails, are rudimentary or nonexistent.

National Self-interest or Shangri-La Isolationism?

In the world order, more or less coherent systems of national interests and strategies of interest-promotion come into contact and conflict. . . . For the effective and continued pursuit of interests, including above all lasting material and spiritual satisfactions at home, force alone is, as political thinkers have known for centuries, an instrument of any nation, to generate power as influence on, and persuasion of, other nations. Such power may be generated bilaterally, and even multilaterally to a certain point, by appeal to common or complementing selfishness. But ultimately it has to rest on a larger common appeal, directed to universal interests, even though these are distorted by the particular immediacies of the power making the appeal and of the power or powers to whom it is made. Such distortion unfortunately gives aid and comfort to proponents of power politics, as it does more generally to those who argue that in the conduct of international relations it is sufficient to rely on the immediate and narrowed interests of neighbors and temporary allies, supported by military preparedness. Perhaps, to put it more fundamentally, this distortion tends to disguise, if not to hide completely, the deeper common principles which nations in truth share and which give meaning to their very immediate self-interests. Undoubtedly, the essential moral weakness of the international order is the absence of an impartial judge and interpreter of claims to rights. . . . Such a lack is doubly evil: it prevents genuine adjudication of disputes, and it hides the reality of those common rights which are in truth shared interests to be interpreted. . . . The logic of force only is no consent. Its consequence, because it cannot create power based on the sympathy or co-operation of others, is the need to eliminate. The particular nation which takes such a view necessarily proclaims itself, by prideful ambition, the sole state in the world. It rejects international politics; it rejects the possibility of creating and using power in an international order to pursue its real, but limited, interests.

The Harmonization of National Self-interests

. . . The sponsorship by a major power of a moral appeal based on universalism, though addressed to specific national interests and needs, today is urgently required for the very generation of power. The furtherance of particular national interests necessitates their identification with the interests of other peoples, as the latter does in fact conceive them, or can be persuaded to conceive and formulate them. The first and chief weapon of national interest, in time as in effect, is then ideas, which are essentially moral doctrines. Effectively to pursue its own interests, the nation has to profess to be universal in interest, and to accept the equality of persons and peoples. Indeed, the utilization of a national interest concept based upon a moral appeal as the firmament of our foreign policy, holds out the greatest promise for meeting the challenge of events that lie ahead.

One testimony to the truth of this thesis is the common use by East and West of the term "democracy." The significance of its use is not lessened by differences in interpretation. Nor is it diminished by possible insincerity in its actual utilization or, where influence or control would permit, in implementation, by one of the parties. In a world where isolation seems impractical and extermination of all peoples save one improbable, even were it desired, the process of furthering national interests necessitates limited identification, appeals to shared purposes, and the generation of power primarily through ideas essentially moral in character. Force, which is but a portion of power, not its prime creator, is indeed relevant as pressure, the utilization of which reflects a lack of an impartial judge under an established law; yet force corrupts the purity and perverts the use of moral ideas. It is finally these ideas—of equality, of sharing, and of liberty, common to the great world religions and philosophies, including Marxism itself—which play a vital role in international politics.

Idealism, far from being utopian and destructive of realistic foreign policy, is basic to such policy. It is likewise basic to the idea that force itself, in the form of warfare, is but a means to creative peace. The purpose of force is to redress evils which, as Grotius first clearly stated and the whole Catholic school of international law has continuously affirmed, stand in the way of man's self-realization through a just social order. The corruption and perversion of moral ideals by simplified propaganda may indeed lead at times to a very unrealistic representation of other peoples or nations collectively as devils, to the detriment both of national and of general human interests. Such falsification can create the belief that, once the devils are destroyed, no further effort is needed: men may then live happily ever after. The error here, however, should not be attributed to idealism; instead, it indicates the necessity for the integrity of factual reality as the basis for moral judgment, just as, on a different level, it is an argument for the proper maintenance and use of force. A moral use of force always necessitates the subordination and service of that force to ethical aspiration. Force is not properly set in balance against idealism itself. Rather, its right application is always subject to moral judgment, even as sound morality necessitates its availability. That curious professed realism which insists that moral ideas are a protective coloration for exclusive and antagonistic interests, is in truth at once immoral and unrealistic. Moreover, to profess it deceives its exponent far more than it deceives those to whom the "realism" is professedly addressed. As a consequence, its potency as a creator of effective power is doubly diminished.

A genuine foreign policy necessitates absence of hypocrisy. Under present conditions it necessitates proceeding beyond the self-delusion that the road to the promotion of political self-interests is military and economic aid to others for selfish reasons only. Effective promotion of American national interests, for instance, requires concern for the real well-being of our NATO allies. It requires, more profoundly, the pursuit of commonly shared ideas and interests beyond the chance parallelism of the moment. It necessitates abandonment of the attempt to create, or, when needed, to recreate, an always precarious favorable balance of power against some other major power, at the present moment Russia. It must be based on a long-term parallelism of interests. It must possess an awareness that universalist moral insight is requisite also from the point of view of technology and communication and must envisage the ultimate creation of corresponding world political institutions. Such institutions, not possible at present, must yet be held desiderata which can be achieved in a foreseeable future.

At the present moment it is vital to pursue and effectuate ideas and policies compatible with the recognized and shared universal interests of those devoted to the ideals of free society and questing man. Certainly these interests necessitate the nurturing and development of the rich diversities of peoples, whose elimination would be impoverishing even were it practicable. Realistic policy is the proof in action of the reality of sharing, despite cultural differences, and beyond any desire to destroy them. It necessitates, above all, the combatting of a hard-boiled, niggardly realism at home. Such realism not only harms our own moral stature, but also gives genuine warrant for realistic insight abroad into the nature of our realism within the confines of its own concepts. The net result is the destruction of the effectiveness of our attempted appeal to moral ideas. Yet we have seen that such ideas are the fundamental generators of power. The essence of the thesis here propounded is that our national power, the organized social creativity of our people, does not diminish, but increases where it works to supplement and to reinforce the generically similar, though in specific content different, creativity in other peoples. The so-called realistic theory of national interest and the balance of power doctrine, insofar as it rests on that theory, constitute in truth a belated translation and preservation of the old economic wage-fund doctrine as a power-fund theory.

Idealism in a Bipolar World

In the bipolar world as it is today, a major power has to be global in interest and commitment. For one thing, it must recruit support from all lesser and uncommitted powers. It must do so by persuasive demonstration that its doctrines of personality and of democracy and its concept of the compatibility of diverse cultures embraced within a world community, are more sincere and more promising to others, from the point of view of their own national interests, than the alternatives offered. . . .

* * *

Total commitment and a total idealism which is yet self-interest are our appropriate answers to Soviet totalitarianism.

They are the means to success in total war, should it come. They are also the most probable grounds for a lasting peace based on positive policies. These policies must be conceived and geared to the preservation of continuity in ever-changing situations, just as they must be directed finally toward the creation of more effective international institutions.

An effective, because long-term, concept of national interest cannot, of course, rest solely on the grim alternative "we or they." It must accept a commonly shared universe of aspiration, at the same time that it necessarily condemns the forceful imposing of unity. It must aim to create a situation in which effective power at once discourages aggression by, and stimulates transformation in, Russia. American ideological power is in this context a leverage. Such power must be backed by a collective force, with the will to use it, which is organized though not created by itself. Possible transformation in Russia, long hoped for from without and implicitly promised from within, has been prevented first by fear and then by national pride. The shared aspirations of humanity have been hidden by the short-sightedness of some putative American interests, promoted and defended by actually irrelevant dogmas. In Russia they have been corrupted by a yet narrower dogma, progressively perverted and misused. Yet these aspirations may still be realized, provided that American policy generates power through sincerity.

This last proviso necessitates a refusal to appease, which is not synonymous with a refusal to comprehend or, consistently with principle, to conciliate. Apart from direct appeasement, which compounds injustice and sacrifices others after the manner of Munich, it is also possible indirectly to appease by our own refusal to commit ourselves to risks and dangers, a refusal supported by narrowly defined and ungenerous interests at home. Nonetheless, it is vital for America to abandon the position of an infallible and absolutely just deity sitting in judgment, a position even more dangerous when sincere than when hypocritical. It is necessary to reject the dogma that diversity of political and social philosophy is incompatible with fundamental universality. It is essential to probe behind the evils of the present regime of Russia and to perceive the justified realities of its economic and cultural national interests and aspirations. It is vital to understand the genuine relevance of Marxism to the organization of Russia as a would-be industrial country, even as it is necessary to condemn the perversion of Marxist teaching and the misuse of it. This means that it is necessary to understand the ethical side of Marxist philosophy, with its broad appeal in countries which would avoid Soviet domination as they would avoid dictatorship. It is, finally, necessary to clarify our own theory and practice of a classless society, which is not incompatible with the essential insights of Marx. This society we have been slowly achieving, during a century and more of peaceful change, by an effective wedding of constitutional democracy, here federal and anti-statist, with a highly productive industrial technology, the fruits and blessings of which have been distributed ever more widely and equally. It is necessary to show that this concept is now closer to realization; that our own national interest and purpose is to help its realization; that it promotes social and economic welfare without the necessity of sacrificing individual freedom or the creative method of constitutional democracy. The preservation and the extension of these last, which can only come through voluntary acceptance, are surely the essence of our national interest.

Our interest is the fulfillment compatibly of diverse persons and, by analogy, of diverse peoples. Based on Christian ethics it is a doctrine of method in coping pragmatically with the realities of differences among men and of imperfections in men. Foreign policy consistently conceived in the light of this tradition and insight at once proclaims, and persuades others of, the realism of idealism.

Realism and Idealism
in International Politics

QUINCY WRIGHT

A PHILOSOPHY MAY BE USEFUL BECAUSE IT GUIDES EFFORTS TOWARD MAKING A WORLD THAT BETTER SATISFIES HUMAN WISHES OR BECAUSE IT RECONCILES THE INDIVIDUAL TO BEING SATISFIED WITH THE CONDITIONS IN WHICH HE LIVES. A philosophy which centers around a distinction between "realism" and "idealism" would seem to have neither of these utilities but would engender lethargy and inaction because it asserts that ideals are not real, or despair because it asserts that reality cannot be ideal. Such thinking is ethically and politically useless and lacks the scientific virtue of looking at human and political activity as it is—a complex in which both values and conditions play a part and which can in a degree be predicted and manipulated toward desired goals, and to which one can in a measure adapt oneself by rethinking the situation. Absolutism has no place in political thinking. . . .

The history of the period since World War I would certainly provide no clear evidence that policies which could be identified with internationalism were less "realistic" than policies which could be identified with nationalism. Neither Mussolini nor Hitler, the high priests of nationalism, did very well for themselves or their states. The other great powers were only a trifle less nationalistic. Public opinion in none of these states was

From "Realism and Idealism in International Affairs" by Quincy Wright. *World Politics*, October, 1952. Reprinted by permission of Princeton University Press.

dominantly "internationalistic" and it is therefore not surprising that the policies of government could in all cases be better described as nationalistic than as internationalistic. It is, however, possible that statesmen would have come out better if they had attempted and been able to win favorable attention to the League of Nations and other symbols of internationalism, and to pursue the policies which those symbols suggested.

It will be said that it was impossible for them to do so because "realism" should have taught them that national power is the end of policy. But does this mean that people today attach high value to national power or does it mean that people are by nature nationalists? The "realists" have been uncertain whether their key terms refer to necessary assumptions or to desirable goals and they have also been uncertain as to the respective roles of observation and of values in either.

This analysis suggests that "realism" and "idealism" have functioned as propaganda terms according to which everyone sought to commend whatever policy he favored by calling it "realistic." The terms do not, in other words, throw light on the policies, institutions, personalities, or theories which they are used to qualify but only on the attitude toward them of the speaker and, it is hoped, of the listener. From this usage we learn that in the past two decades political propagandists have regarded "realism" as a plus term and "idealism" as a minus term.

"Realism" has been associated by some philosophers with the acceptance of the necessary consequences of necessary assumptions. . . . The political "realists" insist it is "realistic" to accept the proposition that "states seek to enhance their power" as axiomatic and not to shrink from any conclusions which follow from it by irresistible logic. The opposite of "realism" in this sense is to reject assumptions which, however self-evident, are disliked and to reject unpalatable results which logically flow from them. It is difficult to see why such irrationality should be called "idealism." It is obvious, however, that few people are ready to denominate themselves "idealists," when that term is made synonymous with foolishness.

There is a flaw in the application of this geometric analogy to international politics. Few assumptions are completely uncontroversial. . . . The alleged axiom about the disposition of states to enhance their power is even more questionable. Modern "realists" recognize that this disposition is more developed in some states than in others, and classify states as "status quo" or "imperialistic" according as they use power to maintain or to change the existing distribution of territory and power. This qualification suggests that power is an instrument for the achievement of values. It is not a necessary property of states. . . . Consequently one cannot hope to deduce from the alleged disposition to enhance power consequences which can be verified by observations under different conditions and circumstances, thus providing the basis for a science predicting the behavior of states. Instead one has to acknowledge that both the magnitude and the utilization of power by a state are influenced by the values it holds and the policies it pursues. Does it want stability or progress? Does it want order or justice? Does it want peace or plenty? It is true that a state's values may also be influenced by the power at its disposal. Policy, in the sense of propositions describing a state's probable action in given circumstances, is a function of both its power and its values, of both the means at its disposal and the ends dictated by its values.

Since the pursuit of values is often associated with "idealism," some "realists" shrink from this conclusion and, to justify the assumption that states act to enhance their power, assert that power is the supreme value for which states strive. In other words, states utilize power to augment power—power is both means and end—but the jump from assuming that the pursuit of power is an inherent property of states to asserting that states pursue power as their supreme value changes the point of view from that of science to that of philosophy. Values can, it is true, be spoken of scientifically as facts manifested in particular cultures, but they are usually spoken of philosophically as subjective appraisals of what ought to be.

Thus when it is said that states pursue power as their supreme value, the philosophical question is at once raised: Ought power to be the supreme value of states? The "realist" answers affirmatively, asserting that states should pursue their national interests and the supreme national interest is the augmentation of the state's power position. They are, however, then asserting not a self-evident axiom but an ethical norm, and an ethical norm which is by no means uncontroversial. Can it be said that the Alexanders, Caesars, Napoleons, and Hitlers who appeared to make power their goal are better examples of statesmanship than the Washingtons, Jeffersons, Lincolns, and Wilsons who appeared to subordinate power to other values? It is admittedly difficult to assess the weight of power as end and power as means in the thinking or action of any political leader.

It is also difficult to assess the relative importance of the various elements of political power—armament, potential, morale, reputation—under given conditions of culture and technology. What contribution may a value system itself make to a state's power? May not a state which attributes high value to the observance of promises, the exercise of power with moderation, the toleration of divergent values, and respect for differences of opinion be usually in a better position to achieve its policies than a state which has a reputation for repudiating promises, and for behaving with brutality, intolerance, and disrespect? The advantage of larger armies, navies, and air forces may be overweighed by superior capacity to gain allies. It is said, without complete accuracy, that Washington lost all his battles but the last, and that Napoleon won all of his but the last. Washington with the help of Franklin succeeded in getting France, the Netherlands, and Spain on his side and Prussia, Russia, and Sweden in benevolent neutrality before the Revolutionary War ended, but Napoleon found himself fighting alone against Europe at Leipzig and Waterloo. While exceptions can be found, it is roughly true that policies and values generally appraised as good win allies and wars, while those generally appraised as bad lose both. Observance of law is a value generally appraised as good and it may be wise policy. "Just as the national," wrote Grotius, "who violates the law of his country in order to obtain an immediate advantage breaks down that by which the advantages of himself and his posterity are for all future time assured, so the state which transgresses the laws of nature and of nations cuts away also the bulwarks which safeguard its own future peace."

The lesson to be drawn is that in social and political affairs values cannot be eliminated from the discussion as they can in dealing with atoms and planets. Values, no less than arms, are among the "facts" which determine state behavior. All terms of politics—power, policy decision, action—involve both values and conditions, both human purposes and material instruments, both goals expressed by symbols and means manifested by procedures, weapons, and propagandas.

Finally, is it certain that political values should be appraised in relation to the state? Is man for the state or is the state for man? The less discouraged of our age may assume that today, in 1776, 1688, 1215, and further back, men and women regard the opportunity to enjoy life and liberty and to pursue happiness as a primary value and that they consider it the function of the state and other institutions to forward that value. In a world which is likely to continue to shrink and to change at an accelerating rate under the influence of advancing science and technology, and in which war is likely to be more destructive and less localizable, these values can hardly develop unless the peoples of the world are so organized that nations and factions will be deterred from war. Such organization is hardly to be expected unless men are educated to world citizenship and opinion is cultivated to support universal institutions. Goals such as these are not achieved in a day or in a decade. The steps toward them must often be deflected by necessities which require that states be strong and opinion be behind them, but unless the goal is recognized it is not likely to be approached.

These conclusions in regard to long-run policy may be characterized as "idealism." Their opposite would counsel a continued education of people to worship the sovereignty of the nation-state, continued propaganda of opinion to strengthen those states and to weaken international institutions, and continuance of the arms race. The result to be expected is further bi-polarizing of the world in hostile alliances, increasing taxes, regimentation of persons, declining standards of living, less enjoyment of human rights, and eventually atomic war, after which the prospects of any large number of people enjoying life and liberty and pursuing happiness as they have been doing during the last few centuries would be slight indeed. If long-run policies with these objectives are called "realism," then realism seems a close neighbor of foolishness.

If the demand for "realism" in international politics means to deny that words are weapons, that values and ideas have influence, and that ideas give power, it can find little to sustain it in modern social thought. If it means that men should not reflect on the probable consequences of their actions but act on impulse and a blind urge for dominance, it is suicidal. If it means that men should calculate the probable consequences of alternative policies in the existing distribution of power, it is sensible, but such action could equally well be called "idealism." If it means that men should avoid absolutistic principles, should appreciate the relativity of all values to time and circumstance, it may be sound advice, but such pragmatism is no less "idealism" than it is "realism." "Idealists" and "realists" seem to agree that calculation of the power situation and of the disposition of states to enhance their power is important in policy-making. The issue is what other factors are important to have in mind in choosing among alternatives if long-run progress is not to be frustrated in meeting short-run exigencies. "Idealists" refuse to conclude that our civilization has made the fatal turn and is going the way of Egypt, Babylon, and Rome. They believe men, by taking thought, can contribute to the development of conditions in which "the dignity and worth of the human person," justice, and respect for the obligations arising from treaties and other sources of international law can be maintained.

Machiavelli suggests that the fundamental norms for the behavior of individuals in a society and for statemen in international relations are different. They are, of course, different because the conditions and circumstances are different. In the same sense, the proper norms of behavior in China, in London, and in Timbuktu, in the age of the horse-borne archer, the tractor-borne gun, and the air-borne atomic bomb are different.

The applicability of any norms can hardly be judged except in the light of the total situation, including the culture and the technology in which they are to be applied. The Machiavellian distinction could hardly have been made except against the background of a culture which assumed that there are absolute moral norms of human behavior to be observed in all cultures and in all situations. A philosophy suitable for our varied and changing world appreciates that justice may resemble long-run expediency if all aspects of the situation are considered. "Honesty," as Franklin said, "may be the best policy." Here "idealism" and "realism" meet.

The ambiguity in the terms "realism" and "idealism" makes them of doubtful service in the field of international relations. If they are used to indicate an antithesis more objective than that of pessimism and optimism or than that of approval and disapproval, it seems to me they can best distinguish short-run from long-run policies, national from human policies, and oppositional from cooperative policies. These distinctions are clearly relative. Thus "realism" demands that immediate necessities and short-run requirements be not neglected in working for long-run goals, and "idealism" demands that long-run goals be not neglected in meeting immediate necessities and short-run requirements. "Realism" also insists that even in the long run it is to be expected that the nation will continue to be the predominant political value of the citizens and, consequently, policy should be guided by the national interest, whether of stability or expansion, with only secondary concern for the individual or humanity. "Idealism," on the other hand, insists that in the long run man will persist but nations and institutions will rise and fall; consequently, dominant values are human, and long-run policy should be guided by them and seek to adjust national policy and develop international institutions to serve them in a changing world, whether those values are stability or progress. Finally, "realism" insists that opposition to any policy is to be expected, while "idealism" sees that most policies are shared by some others and cooperation is possible. They agree that the remedy for opposition is cooperation with others—"Fight 'em or join 'em," say the politicians

—"Know your enemy," say the preachers. The fight may be most important in the short run, but the results of cooperation may be more enduring.

This distinction is supported by usage. The "real" is usually taken to mean the actual, the present, the known, or the expected, and the "ideal" is taken to mean the perfect, the remote, the conceived, or the desired. Short-run policies are more closely related to the actual, the present, the known, and the expected than are long-run policies and so lend themselves to more "realistic" treatment. Furthermore, in our period of history the needs of each nation are more actual, present, known, and anticipated by its people than are the needs of other nations or of humanity, and defense from enemies is more pressing than cooperation with friends for distant goals. Consequently, it is "realistic" to give primary attention to national interests and foreign enemies.

On the other hand, long-run policies must be based upon future contingencies which are remote and merely conceived, and can only be justified by their perfection and desirability, at least until the social sciences make possible prediction and control over longer periods and of far more accuracy than they do today. Consideration of such policies must, therefore, be in large measure "idealistic." Furthermore, say the "idealists," in the rapidly changing world the character, relative power, and even existence of present nations cannot be predicted through long periods of time; therefore, long-run policy ought to be based on more "idealistic" factors, such as the goals of human progress, human potentialities, and human needs, hopes, and desires, which are in fact more stable over long periods of time. Here the "idealists" differ from the "realists," insisting that as consideration is given to an increasingly distant future, it is more "realistic" to be "idealistic." The "realists" may retort that it is idle to waste energy on policy aimed at such a long run that efforts to predict the conditions upon which it must be based are mere speculation. To this the "idealist" replies that short-run policies of today create the conditions of the future, so it is suicidal not to give such intelligent consideration as we can to the conditions which are possible and the goals which are desired in the long run. If this is not done, say the "idealists," policy becomes a drift toward dangerous rapids which may not be very far ahead in a rapidly changing world. In any case, they say, it is clear that the world has so shrunk and interdependencies are so pervasive that the horizon of policy-making must be lifted from the nation to the world, from immediate antagonisms to more permanent ends enlisting general cooperation.

I conclude that statesmen should guide their policies by a philosophy of "realistic idealism" or "idealistic realism." Realism will teach them that both power and values, both conditions and symbols, both passion and reason, both necessities and choices have influence in human affairs, and will urge them to appraise their relative influence in the changing situations with which they are faced. Idealism will suggest attention to the wisdom of Pascal, echoing Solon and Grotius: "Justice without force is impotent; force without justice is tyrannical. It is necessary therefore to unite justice and force and to make that which is just strong and that which is strong just."

The Melian Conference

THUCYDIDES

THE NEXT SUMMER ALCIBIADES SAILED WITH TWENTY SHIPS TO ARGOS AND SEIZED THE SUSPECTED PERSONS STILL LEFT OF THE LACEDAEMONIAN FACTION TO THE NUMBER OF THREE HUNDRED, WHOM THE ATHENIANS FORTHWITH LODGED IN THE NEIGHBOURING ISLANDS OF THEIR EMPIRE. The Athenians also made an expedition against the isle of Melos with thirty ships of their own, six Chian,

From *The History of the Peloponnesian War,* translated by Richard Crawley. Everyman's Library Edition. Reprinted by permission of E. P. Dutton and Co., Inc. and J. M. Dent & Sons Ltd., London.

and two Lesbian vessels, sixteen hundred heavy infantry, three hundred archers, and twenty mounted archers from Athens, and about fiften hundred heavy infantry from the allies and the islanders. The Melians are a colony of Lacedaemon that would not submit to the Athenians like the other islanders, and at first remained neutral and took no part in the struggle, but afterwards upon the Athenians using violence and plundering their territory, assumed an attitude of open hostility. Cleomedes, son of Lycomedes, and Tisias, son of Tisimachus, the generals, encamping in their territory with the above armament, before doing any harm to their land, sent envoys to negotiate. These the Melians did not bring before the people, but bade them state the object of their mission to the magistrates and the few; upon which the Athenian envoys spoke as follows:

Athenians.—"Since the negotiations are not to go on before the people, in order that we may not be able to speak straight on without interruption, and deceive the ears of the multitude by seductive arguments which would pass without refutation (for we know that this is the meaning of our being brought before the few), what if you who sit there were to pursue a method more cautious still! Make no set speech yourselves, but take us up at whatever you do not like, and settle that before going any farther. And first tell us if this proposition of ours suits you."

The Melian commissioners answered:

Melians.—"To the fairness of quietly instructing each other as you propose there is nothing to object; but your military preparations are too far advanced to agree with what you say, as we see you are come to be judges in your own cause, and that all we can reasonably expect from this negotiation is war, if we prove to have right on our side and refuse to submit, and in the contrary case, slavery."

Athenians.—"If you have met to reason about presentiments of the future, or for anything else than to consult for the safety of your state upon the facts that you see before you, we will give over; otherwise we will go on."

Melians.—"It is natural and excusable for men in our position to turn more ways than one both in thought and utterance. However, the question in this conference is, as you say, the safety of our country; and the discussion, if you please, can proceed in the way which you propose."

Athenians.—"For ourselves, we shall not trouble you with specious pretences—either of how we have a right to our empire because we overthrew the Mede, or are now attacking you because of wrong that you have done us—and make a long speech which would not be believed; and in return we hope that you, instead of thinking to influence us by saying that you did not join the Lacedaemonians, although their colonists, or that you have done us no wrong, will aim at what is feasible, holding in view the real sentiments of us both; since you know as well as we do that right, as the world goes, is only in question between equals in power, while the strong do what they can and the weak suffer what they must."

Melians.—"As we think, at any rate, it is expedient—we speak as we are obliged, since you enjoin us to let right alone and talk only of interest—that you should not destroy what is our common protection, the privilege of being allowed in danger to invoke what is fair and right, and even to profit by arguments not strictly valid if they can be got to pass current. And you are as much interested in this as any, as your fall would be a signal for the heaviest vengeance and an example for the world to mediate upon."

Athenians.—"The end of our empire, if end it should, does not frighten us: a rival empire like Lacedaemon, even if Lacedaemon was our real antagonist, is not so terrible to the vanquished as subjects who by themselves attack and overpower their rulers. This, however, is a risk that we are content to take. We will now proceed to show you that we are come here in the interest of our empire, and that we shall say what we are now going to say, for the preservation of your country; as we would fain exercise that empire over you without trouble, and see you preserved for the good of us both."

Melians.—"And how, pray, could it turn out as good for us to serve as for you to rule?"

Athenians.—"Because you would have the advantage of submitting before suffering the worst, and we should gain by not destroying you."

Melians.—"So that you would not consent to our being neutral, friends instead of enemies, but allies of neither side."

Athenians.—"No; for your hostility cannot so much hurt us as your friendship will be an argument to our subjects of our weakness, and your enmity of our power."

Melians.—"Is that your subjects' idea of equity, to put those who have nothing to do with you in the same category with peoples that are most of them your own colonists, and some conquered rebels?"

Athenians.—"As far as right goes they think one has as much of it as the other, and that if any maintain their independence it is because they are strong, and that if we do not molest them it is because we are afraid; so that besides extending our empire we should gain in security by your subjection; the fact that you are islanders and weaker than others rendering it all the more important that you should not succeed in baffling the masters of the sea."

Melians.—"But do you consider that there is no security in the policy which we indicate? For here again if you debar us from talking about justice and invite us to obey your interest, we also must explain ours, and try to persuade you, if the two happen to coincide. How can you avoid making enemies of all existing neutrals who shall look at our case and conclude from it that one day or another you will attack them? And what is this but to make greater the enemies that you have already, and to force others to become so who would otherwise have never thought of it?"

Athenians.—"Why, the fact is that continentals generally give us but little alarm; the liberty which they enjoy will long prevent their taking precautions against us; it is rather islanders like yourselves, outside our empire, and subjects smarting under the yoke, who would be the most likely to take a rash step and lead themselves and us into obvious danger."

Melians.—"Well then, if you risk so much to retain your empire, and your subjects to get rid of it, it were surely great baseness and cowardice in us who are still free not to try everything that can be tried, before submitting to your yoke."

Athenians.—"Not if you are well advised, the contest not being an equal one, with honour as the prize and shame as the penalty, but a question of self-preservation and of not resisting those who are far stronger than you are."

Melians.—"But we know that the fortune of war is sometimes more impartial than the disproportion of numbers might lead one to suppose; to submit is to give ourselves over to despair, while action still preserves for us a hope that we may stand erect."

Athenians.—"Hope, danger's comforter, may be indulged in by those who have abundant resources, if not without loss at all events without ruin; but its nature is to be extravagant, and those who go so far as to put their all upon the venture see it in its true colours only when they are ruined; but so long as the discovery would enable them to guard against it, it is never found wanting. Let not this be the case with you, who are weak and hang on a single turn of the scale; nor be like the vulgar, who, abandoning such security as human means may still afford, when visible hopes fail them in extremity, turn to invisible, to prophecies and oracles, and other such inventions that delude men with hopes to their destruction."

Melians.—"You may be sure that we are as well aware as you of the difficulty of contending against your power and fortune, unless the terms be equal. But we trust that the gods may grant us fortune as good as yours, since we are just men fighting against unjust, and that what we want in power will be made up by the alliance of the Lacedaemonians, who are bound, if only for very shame, to come to the aid of their kindred. Our confidence, therefore, after all is not so utterly irrational."

Athenians.—"When you speak of the favour of the gods, we may as fairly hope for that as yourselves; neither our pretensions nor our conduct being in any way contrary to what men believe of the gods, or practice among themselves. Of the gods we believe, and of men we know, that by a necessary law of their nature they rule wherever they can. And it is not as if we were the first to make this law, or to act upon it when made: we found it existing before us, and shall leave it to exist for ever after us; all we do is to make use of it, knowing that you and everybody else, having the same power as we have, would do the same as we do. Thus, as far as the gods are concerned, we have no fear and no reason to fear that we shall be at a disadvantage. But when we come to your notion about the Lacedaemonians, which leads you to believe that shame will make them help you, here we bless your simplicity but do not envy your folly. The Lacedaemonians, when their own interests or their country's laws are in question, are the worthiest men alive; of their conduct towards others much might be said, but no clearer idea of it could be given than by shortly saying that of all the men we know they are most conspicuous in considering what is agreeable honourable, and what is expedient just. Such a way of thinking does not promise much for the safety which you now unreasonably count upon."

Melians.—"But it is for this very reason that we now trust to their respect for expediency to prevent them from betraying the Melians, their colonists, and thereby losing the confidence of their friends in Hellas and helping their enemies."

Athenians.—"Then you do not adopt the view that expediency goes with security, while justice and honour cannot be followed without danger; and danger the Lacedaemonians generally court as little as possible."

Melians.—"But we believe that they would be more likely to face even danger for our sake, and with more confidence than for others, as our nearness to Peloponnese makes it easier for them to act, and our common blood insures our fidelity."

Athenians.—"Yes, but what an intending ally trusts to, is not the goodwill of those who ask his aid, but a decided superiority of power for action; and the Lacedaemonians look to this even more than others. At least, such is their distrust of their home resources that it is only with numerous allies that they attack a neighbour; now is it likely that while we are masters of the sea they will cross over to an island?"

Melians.—"But they would have others to send. The Cretan sea is a wide one, and it is more difficult for those who command it to intercept others, than for those who wish to elude them to do so safely. And should the Lacedaemonians miscarry in this, they would fall upon your land, and upon those left of your allies whom Brasidas did not reach; and instead of places which are not yours, you will have to fight for your own country and your own confederacy."

Athenians.—"Some diversion of the kind you speak of you may one day experience, only to learn, as others have done, that the Athenians never once yet withdrew from a siege for fear of any. But we are struck by the fact, that after saying you would consult for the safety of your country, in all this discussion you have mentioned nothing which men might trust in and think to be saved by. Your strongest arguments depend upon hope and the future, and your actual resources are too scanty, as compared with those arrayed against you, for you to come out victorious. You will therefore show great blindness of judgment, unless, after allowing us to retire, you can find some counsel more prudent than this. You will surely not be caught by that idea of disgrace, which in dangers that are disgraceful, and at the same time too plain to be mistaken, proves so fatal to mankind; since in too many cases the very men that have their eyes perfectly open to what they are rushing into, let the thing called disgrace, by the mere influence of a seductive name, lead them on to a point at which they become so enslaved by the phrase as in fact to fall wilfully into hopeless disaster, and incur disgrace more disgraceful as the companion of error, than when it comes as the result of misfortune. This, if you are well advised, you will guard against; and you will not think it dishonourable to submit to the greatest city in Hellas, when it makes you the moderate offer of becoming its tributary ally, without ceasing to enjoy the country that belongs to you; nor when you have the choice given you between war and security, will you be so blinded as to choose the worse. And it is certain that those who do not yield to their equals, who keep terms with their superiors, and are moderate towards their inferiors, on the whole succeed best. Think over the matter, therefore, after our withdrawal, and reflect once and again that it is for your country that you are consulting, that you have not more than one, and that upon this one deliberation depends its prosperity or ruin."

The Athenians now withdrew from the conference; and the Melians, left to themselves, came to a decision corresponding with what they had maintained in the discussion, and answered, "Our resolution, Athenians, is the same as it was at first. We will not in a moment deprive of freedom a city that has been inhabited these seven hundred years; but we put our trust in the fortune by which the gods have preserved it until now, and in the help of men, that is, of the Lacedaemonians; and so we will try and save ourselves. Meanwhile we invite you to allow us to be friends to you and foes to neither party, and to retire from our country after making such a treaty as shall seem fit to us both."

Such was the answer of the Melians. The Athenians now departing from the conference said, "Well, you alone, as it seems to us, judging from these resolutions, regard what is future as more certain than what is before your eyes, and what is out of sight, in your eagerness, as already coming to pass; and as you have staked most on, and trusted most in, the Lacedaemonians, your fortune, and your hopes, so will you be most completely deceived."

The Athenian envoys now returned to the army; and the Melians showing no sign of yielding, the generals at once betook to hostilities, and drew a line of circumvallation round the Melians, dividing the work among the different states. Subsequently the Athenians returned with most of their army, leaving behind them a certain number of their own citizens and of the allies to keep guard by land and sea. The force thus left stayed on and besieged the place.

. . . Meanwhile the Melians attacked by night and took the part of the Athenian lines over against the market, and killed some of the men, and brought in corn and all else that they could find useful to them, and so returned and kept quiet, while the Athenians took measures to keep better guard in future.

Summer was now over. The next winter the Lacedaemonians intended to invade the Argive territory, but arriving at the frontier found the sacrifices for crossing unfavourable, and went back again. This intention of theirs gave the Argives suspicions of certain of their fellow-citizens, some of whom they arrested; others, however, escaped them. About the same time the Melians again took another part of the Athenian lines which were but feebly garrisoned. Reinforcements afterwards arriving from Athens in consequence, under the command of Philocrates, son of Demeas, the siege was now pressed vigorously; and some treachery taking place inside, the Melians surrendered at discretion to the Athenians, who put to death all the grown men whom they took, and sold women and children for slaves, and subsequently sent out five hundred colonists and inhabited the place themselves.

II WHAT CAUSES WAR?

The Wish for War

ALDOUS HUXLEY

EVERY ROAD TOWARDS A BETTER STATE OF SOCIETY IS BLOCKED, SOONER OR LATER, BY WAR, BY THREATS OF WAR, BY PREPARATIONS FOR WAR. That is the truth, the odious and unescapable truth. . . .

Let us very briefly consider the nature of war, the causes of war and the possible alternatives to war, the methods of curing the mania of militarism afflicting the world at the present time.

Nature of War

(i) War is a purely human phenomenon. The lower animals fight duels in the heat of sexual excitement and kill for food and oc-. casionally for sport. But the activities of a wolf eating a sheep or a cat playing with a mouse are no more warlike than the activities of butchers and foxhunters. Similarly, fights between hungry dogs or rutting stags are like pot-house quarrels and have nothing in common with war, which is mass murder organized in cold blood. Some social insects, it is true, go out to fight in armies; but their attacks are always directed against members of another species. Man is unique in organizing the mass murder of his own species.

(ii) Certain biologists, of whom Sir Arthur Keith is the most eminent, consider that war acts as "nature's pruning hook," ensuring the survival of the fittest among civilized individuals and nations. This is obviously nonsensical. War tends to eliminate the young and strong and to spare the unhealthy. Nor is there any reason for supposing that people with traditions of violence and a good technique of war-making are superior to other peoples. The most valuable human beings are not necessarily the most warlike. Nor as a matter of historical fact is it always the most warlike who survive. We can sum up by saying that, so far as individuals are concerned, war selects dysgenically; so far as nations and peoples are concerned it selects purely at random, sometimes ensuring the domination and survival of the more warlike peoples, sometimes, on the contrary ensuring their destruction and the survival of the unwarlike.

(iii) There exist at the present time certain primitive human societies, such as that of the Eskimos, in which war is unknown and even unthinkable. All civilized societies, however, are warlike. The question arises whether the correlation between war and civilization is necessary and unavoidable. The evidence of archaeology seems to point to the conclusion that war made its appearance at a particular moment in the history of early civilization. There is reason to suppose that the rise of war was correlated with an abrupt change in the mode of human consciousness. This change, as Dr. J. D. Unwin suggests, may have been correlated with increased sexual continence on the part of the ruling classes of the warlike societies. The archaeological symptom of the change is the almost sudden appearance of royal palaces and elaborate funerary monuments. The rise of war appears to be connected with the rise of self-conscious leaders, preoccupied with the ideas of personal domination and personal survival after death. Even today when economic considerations are supposed to be supreme, ideas of "glory" and "immortal fame" still ferment in the minds of the dictators and generals, and play an important part in the causation of war.

(iv) The various civilizations of the world have adopted fundamentally different attitudes towards war. Compare the Chinese and Indian attitudes towards war with the European. Europeans have always worshipped the military hero and, since the rise of Christianity, the martyr. Not so the Chinese. The ideal human being, according to Confucian standards, is the just, reasonable, humane and cultivated man, living at peace in an ordered and harmonious society. Confucianism, to quote Max Weber, "prefers a wise prudence to mere physical courage and declares that an untimely sacrifice of life is unfitting for a wise man." Our European admiration for military heroism and martyrdom has tended to make men believe that a good death is more important than a good life and that a long course of folly and crime can be cancelled out by a single act of physical courage. The mysticism of Lao Tsú (or whoever was the author of the Tao Téh Ching) confirms and completes the rationalism of Confucious. The Tao is an eternal cosmic principle that is, at the same time, the inmost root of the individual's being. Those who would live in harmony with Tao must refrain from assertiveness, self-importance and aggressiveness, must cultivate humility and return good for evil.

Since the time of Confucius and Lao Tsu, Chinese ideals have been essentially pacifistic. European poets have glorified war; European theologians have found justification for religious persecution and nationalistic aggression. This has not been so in China. Chinese philosophers and Chinese poets have almost all been anti-militarists. The soldier was regarded as an inferior being, not to be put on the same level with the scholar or administrator. It is one of the tragedies of history that the Westernization of China should have meant the progressive militarization of a culture which, for nearly three thousand years, has consistently preached the pacifist ideal. Conscription was imposed on large numbers of Chinese in 1936, and the soldier is now held up for admiration. Comic, but significant, is the following quotation from the *New York Times* of June 17, 1937. "Sin Wan Pao, Shanghai's leading Chinese language newspaper, advised Adolf Hitler and Benito Mussolini to-day to follow the examples of General Yang Sen . . . war lord and commander of the Twentieth Army in Szechwan Province. The general has twenty-seven wives. 'Only 40 years old, General Yang has a child for every year of his life,' the newspaper said. 'General Yang has established complete military training for his offspring. It begins when a young Yang reaches the age of 7, with strict treatment by the time the child is 14. The family has an exclusive military camp. When visitors come, the Yang children hold a military reception and march past the guests in strict review order.'" One laughs; but the unfortunate truth is that General Yang and the forty little Yangs in their strict review order are grotesquely symptomatic of the new, worse, Western spirit of a China that has turned its back on the wisdom of Confucius and Lao Tsu and gone whoring after European militarism. Japanese aggression is bound to intensify this new militaristic spirit in China. Within a couple of generations, it is possible that China will be an aggressive imperialist power.

Indian pacifism finds its completest expression in the teaching of Buddha. Buddhism, like Hinduism, teaches *ahimsa*, or harmlessness towards all living beings. It forbids even laymen to have anything to do with the manufacture and sale of arms, with the making of poisons and intoxicants, with soldiering or the slaughter of animals. Alone of all the great world religions, Buddhism made its way without persecution, censorship or inquisition. In all these respects its record is enormously superior to that of Christianity, which made its way among people wedded to militarism and which was able to justify the bloodthirsty tendencies of its adherents by an appeal to the savage Bronze-Age literature of the Old Testament. For Buddhists, anger is always and unconditionally disgraceful. For Christians, brought up to identify Jehovah with God, there is such a thing as "righteous indignation." Thanks to this possibility of indignation being righteous, Christians have always felt themselves justified in making war and committing the most hideous atrocities.

The fact that it should have been possible for the three principal civilizations of the world to adopt three distinct philosophic attitudes towards war is encouraging; for it proves that there is nothing "natural" about our present situation in relation to war. The existence of war and of our political and theological justifications of war is no more "natural" than were the sanguinary manifestations of sexual jealousy, so common in Europe up to the beginning of the last century and now of such rare occurrence. To murder one's unfaithful wife, or the lover of one's sister or mother, was something that used to be "done." Being socially correct, it was regarded as inevitable, a manifestation of unchanging "human nature." Such murders are no longer fashionable among the best people, therefore no longer seem to us "natural." The malleability of human nature is such that there is no reason why, if we so desire and set to work in the right way, we should not rid ourselves of war as we have freed ourselves from the weary necessity of committing a *crime passionnel* every time a wife, mistress or female relative gets herself seduced. War is not a law of nature, not even a law of human nature. It exists because men wish it to exist; and we know as a matter of historical fact, that the intensity of that wish has varied from absolute zero to a frenzied maximum. The wish for war in the contemporary world is widespread and of high intensity. But our wills are to some extent free; we can wish otherwise than we actually do. It is enormously difficult for us to change our wishes in this matter; but the enormously difficult is not the impossible. We must be grateful for even the smallest crumbs of comfort.

Causes of War

War exists because people wish it to exist. They wish it to exist for a variety of reasons.

(i) Many people like war because they find their peace-time occupations either positively humiliating and frustrating, or just negatively boring. In their studies on suicide Durkheim and, more recently, Halbwachs have shown that the suicide-rate among non-combatants tends to fall during war-time to about two-thirds of its normal figure. This decline must be put down to the following causes: to the simplification of life during war-time (it is in complex and highly developed societies that the suicide rate is highest); to the intensification of nationalist sentiment to a point where most individuals are living in a state of chronic enthusiasm; to the fact that life during war-time takes on significance and purposefulness, so that even the most intrinsically boring job is ennobled as "war work"; to the artificial prosperity induced, at any rate for a time, by the expansion of war industries; to the increased sexual freedom which is always claimed by societies, all or some of whose members live under the menace of sudden death. Add to this the fact that life in war-time is (or at least was in previous wars) extremely interesting, at least during the first years of the war. Rumour runs riot, and the papers are crammed every morning with the most thrilling news. To the influence of the press must be attributed the fact that, whereas during the Franco-Prussian War the suicide rate declined only in the belligerent countries, during the World War a considerable decline was registered even in the neutral states. In 1870 about half the inhabitants of Europe were unable to read, and newspapers were few and expensive. By 1914 primary education had everywhere been compulsory for more than a generation and the addiction to newspaper reading had spread to all classes of the population. Thus, even neutrals were able to enjoy, vicariously and at second hand, the exciting experience of war.

Up to the end of the last war non-combatants, except in countries actually subject to invasion, were not in great physical danger. In any future war it is clear that they will be exposed to risks almost, if not quite, as great as those faced by the fighting men. This will certainly tend to diminish the enthusiasm of non-combatants for war. But if it turns out that the effects of air bombardment are less frightful than most experts at present believe they will be, this enthusiasm may not be extinguished altogether, at any rate during the first months of a war. During the last war, a fair proportion of the combatants actually enjoyed some phases at least of the fighting. The escape from the dull and often stultifying routines of peace-time life was welcomed, even though that escape was bought at a price of physical hardship and the risk of death and mutilation. It is possible that conditions in any future war will be so appalling that even the most naturally adventurous and combative human beings will soon come to hate and fear the process of fighting. But until the next war actually breaks out, nobody can have experience of the new conditions of fighting. Meanwhile, all the governments are actively engaged in making a subtle kind of propaganda that is directed against potential enemies but not against war. They warn their subjects that they will be bombarded from the air by fleets of enemy planes; they persuade or compel them to subject themselves to air-raid drills and other forms of military discipline; they proclaim the necessity of piling up enormous armaments for the purpose of counter-attack and retaliation and they actually build those armaments to the tune, in most European countries, of nearly or fully half the total national revenue. At the same time they do all in their power to belittle the danger from air raids. Millions of gas masks are made and distributed with assurances that they will provide complete protection. Those who make such assurances know quite well that they are false. Gas masks cannot be worn by infants, invalids or the old and give no protection whatsoever against vesicants and some of the poisonous smokes, which for this reason will be the chemicals chiefly used by the air navies of the world. Meanwhile warnings by impartial experts are either officially ignored or belittled. (The attitude of the government's spokesman at the British Medical Association meeting at Oxford in 1936 and that of the *Times* in 1937 towards the Cambridge scientists who warned the public against the probable effects of air bombardment are highly significant in this context.) The whole effort of all the governments is directed, I repeat, to making propaganda against enemies and in favour of war; against those who try to tell the truth about the nature and effects of the new armaments and in favour of manufacturing such armaments in ever increasing quantities. There are two reasons why such propaganda is as successful as it is. The first, as I have explained in this paragraph, must be sought in the fact that, up to the present, many non-combatants and some combatants have found war a welcome relief from the tedium of peace. The second reason will be set forth in the following paragraph, which deals with another aspect of the psychological causation of war.

(ii) A principal cause of war is nationalism, and nationalism is immensely popular because it is psychologically satisfying to individual nationalists. Every nationalism is an idolatrous religion, in which the god is the personified state, represented in many instances by a more or less deified king or dictator. Membership of the *ex-hypothesi* divine nation is thought of as imparting a kind of mystical pre-eminence. Thus, all "God's Englishmen" are superior to "the lesser breeds without the law" and every individual God's-Englishman is entitled to think himself superior to every member of the lesser breed, even the lordliest and wealthiest, even the most intelligent, the most highly gifted, the most saintly. Any man who believes strongly enough in the local nationalistic idolatry can find in his faith an antidote against even the most acute inferiority complex. Dictators feed the flames of national vanity and reap their reward in the gratitude of millions to whom the conviction that they are participants in the glory of the divine nation brings relief from the gnawing consciousness of poverty, social unimportance and personal insignificance.

Self-esteem has as its complement disparagement of others. Vanity and pride beget contempt and hatred. But contempt and hatred are exciting emotions—emotions from which people "get a kick." Devotees of one national idolatry enjoy getting the kick of hatred and contempt for devotees of other idolatries. They pay for that enjoyment by having to prepare for the wars which hatred and contempt render almost inevitable. Another point. In the normal course of events most men and women behave tolerably well. This means that they must frequently repress their anti-social impulses. They find a vicarious satisfaction for these impulses through films and stories about gangsters, pirates, swindlers, bad bold barons and the like. Now, the personified nation, as I have pointed out already, is divine in size, strength and mystical superiority, but sub-human in moral character. The ethics of international politics are precisely those of the gangster, the pirate, the swindler, the bad bold baron. The exemplary citizen can indulge in vicarious criminality, not only on the films, but also in the field of international relations. The divine nation of whom he is mystically a part bullies and cheats, blusters and threatens in a way which many people find profoundly satisfying to their sedulously repressed lower natures. Submissive to the wife, kind to the children, courteous to the neighbors, the soul of honesty in business, the good citizen feels a thrill of delight when his country "takes a strong line," "enhances its prestige," "scores a diplomatic victory," "increases its territory"—in other words when it bluffs, bullies, swindles and steals. The nation is a strange deity. It imposes difficult duties and demands the greatest sacrifices and, because it does this and because human beings have a hunger and thirst after righteousness, it is loved. But it is also loved because it panders to the lowest elements in human nature and because men and women like to have excuses to feel pride and hatred, because they long to taste even at second hand the joys of criminality.

* * *

Cure for War

(i) War, as we have seen, is tolerated, and by some even welcomed, because peace-time occupations seem boring, humiliating and pointless.

The application of the principle of self-government to industry and business should go far to deliver men and women in subordinate positions from the sense of helpless humiliation which is induced by the need of obeying the arbitrary orders of irresponsible superiors; and the fact of being one of a small co-operative group should do something to make the working life of its members seem more interesting. Heightened interest can also be obtained by suitably rearranging the individual's tasks. Fourier insisted long ago on the desirableness of variety in labour, and in recent years his suggestion has been acted upon, experimentally, in a number of factories in Germany, America, Russia, and elsewhere. The result has been a diminution of boredom, and in many cases, an increase in the volume of production. Tasks may be varied slightly, as when a worker in a cigarette factory is shifted from the job of feeding tobacco into a machine to the job of packing and weighing. Or they may be varied radically and fundamentally, as when workers alternate between industrial and agricultural labour. In both cases the psychological effects seem to be good.

(ii) It was suggested that the war-time decline in the suicide rate was due, among other things, to the heightened significance and purposefulness of life during a national emergency. At such a time the end for which all are striving is clearly seen; duties are simple and explicit; the vagueness and uncertainty of peace-time ideals gives place to the sharp definition of the war-time ideal, which is: victory at all costs; the bewildering complexities of the peace-time social patterns are replaced by the beautifully simple pattern of a community fighting for its existence. Danger heightens the sense of social solidarity and quickens patriotic enthusiasm. Life takes on sense and meaning and is lived at a high pitch of emotional intensity.

The apparent pointlessness of modern life in time of peace and its lack of significance and purpose are due to the fact that, in the western world at least, the prevailing cosmology is what Mr. Gerald Heard has called the "mechanomorphic" cosmology of modern science. The universe is regarded as a great machine pointlessly grinding its way towards ultimate stagnation and death; men are tiny offshoots of the universal machine, running down to their own private death; physical life is the only real life; mind is a mere product of body; personal success and material well-being are the ultimate measures of value, the things for which a reasonable person should live. Introduced suddenly to this mechanomorphic cosmology, many of the Polynesian races have refused to go on multiplying their species and are in process of dying of a kind of psychological consumption. Europeans are of tougher fibre than the South Sea Islanders and besides they have had nearly three hundred years in which to become gradually acclimatized to the new cosmology. But even they have felt the effects of mechanomorphism. They move through life hollow with pointlessness, trying to fill the void within them by external stimuli—newspaper reading, day dreaming at the films, radio music and chatter, the playing and above all the watching of games, "good times" of every sort. Meanwhile any doctrine that offers to restore point and purpose to life is eagerly welcomed. Hence the enormous success of the nationalistic and communistic idolatries which deny any meaning to the universe as a whole, but insist on the importance and significance of certain arbitrarily selected parts of the whole—the deified nation, the divine class.

Nationalism first became a religion in Germany, during the Napoleonic wars. Communism took its rise some fifty years later. Those who did not become devotees of the new idolatries either remained Christians, clinging to doctrines that became intellectually less and less acceptable with every advance of science, or else accepted mechanomorphism and became convinced of the pointlessness of life. The World War was a product of nationalism and was tolerated and even welcomed by the great masses of those who found life pointless. War brought only a passing relief to the victims of mechanomorphic philosophy. Disillusion, fatigue and cynicism succeeded the initial enthusiasm and when it was over, the sense of pointlessness became a yawning abyss that demanded to be filled with ever more and intenser distractions, even better "good times." But good times are not a meaning or a purpose; the void could never be filled by them. Consequently when the nationalists and communists appeared with their simple idolatries and their proclamation that, though life might mean nothing as a whole, it did at least prossess a temporary and partial significance, there was a powerful reaction away from the cynicism of the post-war years. Millions of young people embraced the new idolatrous religions, found a meaning in life, a purpose for their existence and were ready, in consequence, to make sacrifices, accept hardships, display courage, fortitude, temperance and indeed all the virtues except the essential and primary ones, without which all the rest may serve merely as the means for doing evil more effectively. Love and awareness—these are the primary, essential virtues. But nationalism and communism are partial and exclusive idolatries that inculcate hatred, pride, hardness, and impose that intolerant dogmatism that cramps intelligence and narrows the field of interest and sympathetic awareness.

The "heads" of pointlessness has as its "tails" idolatrous nationalism and communism. Our world oscillates from a neurasthenia that welcomes war as a relief from boredom to a mania that results in war being made. The cure for both these fearful maladies is the same—the inculcation of a cosmology more nearly corresponding to reality than either mechanomorphism or the grotesque philosophies underlying the nationalistic and communistic idolatries.

What Is War?

EMERY REVES

IT IS COMMONLY TAKEN FOR GRANTED THAT WE CAN NEVER ABOLISH WAR BETWEEN NATIONS, BECAUSE WAR IS IN THE NATURE OF MAN. It is even more widely accepted that war has innumerable causes and that to try to abolish all of them would be a hopeless task.

We must refuse to accept such apparently true but basically deceptive statements, if we would avoid becoming the helpless victims of superstition. No one knows just what "human nature" is. Nor is this a relevant question. Assuming or even admitting that certain evils *are* part of "human nature," this does not mean that we should sit passively and refuse to investigate the conditions which cause the evils to become deadly and the possibility of avoiding their devastating effects.

Since man began to think about life and himself, it has been generally accepted that appendicitis and gallstones were in the nature of man. Indeed, they are. But after thousands of years, during which men died from these fatal evils of "human nature," some people had the courage to take a knife and cut open the diseased part to see what was happening. Appendicitis and gallstones continue to be "in the nature of man." But now man does not necessarily die from them.

Superficially, it looks as though wars have been waged for a great variety of reasons. The struggle for food and mere survival among primitive tribes, feuds between families and dynasties, quarrels between cities and provinces, religious fanaticism, rival commercial interests, antagonistic social ideals, the race for colonies, economic competition and many other forces have exploded in fatal and devastating wars.

Since time immemorial, among primitive people, families, clans and tribes have fought, enslaved and exterminated each other for food, shelter, women, pastures, hunting grounds. Each group had a "religion," a demon, a totem, a god, or several of each, whose divine and supreme will was interpreted by priests, medicine men and magicians, and who protected them from the dangers and depredations of other clans; inspired and incited them to war upon and to annihilate their neighbors. Life at that stage of society was no different from the life of fish in the deep and beasts in the jungle.

Later, at a higher level of civilization, we see larger settlements and city communities fighting and warring with each other. Nineveh, Babylon, Troy, Cnossos, Athens, Sparta, Rome, Carthage and many other similar rival settlements continuously battled, until all of them were finally destroyed.

Under the inspiration and leadership of dynamic personalities, powerful clans and races set out upon wars of conquest so that they might rule over new lands and subjects in safety and wealth. Tiglath Pileser, Nebuchadnezzar, Darius, Alexander, Attila, Genghis Khan and other conquerors in history waged large-scale wars to subdue the world as it was known to them.

For centuries after the fall of Rome, European society was rocked by endless clashes and battles among thousands of feudal barons.

After the consolidation of the three world religions originating in Judaism—Catholicism, Islamism and Protestantism—a long series of wars were fought by the followers of these expanding and conflicting faiths. Kings, princes and knights took part in crusades to defend and spread their own creeds, to destroy and exterminate the believers in the other creeds. The great wars fought by Constantine, Charles V, Suleiman, Philip II, Gustavus Adolphus and other mighty rulers of the Middle Ages were mostly attempts to unify the Western world under one religion.

Following the collapse of the feudal system, with the development of craftsmanship, trade and shipping, a middle class of modern bourgeois citizenry emerged and began to crystallize. The field of conflict again shifted, and wars were fought by great commercial centers, Venice, Florence, Augsburg, Hamburg, Amsterdam, Ghent, Danzig and other city units, which impressed their own citizens and hired mercenaries.

Then another series of wars were waged by absolute monarchs in the interest of their dynasties, to widen the domains of the great royal houses. The Hapsburg, Bourbon, Wittelsbach, Romanoff and Stuart monarchies and dozens of minor dynasties led their subjects into battle to defend and extend their power and rule.

A different type of war was waged between smaller kingdoms and principalities to obtain supremacy within a particular system of monarchy, such as the wars between England and Scotland; Saxony, Bavaria and Prussia; Tuscany, Piedmont and Parma; Burgundy, Touraine and Normandy.

And finally, the creation of modern nation-states at the end of the eighteenth century has brought about a series of gigantic conflicts between whole conscripted nations, culminating in the first and second world wars.

Looking back over history, war appears a hundred-headed

hydra. As soon as the peacemakers chop off one head, new ones immediately appear on the monster. Yet, if we analyze what seem to be the manifold causes of past wars, it is not difficult to observe a thread of continuity running through these strange historical phenomena.

Why did cities once wage wars against each other and why do municipalities no longer fight each other with weapons today? Why, at certain times, have great landowner barons warred with each other and why have they now ceased that practice? Why did the various churches plunge their adherents into armed warfare and why today are they able to worship side by side without shooting each other? Why did Scotland and England, Saxony and Prussia, Parma and Tuscany, at a certain period in their history, go to battle against each other and why have they ceased fighting today?

A careful study of human history reveals that the assumption that war is inherent in human nature—and therefore eternal— is shallow and faulty, that it is only a superficial impression. Far from being inexplicable or inevitable, we can invariably determine the situations that predispose to war, and the conditions which lead to war.

The real cause of all wars has been the same. They have occurred with the mathematical regularity of a natural law at clearly determined moments as the result of clearly definable conditions.

If we try to detect the mechanism visibly in operation, the single cause ever-present at the outbreak of each and every conflict known to human history, if we attempt to reduce the seemingly innumerable causes of war to a common denominator, two clear and unmistakable observations emerge.

1. Wars between groups of men forming social units always take place when these units—tribes, dynasties, churches, cities, nations—exercise unrestricted sovereign power.

2. Wars between these social units cease the moment sovereign power is transferred from them to a larger or higher unit.

From these observations we can deduce a social law with the characteristics of an axiom that applies to and explains each and every war in the history of all time.

War takes place whenever and wherever non-integrated social units of equal sovereignty come into contact.

War between given social units of equal sovereignty is the permanent symptom of each successive phase of civilization. Wars always ceased when a higher unit established its own sovereignty, absorbing the sovereignties of the conflicting smaller social groups. After such transfers of sovereignty, a period of peace followed, which lasted only until the new social units came into contact. Then a new series of wars began.

The causes and reasons alleged by history to have brought about these conflicts are irrelevant, as they continued to exist long after the wars had ceased. Cities and provinces continue to compete with each other. Religious convictions are just as different today as they were during the religious wars.

The only thing that did change was the institutionalization of sovereignty, the transfer of sovereignty from one type of social unit to another and a higher one.

Just as there is one and only one cause for wars between men on this earth, so history shows that peace—not peace in an absolute and utopian sense, but concrete peace between given social groups warring with each other at given times—has always been established in one way and only in one way.

Peace between fighting groups of men was never possible and wars succeeded one another until some sovereignty, some sovereign source of law, some sovereign power was set up *over* and *above* the clashing social units, integrating the warring units into a higher sovereignty.

Once the mechanics and the fundamental causes of wars—of all wars—are realized, the futility and childishness of the passionate debates about armament and disarmament must be apparent to all.

If human society were organized so that relations between groups and units in contact were regulated by democratically controlled law and legal institutions, then modern science could go ahead, devise and produce the most devastating weapons, and there would be no war. But if we allow sovereign rights to reside in the separate units and groups without regulating their relations by law, then we can prohibit every weapon, even a penknife, and people will beat out each other's brains with clubs.

It is tragic to witness the utter blindness and ignorance of our governments and political leaders in regard to this all-important and vital problem of the world.

Voices are now being raised in the United States and in Great Britain demanding compulsory military service and the maintenance of extensive armaments in peacetime. The argument is that if in 1939 the United States and Great Britain had been armed, Germany and Japan would never have dared to start a war. The Western democracies must not be caught unprepared again. If conscription is introduced and America and England have large armed forces ready to fight at a moment's notice, no other power will dare attack them, and they will not be forced into war. That sounds logical. But what about France, the Soviet Union, Belgium, Czechoslovakia, Yugoslavia and the other countries which always had conscription and large standing armies? Did this save them from war?

After 1919, the peacemakers were obsessed by the idea that armaments lead to wars, that a *sine qua non* for world peace is the general limitation and reduction of armaments on sea, land and in the air. Disarmament completely dominated international thought for fifteen years after the signature of the Covenant. Tremendous amounts of propaganda were poured into the public ear by printed and spoken words, to the effect that "armament manufacturers" were the real culprits responsible for wars, that no nation should build battleships bigger than thirty-five thousand tons, that the caliber of guns should be reduced, submarine and gas warfare prohibited, military service shortened and so forth.

These views found the democratic victors receptive and persuaded them to disarm to a large extent. But naturally they were without effect on the vanquished who sought revenge and a revision of the *status quo* by force. The outbreak of the second World War proved conclusively the complete fallacy and uselessness of seeking peace betwen nations through disarmament.

Now our leaders are preaching the exact opposite. We are told today that only powerful armaments can maintain peace, that the democratic and so-called peace-loving nations must maintain omnipotent national navies, air forces and mechanized armies, that we must control strategic military bases spread around the globe, if we would prevent aggression and maintain peace.

This idea, the idea of maintaining peace by armaments, is just as complete a fallacy as the idea of maintaining peace through disarmament. Technical equipment, arms, have as much to do with peace as frogs with the weather. Conscription and large armies are just as incapable of maintaining peace as no conscription and disarmament.

The problem of peace is a social and political problem, not a technical one.

War is never the disease itself. War is a reaction to a disease of society, the symptom of disease. It is just like fever in the human body. We shall never be able to prevent all wars in advance, because it is impossible to foresee future differentiations of human society, exactly where divisions and splits of society will take place. In the twenty-fifth century perhaps the great conflict will be between the orange growers and the believers in Taoism. We do not know.

What we do know is that war is the result of contact between non-integrated sovereign units, whether such units be families, tribes, villages, estates, cities, provinces, dynasties, religions, classes, nations, regions or continents.

We also know that today, the conflict is between the scattered units of nation-states. During the past hundred years, all major wars have been waged between nations. This division among men is the only condition which, in our age, can create—and undoubtedly will create—other wars.

The task therefore is to prevent wars between the nations—international wars.

Logical thinking and historical empiricism agree that there *is* a way to solve this problem and prevent wars between the nations once and for all. But with equal clarity they also reveal that there is *one* way and one way alone to achieve this end: The integration of the scattered conflicting national sovereignties into one unified, higher sovereignty, capable of creating a legal order within which all peoples may enjoy equal security, equal obligations and equal rights under law.

The Scourge of War

ABRAHAM LINCOLN

SECOND INAUGURAL ADDRESS (March 4, 1865)

* * *

On the occasion corresponding to this four years ago, all thoughts were anxiously directed to an impending civil war. All dreaded it—all sought to avert it. While the inaugural address was being delivered from this place, devoted altogether to *saving* the Union without war, insurgent agents were in the city seeking to *destroy* it without war—seeking to dissolve the Union, and divide effects, by negotiation. Both parties deprecated war; but one of them would make war rather than let the nation survive; and the other would *accept* war rather than let it perish. And the war came.

One eighth of the whole population were colored slaves, not distributed generally over the Union, but localized in the Southern part of it. These slaves constituted a peculiar and powerful interest. All knew that this interest was, somehow, the cause of the war. To strengthen, perpetuate, and extend this interest was the object for which the insurgents would rend the Union, even by war; while the government claimed no right to do more than to restrict the territorial enlargement of it. Neither party expected for the war, the magnitude, or the duration, which it has already attained. Neither anticipated that the *cause* of the conflict might cease with, or even before, the conflict itself should cease. Each looked for an easier triumph, and a result less fundamental and astounding. Both read the same Bible, and pray to the same God; and each invokes His aid against the other. It may seem strange that any men should dare to ask a just God's assistance in wringing their bread from the sweat of other men's faces; but let us judge not that we be not judged. The prayers of both could not be answered; that of neither has been answered fully. The Almighty has His own purposes. "Woe unto the world because of offences! for it must needs be that offences come; but woe to that man by whom the offence cometh!" If we shall suppose that American Slavery is one of those offences which, in the providence of God, must needs come, but which, having continued through His appointed time, He now wills to remove, and that He gives *to both North and South,* this terrible war, as the woe due to *those by whom the offence came,* shall we discern therein any departure from those divine attributes which the believers in a Living God always ascribe to Him? Fondly do we hope—fervently do we pray—that this mighty scourge of war may speedily pass away. Yet, if God wills that it continue, until all the wealth piled by the bond-man's two hundred and fifty years of unrequited toil shall be sunk, and until every drop of blood drawn with the lash, shall be paid by another drawn with the sword, as was said three thousand years ago, so still it must be said "the judgments of the Lord, are true and righteous altogether."

With malice toward none; with charity for all; with firmness in the right, as God gives us to see the right, let us strive on to finish the work we are in; to bind up the nation's wounds; to care for him who shall have borne the battle, and for his widow, and his orphan—to do all which may achieve and cherish a just and lasting peace, among ourselves, and with all nations.

LETTER TO THURLOW WEED

Executive Mansion
Washington, March 15, 1865

Thurlow Weed, Esq.
My dear Sir.

Every one likes a compliment. Thank you for yours on . . . the recent Inaugural Address. I expect it to wear as well as—perhaps better than—anything I have produced; but I believe it is not immediately popular. Men are not flattered by being shown that there has been a difference of purpose between the Almighty and them. To deny it, however, in this case, is to deny that there is a God governing the world. It is a truth which I thought needed to be told; and as whatever of humiliation there is in it, falls most directly on myself, I thought others might afford for me to tell it.

Yours truly,
A. Lincoln

The Origin of War

PLATO

"THE ORIGIN OF A CITY," I SAID, "IS, IN MY OPINION, DUE TO THE FACT THAT NO ONE OF US IS SELF-SUFFICIENT, BUT EACH MAN IS IN NEED OF MANY THINGS. Or do you think there is any other cause for the founding of cities?"

From *The Republic*, Book II, translated by Dr. A. D. Lindsay, Everyman's Library Edition. Copyright 1950 by E. P. Dutton and Company, Inc. Reprinted by permission of E. P. Dutton & Co., Inc. and J. M. Dent & Sons Ltd., London.

"No," he said, "none."

"Then men, being in want of many things, gather into one settlement many partners and helpers; one taking to himself one man, and another another, to satisfy their diverse needs, and to this common settlement we give the name of city. Is not that so?"

"Certainly."

"And when they exchange with one another, giving or receiving as the case may be, does not each man think that such exchange is to his own good?"

"Certainly."

"Come, then," I said. "Let us in our argument construct the city from the beginning. Apparently it will be the outcome of our need?"

"Surely."

"But the first and greatest of our needs is the provision of food to support existence and life?"

"Yes, assuredly."

"The second the provision of a dwelling-place, and the third of clothing, and so on?"

"That is so."

"Come, then," I said, "how will our city be able to supply a sufficiency of all those things? Will it not be by having one man a farmer, another a builder, and a third a weaver? Shall we add a shoemaker, and perhaps another provider of bodily needs?"

"Certainly."

"Then the city of bare necessity will consist of four or five men?"

"Apparently."

"Well, then, should each of these men place his own work at the disposal of all in common? For example, should our one farmer provide corn for four and spend fourfold time and labour on the provision of corn, and then share it with the rest; or should he pay no attention to the others, and provide only a fourth part of the corn for himself in a fourth of the time, and spend the other three-fourths of his time in providing a house, clothes, and shoes? Should he not have the trouble of sharing with the others, but rather provide with his own hands what he wants for himself?"

Adeimantus answered: "The first alternative, Socrates, is perhaps the easier."

"Well, it is certainly not strange that it is. For as you were speaking, I myself was thinking that, in the first place, no two of us are by nature altogether alike. Our capacities differ. Some are fit for one work, some for another. Do you agree?"

"I do."

"Well, then, would better work be done on the principle of one man many trades, or of one man one trade?"

"One man one trade is better," he said.

"Yes, for I fancy that it is also evident that, in work, opportunities which we pass by are lost."

"That is evident."

"I fancy that things to be done will not wait the good time of the doer. Rather the doer must wait on the opportunity for action, and not leave the doing of it for his idle moments."

"He must."

"And so more tasks of each kind are accomplished, and the work is better and is done more easily when each man works at the one craft for which nature fits him, that being free from all other occupations he may wait on its opportunities."

"That is certainly the case."

"Then, Adeimantus, we need more citizens than four to provide the above-mentioned necessities. For the farmer, naturally, will not make his own plough if it is to be a good one, nor his mattock, nor any of the other farming tools. No more will the builder, who also needs many tools. And the same will hold of the weaver and the shoemaker, will it not?"

"True."

"Then carpenters and smiths and many other artisans of that kind will become members of our little city, and make it populous?"

"Certainly."

"Yet it would not be so very large if we added herdsmen and

shepherds and others of that class, that the farmers may have oxen for ploughing, and both builders and farmer may have yoke animals for their carting, and that the weavers and shoemakers may have skins and wool."

"Nor so very small if so well provided."

"Again," I said, "it will be almost impossible to have our city so situated that it will need no imports."

"Yes, that will be impossible."

"Then it will need more men still to bring it what it needs from other cities?"

"It will."

"And if they are to get what they need from other people their agent must take with him something that those others want. If he goes empty-handed, he will return empty-handed, will he not?"

"I think so."

"Then the workers of our city must not only make enough for home consumption; they must also produce goods of the number and kind required by other people?"

"Yes, they must."

"Then our city will need more farmers, and more of all the other craftsmen?"

"Yes."

"And among the rest it will need more agents who are to import and export the different kinds of goods. These are merchants, are they not?"

"Yes."

"We shall need merchants, then?"

"Certainly."

"And if the commerce is over sea, we shall need a host of others who are experts in sea-trading."

"Yes, there will be many of them."

"Again, in the city itself how will men exchange the produce of their labors with one another? For this was the original reason of our establishing the principle of community and founding a city."

"Clearly," he said, " by selling and buying."

"This will give us a market-place, and money as a token for the sake of exchange."

"Certainly."

"Then if the farmer or any other craftsman brings his produce into the market-place, and meets there none who wish to exchange their goods with him, is he to sit idle in the market-place when he might be working?"

"Certainly not," said he. "There are men who have taken note of this, and devote themselves to this service. In well-governed cities they are usually those who are weakest in body, and incapable of any other work. They have to stay there in the market-place and exchange money for goods with those who want to sell, and goods for money with those who want to buy."

"Then," I said, "this necessity brings shopkeepers into our city. We give the name of shopkeepers, do we not, to those who serve buyers and sellers in their stations at the market-place, but the name of merchants to those who travel from city to city?"

"Certainly."

"Then are there not other agents also who have no mental gifts to make them at all worthy to share in the community, but who have bodily strength sufficient for hard labour? They sell the use of their strength, and the price they get for it being called hire, they are known, I fancy, as hired laborers?"

"Certainly."

"Then these hired laborers, too, serve to complete our city?"

"I think so."

"Then, Adeimantus, has our city now grown to its perfection?"

"Perhaps."

"Then, where in it shall we find justice and injustice? With which of the elements we have noticed did they make their entry?"

"I cannot see how they came in, Socrates," he said, "unless we find them somewhere in the mutual needs of these same persons."

"Well," I said, "perhaps you are right. But let us consider the matter and not draw back. And first, let us consider what will be the manner of life of men so equipped. Will they not spend their time in the production of corn and wine and clothing and shoes? And they will build themselves houses; in summer they will generally work without their coats and shoes, but in winter they will be well clothed and shod. For food they will make meal from their barley and flour from their wheat, and kneading and baking them they will heap their noble scones and loaves on reeds or fresh leaves, and lying on couches of bryony and myrtle boughs will feast with their children, drink wine after their repast, crown their heads with garlands, and sing hymns to the gods. So they will live with one another in happiness, not begetting children above their means, and guarding against the danger of poverty or war."

Here Glaucon interrupted and said: "Apparently you give your men dry bread to feast on."

"You are right," I said; "I forgot that they would have a relish with it. They will have salt and olives and cheese, and they will have boiled dishes with onions and such vegetables as one gets in the country. And I expect we must allow them a dessert of figs, and peas and beans, and they will roast myrtle berries and acorns at the fire, and drink their wine in moderation. Leading so peaceful and healthy a life they will naturally attain to a good old age, and at death leave their children to live as they have done."

"Why," said Glaucon, "if you had been founding a city of pigs, Socrates, this is just how you would have fattened them."

"Well, Glaucon, how must they live?"

"In an ordinary decent manner," he said. "If they are not to be miserable, I think they must have couches to lie on and tables to eat from, and the ordinary dishes and dessert of modern life."

"Very well," I said, "I understand. We are considering apparently, the making not of a city merely, but of a luxurious city. And perhaps there is no harm in doing so. From that kind, too, we shall soon learn, if we examine it, how justice and injustice arise in cities. I, for my part, think that the city I have described is the true one, what we may call the city of health. But if you wish, let us also inspect a city which is suffering from inflammation. There is no reason why we should not. Well, then, for some people the arrangements we have made will not be enough. The mode of living will not satisfy them. They shall have couches and tables and other furniture; rich dishes too, and fragrant oils and perfumes, and courtesans and sweetmeats, and many varieties of each. Then again we must make more than a bare provision for those necessities we mentioned at the first, houses and clothes and shoes. We must start painting and embroidery, and collect gold and ivory, and so on, must we not?"

"Yes," he said.

"Then we must make our city larger. For the healthy city will not now suffice. We need one swollen in size, and full of a multitude of things which necessity would not introduce into cities. There will be all kinds of hunters and there will be the imitators; one crowd of imitators in figure and color, and another of imitators in music; poets and their servants, rhapsodists, actors, dancers and theatrical agents; and makers of all kinds of articles, of those used for women's adornment, for example. Then, too, we shall need more servants; or do you think we can do without footmen, wet-nurses, dry-nurses, lady's maids, barbers, and cooks and confectioners, besides? Then we shall want swineherds too; we had none in our former city—there was no need—but we shall need great quantities of all kinds of cattle if people are to eat them. Shall we not?"

"Surely."

"Then if we lead this kind of life we shall require doctors far more often than we should have done in the first city?"

"Certainly."

"Then I dare say even the land which was sufficient to support the first population will be now insufficient and too small?"

"Yes," he said.

"Then if we are to have enough for pasture and ploughland, we must take a slice from our neighbors' territory. And they will want to do the same to ours, if they also overpass the bounds of necessity and plunge into reckless pursuit of wealth?"

"Yes, that must happen, Socrates," he said.

"Then shall we go to war at that point, Glaucon, or what will happen?"

"We shall go to war," he said.

"And we need not say at present whether the effects of war are good or bad. Let us only notice that we have found the origin of war in those passions which are most responsible for all the evils that come upon cities and the men that dwell in them."

"Certainly."

The Idea of Cause

LEO TOLSTOY

TOWARDS THE END OF THE YEAR 1811, THERE BEGAN TO BE GREATER ACTIVITY IN LEVYING TROOPS AND IN CONCENTRATING THE FORCES OF WESTERN EUROPE, AND IN 1812 THESE FORCES—MILLIONS OF MEN, RECKONING THOSE ENGAGED IN THE TRANSPORT AND FEEDING OF THE ARMY—MOVED FROM THE WEST EASTWARD, TOWARDS THE FRONTIERS OF RUSSIA, WHERE, SINCE 1811, THE RUSSIAN FORCES WERE BEING IN LIKE MANNER CONCENTRATED.

On the 12th of June the forces of Western Europe crossed the frontier, and the war began, that is, an event took place opposed to human reason and all human nature. Millions of men perpetrated against one another so great a mass of crime—fraud, swindling, robbery, forgery, issue of counterfeit money, plunder, incendiarism, and murder—that the annals of all the criminal courts of the world could not muster such a sum of wickedness in whole centuries, though the men who committed those deeds did not at that time look on them as crimes.

What led to this extraordinary event? What were its causes? Historians, with simple-hearted conviction, tell us that the causes

From *War and Peace*, Part IX, Chapter I; Epilogue, Part II. Random House, Inc., New York. A Modern Library Edition.

of this event were the insult offered to the Duke of Oldenburg, the failure to maintain the continental system, the ambition of Napoleon, the firmness of Alexander, the mistakes of the diplomats, and so on.

According to them, if only Metternich, Rumyantsev, or Talleyrand had, in the interval between a levée and a court ball, really taken pains and written a more judicious diplomatic note, or if only Napoleon had written to Alexander, "I consent to restore the duchy to the Duke of Oldenburg," there would have been no war.

We can readily understand that being the conception of the war that presented itself to contemporaries. We can understand Napoleon's supposing the cause of the war to be the intrigues of England (as he said, indeed, in St. Helena); we can understand how to the members of the English House of Commons the cause of the war seemetd to be Napoleon's ambition; how to the Duke of Oldenburg the war seemed due to the outrage done him; how to the trading class the war seemed due to the continental system that was ruining Europe; to the old soldiers and generals the chief reason for it seemed their need of active service; to the regiments of the period, the necessity of returning to the old traditions; while the diplomatists of the time set it down to the alliance of Russia with Austria in 1809 not having been with sufficient care concealed from Napoleon, and the memorandum, No. 178, having been awkwardly worded. We may well understand contemporaries believing in those causes, and in a countless, endless number more, the multiplicity of which is due to the infinite variety of men's points of view. But to us of a later generation, contemplating in all its vastness the immensity of the accomplished fact, and seeking to penetrate its simple and fearful significance, those explanations must appear insufficient. To use it is inconceivable that millions of Christian men should have killed and tortured each other, because Napoleon was ambitious, Alexander firm, English policy crafty, and the Duke of Oldenburg hardly treated. We cannot grasp the connection between these circumstances and the bare fact of murder and violence, nor why the duke's wrongs should induce thousands of men from the other side of Europe to pillage and murder the inhabitants of the Smolensk and Moscow provinces and to be slaughtered by them.

For us of a later generation, who are not historians led away by the process of research, and so can look at the facts with commonsense unobscured, the causes of this war appear innumerable in their multiplicity. The more deeply we search out the causes the more of them we discover; and every cause, and even a whole class of causes taken separately, strikes us as being equally true in itself, and equally deceptive through its insignificance in comparison with the immensity of the result, and its inability to produce (without all the other causes that concurred with it) the effect that followed. Such a cause, for instance, occurs to us as Napoleon's refusal to withdraw his troops beyond the Vistula, and to restore the duchy of Oldenburg; and then again we remember the readiness or the reluctance of the first chance French corporal to serve on a second campaign; for had he been unwilling to serve, and a second and a third, and thousands of corporals and soldiers had shared that reluctance, Napoleon's army would have been short of so many men, and the war could not have taken place.

If Napoleon had not taken offence at the request to withdraw beyond the Vistula, and had not commanded his troops to advance, there would have been no war. But if all the sergeants had been unwilling to serve on another campaign, there could have been no war either.

And the war would not have been had there been no intrigues on the part of England, no Duke of Oldenburg, no resentment on the part of Alexander; nor had there been no autocracy in Russia, no French Revolution and consequent dictatorship and empire, nor all that led to the French Revolution, and so on further back: without any one of those causes, nothing could have happened. And so all those causes—myriads of causes—coincided to bring about what happened. And consequently nothing was exclusively the cause of the war, and the war was bound to happen, simply because it was bound to happen. Millions of men, repudiating their common-sense and their human feelings, were bound to move from west to east, and to slaughter their fellows, just as some centuries before hordes of men had moved from east to west to slaughter their fellows.

The acts of Napoleon and Alexander, on whose words it seemed to depend whether this should be done or not, were as little voluntary as the act of each soldier, forced out by the drawing of a lot or by conscription. This could not be otherwise, for in order that the will of Napoleon and Alexander (on whom the whole decision appeared to rest) should be effective, a combination of innumerable circumstances was essential, without any one of which the effect could not have followed. It was essential that the millions of men in whose hands the real power lay—the soldiers who fired guns and transported provisions and cannons—should consent to carry out the will of those feeble and isolated persons, and that they should have been brought to this acquiescence by an infinite number of varied and complicated causes.

We are forced to fall back upon fatalism in history to explain irrational events (that is those of which we cannot comprehend the reason). The more we try to explain those events in history rationally, the more irrational and incomprehensible they seem to us. Every man lives for himself, making use of his freewill for attainment of his own objects, and feels in his whole being that he can do or not do any action. But as soon as he does anything, that act, committed at a certain moment in time, becomes irrevocable and is the property of history, in which it has a significance, predestined and not subject to free choice.

There are two aspects to the life of every man: the personal life, which is free in proportion as its interests are abstract, and the elemental life of the swarm, in which a man must inevitably follow the laws laid down for him.

Consciously a man lives on his own account in freedom of will, but he serves as an unconscious instrument in bringing about the historical ends of humanity. An act he has once committed is irrevocable, and that act of his, coinciding in time with millions of acts of others, has an historical value. The higher a man's place in the social scale, the more connections he has with others, and the more power he has over them, the more conspicuous is the inevitability and predestination of every every act he commits. "The hearts of kings are in the hand of God." The king is the slave of history.

History—that is the unconscious life of humanity in the swarm, in the community—makes every minute of the life of kings its own, as an instrument for attaining its ends.

Although in that year, 1812, Napoleon believed more than ever that to shed or not to shed the blood of his peoples depended entirely on his will (as Alexander said in his last letter to him), yet then, and more than at any time, he was in bondage to those laws which forced him, while to himself he seemed to be acting freely, to do what was bound to be his share in the common edifice of humanity, in history.

The people of the west moved to the east for men to kill one another. And by the law of the coincidence of causes, thousands of petty causes backed one another up and coincided with that event to bring about that movement and that war: resentment at the non-observance of the continental system, and the Duke of Oldenburg, and the massing of troops in Prussia—a measure undertaken, as Napoleon supposed, with the object of securing armed peace—and the French Emperor's love of war, to which he had grown accustomed, in conjunction with the inclinations of his people, who were carried away by the grandiose scale of the preparations, and the expenditure on those preparations, and the necessity of recouping that expediture. Then there was the intoxicating effect of the honours paid to the French Emperor in Dresden, and the negotiations too of the diplomatists, who were supposed by contemporaries to be guided by a genuine desire to secure peace, though they only inflamed the self-love of both sides; and millions upon millions of other causes, chiming in with the fated event and coincident with it.

When the apple is ripe and falls—why does it fall? Is it because it is drawn by gravitation to the earth, because its stalk is withered, because it is dried by the sun, because it grows heavier, because the wind shakes it, or because the boy standing under the tree wants to eat it?

Not one of those is the cause. All that simply makes up the

conjunction of conditions under which every living, organic, elemental event takes place. And the botanist who says that the apple has fallen because the cells are decomposing, and so on, will be just as right as the boy standing under the tree who says the apple has fallen because he wanted to eat it and prayed for it to fall. The historian, who says that Napoleon went to Moscow because he wanted to, and was ruined because Alexander desired his ruin, will be just as right and as wrong as the man who says that the mountain of millions of tons, tottering and undermined, has been felled by the last stroke of the last workingman's pickaxe. In historical events great men—so called—are but the labels that serve to give a name to an event, and like labels, they have the least possible connection with the event itself.

Every action of theirs, that seems to them an act of their own freewill, is in an historical sense not free at all, but in bondage to the whole course of previous history, and predestined from all eternity.

* * *

History examines the manifestations of man's freewill in connection with the external world in time and in dependence on cause, that is, defines that freedom by the laws of reason; and so history is only a science in so far as that freedom is defined by those laws.

To history the recognition of the freewills of men as forces able to influence historical events, that is, not subject to laws, is the same as would be to astronomy the recognition of freewill in the movements of the heavenly bodies.

This recognition destroys the possibility of the existence of laws, that is, of any science whatever. If there is so much as one body moving at its freewill, the laws of Kepler and of Newton are annulled, and every conception of the movement of the heavenly bodies is destroyed. If there is a single human action due to frewill, no historical law exists, and no conception of historical events can be formed. . . .

From the point of view from which the science of history now approaches its subject, by the method it now follows, seeking the causes of phenomena in the freewill of men, the expression of laws by science is impossible, since however we limit the freewill of men, so long as we recognize it as a force not subject to law, the existence of law becomes impossible.

By limiting this element of freewill to infinity, that is, regarding it as an infinitesimal minimum, we are convinced of the complete unattainability of causes, and then, instead of seeking causes, history sets before itself the task of seeking laws.

The seeking of those laws has been begun long ago, and the new lines of thought which history must adopt are being worked out simultaneously with the self-destruction towards which the old-fashioned history is going, forever dissecting and dissecting the causes of phenomena. . . .

The other sciences, too, have followed the same course, though under another form. When Newton formulated the law of gravitation, he did not say that the sun or the earth has the property of attraction. He said that all bodies—from the greatest to the smallest—have the property of attracting one another; that is, leaving on one side the question of the cause of the movements of bodies, he expressed the property common to all bodies, from the infinitely great to the infinitely small. The natural sciences do the same thing; leaving on one side the question of cause, they seek for laws. History, too, is entered on the same course. And if the subject of history is to be the study of the movements of peoples and of humanity, and not episodes from the lives of individual men, it too is bound to lay aside the idea of cause, and to seek the laws common to all the equal and inseparably interconnected, infinitesimal elements of freewill.

Moral Man
and Immoral Society

REINHOLD NIEBUHR

THE THESIS TO BE ELABORATED IN THESE PAGES IS THAT A SHARP DIS-
TINCTION MUST BE DRAWN BETWEEN THE MORAL AND SOCIAL BEHAVIOR
OF INDIVIDUALS AND OF SOCIAL GROUPS, NATIONAL, RACIAL, AND ECO-
NOMIC; AND THAT THIS DISTINCTION JUSTIFIES AND NECESSITATES PO-
LITICAL POLICIES WHICH A PURELY INDIVIDUALISTIC ETHIC MUST AL-
WAYS FIND EMBARRASSING. The title "Moral Man and Immoral Society" suggests the intended distinction too unqualifiedly, but it is
nevertheless a fair indication of the argument to which the following pages are devoted. Individual men may be moral in the sense
that they are able to consider interests other than their own in
determining problems of conduct, and are capable, on occasion,
of preferring the advantages of others to their own. They are
endowed by nature with a measure of sympathy and consideration for their kind, the breadth of which may be extended by an
astute social pedagogy. Their rational faculty prompts them to
a sense of justice which educational discipline may refine and
purge of egoistic elements until they are able to view a social
situation, in which their own interests are involved, with a fair
measure of objectivity. But all these achievements are more
difficult, if not impossible, for human societies and social groups.
In every human group there is less reason to guide and to check
impulse, less capacity for self-transcendence, less ability to comprehend the needs of others and therefore more unrestrained

egoism than the individuals, who compose the group, reveal in their personal relationships.

The inferiority of the morality of groups to that of individuals is due in part to the difficulty of establishing a rational social force which is powerful enough to cope with the natural impulses by which society achieves its cohesion; but in part it is merely the revelation of a collective egoism, compounded of the egoistic impulses of individuals, which achieve a more vivid expression and a more cumulative effect when they are united in a common impulse than when they express themselves separately and discreetly.

Inasfar as this treatise has a polemic interest it is directed against the moralists, both religious and secular, who imagine that the egoism of individuals is being progressively checked by the development of rationality or the growth of a religiously inspired goodwill and that nothing but the continuance of this process is necessary to establish social harmony between all the human societies and collectives. Social analyses and prophecies made by moralists, sociologists and educators upon the basis of these assumptions lead to a very considerable moral and political confusion in our day. They completely disregard the political necessities in the struggle for justice in human society by failing to recognise those elements in man's collective behavior which belong to the order of nature and can never be brought completely under the dominion of reason or conscience. They do not recognise that when collective power, whether in the form of imperialism or class domination, exploits weakness, it can never be dislodged unless power is raised against it. If conscience and reason can be insinuated into the resulting struggle they can only qualify but not abolish it.

The most persistent error of modern educators and moralists is the assumption that our social difficulties are due to the failure of the social sciences to keep pace with the physical sciences which have created our technological civilisation. The invariable implication of this assumption is that, with a little more time, a little more adequate moral and social pedagogy and a generally higher development of human intelligence, our social problems will approach solution. "It is," declares Professor John Dewey, "our human intelligence and our human courage which is on trial; it is incredible that men who have brought the technique of physical discovery, invention and use to such a pitch of perfection will abdicate in the face of the infinitely more important human problem. What stands in the way (of a planned economy) is a lot of outworn traditions, moth-eaten slogans and catchwords that do substitute duty for thought, as well as our entrenched predatory self-interest. We shall only make a real beginning in intelligent thought when we cease mouthing platitudes. . . . Just as soon as we begin to use the knowledge and skills we have, to control social consequences in the interest of a shared, abundant and secured life, we shall cease to complain of the backwardness of our social knowledge. . . . We shall then take the road which leads to the assured building up of social science just as men built up physical science when they actively used techniques and tools and numbers in physical experimentation." In spite of Professor Dewey's great interest in and understanding of the modern social problem there is very little clarity in this statement. The real cause of social inertia, "our predatory self-interest," is mentioned only in passing without influencing his reasoning. . . . The suggestion that we will only make a beginning in intelligent thought when we "cease mouthing platitudes," is itself so platitudinous that it rather betrays the confusion of an analyst who has no clear counsels about the way to overcome social inertia. The idea that we cannot be socially intelligent until we begin experimentation in social problems in the way that the physical scientists experimented fails to take account of an important difference between the physical and the social sciences. The physical sciences gained their freedom when they overcame the traditionalism based on ignorance, but the traditionalism which the social sciences face is based upon the economic interest of the dominant social classes who are trying to maintain their special privileges in society. Nor can the difference between the very character of social and physical sciences be overlooked. Complete rational objectivity in a social situation is impossible. The very social scientists who are so anxious to offer our generation coun-

sels of salvation and are disappointed that an ignorant and sloth-
ful people are so slow to accept their wisdom, betray middle-class
prejudices in almost everything they write. Since reason is always, to some degree, the servant of interest in a social situation,
social injustice cannot be resolved by moral and rational suasion
alone, as the educator and social scientist usually believes. Conflict is inevitable, and in this conflict power must be challenged
by power. That fact is not recognized by most of the educators,
and only very grudgingly admitted by most of the social scientists.

If social conflict be a part of the process of gaining social
justice, the idea of most of Professor Dewey's disciples that our
salvation depends upon the development of "experimental procedures" in social life, commensurate with the experimentalism of
the physical sciences, does not have quite the plausibility which
they attribute to it. Contending factions in a social struggle require morale; and morale is created by the right dogmas, symbols and emotionally potent oversimplifications. These are at
least as necessary as the scientific spirit of tentativity. . . . Modern
educators are, like rationalists of all the ages, too enamored of
the function of reason in life. The world of history, particularly
in man's collective behavior, will never be conquered by reason,
unless reason uses tools, and is itself driven by forces which are
not rational.

The sociologists, as a class, understand the modern social
problem even less than the educators. They usually interpret
social conflict as the result of a clash between different kinds of
"behavior patterns," which can be eliminated if the contending
parties will only allow the social scientist to furnish them with a
new and more perfect pattern which will do justice to the needs
of both parties. With the educators they regard ignorance rather
than self-interest as the cause of conflict. "Apparently," declares
Kimball Young, "the only way in which collective conflicts, as
well as individual conflicts, can be successfully and hygienically
solved is by securing a redirection of behavior toward a more
feasible environmental objective. This can be accomplished most
successfully by the rational reconditioning of attitudes on a
higher neuro-psychic or intellectual symbolic plane to the facts

of science, preferably through a free discussion with a minimum of propaganda. This is not an easy road to mental and social sanity but it appears to be the only one which arrives at the goal." Here a technique which works very well in individual relations, and in certain types of social conflict due to differences in culture, is made a general panacea. . . .

A favorite counsel of the social scientists is that of accommodation. If two parties are in a conflict, let them, by conferring together, moderate their demands and arrive at a *modus vivendi.* . . . Only a very few sociologists seem to have learned that an adjustment of a social conflict, caused by the disproportion of power in society, will hardly result in justice as long as the disproportion of power remains. . . . Most of the social scientists are such unqualified rationalists that they seem to imagine that men of power will immediately check their exactions and pretensions in society, as soon as they have been apprised by the social scientists that their actions and attitudes are anti-social. . . . It may be that despotism cannot endure but it will not abdicate merely because the despots have discovered it to be anachronistic. Sir Arthur Salter, to name a brilliant economist among the social scientists, finishes his penetrating analysis of the distempers of our civilisation by expressing the usual hope that a higher intelligence or a sincerer morality will prevent the governments of the future from perpetrating the mistakes of the past. His own analysis proves conclusively that the failure of governments is due to the pressure of economic interest upon them rather than to the "limited capacities of human wisdom." . . .

Modern religious idealists usually follow in the wake of social scientists in advocating compromise and accommodation as the way to social justice. . . .

What is lacking among all these moralists, whether religious or rational, is an understanding of the brutal character of the behavior of all human collectives, and the power of self-interest and collective egoism in all inter-group relations. Failure to recognise the stubborn resistance of group egoism to all moral and inclusive social objectives inevitably involves them in unrealistic and confused political thought. They regard social conflict either as an impossible method of achieving morally approved ends or as a momentary expedient which a more perfect education or a purer religion will make unnecessary. They do not see that the limitations of the human imagination, the easy subservience of reason to prejudice and passion, and the consequent persistence of irrational egoism, particularly in group behavior, make social conflict an inevitability in human history, probably to its very end.

The romantic overestimate of human virtue and moral capacity, current in our modern middle-class culture, does not always result in an unrealistic appraisal of present social facts. Contemporary social situations are frequently appraised quite realistically, but the hope is expressed that a new pedagogy or a revival of religion will make conflict unnecessary in the future. Nevertheless a considerable portion of middle-class culture remains quite unrealistic in its analysis of the contemporary situation. It assumes that evidences of a growing brotherliness between classes and nations are apparent in the present moment. It gives such arrangements as the League of Nations, such ventures as the Kellogg Pact and such schemes as company industrial unions, a connotation of moral and social achievement which the total facts completely belie. "There must," declares Professor George Stratton, a social psychologist, "always be a continuing and widening progress. But our present time seems to promise distinctly the close of an old epoch in world relations and the opening of a new. . . . Under the solemn teaching of the War, most of the nations have made political commitments which are of signal promise for international discipline and for still further and more effective governmental acts." This glorification of the League of Nations as a symbol of a new epoch in international relations has been very general, and frequently very unqualified, in the Christian churches, where liberal Christianity has given itself to the illusion that all social relations are being brought progressively under "the law of Christ." William Adams Brown speaks for the whole liberal Christiain viewpoint when he declares: "From many different centres and in many different forms the crusade for a unified and brotherly society is being carried on. The ideal of the League of Nations in which all civilised people shall be represented and in which they shall cooperate with one another in fighting common enemies like war and disease is winning recognition in circles which have hitherto been little suspected of idealism. . . . In relations between races, in strife between capital and labor, in our attitudes toward the weaker and more dependent members of society we are developing a social conscience, and situations which would have been accepted a generation ago as a matter of course are felt as an intolerable scandal. . . ." The suggestion that the fight against disease is in the same category with the fight against war reveals the same confusion. Our contemporary culture fails to realise the power, extent and persistence of group egoism in human relations. It may be possible, though it is never easy, to establish just relations betwen individuals within a group purely by moral and rational suasion and accommodation. In inter-group relations this is practically an impossibility. The relations between groups must therefore always be predominantly political rather than ethical, that is, they will be determined by the proportion of power which each group possesses at least as much as by any rational and moral appraisal of the comparative needs and claims of each group. The coercive factors, in distinction to the more purely moral and rational factors, in political relations can never be sharply differentiated and defined. It is not possible to estimate exactly how much a party to a social conflict is influenced by a rational argument or by the threat of force. It is impossible, for instance, to know what proportion of a privileged class accepts higher inheritance taxes because it believes that such taxes are good social policy and what proportion submits merely because the power of the state supports the taxation policy. Since political conflict, at least in times when controversies have not reached the point of crisis, is carried on by the threat, rather than the actual use, of force, it is always easy for the casual or superficial observer to overestimate the moral and rational factors, and to remain oblivious to the covert types of coercion and force which are used in the conflict.

Whatever increase in social intelligence and moral goodwill may be achieved in human history, may serve to mitigate the brutalities of social conflict, but they cannot abolish the conflict itself. That could be accomplished only if human groups, whether racial, national or economic, could achieve a degree of reason and sympathy which would permit them to see and to understand the interests of others as vividly as they understand their own, and a moral goodwill which would prompt them to affirm the rights of others as vigorously as they affirm their own. Given the inevitable limitations of human nature and the limits of the human imagination and intelligence, this is an ideal which individuals may approximate but which is beyond the capacities of human societies. Educators who emphasize the pliability of human nature, social and psychological scientists who dream of "socialising" man and religious idealists who strive to increase the sense of moral responsibility, can serve a very useful function in society in humanising individuals within an established social system and in purging the relations of individuals of as much egoism as possible. In dealing with the problems and necessities of radical social change they are almost invariably confusing in their counsels because they are not conscious of the limitations in human nature which finally frustrate their efforts.

'Plato told'

e. e. cummings

plato told

him:he couldn't
believe it(jesus

told him;he
wouldn't believe
it)lao

tsze
certainly told
him,and general
(yes

mam)
sherman;
and even
(believe it
or

not)you
told him:i told
him;we told him
(he didn't believe it, no

sir)it took
a nipponized bit of
the old sixth

avenue
el;in the top of his head:to tell

him

The Drive for Power

PLUTARCH

THERE WAS ONE CINEAS, A THESSALIAN, CONSIDERED TO BE A MAN
OF VERY GOOD SENSE, A DISCIPLE OF THE GREAT ORATOR DEMOS-

From *Plutarch's Lives, The Lives of the Noble Grecians and Romans*, translated by John Dryden and revised by Arthur Hugh Clough. Random House,
Inc., New York. A Modern Library Edition.

THENES, WHO, OF ALL THAT WERE FAMOUS AT THAT TIME FOR SPEAKING WELL, MOST SEEMED, AS IN A PICTURE, TO REVIVE IN THE MINDS OF THE AUDIENCE THE MEMORY OF HIS FORCE AND VIGOUR OF ELOQUENCE; AND BEING ALWAYS ABOUT PYRRHUS, AND SENT ABOUT IN HIS SERVICE TO SEVERAL CITIES, VERIFIED THE SAYING OF EURIPIDES, THAT:

> "——— the force of words
> Can do whate'er is done by conquering swords."

And Pyrrhus was used to say, that Cineas had taken more towns with his words than he with his arms, and always did him the honour to employ him in his most important occasions. This person, seeing Pyrrhus eagerly preparing for Italy, led him one day when he was at leisure into the following reasonings: "The Romans, sir, are reported to be great warriors and conquerors of many warlike nations; if God permit us to overcome them, how should we use our victory?" "You ask," said Pyrrhus, "a thing evident of itself. The Romans once conquered, there is neither Greek nor barbarian city that will resist us, but we shall presently be masters of all Italy, the extent and resources and strength of which any one should rather profess to be ignorant of than yourself." Cineas after a little pause, "And having subdued Italy, what shall we do next?" Pyrrhus not yet discovering his intention, "Sicily," he replied, "next holds out her arms to receive us, a wealthy and populous island, and easy to be gained; for since Agathocles left it, only faction and anarchy, and the licentious violence of the demagogues prevail." "You speak," said Cineas, "what is perfectly probable, but will the possession of Sicily put an end to the war?" "God grant us," answered Pyrrhus, "victory and success in that, and we will use these as forerunners of greater things; who could forbear from Libya and Carthage then within reach, which Agathocles, even when forced to fly from Syracuse, and passing the sea only with a few ships, had all but surprised? These conquests once perfected, will any assert that of the enemies who now pretend to despise us, any one will dare to make further resistance?" "None," replied Cineas, "for then it is manifest we may with such mighty forces regain Macedon, and make an absolute conquest of Greece; and when all these are in our power what shall we do then?" Said Pyrrhus, smiling, "We will live at our ease, my dear friend, and drink all day, and divert ourselves with pleasant conversation." When Cineas had led Pyrrhus with his argument to this point: "And what hinders us now, sir, if we have a mind to be merry, and entertain one another, since we have at hand without trouble all those necessary things, to which through much blood and great labour, and infinite hazards and mischief done to ourselves and to others, we design at last to arrive?" Such reasonings rather troubled Pyrrhus with the thought of the happiness he was quitting, than any way altered his purpose, being unable to abandon the hopes of what he so much desired.

||| THE COLD WAR

Russia and America

ALEXIS DE TOCQUEVILLE

THERE ARE AT THE PRESENT TIME TWO GREAT NATIONS IN THE
WORLD, WHICH STARTED FROM DIFFERENT POINTS, BUT SEEM TO
TEND TOWARD THE SAME END. I allude to the Russians and the
Americans. Both of them have grown up unnoticed; and while
the attention of mankind was directed elsewhere, they have suddenly placed themselves in the front rank among the nations,
and the world learned their existence and their greatness at
almost the same time.

All other nations seem to have nearly reached their natural
limits, and they have only to maintain their power; but these are
still in the act of growth. All the others have stopped, or continue to advance with extreme difficulty; these alone are proceeding with ease and celerity along a path to which no limit
can be perceived. The American struggles against the obstacles
that nature opposes to him; the adversaries of the Russian are

From *Democracy in America*, Vol. I. (1835).

men. The former combats the wilderness and savage life; the latter, civilisation with all its arms. The conquests of the American are therefore gained by the plowshare; those of the Russian by the sword. The Anglo-American relies upon personal interest to accomplish his ends and gives free scope to the unguided strength and common sense of the people; the Russian centers all the authority of society in a single arm. The principal instrument of the former is freedom; of the latter, servitude. Their starting-point is different and their courses are not the same; yet each of them seems marked out by the will of Heaven to sway the destinies of half the globe.

An Inquiry into Soviet Mentality

GERHART NIEMEYER

AMERICAN FOREIGN POLICY IS GEARED TO THE DYNAMICS OF A RELATIONSHIP WITH ANOTHER POWER UNLIKE ANY OTHER IN AMERICAN HISTORY. The fate of the United States—as well as the fate of the civilized world—depends on how well Americans can learn to understand this relationship. The new and unknown quality in it is a power possessed by a revolutionary ideology that aims at refashioning the entire world, including human nature. Or, from a different angle, it is a political and secular religion, possessed of the vast power of a major industrial nation. The rulers of this formidable complex of emotional and material forces behave like no other government has behaved in the history of modern diplomacy. The normal assumptions of international relations do not seem to fit their conduct. Their motives are not confined to

From *An Inquiry into Soviet Mentality*. Frederick A. Praeger, Inc., 1956. Reprinted by permission.

the pursuit of national interests. How are we to gauge the policies of such a power? How are we to read the minds of its masters? How are we to influence them by our actions? These are the questions which that puzzling relationship continuously poses for us. . . .

Are we dealing with a state whose leaders are "neither criminal nor insane," but, as is often alleged, "intelligent," "cautious," "calculating," "prudent," "sober"? These questions, we should remember, arise here in the context of international relations rather than of clinical psychology. There is no accepted methodology to guide us in this study of rationality in Soviet-American relations. The only criterion to guide us is that of utility. From this point of view one can say that we need to know (1) whether the Soviet rulers are reasonable, (2) whether the Soviet policies are predictable, and (3) whether our policies and theirs can communicate meaningfully with each other.

To put it in other words: We should like to know whether the Soviets are reasonable in the sense that they pursue rational political ends, and whether they maintain a proportionality between their ends and the cost of attaining them which we can understand and share. Reasonableness in foreign relations is primarily a sense of community and reciprocity in the pursuit of competing national interests which in turn flows from a rational conception of the function of government in human affairs. In order to find out about the reasonableness of Soviet leaders, we must therefore inquire into their ideas about government, particularly the function of their government as compared with that of other governments. But apart from the rationality or irrationality of their ends we also are interested in the consistency of their conduct, given their premises. Whatever the Soviet goals are, they might or might not proceed rationally toward thir realization, and knowledge of such an instrumental rationality would of course be relevant to our foreign policy. Finally, we would like to know, again regardless of whether their conception of politics or its instruments is rational, whether communication between them and us is possible in the sense that the policy-makers in each camp understand in some measure one another's behavior.

It is a function of foreign policy to convey important impressions and ideas to other governments. The degree to which this exchange of signals is possible often determines the chances of peace and war. It certainly determines the degree of mutuality and reciprocity that can be achieved between two powers. It is a matter of vital importance to the West whether or not its policy is actually reacting and responding to Soviet policy and vice versa.

The Policy of Containment

GEORGE F. KENNAN

THE RUSSIANS BELIEVE THERE IS AN INNATE ANTAGONISM BETWEEN CAPITALISM AND SOCIALISM. . . . If the Soviet Government occasionally sets its signature to documents which would indicate the contrary, this is to be regarded as a tactical maneuver. . . . The secretiveness, the lack of frankness, the duplicity, the war suspiciousness, and the basic unfriendliness of purpose . . . are there to stay for the foreseeable future. . . .

This means that we are going to continue for a long time to find the Russians difficult to deal with. . . .

The Kremlin has no compunction about retreating in the face of superior force. . . . Its political action is a fluid stream which moves constantly, wherever it is permitted to move, toward a given goal. . . . But if it finds unassailable barriers in its path, it accepts these philosophically and accommodates itself to them. The main thing is that there should always be pressure, in-

From *American Diplomacy, 1900-1950* by George F. Kennan. Published by The University of Chicago Press. Copyright 1951. Reprinted by permission. The selection on page 122 is from *The Realities of American Foreign Policy* by George F. Kennen. Princeton, 1954.

creasing constant pressure, toward the desired goal. There is no trace of any feeling in Soviet psychology that that goal must be reached at any given time. . . .

In these circumstances it is clear that the main element of any United States policy toward the Soviet Union must be that of a long term, patient but firm and vigilant containment of Russian expansive tendencies. It is important to note, however, that such a policy has nothing to do with outward "toughness." While the Kremlin is basically flexible in its reaction to political realities, it is by no means unamenable to considerations of prestige. Like almost any other government, it can be placed by tactless and threatening gestures in a position where it cannot afford to yield even though this might be dictated by its sense of realism. . . . It is a *sine qua non* of successful dealing with Russia that the foreign government in question should remain at all times cool and collected and that its demands on Russian policy should be put forward in such a manner as to leave the way open for a compliance not too detrimental to Russian prestige.

In the light of the above, it will be clearly seen that the Soviet pressure against the free institutions of the Western world is something that can be contained by the adroit and vigilant application of counterforce at a series of constantly shifting geographical and political points, corresponding to the shifts and maneuvers of Soviet policy.

❈ ❈ ❈

An attempt at an over-all agreement with the Soviet leaders is not really an alternative. The dynamism of world communism would not be seriously affected by such an agreement. Words would still mean different things to the Russians than they mean to us. The agreement would be worth precisely what the realities of world power made it worth, including ourselves, maintained by a vigorous resistance to Soviet Communist political expansion whenever possibilities for such resistance presented themselves, these realities would rapidly deteriorate from our standpoint and with them the value of the agreement. Not to mention the fact that, in any over-all agreement, the Russians would doubtless insist on provisions which would be interpreted everywhere as an acceptance and approval, on our part, of the system of colonial oppression and exploitation which they have opposed upon other people in Eastern Europe and elsewhere.

* * *

There can be no genuine stability in any system which is based on the evil and weakness in man's nature—which attempts to live by man's degradation. . . .

Despotism can never live just by the fears of the jailers and hangmen alone; it must have behind it a driving political will. . . . The modern police state does not have these qualities. . . .

The day must come—soon or late, and whether by gradual process or otherwise—when that terrible system of power which has set a great people's progress back for decades and has lain like a shadow over the aspirations of all civilization will be distinguishable no longer as a living reality, but only as something surviving partly in recorded history and partly in the sediment of constructive, organic change which every great human upheaval, however unhappy its other manifestations, manages to deposit on the shelf of time.

Communist penetration in the non-communist world is not solely a matter of Soviet initiative or support, but contains a very important component of local origin, in the weaknesses and illnesses of a given society. . . .

There are great areas of softness and vulnerability in the non-communist world, areas which it lies wholly in the competence of non-communist authority to remove. If certain of these areas could be removed, there would be, I think, no further expansion of Soviet power.

Thus the problem of containment is basically a problem of the reactions of people within the non-communist world. It is true that this condition depends upon the maintenance by ourselves and our allies, at all times, of an adequate defense posture, designed to guard against misunderstandings and to give confidence to the weak and the fainthearted. But so long as that posture is maintained, the things that need most to be done to prevent the further expansion of Soviet power are not, so far as we are concerned, things we can do directly in our relations with the Soviet Government; they are things we must do in our relations with the peoples of the non-communist world. . . .

Whatever we do that serves to bring hope and encouragement and self-confidence to peoples outside the Soviet orbit has a similar effect on the peoples inside, and constitutes the most potent sort of argument for prudence and reasonableness on the part of the Soviet leaders.

* * *

The Soviet leaders are not going to dismantle their power in Eastern Europe for the love of our beautiful eyes, or because we set out to huff and puff and to blow their house in. Their power does not rest on the consent of the governed; and it it not the sort that would be easily shaken by propaganda to the subject peoples, even if there were effective things that we could say. The very attempt to shake it by external action is exactly the thing that would make it impossible for the Soviet leaders to yield any portion of it except under the pressure of war.

You cannot expect a group of totalitarian rulers to step down from the scene of world history and to acquiesce in the destruction of their political system for the sake of the preservation of peace. These people have no future outside of their own political power. There is no place for them to go. Their chances for personal survival would be minimal if that power were really weakened. Let no one think that they could give up a portion of it by way of submission to some foreign ultimatum, and still retain the remainder, unaffected. One of the great realities of political life is the cumulative nature of all political change, the factors of momentum in human affairs, the dynamic character of all alterations in political prestige. The Soviet leaders know this; and it explains why they are sensitive about yielding anything under pressure, even at the remotest ends of their empire.

I can conceive that Soviet power will some day recede from

its present exposed positions, just as it has already receded in Finland and Yugoslavia and northern Iran. But I can conceive of this happening only precisely in the event that the vital prestige of Soviet power is not too drastically and abruptly engaged in the process, in the event that the change is permitted to come gradually and inconspicuously and as the result of compulsions resident within the structure of Soviet power itself, not created in the form of threats or ultimata or patent intrigues from outside.

Report on Moscow Conference

NIKITA KHRUSHCHEV

Moscow, Soviet Home Service, Jan. 19, 1961, 0800 GMT—L

Text of Nikita Khrushchev's report, "For New Victories of the World Communist Movement," at the meeting of party organizations of the Higher Party School, the Academy of Social Sciences, and the Institute of Marxism-Leninism attached to the Central Committee of the CPSU on January 6, as published in Kommunist, No. 1, January 1961.

* * *

Comrades: Our epoch is the epoch of the triumph of Marxism-Leninism:

 The analysis of the world situation at the beginning of the sixties can only evoke in every fighter in the great Communist movement feelings of profound satisfaction and legitimate pride. Indeed, comrades, life has greatly surpassed even the boldest and most optimistic predictions and expectations. Once it was

From *Analysis of the Khrushchev Speech of January 6, 1961.* United States Government Printing Office. Washington, 1961.

customary to say that history was working for socialism; at the same time, one remembered that mankind would dump capitalism and that socialism would be victorious. Today, it is possible to assert that socialism is working for history, for the basic content of the contemporary historical process constitutes the establishment and consolidation of socialism on an international scale.

In 1913, 4 years before the October revolution, our immortal leader and teacher, Vladimir Ilich Lenin, wrote that since the time of the Communist Manifesto world history had been distinctly divided into three major periods: (1) From the 1848 revolution to the Paris Commune in 1871, (2) from the Paris Commune to the Russian revolution in 1905, and (3) since the Russian revolution. He concluded the description of these periods this way: Since the emergence of Marxism each of the three great epochs in world history has been supplying it with new confirmations and new triumphs; but Marxism, as the teaching of the proletariat, will be supplied with even greater triumphs by the present historical epoch. These are prophetic words. They became reality with striking force and accuracy. The historical epoch brilliantly foreseen by Vladimir Ilich Lenin has become a qualitative, basic, new era in world history. Not a single preceding era can be compared to it.

These were the eras when the working class was gaining strength, when its heroic struggle, though shaking the foundations of capitalism, was as yet unable to solve the major problem of the transfer of power into the hands of the workers.

The new era differs from all the preceding ones in the universal historic triumph of socialism initiated in October 1917. Since then Marxist-Leninist teaching has been achieving one triumphal victory after another, and now its great strength and its transforming role are felt not only within individual countries and continents but in social development in all parts of the world.

There are a number of reasons which make the march of socialism invincible. In the first place, Marxism-Leninism today dominates the minds of literally hundreds of millions of people and thereby constitutes, if one is to apply Marx's words, a mighty material force. Furthermore, Marxism-Leninism now appears before mankind not only as a theory but as a living reality. The Socialist society which is being created in the boundless expanses of Europe and Asia today represents this teaching.

Now a force does not exist in the world, nor can one exist, that can hold back the increasing tendency by which the masses see with their own eyes and, so to speak, feel with their own hands, what socialism is like—no, not in books and manifestoes, but in life, in practice. There is now no force in the world that can stem the movement toward socialism by the peoples in all the new countries.

* * *

What requirements should a Marxist-Leninist appraisal of our epoch meet? It should provide a clear idea of which class stands in the center of the era and what the essence, direction, and tasks of social development are. It should cover the whole revolutionary process from the formation of socialism to the full victory of communism. It should indicate the forces which side with the working class, standing in the center of our era, and the movements which contribute to the general anti-imperialist stream.

Socialist revolution has achieved victory in a large number of countries, socialism has become a powerful world system, the colonial system of imperialism verges on complete disintegration, and imperialism is in a state of decline and crisis. The definition of our epoch must reflect these decisive events.

The statement of the conference provides the following definition of our era: Our era, whose essence is the transition from capitalism to socialism begun by the great October Socialist revolution, is an era of the struggle of two diametrically opposed social systems, an era of Socialist revolutions and national liberation revolutions; an era of the collapse of capitalism and of liquidation of the colonial system; an era of the change to the road of socialism by more and more nations; and of the triumph of socialism and communism on a world scale.

This definition of the nature of the current era can be regarded as an example of the creative, truly scientific solution of a big, weighty problem. The strength of this definition is that it correctly characterizes the main achievement of the world liberation movement and opens before the Communist and workers movement clear prospects for the worldwide victory.

Defining the essence and nature of the entire current era, it is highly important that we understand the chief peculiarities and distinctive characteristics of its present stage. If one approaches an evaluation of the post-October period from the point of view of its principal motive forces, this period is clearly divided into two stages:

The first began with the victory of the October revolution. This was the period of the assertion and development of, as Lenin put it, the national dictatorship of the proletariat; i.e., the dictatorship of the proletariat within the national boundaries of Russia alone. Although the Soviet Union, from the very first days of its existence, exercised an exceptional influence on international life, imperialism, nevertheless, greatly determined the course and nature of international relations. But even then imperialism proved itself unable to smash the Soviet Union, to prevent its becoming the mighty industrial power which became the stronghold of the cause of progress and civilization, the center of attraction of all forces opposing imperialist oppression and Fascist enslavement.

The second stage of development of the current era is connected with the formation of the world Socialist system. This is a revolutionary process with universal historic importance.

The October revolution broke one link in the chain of imperialism. Then a frontal assault on the chain of imperialism was carried out. Previously one had spoken of a breach in the chain of imperialism through one or a number of links, but now, as a matter of fact, there no longer exists an all-enveloping chain of imperialism. The dictatorship of the working class has stepped out of the boundaries of one country, has become an international force.

Imperialism has lost not only those countries in which socialism was victorious; it is rapidly losing almost all its colonies. It is quite understandable that as a result of such blows and losses the general crisis of capitalism has greatly increased, and the balance of forces in the world arena undergone radical changes in favor of socialism.

The principal distinguishing feature of our time is the fact that the world socialist system is becoming a decisive factor in the development of human society. This has been directly reflected also in the sphere of international relations. Under present conditions, prerequisites have been created for socialism to increasingly determine the nature, methods, and ways of international relations. This does not mean that imperialism represents an infinitesimal quantity which can be disregarded. Not at all. Imperialism still possesses great strength. It possesses a strong military machine. Now imperialism has created, under peacetime conditions, a gigantic apparatus of war and a widespread system of blocs, and has subjected their economy to the arms race. American imperialists lay claim to the whole world living under their heel and threaten humanity with a rocket and nuclear war.

Contemporary imperialism is being characterized to an ever-increasing degree by decay and parasitism. In their evaluation of the prospects of international development, Marxist-Leninists do not permit and cannot permit any illusions concerning imperialism. There is countless evidence that imperialists are pursuing a policy of base provocations and aggressions. This is nothing new. What is new is that any intrigues by the imperialists not only are completely exposed but are also resolutely rebuffed, and their attempts to unleash local wars are being cut short.

For the first time in history, the present balance of power in the world arena enables the Socialist camp and other peace-loving forces to pursue the completely realistic task of compelling the imperialists, under the threat of the downfall of their system, not to unleash a world war.

Comrades, the world Socialist [system] is the greatest moving force in modern times. The international working class and its Communist vanguard regard it as their duty to strengthen in every way the might and cohesion of the Socialist camp—the stronghold of peace, freedom, and independence. It is well known that the conference devoted a great deal of attention to the further development of the world Socialist system. The statement set forth important theoretical and political tenets of this development. I would like to dwell now on some of them.

As pointed out in the statement, the primary task of Socialist countries is to exploit possibilities inherent in socialism to outstrip, as soon as possible, the world capitalist system in absolute volume of industrial and agricultural production, and then to overtake the most developed capitalist countries in per capita production and living standards.

The period since the 1957 conference of representatives of Communist and Workers Parties is characteristic of the vigorous growth of the economic might and international influence of the world Socialist system.

Since then the volume of industrial production in the Socialist countries rose 37.1 percent and the industrial output in the capitalistic countries increased 7.4 percent. During the same time industrial production in the U.S.S.R. rose by 23 percent and in the United States by only 4.6 percent. The average annual rate of increase in all the Socialist countries amounted to 17 percent, and in the capitalist countries to 3.6 percent. The average annual rate of increase in the U.S.S.R. in that period amounted to 10.9 percent and in the United States to 2.3 percent.

Socialism has wrought such profound changes in all spheres of life in the people's democracies that today we can assert with legitimate pride that by now not only in the U.S.S.R. but in all countries of the Socialist camp the social-economic possibilities for the restoration of capitalism have been liquidated.

The world Socialist system has entered a new stage of development. . . .

* * *

The time is approaching when, in its share in world production, socialism will take first place. Capitalism will have been dealt a defeat in the decisive sphere of human activity—the sphere of material production.

Already as a result of fulfillment and overfulfillment of the 7-year plan, and of the high rate of development of the economies of the people's democracies, the countries of the world Socialist system will be producing more than half of the world's entire industrial production.

The victory of the U.S.S.R. in economic competition with the United States, the victory of the whole Socialist system over the Capitalist system, will be the biggest turning point in history, will exert a still more powerful, revolutionizing influence on the workers movement all over the world. Then, even to the greatest skeptics, it will become clear that it is only socialism that provides everything necessary for the happy life of man, and they will make their choice in favor of socialism.

To win time in the economic contest with capitalism is now the main thing. The quicker we increase economic construction, the stronger we are economically and politically, the greater will be the influence of the Socialist camp on historical development, on the destiny of the world.

* * *

The prevention of a new war is the question of all questions: Comrades, questions of war and peace were at the center of attention at the conference. The participants were fully aware that the problem of preventing a global thermonuclear war is the most burning and vital problem for mankind. V. I. Lenin pointed out that since World War I the question of war and peace has become the cardinal question in the entire policy of all countries on earth, a question of life and death for tens of millions of people. These words of Lenin resound with increased force in our days, when an application of the new means of mass destruction threatens unprecedented devastation and the death of hundreds of millions of people.

There is now no more urgent task than the prevention of such a catastrophe. The conference has discovered and outlined ways of using even more effectively the new opportunities of preventing a world war which emerged as a result of the formation of the Socialist camp, the growth of its might, and the new balance of power. The peoples believe that Communists will use the entire might of the Socialist system and the increased strength of the international working class to deliver mankind from the horrors of war. Marx, Engels, and Lenin considered that the historic mission of the working class and its Communist vanguard consisted not only in abolishing the oppression of exploitation, poverty, and lack of rights, but in ridding mankind of bloody wars.

V. I. Lenin nurtured our party in a spirit of implacable struggle against imperialism, for stable peace and friendship among all peoples. These principles have always been and continue to be the essence of our foreign policy. Our party remembers Lenin's words to the effect that while dying and disintegrating, capitalism is still capable of causing great calamities to mankind. The party always maintains the greatest vigilance regarding the danger emanating from imperialism. It nurtures the Soviet people in this spirit and does everything necessary to make it impossible for the enemy ever to catch us unawares.

We warn of a threat of war in order to raise the vigilance and energy of the peoples and to mobilize them for the struggle to prevent world war. The attitude of the CPSU toward problems of war and peace are generally known. It has been more than once expounded in decisions of congresses and in other documents of our party.

Wars have followed the division of the society into classes, i.e., the basis for the beginning of all wars will be finally eliminated only when the division of the society into hostile antagonistic classes is abolished. The victory of the working class throughout the world and the victory of socialism will bring about the removal of all social and national causes of the outbreak of wars, and mankind will be able to rid itself forever of that dreadful plight.

In modern conditions the following categories of wars should be distinguished: World wars, local wars, liberation wars, and popular uprisings. This is necessary to work out the correct tactics with regard to these wars.

Let us begin with the question of world wars. Communists are the most determined opponents of world wars, just as they are generally opponents of wars among states. These wars are needed only by imperialists to seize the territories of others, and to en-slave and plunder other peoples. Before the formation of the world Socialist camp the working class had no opportunity to make a determining impact on the solution of the question of whether there should or should not be world wars. In these con-ditions the best representatives of the working class raised the slogan of turning imperialist wars into civil wars, or to exploit the situation that had arisen to seize power.

This kind of situation arose during the World War I and was classically used by the Bolshevik Party and Lenin. In our times different conditions have developed. The world Socialist camp is making an ever-growing impact, through its economic might and its armed forces, on the solution of problems of war and peace.

Of course, there also are among the imperialist countries acute contradictions and antagonisms, as well as the desire to profit at the expense of others who are weaker; yet imperialists now must keep an eye on the Soviet Union and the whole Socialist camp, and are afraid of starting wars among themselves. They are trying to play down their differences; they have set up military blocs in which they have involved many capitalist countries. Although these blocs are being torn by internal struggle, their members—as they themselves say—are united in their hatred of communism and, of course, by the nature and aspirations of imperialism.

In present conditions, the most probable wars are wars among capitalist and imperialist countries, and this too should not be ruled out.

Wars are chiefly prepared by imperialists against Socialist countries, and in the first place against the Soviet Union as the most powerful of the Socialist states. Imperialists would wish to undermine our might and thus reestablish the former domination of monopolistic capital. The task is to create impassable obstacles against the unleashing of wars by imperialists. We possess in-creasing possibilities for placing obstacles in the path of the warmongers. Consequently, we can forestall the outbreak of a world war.

Of course, as yet we are unable to completely exclude the possibility of wars, for the imperialist states exist. However, the unleashing of wars has become a much more complicated business for the imperialists than it was before the emergence of the mighty Socialist camp. Imperialists can unleash a war, but they must think hard about the consequences.

I already said that even if the crazy Hitler had realized what a devastating rout was in store for his bloody gamble and had seen that he would have to commit suicide, he would have thought twice before starting a war against the Soviet Union. Then there were but two Socialist countries, the Soviet Union and the Mongolian People's Republic, and yet we routed the aggressors, having also exploited the contradictions between imperialistic states.

The picture now is quite different: the Socialist countries, which represent a mighty force, now oppose the imperialist camp. It would be a mistake to minimize the strength of the Socialist camp and its influence on the course of world events and thus on the solution of the question of whether wars will take place. In conditions where a mighty Socialist camp exists, possessing powerful armed forces, the peoples, by mobilization of all their forces for active struggle against the warmonging imperialists, can indisputably prevent war and thus insure peaceful coexistence.

A word or two about local wars. A lot is being said nowadays in the imperialist camp about local wars, and they are even making small-caliber atomic weapons for use in such wars; a special theory of local wars has been concocted. Is this fortuitous? Of course not. Certain imperialist circles, fearing that world war might end in the complete collapse of capitalism, are putting their money on unleashing local wars.

There have been local wars and they may occur again in the future, but opportunities for imperialists to unleash these wars too are becoming fewer and fewer. A small imperialist war, regardless of which imperialist begins it, may grow into a world thermonuclear rocket war. We must therefore combat both world wars and local wars.

* * *

The Communists fully support . . . just wars and march in the front rank with the peoples waging liberation struggles.

Comrades, mankind has come close to the historic point where it can solve all problems which were beyond the strength of former generations. This also concerns the most vital issue, the prevention of a world war. The working class, which already leads a large part of the world—and the time will come when it will lead the whole world—cannot allow the forces doomed to ruin to drag hundreds of millions of people to the grave with them.

A world war in present conditions would be a rocket and nuclear war, the most destructive war in history. Among hydrogen bombs already tested are those in which the power of one bomb exceeds by several times the force of all explosions during the World War II—and even during all of mankind's existence. According to scientific calculations, the explosion of a single hydrogen bomb in an industrial area can destroy up to 1.5 million people, and cause death from radiation to another 400,000.

Even a medium-sized hydrogen bomb is sufficient to wipe a large town off the face of the earth. British scientists have concluded that four megaton bombs, one each for London, Birmingham, Lancashire, and Yorkshire would destroy at least 20 million people. According to data submitted to the Senate by American experts, losses after 24 hours of nuclear war are expected to total 50 to 75 million people.

Pauling, a well-known American scientist, states: The area likely to suffer strong nuclear blows are inhabited by about 1 billion people. In 60 days from the moment of atomic attack, 500 to 750 million people could perish. Nuclear war would also bring innumerable hardships to the peoples of those countries not directly subjected to bombing; in particular, many millions would perish as a result of the lethal consequences of radiation.

We know that if the imperialist madmen unleash a world war capitalism would be wiped out and annihilated by the peoples. But we are resolutely opposed to war, first of all because we are concerned for the destiny of mankind, its present and its future. We know that in the event of war it is the working people and their vanguard, the working class, that would suffer most. We remember how Vladimir Illich Lenin formulated the question of the destiny of the working class. As early as in the first few years after the revolution, when the world's first state of workers and peasants was in a state of siege, Illich taught that if we save the working man, the main producing force of mankind, we will save everything, but we will perish if we fail to save him.

Now there is more than one worker-peasant state in the world, there is an entire system of Socialist states. Our duty to history is to insure peace and peaceful development of this great offspring of the international working class and to protect the peoples of all countries from another destructive war. The victory of socialism throughout the world, which is inevitable because of the laws of historic development, is now near. For this victory, wars among states are not necessary.

* * *

The entire foreign policy of the Soviet Union is directed toward the strengthening of peace. The growing might of our state has been used by us and will in the future be used not to threaten anyone, not to fan the fear of war, but to steadfastly pursue a policy of struggle against the danger of war, for the prevention of a world war. We have been and are prompted by the desire to maintain and strengthen friendly relations with all peoples in the interests of peace on the basis of the principles of peaceful coexistence.

Comrades, life itself bears out the correctness of the Leninist policy of peaceful coexistence of states with diverse social systems, consistently pursued by the Soviet Union and the other Socialist countries. Our party considers the policy of peaceful coexistence, which has been handed down to us by Lenin, to be the general line of our foreign policy. Peaceful coexistence is the high road of international relations between Socialist and Capitalist countries. The consistent implementation of the policy of peaceful coexistence strengthens the position of the world Socialist system, promotes the growth of its economic might, its international prestige and influences among the people's masses, and creates for it favorable foreign-political possibilities in peaceful competition with capitalism.

* * *

Comrades, we live at a splendid time: communism has become the invincible force of our century. The further successes of communism depend to an enormous degree on our will, our unity, our foresight and resolve. Through their struggle and their labor, Communists, the working class, will attain the great goals of communism on earth. Men of the future, Communists of the next generations will envy us. In their thoughts they will always revert to our days when the lines from the party anthem "We shall build our own new world and those who were nothing will become everything!" resounded with particular force.

The CPSU has been, is, and shall be true to the teaching of Marxism-Leninism, to proletarian internationalism, and friendship among peoples. It will always struggle for universal peace, for the victory of communism as we were taught by great Lenin.

The All-Purpose Khrushchev Speech by Uniquack

JAMES RESTON

FIERY RUN, VA., JUNE 24—For the benefit of researchers who do not have time to memorize seven speeches a week by Nikita Sergeyevich Khrushchev, the following all-purpose Khrushchev speech has been summarized by Uniquack, the electronic truth detector:

From *The New York Times*, June 25, 1961. © 1961 by The New York Times Company. Reprinted by permission.

Comrades: As is well known, capitalism is a worn out mare while socialism is new, young, and full of teeming energy (prolonged laughter). Our epoch is the epoch of the triumph of Marxism-Leninism (prolonged cheers). I will refer to Stalin and Mao Tse-tung later (prolonged boos and throwing of chairs from the balcony).

How should a Marxist-Leninist view the present time? We must learn to think in centuries, regarding the whole story of mankind. Thus it is clear that from the beginning of time conflict has been the inevitable lot of the human race. Adam was a good Marxist who wished to see the equal distribution of the world's goods. Eve was the first usurer and exploiter of man, a monopolist and imperialist who did not understand "peaceful co-existence."

During this entire period between Adam and Marx there was no hope for mankind, but since Marx history has been divided into three phases: 1. From the 1848 Revolution to the Paris Commune of 1871; 2. From the Paris Commune to the Russian Revolution of 1905; and 3. Since the Russian Revolution.

When I say this is now the epoch of the triumph of Marxism-Leninism, what do I mean? (Cries from the audience: "Yes, what *do* you mean?") I mean that after the triumph of socialism within the U.S.S.R. we won the last war despite the activities of the American imperialists and started the great world-wide movement toward socialism. Prior to the second World War the U.S.S.R. was the only Socialist country in the world. At present the Socialist countries cover about one-fourth of the territory of the globe, have one-third of its population and one-third of its industrial production. (Tumultuous cheers and cries of "Good old Nik," and "When do we bury them?").

We must be patient. The capitalists are crumbling, but they are still strong. They have vowed to "stand firm" in Berlin, but as Lenin said, "Those who stand firm get a sore back." Our major problem is to wipe out the vestiges of the last war we don't like, such as the Western presence in Berlin, but to solidify the vestiges of the last war we do like, such as the great Socialist Government of East Germany.

For this purpose we have devised the "doctrine of the three wars." World wars we rule out, for while we would obliterate the German militarists and revanchists, and wipe out the American monopolists, millions of our own people would also be killed and we would be left with over 700,000,000 of our dear Chinese brethren on our borders. I need not say what they would mean (prolonged boos).

Therefore we rule out world wars. We also rule out limited wars like Suez, but wars of national liberation are totally different and we must be clear about this distinction. If the British and French invade Suez, that is an imperialist war and therefore inadmissible. If, however, we help our comrades invade Laos or South Korea, that is a war of liberation. Similarly, if Castro in Cuba rises against Batista, that is a war of liberation, but if the American imperialists help other Cubans to fight Castro, that is counter-revolution. Is this clear? (Cries of No! and scuffling in the balcony).

What we must do, therefore, is to persuade or intimidate Kennedy into accepting our idea of what is an admissible and what is an inadmissible war. The distinction is perfectly clear: an admissible war is one which benefits us; an inadmissible war is one that benefits them.

This brings me to the question of our internal situation, and particularly to the question of food. (Storms of applause and prolonged shouting and whistling!) As is well known, we will pass the United States in the production of grains and meat on Oct. 9, 1973. (Cries of Meat! Meat!). However, here again we must see this internal problem in historic terms. The first phase of socialism (1905-30) was the phase of No Meat. The second, or Stalinist phase, was the phase of Some Meat, not much but some. As I said in Kazakhstan on June 23, we are now entering another phase, the phase of Horse Meat. This is progress which no capitalist country can claim.

Comrades: Down with the imperialists! (Cheers). Down with Hitler and Adenauer! (Prolonged cheers.) Down with war! (Tumultuous cheers.) On to Berlin! (Dead silence).

The Cold War: Status and Prospects

MILTON RAKOVE

THE COLD WAR HAS NOW ENTERED ITS TWENTIETH YEAR. The Soviet-American struggle, which began in 1945 and was formalized in 1947, shows no signs of coming to an end and indeed, bids fair to continue into the indefinite future.

The Cold War had its origins in the almost immediate breakdown of the Yalta agreements in 1945, in particular those agreements dealing with Eastern Europe.

With Stalin's blatant and open disregard of the agreements, and with the death of Roosevelt and the defeat of Churchill in the British election of July, 1945, the breach between the wartime allies that opened up in March, 1945, steadily widened. The lines of demarcation dividing Germany into zones of occupation for military and administrative purposes became the borders of a permanently divided Germany, with both sides engaged in a struggle for the good will of the just defeated erstwhile enemy. Any possibility for collaboration and cooperation in Europe or the Far East became an illusion and the lines were drawn for a long term struggle for mastery of the world, or failing that, an armed truce between the two great antagonists.

In 1945 two rational alternatives were open to American policy makers with regard to Eastern Europe. They could have recognized Russian control of the area, written it off and prepared to do business with the Russians in a traditional power politics mi-

From *The Chicago Jewish Forum,* Fall, 1965. Reprinted by permission.

lieu. Or they could have told the Russians to get out of Eastern Europe or we would throw them out. The first alternative would have forced them to compromise their moral sensibilities and principles, which they could not bring themselves to do. The second alternative would have posed the possibility of a war with the Soviet Union, an alternative they shrank from especially in view of the "bring the boys home" climate of opinion in the United States and among the enlisted men in the armed services.

Being unable to face up to the consequences of either of these two policies they chose a third, which consisted of telling the Russians we would not recognize their seizure of Eastern Europe, but that we would not do anything about it. Thus, they maintained a semblance of their moral integrity and avoided an armed clash. The Russians, being free to solidify their position in Eastern Europe, remained content with the status quo, occasionally probing a soft spot in the West, but not doing anything drastic for fear of provoking a serious American countermove.

Thus was born the policy of Containment, the policy spelled out in 1947 by George Kennan, the first chief of the newly created Policy Planning Staff in the Department of State. The policy was based on the assumption that the Soviets could be blocked from further expansion by "a long term, patient but firm and vigilant containment of Russian expansive tendencies" and an "adroit and vigilant application of counterforce at a series of constantly shifting geographical and political points, corresponding to the shifts and maneuvers of Soviet policy." The policy was not, however, envisaged merely as a negative reaction to Soviet initiatives. It was also based on the belief that such a policy would, in time, lead to a slow Russian retreat to the original borders of the Soviet Union, especially since the dictatorship could not survive the internal and external pressures of a long term, continuing cold war. The Soviet system, Kennan believed, contained within itself the seeds of its own destruction. This was essentially Marxism in reverse.

If Containment was going to work, then it was imperative for the United States to rebuild the economies of the Western European nations, aid them in establishing stable political systems, and bring them into a military defense system which would both guarantee their security and gradually reduce the costs and commitments of the United States. Also the newly freed under-developed nations of the world were to be safeguarded from communist imperialism by military, political and economic aid from the United States. The Truman Doctrine, the Marshall Plan, NATO, and a massive program of economic development were the tools with which these objectives were to be accomplished.

While these long range objectives were being accomplished there would be no negotiations with the Soviets which would recognize the Russian conquests. Only when the United States and its allies had achieved a preponderance of power over the Soviets would we deal with them. This was the essence of the policy of negotiation from strength. It was assumed that in-evitably time would be on the side of the West and the dis-parity in the relative strength of the two sides would slowly but surely shift in favor of the West.

In the meantime the Russians would have to reform and stop acting like communists. They would have to stop their aggressive tactics, call an end to subversion of the Western nations from within, hold free elections in Germany, Korea and the Eastern European nations, and withdraw from those nations within the original Soviet borders. This, in essence, was the policy pursued by the Truman Administration.

The Eisenhower Administration, coming to office in 1953, con-tinued for eight years to pursue essentially the same policy laid down by Truman, Marshall and Acheson. Despite Mr. Dulles' bombastic utterances about liberation, massive retaliation, ago-nizing reappraisal and unleashing Chiang Kai-shek, the basic policy remained containment of Russia, a refusal to negotiate an overall settlement, and an unwillingness to attempt to push the Soviets back at the risk of war. The Kennedy Administration, in its three years in office, continued to pursue basically the same policies toward Russia as the two previous administrations. And so did President Johnson. . . .

Thus, it is clear that for eighteen years American policy has been characterized by a bipartisan continuity which has not changed significantly, regardless of the political composition of the administration in Washington.

How well have these policies succeeded and where have they failed?

An objective appraisal of the Containment policy would indicate that in our basic objective of preventing further Soviet encroachment or expansion into Western Europe, we have been eminently successful. The Russians have not gained a single inch in Europe or indeed anywhere else in the world since 1945 through direct Soviet intervention. The only nation in Europe which passed under Russian control since 1945 was Czechoslovakia, which was lost through an internal *coup d' état* in 1948. Communism has ceased to be a serious internal threat in Italy, France and Greece. The economies of Western Europe have been rebuilt and a measure of political stability has been established. The military threat of a Russian attack has been all but eliminated. The military adventure in Korea failed. The attempt to alter the status quo in Germany and Berlin has been stalemated. The prophesied communist penetration and subversion of the Middle East and Africa has not materialized. Japan has been rebuilt as a western bastion.

What of the other side of the balance sheet? Here some red ink does appear on the ledger. The Russian exploitation of the Cuban nationalistic revolution has been blunted but not eliminated. Internal subversion remains something of a problem in parts of Latin America and the underdeveloped countries. But any successes in these areas have not been due so much to Russian efficiency as to internal, inherent domestic problems, many of which defy the quick and easy solutions those nations seek. The loss of China to Communism was, of course, a disaster of the first magnitude, but as has been so often pointed out, China was not really ours to win or lose. Since 1949, however, except for minor successes in Laos, Tibet, and the escalating conflict in Vietnam, China has been effectively contained. The collapse of Indian military power was a blow to Western hopes for a strong counterweight to China in Southeast Asia, but the Chinese aggression and the Indian humiliation has marked the collapse of

Nehru's policy of neutralism. With his passing will almost certainly come a closer alignment of India to the West. For, according to the traditional rules of the balance of power, where else can a threatened nation turn for aid except to the enemies of its enemies?

What of the long range objective of Containment, the gradual reduction of Soviet power and influence in Eastern Europe and the freeing of the satellite nations? Here, Containment has been an absolute, unmitigated failure. The Soviet Union has slowly amalgamated the area as a communist bloc under its control and direction and the United States has accepted the loss of Eastern Europe, although our leaders do not say so publicly. One has only to go back and read the speeches of our politicians for the past few years to document the fact that the once continuous insistence on liberation or free elections has all but disappeared, except as an occasional sop to the East European minorities in our major cities. The failure to take any action whatsoever during the Hungarian revolution in 1956 drove the final nail into the coffin of the liberation policy. A divided Germany, with the consequent loss of the eastern zone to the West, is a *fait accompli* that will almost certainly be a part of the European landscape for some time to come.

If we were to use a single word for the current status of the Cold War, that word would have to be stalemate. Those right wing conservatives who have been insisting for years that we have a no-win policy and are losing the cold war are politically naive. Those professional optimists who insist that victory is in sight or will be soon will surely be disillusioned. The dedicated activists on both sides, liberals and conservatives, who insist that we must win because the world cannot exist half-slave and half-free will almost certainly be disappointed. We have not lost and we have not won and the same thing can be said for the Russians. We have won a few and lost a few and so have the Soviets.

If this is so, then we must ask ourselves why it is so. The answer is simple and clear. It lies in the fact that the central political problem of our time is not the Cold War, but the revolution in military technology. In the nuclear age the traditional practices of international politics are subordinated to and governed by the monsters we have created. We all live under the mushroom cloud in what Winston Churchill called the balance of terror. We are all impaled on the horns of the dilemma of the relationship of force and foreign policy in the nuclear age. No nuclear power can go to war with another nuclear power. But no great nation can pursue its foreign policy successfully unless it is willing to go to war. In the nuclear world, neither side can go to war, but both sides must swear that they will go to war if necessary. This peculiar relationship is complicated even further because both sides have to believe that the other side means what is says. As Lewis Carroll's Alice in Wonderland would put it, "Our world gets curiouser and curioser."

The existing stalemate and the balance is the result of the fact that both the Marxists and their opponents have been wrong. Time has been on neither side and the inner contradictions of neither system have been strong enough to destroy that system from within. Since neither side can destroy the other from without except at the cost of its own destruction, and since both sides have demonstrated enough vitality to maintain themselves internally, the stalemate continues.

But politics, like life, is not a static process. The existing stalemate is already in the process of transition. President De Gaulle has proclaimed the end of the Cold War in its traditional state. With American and Soviet power cancelling each other out, with the Chinese specter haunting the Russians on their eastern border and with the possibility of an American return to its traditional interests in the Western Hemisphere, De Gaulle sees an opportunity for Western Europe to reassert itself under French leadership as a power center and third force between the two colossi. If the Soviet Marxists have lost their dynamism and have become more conservative, why not bring them back into a European system, thus serving two purposes, the protection of Europe from China and the containment of Germany? The latter objective could be accomplished by building a loose European federation dominated by France, or, failing that, a Franco-Russian condominium in which the mutuality of interests *vis a vis* Germany would serve as the mortar for the bricks.

If De Gaulle is correct in his assumptions, we are entering a new period in the Cold War. The French president has almost single-handedly brought the whole Western world up short and forced it to reevaluate the contemporary world situation. What we may well be witnessing is not only a revival of Western European power, but a relationship between Western and Eastern Europe, based not so much on conflict, but rather on an ability to live together and draw closer, gradually reducing the tensions and barriers which divide Europe. The 1960's may also presage the revival of an intra European power politics with France, Germany and Russia as the major players in the game, lining up the smaller nations in traditional great power-small power relationships. In such a system France will almost inevitably emerge as the weakest of the three great European powers. However, if France can manage to become a nuclear power in her own right, the criteria for measuring strength and weakness in military terms will be relatively meaningless, since a European nuclear balance of terror will suffice to protect French interests and French security.

If De Gaulle is right, as he probably is, that American nuclear power will not and cannot be used to defend Western Europe from a Russian armed with commensurate nuclear power, then France and Germany will have to develop their own nuclear capabilities to safeguard their security, not only from Russia, but also from each other. For, as Hans Morgenthau has pointed out, not only would the United States probably not defend Western Europe at the cost of the obliteration of our own country, but France would not defend Germany against a Russian assault, nor would Germany defend France. In the Nth country nuclear age, no nation will defend any other nation, so every nation will have to take care of itself. The traditional basis for alliances will have been swept away. A worthwhile alliance is a relationship between two nations in which they agree to defend each other out of consideration for their own security. But if the price of my coming to your aid would mean my death I would surely choose to live by refusing to honor my commitments.

What is the probable course for the United States for the foreseeable future?

Perhaps we had best begin again by looking back to where we have been. In the early stages of the Cold War we had four possible alternatives open to us in dealing with the Soviet Union: we could have reverted to our traditional isolationism; we could have negotiated a settlement with the Russians granting them hegemony over Eastern Europe; we could have gone to war to achieve our aims; or we could have temporarily accepted the status quo with the aim of altering it in our favor by building up our power to the point where we could dictate terms to the Soviets.

We rejected the first three alternatives and adopted the fourth as our policy, combining Containment with a massive, continuing effort to build up a preponderance of power.

It is clear that the policy has been both a success and a failure. We have contained the Soviet Union from further expansion but we have been unable either to force her to retreat or to gain the necessary preponderance of power. War is unthinkable (despite Herman Kahn's mandate to think the unthinkable), the achievement of a preponderance of power is unlikely and a formal negotiated settlement is improbable.

Does this mean a return to isolationism? There are indications that we have been slowly reversing our field and heading for the sidelines again. The disillusionment with the foreign aid program . . . the hostility toward De Gaulle, the economic competition with Western Europe, our almost unilateral policy in Vietnam and Latin America, the continuing burden of rising costs, and frustration with the inability to win the Cold War, are all signs of a possible swing of the pendulum back toward withdrawal.

However, it is also clear that most thinking Americans recognize both the impossibility of war and of a return to isolationism. Despite the mouthings of the right wing radicals it is clear that, as a nation, we have accepted coexistence with the Soviet Union and Communist China as the basis of our contemporary policy. We have written off Eastern Europe and the Soviets have lost any chance to take Western Europe, either by force or subversion. The Western Hemisphere is still our back yard. Despite the nuisance of Castro's Cuba, there is little the Russians can do here. China is a great power on the continent of Asia and there is little possibility that much can be done about that. But we are surely strong enough to hold Japan, build up India, defend the Western Pacific and contain China on the continent not allowing her to move into the Pacific or too far into Southeast Asia. When China becomes a nuclear power the Chinese activists will have to speak more softly. It is easy for Mao to prattle about being able to afford a nuclear conflict as long as the danger does not exist. But once such a conflict becomes a real possibility the Chinese leaders will be faced with the same dilemma which confronts the United States and Russia. Africa and the Middle East are beyond the reach of either side for some time to come.

Neither Johnson nor Kosygin can openly admit that the stalemate exists. Kosygin cannot tell the Russians that the dream of world revolution is a myth and cannot be achieved. Nor can Johnson, a Democratic president, admit to the East European minorities and the right wing radicals that Eastern Europe is gone. But there is an informal understanding, accepting the status quo, qualified only by the unwillingness of both sides to admit publicly that it exists, and aggravated slightly by the efforts of both sides to create irritations and nuisances in the other side's world and in the peripheral areas.

What is more likely than a return to isolationism for the United States under these conditions is a gradual move toward unilateralism. We cannot withdraw from the world but we can, in all likelihood, go it alone much more than we have been doing for the past twenty years. If the ties to the Western European nations are somewhat formally weakened, the basic similarity of interests will still serve to keep us on the same side. If they are capable and desirous of becoming independent nuclear powers we cannot stop them and it will lift a significant financial and military burden from our shoulders.

The great danger that the escalating conflict in Vietnam presents is that it may disrupt the slowly built up coexistence relationship between the United States and the Soviet Union.

With the Johnson Administration committing more and more

American power to the conflict and laying the prestige of the United States on the line in Vietnam, the breach between the great powers may widen again significantly. For the Soviet Union, the major communist world power, cannot afford the loss of prestige that an American victory in Vietnam would entail.

It is true that the objective of American policy today is not victory in Vietnam, but a stalemate. But conflicts have a way of getting out of control and expanding into unforeseen areas.

There is little chance of a direct Soviet-American confrontation or conflict in Vietnam. The most serious consequences would probably be a renewed Cold War and a much more intransigent, belligerent Russia, forced to play the game in the Chinese Communist manner. Should this come about we could wipe away many of the gains of the last few years. Such a development would be a setback, not just for relationships between the two great powers but for the free world, the Soviet satellites in Eastern Europe, the neutral nations, and the beleaguered United Nations. We would be heading back to where we began twenty years ago. The sole beneficiary of such a development would be the Chinese Communists who have been preaching the irreconcilability of our world and the communist world.

We must recognize that under the nuclear threat neither side can win the Cold War. In fact it would be extremely dangerous for either side to really try. But it is also quite likely that neither side will lose. We will have to coexist, with neither of us being too happy about it. However, since most people are happy only for very infrequent short intervals, this is a normal state of affairs. And we will at least be alive, fairly prosperous and somewhat free.

This policy may not please the activists, who insist we must win the Cold War, or the One Worlders or Atlantic Unionists who have pinned their hopes on a world or Western federation. But it is the most likely possibility in the years ahead. Such a policy will require tolerance and forbearance on the part of both our political leaders and our people. But, if the last twenty years are a criterion of our ability to adapt to changing world conditions, we should be able to shift our gears without stripping them.

During the War of 1812, when the American gunners were firing over the heads of the British redcoats at the battle of New Orleans, Andrew Jackson was reported to have said, "Elevate them guns a little lower." Perhaps that is what we need to do in foreign policy. Not to withdraw, not to plunge ahead full force, but to "elevate them guns a little lower."

On Negotiations

HENRY A. KISSINGER

The Intractability of Diplomacy

As armaments have mutiplied and the risks of conflict have become increasingly catastrophic, the demands for a "new approach" to end tensions have grown ever more insistent. No country, it is said, has any alternative except to seek to attain its aims by negotiations. The Cold War must be ended in order to spare mankind the horrors of a hot war: "The stark and inescapable fact is that today we cannot defend our society by war since total war is total destruction and if war is used as an instrument of policy eventually we will have total war," wrote Lester Pearson. "We prepare for war like precocious giants and for peace like retarded pigmies."

There is no doubt that the avoidance of war must be a primary goal of all responsible statesmen. The desirability of maintaining peace cannot be the subject of either intellectual or partisan political controversy in the free world. The only reasonable issue is how best to achieve this objective.

And here there is reason for serious concern. A welter of slogans fill the air. "Relaxation of tensions," "flexibility," "new approaches," "negotiable proposals," are variously put forth, as remedies to the impasse of a Cold War. But the programs to give these phrases meaning have proved much more difficult to define. The impression has been created that the missing ingredient has been a "willingness to negotiate." While this criticism is correct for some periods, particularly John Foster Dulles' incumbency as Secretary of State, it is not a just comment when applied to the entire post-war era. Hardly a year has passed without at least some negotiation with the Communist countries. There have been six Foreign Ministers' Conferences and three summit meetings. Periods of intransigence have alternated with spasmodic efforts to settle all problems at one fell swoop. The abortive summit meeting of 1960 proved that tensions have sometimes been increased as much by the manner in which diplomacy has been conducted as by the refusal to negotiate. The Cold War has been perpetuated not only by the abdication of diplomacy but also by its emptiness and sterility.

What, then, has made the conduct of diplomacy so difficult? Why have tensions continued whether we negotiated or failed to negotiate? There are four basic causes: (1) the destructiveness of modern weapons, (2) the polarization of power in the contemporary period, (3) the nature of the conflict, (4) national attitudes peculiar to the West and particularly to the United States.

It is not an accident that the diplomatic stalemate has become more intractable as weapons have grown more destructive. Rather than facilitating settlement, the increasing horror of war has made the process of negotiation more difficult. Historically, negotiators have rarely relied exclusively on the persuasiveness of the argument. A country's bargaining position has traditionally depended not only on the logic of its proposals but also on the penalties it could exact from the other side's failure to agree. An abortive conference rarely returned matters to the starting point. Rather, diplomacy having failed, other pressures were brought into play. Even at the Congress of Vienna, long considered the model diplomatic conference, the settlement which maintained the peace of Europe for a century was not achieved without the threat of war.

As the risks of war have become more cataclysmic, the result has not been a universal reconciliation but a perpetuation of all disputes. Much as we may deplore it, most historical changes have been brought about to a greater or lesser degree by the threat or the use of force. Our age faces the paradoxical problem that because the violence of war has grown out of all proportion to the objectives to be achieved, no issue has been resolved. We cannot have war. But we have had to learn painfully that peace is something more than the absence of war. Solving the problem of peaceful change is essential; but we must be careful not to deny its complexity.

The intractability of diplomacy has been magnified by the polarization of power in the post-war period. As long as the international system was composed of many states of approximately equal strength, subtlety of maneuver could to some extent substitute for physical strength. As long as no nation was strong enough to eliminate all the others, shifting coalitions could be used for exerting pressure or marshaling support. They served in a sense as substitutes for physical conflict. In the classical periods of cabinet diplomacy in the eighteenth and nineteenth centuries, a country's diplomatic flexibility and bargaining position depended on its availability as a partner to as many other countries as possible. As a result, no relationship was considered permanent and no conflict was pushed to its ultimate conclusion. Disputes were limited by the tacit agreement that the maintenance of the existing system was more important than any particular disagreement. Wars occurred, but they did not involve risking the national survival and were settled in relation to specific, limited issues.

Whenever the number of sovereign states was reduced, diplomacy became more rigid. When a unified Germany and Italy emerged in the nineteenth century, they replaced a host of smaller principalities. This reflected the dominant currents of nationalism. But from the point of view of diplomatic flexibility, some of the "play" was taken out of the conduct of foreign policy. To the extent that the available diplomatic options diminished, the temptation to achieve security by mobilizing a country's strength increased. The armaments race prior to World War I was as much the result as the cause of the inflexibility of diplomacy. France and Germany were in fundamental conflict. And neither state could organize an overwhelming coalition. As a result, power had to substitute for diplomatic dexterity and the period prior to World War I witnessed a continuous increase of the standing armies.

World War I accelerated the polarization of power. By the end of World War II only two major countries remained—major in the sense of having some prospect of assuring their security by their own resources. But a two-power world is inherently unstable. Any relative weakening of one side is tantamount to an absolute strengthening of the other. Every issue seems to involve life and death. Diplomacy turns rigid, for no state can negotiate about what it considers to be the requirements of its survival. In a two-power world these requirements are likely to appear mutually incompatible. The area where diplomacy is most necessary will then appear most "unnegotiable."

The inherent tensions of a two-power world are compounded by the clash of opposing ideologies. For over a generation now the Communist leaders have proclaimed their devotion to the overthrow of the capitalist world. They have insisted that the economic system of their opponents was based on exploitation and war. They have never wavered from asserting the inevitability or the crucial importance of their triumph. To be sure, periods of peaceful coexistence have alternated with belligerence, particularly since the advent of Mr. Khrushchev. But one of the principal Communist justifications for a *detente* can hardly prove very reassuring to the free world; peace is advocated not for its own sake but because the West is said to have grown so weak that it will go to perdition without a last convulsive upheaval. At the height of the spirit of Camp David, Khrushchev said: "The capitalist world is shaking under the blows of the Socialist camp. What shakes it even more than the rockets is the attitude of our workers towards their work. . . . We have the will to win."

Negotiations with Communist leaders are complicated by one of the key aspects of Leninist theory: the belief in the predominance of "objective" factors. One of the proudest claims of the Communist leaders is that in Marxist-Leninist theory they posses a tool enabling them to distinguish appearance from reality. "True" reality consists not of what statesmen say but of the productive processes—the social and economic structure—of their country. Statesmen, particularly capitalist statesmen, are powerless to alter the main outlines of the policy their system imposes on them. Since everything depends on a correct understanding of these "objective factors" and the relation of forces they imply, "good will" and "good faith" are meaningless abstractions. One of the chief functions of traditional diplomacy—to persuade the opposite party of one's view point—becomes extremely difficult when verbal declarations are discounted from the outset. Khrushchev said in 1959: "History teaches us that conferences reflect in their decisions an established balance of forces resulting from victory or capitulation in war or similar circumstances."

Much of the diplomatic stalemate has therefore little to do with lack of good will or ingenuity on the part of the statesmen. Without an agreement on general principles, negotiations become extremely difficult. What will seem most obvious to one party will appear most elusive to the other. When there is no penalty for failing to agree and when at the same time the balance of power is so tenuous, it is no accident that the existing dividing lines are rigidly maintained. For the *status quo* has at least the advantage of familiarity while any change involves the possibility of catastrophe. At the same time, since these dividing lines are contested, protracted tension is nearly inevitable.

This impasse has led either to long periods in which diplomacy has for all practical purposes abdicated its role; or else it has produced a form of negotiations which has almost seemed to revel in *not* coming to grips with the issues dividing the world. The reference which is often made to the coexistence achieved by Mohammedanism and Christianity or by Protestantism and Catholicism is not fully relevant to the contemporary problem.

In both cases, coexistence was the result of protracted, often ruinous, warfare—the very contingency diplomacy is now asked to prevent. We must be aware that the factors that intensify the desire to resolve the impasse of the Cold War may also make a creative response more difficult.

These obstacles to serious negotiations are magnified by Western, and in particular American, attitudes towards negotiating with the Communists. A *status quo* power always has difficulty in coming to grips with a revolutionary period. Since everything it considers "normal" is tied up with the existing order, it usually recognizes too late that another state means to overthrow the international system. This is a problem especially if a revolutionary state presents each demand as a specific, limited objective which in itself may seem quite reasonable. If it alternates pressure with campaigns for peaceful coexistence, it may give rise to the belief that only one more concession stands in the way of the era of good feeling which is so passionately desired. All the instincts of a status *quo power* tempt it to gear its policy to the expectation of a fundamental change of heart of its opponent—in the direction of what seems obviously "natural" to it.

Were it not for this difficulty of understanding, no revolution would ever have succeeded. A revolutionary movement always starts from a position of inferior strength. It owes its survival to the reluctance of its declared victims to accept its professions at face value. It owes it success to the psychological advantage which single-minded purpose confers over opponents who refuse to believe that some states or groups may prefer victory to peace. The ambiguity of the Soviet challenge results in part from the skill of the Soviet leadership. But it is magnified by the tendency of the free world to choose the interpretation of Soviet motivations which best fits its own preconceptions. Neither Lenin's writings, nor Stalin's utterances, nor Mao's published works, nor Khrushchev's declarations has availed against the conviction of the West that a basic change in Communist society and aims was imminent and that a problem deferred was a problem solved.

It is only to posterity that revolutionary movements appear unambiguous. However weak it may be at the beginning, a revolutionary state is often able to substitute psychological strength for physical power. It can use the very enormity of its goals to defeat an opponent who cannot come to grips with a policy of unlimited objectives.

The United States has had particular difficulty in this respect. From the moment in our national history when we focused our attention primarily on domestic development, we met very few obstacles that were really insuperable. We were almost uniquely blessed with the kind of environment in which the problems that were presented—those at least that we really wanted to solve— were difficult but manageable. Almost from our colonial infancy we have been trained to measure a man, a government, or an era by the degree of energy with which contemporary problems have been attacked—and hence by the success in finding a final, definite solution. If problems were not solved, this was because not enough energy or enough resolution had been applied. The leadership or the government was clearly at fault. A better government or a better man would have mastered the situation. Better men and a better government, when we provide them, *will* solve all issues *in our time*.

As a result, we are not comfortable with seemingly insoluble problems. There must be *some* way to achieve peace if only the correct method is utilized. Many of the erratic tendencies in American policy are traceable to our impatience. The lack of persistence, the oscillation between rigid adherence to the *status quo* and desire for novelty for its own sake show our discomfort when faced with protracted deadlock. We grow restless when good will goes unrewarded and when proposals have to be maintained over a long period of time.

When reality clashes with its anticipated form, frustration is the inevitable consequence. We have, therefore, been torn between adopting a pose of indignation and seeking to solve all problems at one fell swoop. We have been at times reluctant, indeed seemingly afraid, to negotiate. We have also acted as if all our difficulties could be removed by personal rapport among the statesmen. Periods of overconcern with military security have alternated with periods when we saw in a changed Soviet tone an approach to an end of tensions.

The quest for good will in the abstract has been as demoralizing and as fruitless as the insistence that negotiations are inherently useless. The abortive summit meeting in Paris is as certain a symptom of the perils of a purely formal conciliatoriness as Secretary Dulles' rigidity was a symptom of a largely mechanical intransigence. It is, therefore, necessary to examine Western, and particularly American, attitudes towards negotiations in more detail.

The Notion of War and Peace as Successive Phases of Policy

Perhaps the basic difficulty has been that our historical experience is very much at variance with the world in which we live. What had come to seem to us as the "normal" pattern of international relations has clashed at every turn with the realities of the post-war period. For over a century and a half, America asked little of the rest of the world except to be let alone. For over a century following the War of 1812 we never confronted the danger of foreign attack. Safe behind two oceans, we came to consider out invulnerability natural. The efforts of less favored nations to protect themselves against potential dangers seemed to us shortsighted and petty, indeed a contribution to international distrust. We believed that the measure of our invulnerability was that many nations would be involved long before we could be directly threatened. It is easy to forget that if the safety of the world of 1914 or of 1939 had depended on America's willingness to commit itself, the aggressor would have prevailed without opposition. Neither the invasion of Belgium nor the attack on Poland seemed to Americans of the time to impair our security to the extent that we should run the risks of war.

Because of our distance from the scene and our invulnerability we developed notions of war and peace both mechanical and absolutist. Peace seemed to us the "normal" relation among states. This is another way of saying that we were satisfied with the international order as it was and wished to enjoy its benefits undisturbed. The instrument for settling disputes during periods of peace was diplomacy, which we conceived as being analogous to commercial negotiations, attaching a disproportionate emphasis to bargaining technique. Because the advantages of peace seemed self-evident, we necessarily had to ascribe the cause of war to the machinations of wicked men. Our military actions were thereby transformed into crusades to punish the aggressor. Once this was accomplished, the "normal" pattern of international relations would reassert itself. Since we were satisfied with the existing international system—it seemed so natural to us that we never thought of it as a system—we rarely addressed ourselves to the problem of the nature of a stable international order.

The notion that war and peace were separate and successive phases of policy has been at the root of much of our post-war policy. It came to expression in the dominant Western policy of the post-war period: the policy of containment. This was based on the assumption that a substantial effort to rebuild Western strength had to *precede* any serious negotiation with the Soviet Union. Conferences would be futile until the Communist countries found themselves confronted by preponderant strength all around their periphery. "What we must do," said Secretary Acheson, "is to create situations of strength; we must build strength; and if we create that strength then I think the whole situation in the world begins to change. . . . With that change there comes a difference in the negotiating position of the various parties and out of that I should hope that there would be a willingness on the part of the Kremlin to recognize the facts . . . and to begin to solve at least some of the difficulties between East and West."

In the context of 1951, these statements were highly plausible. After three years of Communist provocation, after the Berlin blockade and the invasion of Korea, it was understandable that we should have given priority to achieving security against Soviet invasion. How the strength we were building was to be conveyed to the Communist leaders, and how precisely one went about negotiating from strength seemed then questions not worth considering. Expansionism was believed inherent in Stalinist Communism. Thwarted in the possibility of foreign adventures,

Communism would have to transform itself. At that point fruitful negotiations would be possible.

Given the atmosphere of disillusionment after the wartime hopes of a reconciled humanity, this view of the nature of negotiations was inevitable when it was first formulated. But as the containment theory came to be applied under Secretary Dulles, what had originally been considered the condition of policy—security against aggression—seemed to become its only goal. The Baghdad Pact, SEATO, the Eisenhower Doctrine marked steps of a policy which seemed unable to articulate any purpose save that of preventing an expansion of the Soviet sphere.

In the process, many of the difficulties which earlier had been obscured by the fear of imminent Soviet aggression became apparent. As Soviet pressure grew more subtle, the pre-occupation with the military aspect of containment made it increasingly difficult to rally the people of the West for the effort needed to ensure their security. The longer we deferred negotiations, the easier it became for the Soviet leaders to maneuver us into the position of being the intransigent party. The closer we approached the theoretical point at which, according to the containment theory, fruitful negotiations should have been possible, the more elusive they seemed.

Our literal view of containment caused us to be mesmerized by the vast Soviet ground strength. Though the Soviet Union could have overrun Europe at any time, it was in a very inferior position for a showdown until 1956 at least. Because of our obsession with building strength, we overlooked the fact that our relative military position would never be better than it was at the very beginning of the containment policy. We were so aware of the vulnerability of our allies that we underestimated the bargaining power inherent in our industrial potential and our nuclear superiority. By deferring negotiations until we had mobilized more of our military potential, we in fact gave the Soviet Union time —the most precious commodity considering its losses in World War II, its inferiority in the nuclear field, and its need to consolidate its conquests.

The Western statesman who understood this problem best

was Sir Winston Churchill. His repeated calls for a diplomatic confrontation in 1948 and 1949 were based on the realization that a failure to negotiate would mortgage the future. In a major, much-neglected speech, he said in 1948:

> The question is asked: What will happen when they get the atomic bomb themselves and have accumulated a large store? You can judge yourselves what will happen then by what is happening now. If these things are done in the green wood, what will be done in the dry? If they can continue month after month disturbing and tormenting the world, trusting to our Christian and altruistic inhibitions against using this strange new power against them, what will they do when they themselves have large quantities of atomic bombs? . . . No one in his senses can believe that we have a limitless period of time before us. We ought to bring matters to a head and make a final settlement. We ought not to go jogging along improvident, incompetent, waiting for something to turn up, by which I mean waiting for something bad for us to turn up. The Western Nations will be far more likely to reach a lasting settlement, without bloodshed, if they formulate their demands while they have the atomic power and before the Russian Communists have got it too.

Particularly after the death of Stalin, the rigid persistence in the patterns appropriate to an earlier period afforded the new Soviet leadership the breathing spell it required to establish itself without making any concessions on the issues which had produced the Cold War. During the period of maximum confusion in the Kremlin, the West seemed afraid of diplomatic contact. When the possibility was greatest that the new Soviet leadership might break with its past, if only to consolidate itself, we procrastinated. The longer we deferred negotiations, the more committed the new Soviet leadership became to the empire it had inherited and the more it was tempted into adventures by the upheavals associated with the rise of the new nations. The more uncertain our performance, the more confident the successors of Stalin became.

During this period, it became increasingly apparent that the guiding notion of our strategic planning—the concept of deterrence—could not support the key assumption of the containment theory that strength would more or less automatically lead to negotiation. Deterrence is tested negatively by actions which do *not* happen. But, unless there is aggression, our strength is not demonstrated and can supply no incentive to negotiate. Since Secretary Dulles was unwilling to assume the diplomatic initiative, a stalemate was the inevitable consequence.

As ever more destructive weapons entered the weapons arsenals and as the notion that war was unthinkable began to gain currency, many of the benefits we had once expected to realize from a position of strength failed to materialize. At the precise moment when, according to the theory of containment, positions of strength should have led to fruitful negotiations, the peoples of the Western world began to waver. Because strength proved so elusive and because the Cold War persisted, many drew the conclusion that the containment policy had been wrong altogether. Containment was not critized for being too one-sided. Rather, the preposterous argument was advanced in many quarters that, since the quest for strength had produced a stalemate, weakness, by reassuring the Soviet Union, might lead to a settlement. The assumption of an automatic connection between a position of strength and an effective diplomacy was countered by arguments which implied that power was irrelevant, if not an obstacle to the conduct of negotiations.

The gulf between strategy and diplomacy reduced the effectiveness of both. While we were in the phase of building strength, this separation caused us to delay defining for ourselves the kind of world for which we were striving. When we did address ourselves to the problem of negotiations, there was a great deal of talk about peace as the ultimate goal. But too frequently we seemed to have in mind a kind of terminal point at which the need for further effort would disappear. The slogan of peace was rarely coupled with an effort to give it content, thus reflecting the typical American nostalgia: since peace is the "natural condition," it need only be wanted; its nature being self-evident, it requires no definition.

Keeping the Strategic Balance

CARL KAYSEN

THE SOVIET UNION AND THE UNITED STATES ARE RIVAL SUPERPOWERS NOT SIMPLY BECAUSE OF THEIR WEALTH, NUMBERS, SIZE, GEOGRAPHICAL POSITION, SOCIAL COHESION, STRONG GOVERNMENT, BUT BECAUSE THEY HAVE TRANSLATED THESE POTENTIALITIES INTO OVERWHELMINGLY STRONG MILITARY FORCES WHICH, MEASURED ON ANY HISTORIC OR CURRENT STANDARD, ARE COMPARABLE ONLY WITH EACH OTHER. For nearly fifteen years, the central strength of these forces has been their respective long-range strategic striking arms, each designed to be capable of a large-scale attack with nuclear weapons on the home territory of the other. Over the past decade, more or less, each nation has become increasingly aware that the chief utility of his strategic force was to prevent his adversary from using his own. This result was achieved primarily by offering the adversary the prospect that any attack by his strategic forces would be met by a counterblow so devastating as to convert a decision to attack into a suicide pact. So the strategic equilibrium commonly termed "mutual deterrence" was recognized.

For our (or the Soviets') strategic forces to provide effective deterrence, they must be in such numbers, of such nature and so deployed as to be capable of delivering the required counterattack *after* the other side has struck; thus effective deterrence is measured by the usable strength of the survival second-strike force. We were perhaps earlier than the Soviets in recognizing this, but we were far from perceiving it from the first. Once we recognized the need, we sought survivable forces in

From *Foreign Affairs*, July, 1968. Copyright 1968 by the Council on Foreign Affairs, Inc., New York. Reprinted by special permission.

different ways as technological possibilities changed over the period. Increase in the size of the force, geographical dispersal to increase the number of targets presented by a given force, active defense, hardening to survive attack, warning and movement capability to take advantage of warning, all played a part in the quest for a secure second-strike force. If surviving forces are to be usable, equally essential requirements are imposed for ensuring the survival of a complex network of reporting and communication facilities, command organization and commanders, all of which occasion their own technical and organizational problems. With missiles having displaced aircraft as the most important component of the second-strike force for both sides, hardening to ensure survival through an attack, combined with concealment and mobility for the sea-based portion of our force, provide our main means of ensuring survivability. The Soviets, with—at this moment—smaller and less effective seaborne forces, rely more heavily on hardening.

Strong and survivable long-range striking forces provide each superpower with something more in relation to the other than deterrence against direct nuclear attack, though the precise specification of the extra effect is difficult. First, they provide a substantial incentive for each nation to refrain from initiating any military action against the other, lest the conditions under which rational calculation can be expected to dominate decision and action disappear in one or both. These incentives become stronger the larger the forces and interests involved, thus leading to a kind of built-in brake on the growth of military incidents in situations where the military forces of the superpowers face each other directly, or could readily do so in their worldwide movements. By extension, the same incentives operate with respect to political confrontations that might in turn lead to military action, but more weakly the more remote the military steps appear to be in the chain of potential actions and reactions. Together these effects add up to a kind of indirect or second-order deterrence, which could tend to stablilize the behavior of the two superpowers in relation to each other over a wide range of actions and deter unilateral attempts by either to change the status quo forcibly or suddenly. This might be called the self-deterrent effect of strategic nuclear forces.

However, the history of the last two decades makes the strength, steadiness and symmetry with which these incentives have operated questionable, and emphasizes their relation to broader military and political contexts. In the earlier part of the period, the Soviets seem to have acted at a higher margin of risk than the United States; more recently, the reverse appears to be true. These changes are not the simple consequence of shifts in the balance of strategic forces; on the contrary, any shift has probably moved steadily against the United States over most of this period. This is not the place to discuss the reasons for these apparent shifts in behavior, but they do illustrate the problems of delimiting the reach of the broader deterrent effects of nuclear striking forces.

In analyzing the concept of effective deterrence and trying to understand on what relation of forces it depends, it is conventional and useful to examine it in the context of a spectrum of possible strategic purposes and the striking forces appropriate to them, that stretches from what might be termed a credible first strike at one end to a minimum deterrent at the other. A first-strike force would be one whose size, reliability, accuracy, control arrangements, etc., were such, in relation to the adversary's forces, as to make possible an attack that would, with a high degree of assurance, destroy essentially all of the adversary's force and still leave the attacker a substantial unspent reserve force. In this context, the sense of "essentially all" of the adversary's force is that whatever residual might escape destruction could not inflict major damage on the attacker or prevent his reserve force from being used to a very substantial extent. For a first strike to be further characterized as "credible," the relation of forces described above would have to be clearly perceived by both adversaries, and the "high degree" of assurance involved might have to be set at 99 percent or more. In such circumstances, it is just conceivable that the superior adversary could use this power for what has been termed "compellance" as opposed to deterrence: the threat of a strike used as a means of compelling specified behavior by the adversary. Just after the Second World War, when the United States still had a monopoly on nuclear weapons and expected to maintain it, there were some who argued in favor of policies based on "compellance." Whatever the wisdom of the policies, the forces then at our command were never such as to provide that power in relation to the Soviets; it is doubtful if there ever was a moment when they were; and it is as certain as any judgment in these matters can be that we cannot now or in the foreseeable future achieve it.

At the other end of the spectrum, a minimum deterrent force would be one which would provide high assurance of the survival, for use in a second strike, of an effective, usable force large enough to inflict unacceptable damage on the adversary defined in terms of some absolute level of expected casualties, urban and industrial destruction, etc.

Since 1961, under the guidance of Secretary McNamara, our strategic forces have been programed in terms of deterrence-plus. We have never sought a first strike-capacity, and indeed from his first budget message, the Secretary denied both the possibility and desirability of attaining one: secure Soviet striking capacity was and would be maintained at a high enough level to make a U.S. first strike irrational. But, in the first two full budgets of the Kennedy Administration—which laid down guidelines governing the size of the strategic striking forces that are still in effect today—the programed missile and long-range bomber forces were larger in relation to projected Soviet forces than would have been required for minimum deterrence alone, even allowing for a generous margin of uncertainty on the growth of Soviet forces, their effectiveness and the post-attack performance of our own programed forces. The margin over deterrence was justified in terms of the idea of "damage limitation," should deterrence fail—a contingency that could not be ignored. Should sufficient warning of preparations for a Soviet strike or actual launching of one be available, U.S. missiles could be launched against Soviet missile sites and airfields, thus limiting to an extent depending on warning time the damage that the Soviet strike would inflict.

A large enough effort at "damage limitation" of course shades off into a first-strike posture; a small enough one becomes indistinguishable from the safety margin for deterrence. After the third McNamara budget, the emphasis on damage limitation vanished, to be replaced by deterrence, under the terminology of "assured destruction," referring to the capacity of our strategic forces to survive a Soviet attack and achieve with high probability a level of death and destruction in the Soviet Union that would rule out nuclear war as a rational policy for them.

The decisions of 1961 and 1962 called for the build-up by 1965 of a U.S. strategic force of nearly 1,800 missiles capable of reaching Soviet targets; somewhat more than a third were to be submarine-launched. In addition, some 600 long-range bombers would be maintained. This was projected against an expected Soviet force of fewer than a third as many missiles and a quarter as many bombers capable of reaching the United States. Further, the Soviets were expected to possess an equal number of shorter-range missiles and a much larger number of medium bombers that could be used against European targets. These decisions were taken by a new administration in the aftermath of the missile-gap argument that had been a prominent feature of the election campaign; it was a time, too, when American intelligence estimates of Soviet programs for their strategic forces were undergoing sharp revisions, to the accompaniment of the intragovernmental controversy that such processes always entail. Whether, in another atmosphere, such a program might have been viewed as unnecessarily large for deterrence alone, and whether the articulation of an additional objective of damage limitation would have been avoided from the start is, of course, unknowable. Unknown, and perhaps equally unknowable at least for some time to come, is whether the Soviets' original force goals in 1961–1962 were as modest as our estimates of them at the time—or even more so—and whether their rapid recent build-up, discussed immediately below, was a response to the tremendous acceleration in the growth of our long-range striking forces that the Kennedy Administration brought about. In any event, until 1965 or even into 1966 it was possible for the Administration to deny any wider aim for its strategic posture than deterrence, to argue the futility of seeking to achieve a first-strike force, and yet to avoid the sharp edge of the question of whether we were maintaining "strategic superiority" over the Soviets.

Recent changes in Soviet deployments have given a new bite to this question; corresponding and anticipatory changes in our own have raised even broader questions of how stable our deterrent posture will be in the years ahead.

II

The last two years have shown significant changes in the Soviet strategic forces. The number of their intercontinental and submarine-launched ballistic missiles has grown rapidly. As of late 1967—as estimated by Secretary McNamara in his 1968 budget presentation—the number of land based missiles had grown to 750, or nearly half our total, and most of the growth had taken place in the previous year. This indicates that the number might well continue to grow rapidly. The total number of Soviet missiles targetable against both the United States and NATO countries is already nearly equal to the total number of U.S. missiles that can reach Soviet targets. Further, there are some suggestions that the Soviets are currently building up their missile submarine fleet both qualitatively and quantitatively, so as to achieve—like the United States—a substantial force protected from a first strike by concealment and mobility.

In addition to these changes in offensive forces, the Soviets have deployed an anti-ballistic missile defense system around Moscow. They may be extending this deployment further, but if so, they are doing it slowly rather than rapidly.

So far, we have not responded to these developments by planning an increase in the number of our missile launchers. Rather, we have concentrated on programs for upgrading our present forces by replacing existing missiles with new ones designed to use present launching platforms. The new missiles will be superior to the old in three respects. First, they will be significantly more accurate, which means that a smaller warhead can be used to achieve a particular level of destruction against a specified target. Second, they will contain a variety of decoys and other penetration aids which will make more difficult the defensive task of an ABM system. Finally, and most significant, they will ultimately contain several independently aimed warheads within a single missile (MIRVs or multiple independent reëntry vehicles, to the trade). These, in turn, again make the task of the defensive ABM more difficult. In addition, they raise a new, and as we shall see, somewhat frightening possibility of multiplying greatly the number of warheads which one or the other side can launch, without changing the number of visible missile launchers.

In addition, of course, we have made the decision to deploy a "thin" ABM system, emphasizing primarily area defense against light attacks, a so-called anti-Chinese defense.

In themselves, none of these changes will significantly alter the strategic balance from one of mutual deterrence, if they do not go beyond their present limits. Neither the Soviet ABM nor the growth of Soviet missile forces reduces in an important way our capability to inflict unacceptable damage on the Soviet Union after a Soviet first strike. In his most recent budget presentation, Secretary McNamara estimated that, on the basis of projected force levels in the 1970s, a United States retaliatory attack after a Soviet strike against our strategic forces would result in over 100 million Soviet dead. Similarly, Soviet responses to our proposed ABM deployment, if they were like our own responses to theirs, would be readily within their capabilities and would leave them able to inflict over 100 million fatalities on us in a second strike. Were we to deploy much stronger and more costly defenses, it would remain within the Soviet capability to counter them by corresponding increases in the size of their offensive deployments—which could probably be made at significantly less cost than that of our increased defenses. The Russians would thus retain their capability to inflict high levels of fatalities on us in a second strike.

To be sure, the Administration asserts that our ABM system is being deployed to counter the possibility of a light Chinese attack in the coming years. The Chinese are testing thermonuclear devices and medium-range missiles; within the next decade they could achieve a modest ICBM force. In the same budget testimony, Secretary McNamara argued that the proposed ABM system might hold fatalities from potential Chinese attacks of varying plausible sizes in the next five to eight years to below a million; in the absence of such a system the figure could range from seven to fifteen million. But why deterrence, on which we have relied successfully for many years to restrain the powerful forces of the Soviets, is not expected to work against the small forces of the poorer and weaker Chinese is totally unclear. For some time into the future, at least as far as our present projections and calculations go, we shall have a credible first-strike capacity against the Chinese. In such circumstances, it is difficult to understand on what calculation the Chinese would throw away the only effective restraint on our nuclear force, the strong moral and political inhibitions we have against striking first, by launching an attack.

Only the proposition that there is a special danger of aggressive irrational behavior by some future Chinese Government would make sense of the official argument. Yet there is nothing in the recent record of the Chinese Government in its international relations that provides the basis for such an expectation. Accordingly, it is hard to take the Administration's rationale for deploying a thin ABM defense at face value, especially in the light of its own evaluation of the utility of not only the proposed defense system, but more elaborate, extensive and powerful ones. The decision is much more easily understood as the result of long-standing pressures within the military establishment and the Congress for an antimissile defense. When these were reinforced in recent years by the evidence of initial Soviet deployments, the demand for a "response" finally became irresistible.

While the recent and projected changes in Soviet and American strategic forces have not altered the fundamental strategic situation from one of mutual deterrence, they may have set in motion forces which will undermine the stability of the relation in coming years. Within the Congress, pressures are already beginning to mount for action to offset the large increase in numbers of Soviet missiles, so as to maintain a margin of "strategic superiority," rather than accepting "parity." As the planned deployment of the ABM system goes forward, Congressional and public pressures to upgrade it can be expected to rise; this would be done by adding local defenses of missiles and cities to the present area-defense system. The next Administration will then face the task of making the public case for the explicit acceptance of strategic "parity" with the Soviets, or in the alternative, giving in to these pressures and beginning a new set of developments in our strategic forces, with consequences that are unpleasant to contemplate.

The core of the case for accepting "parity" has already been put, but it bears repetition, and a little elaboration. In essence we cannot expect with any confidence to do more than achieve a secure second-strike capacity, no matter how hard we try. This capacity is not usefully measured by counting warheads or megatons or, above some level, expected casualties. Whether the result comes about with twice as many American as Soviet delivery vehicles—as has been the case in the past—or with roughly equal numbers, or even with an adverse ratio, does not change its basic nature. Further, any significant change in deployments by either major adversary requires a long period of time, and announces itself, either explicitly or through intelligence means, in its early stages. The other, therefore, has notice and time within which to respond. The present level of research, development and production capacity for weapons of both superpowers is such that each has the power to respond to a change in the deployments of the other in a way that leaves it "satisfied" with its new position in relation to the adversary. Each, accordingly, must anticipate such a response. And so the arms race would go on. The expected result of the process can be no more than a new balance at higher force levels, larger expenditures and, most likely, even more unthinkably high levels of destruction in the event that the forces were ever used.

Moreover, there is another and even more troubling consequence of following the competitive path: the stability of mutual deterrence becomes far less certain in a rapidly changing situation. Deterrence is at bottom a political and psychological concept. It rests on the perception and interpretation of the military situation by political decision-makers; and it is as open to influence by changes in their operating environment or the attitudes they bring to their perceptions as by changes in the hard technical facts. This inevitably marks it with a certain elusiveness. How great a capacity to wreak death and destruction on an adversary is enough? Can it be measured in absolute terms in millions of dead and acres of destruction, or only in the fractions of his population, industry and urban area? If one rival's destructive capacity grows while the other's remains constant at a high level, does this reduce the effectiveness of the latter's deterrent? Questions such as these clearly have no unique, well-defined answers that hold for all decision-makers in all circumstances. What is clear is that constant or slowly changing force structures, whose technical performance characteristics are reasonably well understood—subject, of course, to the important fundamental limitation that they have not been and never can be tested in a realistic way—provide a much more stable basis for mutual reliance on and acceptance of deterrence than a rapidly moving process of qualitative and quantitative competition.

The behavior of a whole defensive system in action is difficult to predict, since it depends heavily on specific details of design of both offensive and defensive weapons which are not likely to be well known to both adversaries. The effects of the interaction of two strikes, in which offensive and defensive forces on both sides are involved, multiply the uncertainties. Thus the "adequacy" of any particular second-strike force becomes harder to assure with confidence, and the impulse to compensate for uncertainty by building larger forces will make itself felt on both sides.

Further, current technical developments in weaponry present the possibility of introducing significantly new elements of uncertainty into the situation, which in themselves, even in the absence of further continuing change, would diminish the stability of deterrence. Anti-ballistic missile defenses constitute one example; another is the multiple, independently aimable warheads carried by a single missile. At present, each adversary has a reasonably clear idea of the other's deployments, with enough detail to permit a confident estimate of the balance of forces. Once MIRVs become widespread, it becomes much more difficult for each side to know how many warheads, as opposed to launchers, the other has. How great the uncertainty will be depends, of course, on the specific technical possibilities: two warheads per missile would create one situation; ten, quite another. In the absence of submarine-launched, or equally mobile land-based missiles, the latter situation could give rise to the ugly possibility of each side's possessing a first-strike capability against the other, provided the accuracy of the independently aimed warheads permitted successful attack on hard targets.

III

These frightening possibilities still lie in the future. For the present, and the next year or two ahead, nothing that is currently happening or in prospect justifies anxiety for the continued effectiveness of the U.S. second-strike capability, or its continued power to perform its primary function of deterring the Soviets from using their nuclear forces against us. None of the evidence on the Soviet build-up points beyond an effort to move close to a crude equality with us in numbers of offensive missiles. There is no evidence of a wide program of ABM deployment; indeed, nothing beyond the Moscow system seems to be happening. This is certainly no more imposing than our own proposed defensive system, which we believe to be too weak to affect our calculation of Soviet deterrent capabilities.

The rapidity of the recent build-up in Soviet forces tempts some to project that build-up into the future, and see it as a race for "strategic superiority." The absence of official announcements of force goals by the Soviets—such as the Secretary of Defense makes in his annual budget presentations—reinforces the temptation; and the demonstration of the illusory nature of such a goal seems an insufficient response. Yet our past experience with the projected "bomber gap" of the early fifties and the "missile gap" of 1959–61 shows the problems of such interpretations. In both these cases we clearly over-reacted. In the first, the result was our concentration on the creation of a very large, expensive and vulnerable bomber force, while the Soviets moved on to missiles. In the second, the scale of our reaction has probably been the major factor in stimulating the current Soviet build-up. If our aim remains that of maintaining deterrence, we can clearly afford to wait for the event, rather than begin now to respond to our projections of the future.

Can our aim be more? Should we seek to exploit the opportunities of our new technology as rapidly as possible to reach beyond deterrence ourselves? There are strong forces in the military and the Congress always ready to urge this path. They are undoubtedly supported, and their voices amplified to some extent, by the handful of large contractors who benefit from an increase in expenditures on strategic forces. What is many times more important, they reflect a deeply held and widely shared popular sentiment that our wealth, our power and our virtue entitle us to be "first," and any claim to equality by the morally and economically inferior Soviet Union is at best presumptuous, at worst dangerous.

The facts of weapons technology have long made the pursuit of "virtue" along this path vain and wasteful; now they make it positively dangerous. We are in a position in relation to our superpower adversary in which, for the present and near future, the balance of forces is such as to make possible new and far-reaching arms-control agreements. With not too widely disparate levels of offensive forces, and some deployment of defensive forces on both sides, the possibility of an agreed "freeze" in further deployments of strategic weapons looks more favorable than it has for some time. Such an agreement would clearly present a host of difficult problems, centering around how much control of technical improvement in existing vehicles and warheads was sought, and by what means. No risk-free solution of these difficulties is likely to be found, even in concept, much less in terms of negotiable arrangements between the two countries. Yet, the alternative risks arising from the uncontrolled forward thrust of technical change in weaponry are much greater. The more successful the development of MIRVs in terms of both the number of reëntry vehicles carried by a single warhead and the accuracy with which they can be directed, the more difficult it becomes to be confident about the security of a deterrent force. Wider deployment of ABMs compounds the difficulty by adding to the uncertainties of both sides as to the effectiveness of their own and their rivals' forces. Under such circumstances, arms-control agreements in turn may become much more difficult to reach, since an atmosphere of mutual distrust and fear will hardly promote the success of what will at best be difficult negotiations.

All signs point to the coming of a time when the stability of mutual deterrence can no longer rest reliably on mutual watchfulness and forbearance, without explicit arms-control agreements over strategic weapons deployments. We should do nothing to hasten its arrival, and everything to take advantage of whatever respite we have to move forward to such agreements.

IV THE REJECTION OF FORCE:
PACIFISM

The Price of Power

"Only he who has measured the dominion of force,
and knows how not to respect it, is capable of
love and justice."
                                        —Simone Weil

The Basic Assumption of Present Policy

The basic reason for our failure lies in the nature of our present
commitment to violence. The basic assumption upon which
United States foreign policy rests is that our national interest
can best be served by military preparedness against a Soviet
threat on the one hand, and by constructive and world-wide economic, political, and social programs on the other. The most
common image used to suggest an adequate American policy is
that of a wall of military power as a shield against communism,
behind which the work of democracy, in raising the level of life

From *Speak Truth to Power; A Quaker Search for an Alternative to Violence,* a pamphlet prepared for the American Friends Service Committee,
1955. This excerpt is not a full expression of the American Friends Service
Committee's approach to world peace. Reprinted by permission.

and educating the minds of men, can be carried on. Our material strength must provide the basis of security so that men may have a chance to grow and develop.

This is an appealing image, reflecting both our peaceful intentions and our high aspirations, but we believe it is false and illusory. We believe that whatever may have been true in the past, it is now impossible for a great nation to commit itself both to military preparedness and to carrying forward a constructive and positive program of peacemaking. We believe these two aims have become mutually exclusive, and that a willingness to resort to organized mass violence under any circumstances requires a commitment that condemns all other desires and considerations to relative ineffectiveness. We propose first to explain why we believe this to be so, leaving for [another place] the question whether there is any way out of the dilemma thus created.

The rationale for the military, or containment, part of American policy is that the cool, logical, limited use of force to hold Soviet military power in check will provide the United States with the opportunity to employ other methods and resources to deal with the problems that are the causes of communist totalitarianism and its growth in the world. We believe that this conception of a "limited" commitment to power is unrealistic in terms of the requirements of present day military planning. Today war has its own logic, its own direction. No social institution is firmly enough based to contain it. It bends all to its needs. This is the nature of modern war. It is necessarily also the nature of preparation for war.

We suggest that American experience over the past dozen years bears out this conclusion regarding the all-engulfing nature of a commitment to military preparedness. We are not at this point in our discussion challenging the necessity for the commitment itself. We seek only to establish that it is in its nature an open-ended rather than a limited endeavor, and that it has in fact prevented us from moving in those other directions that so many agree are necessary if peace is to be won.

What then has been our experience in applying this limited restraining power? Has it been possible to act rationally and cooly to balance negative military requirements against the need for more positive and far reaching measures necessary to win the peace?

The Impact of Military Requirements on Our Military Establishment

Even in a simple military sense the idea of a limited commitment to material power appears unrealistic. For it is in the nature of the situation that the limits to an armaments races are set for us by our enemy and for him by us. Here is a clear illustration of the familiar insight that by arming ourselves we do but arm our enemy. Thus in 1948 we were assured that forty-eight air wings were adequate to contain Soviet power. In July 1952 it was ninety-five; three months later, one hundred twenty-four. Recent discussion has centered around the goal of one hundred forty-three wings. It is clear that it is not what we possess, but what we fear others possess that sets the limits. Since this is also true for others, the attempt to find security in military power cannot be a matter of "thus far and no farther," but is a road that, once entered, has no end.

We have said that we would "contain" Soviet power. We have in fact *tried* to contain it. But since this would require a preponderance of force, which it has not been possible to achieve, we have failed. We have succeeded only in diverting large proportions of the economic political and psychological energy of both sides to non-productive and inflammatory purposes. Neither history nor our own recent experience supports the hope that the United States can make a limited commitment to military security in a world where power is concentrated in two blocs, both commanding vast resources.

The Impact of Military Requirements on Our Democratic Structure

Organization for modern warfare is no longer the problem of the military establishment alone. Just as the burden of war itself must now be borne by every citizen as well as by every soldier, so the preparation for war must necessarily be the responsibility of the whole nation. This fact has been brought home to Americans in almost every phase of their lives. The requirements of a military posture in terms of internal security, national unity, and basic values are literally changing the character of American life.

In the first place, preparing ourselves for the eventuality of total war demands that we adopt stringent measures to insure internal security. Traditional American liberties must be sacrificed in the relentless search for subversives in our midst. Where loyalty oaths must be demanded, dissent becomes confused with disloyalty, and orthodoxy is made the badge of patriotism. Individual rights must be submerged in the interest of national security, and we have a widespread and irrational hysteria abroad in the land that strikes at the very heart of our democracy. It destroys our trust in one another, and without trust a free society cannot exist.

Nor does this situation reflect only a passing crisis that will largely disappear with the correction of these excesses that have been introduced by political exploitation of the subversion fear. Excesses can be corrected, but the basic threat to individual liberty will remain, for underneath the present hysteria lies a problem that has been widely recognized by responsible leaders and by a great many other Americans. In an age when a single bomb can destroy a city, and where secrecy may be the price of continued national existence, the pervasiveness of the subversion danger is apparent, and many a thoughtful citizen has been forced to accept the necessity of rigid security precautions. How can our old concepts of individual liberty survive under these circumstances? How indeed can a nation caught up in an atomic arms race find the calm judgment necessary to strike even a reasonable balance between freedom and security?

Secondly, as this suggests, organization for war demands the highest possible degree of national unity. If we are to be ready to act quickly and decisively in any crisis, the nation must be as nearly of one mind as possible. This need has led to the new science of "emotional engineering," the planned development of the mass mind. Though originally a technique employed by total-itarian regimes, it has now been adopted by the democratic West as a necessity of the perilous post-war era. A great nation of one hundred sixty million people, fundamentally anti-war in its values, content with its living standards, and relatively uncon-cerned with the problems of far-away people, cannot be per-suaded to send its young men to fight a war on the other side of the world simply on the grounds that a rational application of power demands it. Something more stirring is needed, something more akin to the "Two Minute Hate" that George Orwell de-scribes in *1984*, in which deep fear and moral outrage are com-bined to induce a kind of mass hysteria. It seems clear to us that our government, acting from the best motives, and in the in-terests of national security, has consciously tried to build a mass mind in America, a mind outraged by our enemies and con-vinced of the moral justification of our own position.

* * *

Thirdly, military requirements have caused profound changes in the basic values by which America has lived. We have already noted the impact on individual freedom and on independence of thought. Now we turn to the demands of military preparation in the spiritual realm. There is strong evidence that our traditional American culture does not produce the kind of man best equipped to meet the needs of combat. . . .

* * *

. . . As long as militarism remains alien to our culture, it will be difficult to convert young Americans into front line fighters. Since we must be militarily strong we must take steps to change our social pattern. It is no accident that our government, in con-flict with a totalitarian opponent, has found it necessary to set up an independent agency, the Rand Corporation, to study prob-lems of social control. Methods of propaganda, social organiza-tion, and control of movements are studied and evaluated by sociologists and psychologists for their usefulness in the stress of war. For the first time in United States history, we have a continuing peacetime draft, as well as unprecedented pressure for permanent universal military training for all eighteen-year-olds. We must build military assumptions into the very warp of our culture. ROTC for high school youngsters must be expanded. Film series—such as "Are You Ready for Service?"—are designed to prepare young people for conscription, and establish military points of view in the minds of thirteen-year-olds. Shall we discover, as Hitler did, that thirteen is also too late, and that we must begin our drilling and shaping with five-year-olds?

. . . Organization for modern war demands fundamental changes in the values of our society. The organizational, cultural, and spiritual framework of a society prepared to wage modern mass warfare is incompatible with the framework of a society that sustains democratic and human values. War preparation now requires organizing society itself as an army, with information and control wholly in the hands of the wielders of power. Obviously, this is incompatible with democracy. We believe therefore that the commitment to violence inherent in our containment policy can only be carried out at the expense of the very democracy we seek to protect.

The Impact of Military Requirements on Our Foreign Policy

If it could be shown that the price that must be paid internally, in terms of vast economic outlays and the sacrifice of democratic principles, would make possible the implementation of constructive foreign policies that attack the causes of conflict, perhaps the sacrifices would be worth making. Unfortunately, the same insatiable demands of military security that dominate the domestic scene operate to inhibit constructive programs in the foreign field. Whatever we may wish to do as a nation, politically, economically, or diplomatically, must inevitably be measured in terms of its impact on national security. We believe therefore that, in the field of foreign policy, an examination of the record over the past ten years will support the conclusion that the effective implementation of constructive, long-range policies is, in fact, impossible as long as military security must also be sought. This we believe to be true in various spheres regardless of how earnestly the American people desire to move toward the positive policies that many have suggested.

1. *The impact on political policies.* One of the cornerstones of American political philosophy has always been an insistence on the right of people to choose their own governments. In pre-war years we generally supported this right of self-determination, and later set an example for the world in granting independence to the Philippines. This position stems from our revolutionary tradition, and was an important factor in building for the United States a great reservoir of good will among exploited and colonial peoples the world over. They regarded us as their champion, and their friendship gave us a position of strength and a loyalty more potent than any that could be purchased with guns. What has happened to this tradition since military containment became the central plank of our foreign policy?

* * *

. . . Our sympathies are still with the oppressed. Most Americans have always wanted independence for the Indo-Chinese, self-determination for African peoples, and liberation of Latin Americans and Asians from the economic bondage in which many millions live. Yet in country after country we find ourselves allied with those forces which stand in the way of the revolutionary changes that are demanded. This is usually not because of selfish economic interests or because we believe in the present ruling powers, but simply because of our belief that the prime danger comes from Soviet military expansion and our reluctant conclusion that we either ally ourselves with those who hold power now, and thus strengthen ourselves militarily, or we sacrifice strategic considerations in allying ourselves with the demand for change. It may be tragic that the United States is coming to be regarded as the guardian of the *status quo* instead of the champion of the oppressed, but it appears to have no choice. Our commitment to containment requires that the price be paid. Is there any evidence of a limited commitment here? Is there any example of moral or political considerations prevailing on colonial questions except as military considerations permit? In theory, the containment concept allows for it; in practice, it has proved impossible.

Nor are colonial and underdeveloped regions the only areas in which political policy is dictated by military necessity. They are only the most striking, since it is around them that much of the discussion centers concerning the basic requirements of peace. Our German policy, for example, is almost wholly oriented around strategic considerations. Moral and political questions involved in German rearmament, or in reconstituting a united Germany, or in ending military occupation, or in dealing adequately with the refugee problem—all must be submitted to the military role of West Germany in the containment program. The same thing is true with regard to Japan. Whether the question is one of rearmament, foreign trade, or international labor relations, the American position is determined finally on the basis of military considerations rather than on what seems right for Japan from a total view of the situation. How else can our policy of discouraging Japanese trade with China be interpreted, when it is clear that such trade is of vital importance to a self-sustaining Japan?

American policy toward the United Nations provides a further example of the impact of military requirements in the political arena. The United Nations was originally conceived of as a world forum for the peaceful settlements of disputes, with eventual forces of its own to back its decisions. As the power struggle has developed, the United States has sought to convert it into a collective military instrument for use against the communist bloc of nations. Although undertaken in the name of collective security, the move has been basically dictated by the demands of the power struggle, and too little thought has been given to the impact of United Nations military action on its crucial role of mediation and peaceful settlement. Moreover, the collective security concept has been applied only when it conformed to the demands of national military policy. Korea and Guatemala provide contrasting examples. In the former, collective action was invoked, in the latter it was discouraged, though in both cases aggression had taken place. Similarly, the whole question of United Nations membership has become tangled up in strategic considerations. Entrance applications are weighed more on the basis of their impact on the cold war than their impact on world organization. We are not here questioning the wisdom of particular policies but only pointing to the fact that in the United Nations, as elsewhere, the commitment to a military containment policy overrides other considerations in the formulation of political decisions.

2. *The impact on economic policies.* Another area in which there is practically unanimous agreement among those who have studied the requirements of peace is in the field of economic policy. Underdeveloped countries must be built up. Trade barriers must be broken down. These are important ways in which poverty, disease, and unemployment can be attacked, and the basic sources of discontent and strife eliminated. But how far have we been able to move toward these goals?

United States participation in UNRRA and its sponsorship of the Marshall Plan provided a fine start, and it is unfortunate that the good effects were in both instances vitiated by the developing demands of the cold war. The international cooperative character of UNRRA, already weakened by a lack of Russian cooperation, was further damaged by the American decision in 1947 to stress bilateral arrangements, while the Marshall Plan came admittedly to be considered by both sides as an anti-communist weapon in the later years of its effective operation. Since the time of these two major recovery efforts, the first test for American economic aid has been whether or not it would strengthen the power position of the United States: Is the prospective recipient prepared to help win a possible war? Need has become a secondary criterion. Even technical assistance, once envisaged as a bold new program to lift the level of life in underdeveloped areas, has become so enmeshed in American military planning that one nation (Burma) rejected aid for fear that it would involve a commitment to American military policy, and others have been troubled by the same implication.

Fully as serious is the generally smaller size of the appropriations that Congress makes available for economic aid and technical assistance. The demands of the military are so great and the pressure against higher taxes so strong, that there are only marginal funds left over for purposes of economic development. Our national leaders frankly admit that until some way can be found to reduce military requirements, large-scale American participation in economic assistance will not be possible. This is to be regretted, of course, but military needs come first, and as long as they are reckoned in the tens of billions, economic assistance will continue to be reckoned in the tens of millions.

* * *

The same situation exists in the field of world trade. Our government is well aware of the long-range benefits that would accrue from expanded trade—benefits that have direct bearing on world peace and stability. But again, military considerations intervene, and we are obliged to adopt a rigid policy of barring trade between East and West. Thus at many points where economic steps might be taken to correct the basic conditions that lead to violence, we find ourselves blocked by the military demands of containment.

3. *The impact on diplomacy.* Post-war diplomacy has become more and more directly related to military power. Negotiation is carried forward not to discover a *modus vivendi,* but to force acceptance of a position through the demonstration of superior power. Where one party yields, it is only because the concession is forced by either internal or external pressures. Under these conditions, international conferences are too often turned into sounding boards for diplomats speaking for home consumption. As long as a primary requisite of military preparedness is a public convinced of the total depravity of the prospective enemy, and the total values of the stakes, rational attempts at peaceful settlement have small chance of success. Under these conditions, great power conferences become only milestones in the cold

war, and even proposals for disarmament are perverted until they become a facade behind which the great powers continue to stockpile armaments. Similarly, though committed to working through the United Nations for peaceful settlement, we find ourselves caught in the web of our own power diplomacy, unable to consider admitting to the forum the very party we must deal with if settlement is to be achieved. We may *want* to reach peaceful settlement. We may *want* to remain in touch with the thinking of the other side. But our dominant military and strategic emphasis so colors our attempts at peaceful settlement as to render them futile. This failure is not an accident, nor is it the result of inadequate political or military leadership. Rather it is the logical outcome of the total endeavor necessary for preparedness for modern war.

4. *The impact on psychological processes.* Even if it were possible, economically, for a nation to support both an expanding military budget and an adequate assistance program, it would be psychologically impossible for the American people to support both. This is not merely because a mounting tax burden and an inflexible diplomatic position require a steadily stimulated attitude of fear or suspicion; it is because, by its very nature, the human will cannot without disaster commit itself at one and the same time to contradictory values and opposed actions. It is psychologically impossible to be devoted at once to the attitudes that alone make possible the destruction of one's fellow men and to the generous and creative relief of their necessities. Man cannot make peace and prepare for war at the same time any more than he can simultaneously support and oppose revolutions. These basic impossibilities have long been recognized in the spiritual realm. Jesus said: "No man can serve two masters; for either he will hate the one, and love the other; or else he will hold to the one, and despise the other." We believe the words apply also in the present day political realm.

* * *

In conclusion, it seems clear to us that we cannot ultimately follow the constructive policies we voice because of the nature of our commitment to violence. Military power is as corrupting to the man who possesses it as it is pitiless to its victims. It is just as devastating to its employer as it is to those who suffer under it.

> Its power of converting a man into a thing is a double one, and its application is double-edged. To the same degree, though in different fashions, those who use it and those who endure it are turned to stone.

We have gone wrong here in America. We close our eyes to the meaning of the subjection of the human spirit to violence. We deceive ourselves even in our practical political judgments.

On the one hand, we want to resolve our difficulties with the Soviet Union peacefully. We want to aid the underprivileged of the world in their demand for a decent standard of life. We want to develop the United Nations as an agency of peaceful settlement and as a nascent center of world law. We want to be free of the burden of an arms race and of the terrible fear of an atomic war. We want to be free to live our lives in a manner befitting our conception of the dignity and worth of individual men.

On the other hand, we want also to find security through our ability to cause pain to others and through the phenomenal development of our nation as a society prepared to wage war.

We cannot do both.

A Choice With Hope

> "Ye have heard that it hath been said, Thou shalt love thy neighbor, and hate thine enemy. But I say unto you, love your enemies . . ."
>
> —Matthew 5:43-44

The False Assumptions of Present Policy

Surely no American, when faced with the choice between war and peace with honor, would choose war. The United States, despite unfair charges to the contrary, has been trying to choose peace with honor since 1945, and Americans are still ready today to sacrifice their blood and their treasure in the effort to obtain it. Foreign policy decisions have been the subject of widespread discussion in Congress and across the country. A great national debate preceded approval of the North Atlantic Treaty Organization. In 1954, the nation was aroused to weigh the merits of intervention in Indo-China. The American people considered carefully the question of relative priority between Europe and Asia in defense plans. They have debated whether to commit the nation to resist aggression when it occurs, or to attempt to prevent it by threatening instant and massive retaliation against the Soviet Union itself. They have argued the wisdom of relying primarily upon air power as against maintaining a balance between all the military forces. Questions of collective or unilateral action, of neutralism, of United Nations memberships—all these have been discussed, and each time the choice is determined by what the majority feels is the most likely to produce peace. Through this period of crisis, American choices have been made as choices for peace.

Yet they have not produced peace. We believe the reason is that they have been content to deal with problems at the level of strategy. Rarely have they examined the assumptions upon which strategy is based, and in our opinion it is here that the difficulty lies. We have suggested that in at least three major respects, the fundamental assumptions of the American people are in error. First, we challenged the assumption that under present circumstances power could be applied rationally, and a constructive program for peace carried on simultaneously with a program for military defense. Second, we challenged the assumption that the Soviet Union is the source of our problems, and that by achieving its disintegration or even its containment we would move toward a peaceful world. Finally, we challenged the assumption that force is the only realistic means of dealing with international problems.

The Real Choice

Obviously, our analysis suggests that America's discussion of peace, however sincere, has been carried forward on too shallow a basis. If the underlying presuppositions of policy are false, discussion of the policies themselves is idle business. We believe the real choice lies between continuing to deal with international problems on the old basis of military power and attempting to deal with them on the new and revolutionary basis of nonviolence.

Faced with such a choice, and cognizant of the dangers of moving into a largely unknown and unexplored area, we must still choose, and urge others to choose, the second alternative.

1. We make this choice for moral reasons. Our faith insists that God did not create men to hate, nor establish His law so that peace could emerge from fury. Man is answerable for his actions, and can neither violate his faith on pleas of urgency nor escape his moral responsibility by the simple device of turning it over to others. The United States government itself insisted on this principle at the Nürnberg war crime trials; we believe it applies equally at home, for we do not recognize the existence anywhere of a double standard of morality that justifies conduct in the name of the state that would be reprehensible in the name of God.

2. We make the choice because we believe that democracy is the noblest philosophy of social organization that man has yet developed, and we are convinced that under modern conditions democracy and militarism are incompatible. Thus, we would rather give up our military strength and accept the risks that this involves, than keep our guns and lose our democracy. Gandhi, who understood the nature of power as well as any man in our time, put it explicitly:

> There is no escape from the impending doom save through a bold unconditional acceptance of the non-violent method. Democracy and violence go ill together. The States that today are nominally democratic have either to become

frankly totalitarian or, if they are to become truly democratic, they must become courageously non-violent.

3. We make this choice because we believe that modern conditions have brought us to the end of the military road. The heavy polarization of power into two world centers, the development of ultimate weapons, and the miracles of communication and transportation are new factors in history that demand new attitudes toward conflict. If men continue to hold on to an old rehearsed response in the presence of these new elements, they will not grow, but die. This is the crisis that all living things periodically have faced. To try to cling to outworn patterns of security rather than face the risks of striving for a new approach, has always meant death. We believe it will again mean death.

The Choice—Untried

The choice we propose is a radical one, requiring new attitudes, news risks, and it may be, new suffering. It is not a choice that the United States has ever made before. It has no relation whatever to what military leaders and patriotic groups like to refer to as the "pacifist virus that undermined America" in the years after the first World War. Campaigns to demobilize and "bring the boys home," pressures for a quick "return to normalcy," insistence on lower taxes and smaller military budgets, and drifts toward isolationism, may be sincere expressions of a war-weary people, but they are not pacifism. These attitudes, stemming as they did from selfish motives, and unaccompanied by concern for the welfare of others, may, indeed, have hastened war in a world where power is necessary to retain privilege and protect position. It does not follow, however, that peace is only for the militarily strong, as Americans are being so insistently advised. Indeed, even if military superiority once did insure a kind of enforced peace, it can do so no longer now that cosmic weapons place cosmic power at the disposal of more than one nation.

We suggest that from now on, peace will not be for the strong, but for the just, and further, that there will neither be peace until men learn to be just, nor justice until men determine to renounce violence.

The Choice—Not Utopian

Thus, we dissociate ourselves from the basically selfish attitude that has been miscalled pacifism, but that might be more accurately described as a kind of irresponsible anti-militarism. We dissociate ourselves also from utopianism. Though the choice of non-violence involves a radical change in men, it does not require perfection.

The renunciation of violence and the creation of a new climate in the world community will certainly be difficult, but we believe human nature, illumined and ennobled by divine power, can bear effective witness in the direction of world community. Man's character is a strange mixture of the petty, the self-centered, the fearful, and the complacent on the one hand, and the compassionate, the patient, the forgiving, and the noble on the other. The redemptive working of God in human lives, perhaps through the person of an inspired leader, can invoke on a large scale the qualities of sacrifice and service which are evidenced daily in common living, and which make up the heart of the non-violent alternative. Man *can* rise to noble heights, but he must first free himself from the compulsions of fear and the pressures of conformity.

* * *

Thus we believe that while man's nature makes war possible, it does not make war inevitable. Under the inspiration of a great cause and with great leadership, human nature can be made adequate to achieve creative solutions to whatever problems confront it. Moreover, man's struggle to control himself has been marked by a confirming series of successes. In the course of history he has gradually learned how to live peacefully in larger and larger units, and consequently to push his savage qualities farther and farther away. His concept of community has grown from a narrow tribal basis to one which embraces half the world. It must now be pushed further, for in our age there can be no stopping short of a global community. We will either find a way to replace savagery with law and government on this last frontier, or there will soon be no community left at all.

The Choice—Necessary

Thus, we insist that if Americans want to live and not die, if they want to lead the way toward a world where peace prevails and the miracles of science are put to work for man's benefit, and not his destruction, they must face individually the need for an ultimate and fundamental break with violence. There is, we believe, no other way to eliminate the scourge of war. Man must put aside his barren militarism and dare to embark courageously on the search for non-violent solutions to his problems. Moreover, the choice is inescapable. It will be made, either deliberately or by default.

In thus insisting on the rejection of violence as a method, we do not imply that all men must become pacifist. Rather our reading of history indicates that without the *unconditional* acceptance of an ideal by a minority, the vision and perseverance required to move the world in the direction of that ideal will be lacking. Specifically in the present situation, we believe the unconditional acceptance of non-violence by a growing number of committed men and women is necessary to provide the dynamic, and create the atmosphere, in which order can replace anarchy in the international community.

* * *

. . . Leadership at a new and deeper level is required; leadership that rejects violence and calls men to a new and revolutionary commitment to practice love in every area of life. Such a commitment will demand a high price, but we believe that those who would lead must be ready to pay it. Great goals are always costly, and we doubt there is any road to peace save that which for many leads through suffering and sacrifice. Indeed, we go further and say that paying this price is the most relevant political and spiritual act of our day. . . .

Force: Christian or Unchristian, Moral or Immoral

WILLMOORE KENDALL

. . . WHILE THERE ARE MANY VARIANTS OF PACIFISM, MANY FORMS ITS PROPOSALS MAY TAKE, MANY RATIONALES ITS PROPONENTS MAY PUT FORWARD, THEY ALL HAVE AT LEAST THIS MAJOR EMPHASIS IN COMMON, NAMELY: THEY DEMAND THE PRINCIPLED REJECTION OF FORCE, OF VIOLENCE, OF THE RECOURSE TO ARMS, EVEN BY LEGALLY CONSTITUTED STATES ATTEMPTING TO DEFEND THEIR JUST INTERESTS, INCLUDING SURVIVAL ITSELF. . . .

That pacifism is alien to the tradition of Western Civilization because that tradition is above all a *Christian* tradition and because pacifism is alien to the Christian tradition. That, more concretely, pacifism—though it appeals to the Christian doctrine of love—is the very negation of that love, that is, a manifestation of a kind of self-love that is hostile to the very meaning and heart of Christianity. That pacifism, though it insinuates itself into the body politic as a higher expression of Christian selflessness, is marked throughout by irresponsibility and callous

From *The Conservative Affirmation,* by Willmoore Kendall. It appears in "War and the Use of Force: Moral or Immoral, Christian or Unchristian," a debate at Stanford University by Willmoore Kendall and Mulford Q. Sibley. Henry Regnery Co., 1963. Reprinted by permission.

indifference towards the wants and needs and rights of the pacifists' fellow-men. That, finally, so-called *Christian pacifism* . . . though often no doubt motivated by a good-will whose roots are indeed to be found in the Christian tradition, is in fact a Christian heresy and, by that very token, a sign of barbarism in our midst.

We shall not, I recognize, understand each other about these theses, about why Christian pacifism must be judged a heresy, until we have said something more about the meaning of orthodoxy—at least this: The mark of a mind civilized by our Christian inheritance and therefore pervaded through and through by *civility*—a term I take from Dr. Johnson—the mark of such a mind, I say, is its ability to entertain intellectually and experience emotionally a complex of propositions whose unity consists, difficult as the idea may be for some persons to grasp, in the very tension among them. We confront here the paradox of intellectual opposites caught up together in a unity that gives vision and therefore peace to the man who possesses it—so that precisely what makes a man an orthodox Christian is his will's assent, under the impetus of the Grace of God, to a vision of reality based upon a fusing of opposites. The man who fails to be moved to that assent by the Grace of God, the man who fails there but is still able to entertain the vision intellectually, is what we may call a civilized unbeliever and not, in our terms, a heretic at all. The heretic is a different kind of man altogether, and his delineation is of central importance for our discussion. . . . The heretic is the man insufficiently civilized to understand —to get through his head—the complex of propositions that make up orthodox Christianity, and are thus a major part of the intellectual inheritance of Western Civilization. He is not, let us note carefully, an unbeliever. The heretic believes, but believes only a portion of the Deposit of Faith; and he believes *this* portion to the exclusion of *that* because (I repeat) he is temporarily or intellectually incapable of getting hold of that fusion of opposites that is the fullness of the Christian faith.

For example: orthodox Christianity maintained from the beginning that Christ was not a being apart from God and man (as an elf is), nor yet a half-human and half not (like a cen-taur) but both at once and both through and through—*very* man and *very* God. The inability to believe this is not heresy, but rather incredulousness. Total rejection of the Incarnation, that is, of the doctrine we have just stated, is easy to imagine in a mind and will annealed in the Judaic experience of civi-lized order, and is not, therefore, an evidence—if I may invert Dr. Johnson's word—of uncivility. It is easy to imagine also in a mind and will annealed in the Classical experience of civilized order, where again it would not be an indication of uncivility. But it is quite otherwise with the mind and will that partially accepts the doctrine and at the same time partially rejects it, for here we have a mind and will both inside and outside the Christian experience of the order of being, both inside and out-side Christian civilization and, insofar as he is outside, by defini-tion a barbarian. The stigmata by which he is to be recognized are the various forms of the wish to live *off* our Civilization and benefit from the commitments it imposes upon others, but not within them. And since that wish derives from his failure to grasp that complex of propositions, to entertain that paradox, to assent to the mystery inherent in it, he is a double threat to Civilization: he consumes the produce of fields that he does not help to till—that are, indeed, tilled by his enemies; he draws his strength from that which he rejects; and society is the weaker both because of that which he consumes and because of that which he should have nurtured but did not nurture. The heretic is a parasite.

Heretic: barbarian: parasite. That is the profane trinity that sums up the pacifist. Christianity—so Chesterton puts it—taught the lion to lie down with the lamb; but the lion did not thereby cease to be leonine, or become lamblike. The paradox of ortho-doxy is this joining together of lion and lamb that remain lion and lamb, of war and peace that are truly war and peace, of violence that is violent and resignation to evil that is resigned. The Christian pacifist, by contrast with the orthodox Christian, seizes upon Christ's injunction to bear evil for His sake, and for-gets or ignores or cannot comprehend the massive truth that

Christ himself used violence when he scourged the money-changers out of the temple. And that He was fond of the company of Roman soldiers. And that He paid one of His highest compliments to a centurion.

We learn from Augustine that the first serious manifestation of the heresy known as pacifism is to be found in the Manicheans. They, you will remember, insisted that there are two principles in reality, the Good and the Evil; that the material universe is the work of Evil and therefore itself evil warp-and-woof; that whatsoever the body does and suffers has no essential bearing upon what the soul thinks and knows and loves—all of this issuing logically in an indifference towards civil society which in due course hardened into opposition, into obstruction, and, eventually, into hatred. They were, in any case, pacifists, who punctuated lives of lethargic indifference to the world with periodic orgies and excesses and then, pure spirits that they were, denied all responsibility for the consequences of their debauchery. We have it from Waldensis that the Manicheans' pacifism was in due course handed down (which brings it a deal closer home) to Wycliffe, who probably received it from the Catharists, a sect whose doctrine on the evil of marriage struck at the very roots of civilized order and the decency of human love. Also in the fourteenth century, pacifism reared its head in the Rhine Valley, where it signalized the internal breakdown of medieval Christendom and the spread of that religious individualism, the negation of Christian charity, which I believe to be the root—both philosophical and theological—of the pacifist malady; a malady which, accordingly, flourishes where it flourishes. (A great deal of foolishness has been talked, and by persons who ought to know better, about the alleged pacifism of the Early Christians. They did indeed refuse to serve in the Roman armies, but not because they regarded the recourse to arms as evil; rather because as Roman soldiers they would have had to burn incense to the gods. As for the martyrs, they did not, to be sure, resist; but the martyrs were precisely not pacifists but saints, and did not pick and choose among the Beatitudes.)

Let us speak now of traditional Christian doctrine concerning the just war, which may safely cite as one of Western Civilization's major defenses against the heretical preachments of the pacifists. In brief summary, it runs as follows: The state is a *natural* society; being that, it possesses under natural law the right to use the means necessary for its preservation and proper functioning. In certain conditions, moreover, the only means by which it *can* preserve itself, or perfect or recover its lawful rights, is war—that is, the recourse to arms. And, given those conditions, it possesses under the natural law the right and the duty to wage war.

The traditional reasoning here has as its underpinning, let us notice at once, a profound metaphysics of Being itself, and one that has nowhere been better articulated than in Abraham Lincoln's blunt assertion that "No state voluntarily wills its own dissolution." The state—so runs the reasoning—has as its end the common good of its citizenry; it therefore is an order of Being, and of the being appropriate to a complex relationship. To say that it must not have recourse to armed might even when its existence is threatened by aggressors from without or within is, in other words, to demand that *an order of Being voluntarily will its own nothingness;* and such a demand is contrary to the structure of reality itself. As Thomas Aquinas puts it: every order of Being, and every being as well, *by its very nature* strives to keep itself in being. As Paul Tillich puts it, Being identical with its own power to be, its own affirmation against its own non-being. In a word: when we say that the lawfully-constituted state must bare its neck to the executioner, must do so though it exists to promote the common good of its citizenry, we as good as say that reality must have a tendency towards non-reality, that existence is one with nothingness. The pacifist in his heresy approaches the heresy of the suicide, and both are powerful artillery pieces trained upon the structure of existence itself. The Jewish tradition of Spinoza, the Catholic tradition of Aquinas, and the Protestant tradition of Tillich are all at one in this conception of the fundamental metaphysics. And the fact that they are at one bespeaks an orthodoxy common to the *entire* West, and it is the essence of pacifism, a doctrine so irresponsible that it refuses to salute even the Flag of Being, that it represents a sharp break with that orthodoxy. It is the Jehovah's Witness *par excellence*.

Let us put the point a little differently: A state which will not wage war in any circumstances, however serious, would condemn itself, we are saying, to extinction. Now: if the natural law demanded that, then God, who is the Author of the natural law, would both *will* and *not will* political society. He would will its end, and at the same time forbid it the means *necessary* for attaining that end, and we say "necessary" because the state that cannot protect the life, liberty, and property of its citizens fails in its appointed function. If, therefore, the state can sometimes perform its function only through the use of force, it must have the right to use force. And, naturally enough, the common orthodoxy of the West has always maintained that among the most precious rights of man is the right to go to war.

In this context, we readily see what is wrong with pacifism as a doctrine. If the pacifist were merely an opponent of militarism, of the use of aggressive war as an instrument of imperialistic expansion, the West would not always have turned a deaf ear to him. But the pacifist contents himself with nothing so modest or sensible: he condemns *all* war, even defensive war, and in doing so logically plunges himself into anarchism—an anarchism which, implicitly and often explicitly, wills the nothingness of civil society. This is a nihilism as dangerous as that of *Zarathustra*—nay, more dangerous, because it masks itself under the cloak of the very Christian responsibility that it denies.

Let us, however, pass on to another chapter of our topic: War, says the common tradition of Western Civilization, is not only *not* intrinsically wrong; it is very often intrinsically right, intrinsically moral. This also emerges from the doctrine of the just war—the conditions for which, under natural law, are as follows: 1) The just or legitimate war must be declared by a lawful authority. (Killing, the doctrine teaches, is clearly wrong when the killer is an individual acting in a private capacity, though no longer wrong when the killer kills in self-defense against private aggression. As for the soldier, he has a clear right to kill when he acts as the legal and publicly-designated agent of his country in the prosecution of a just war; and even public designation is not necessary if the war is a purely defensive one.) 2) Resort to force is permitted only on behalf of a just cause, where we must confess at once that the definition of just cause has given rise to very considerable differences of opinion, though not so many as to prevent our pointing to certain just causes about which there has been general agreement, namely: that of the state that is fighting for its very existence; that of the state which moves to recover that which is rightfully its own; and that of the state whose honor has been wounded so grievously that inaction would plead it guilty of cowardice in the eyes of the world. 3) The use of force is permitted only as a *last resort*. Before a nation launches its just war, that is to say, it must have exhausted every peaceful means consistent with its dignity: negotiation; mediation; arbitration; diplomatic pressure; economic sanctions; ultimata—in a word, every means short of war known to enlightened statesmanship. Otherwise, the doctrine holds, there exists no clear proof that the war is unavoidable, and that there is a proper relation between the good hoped for from the war and the means of achieving that good. 4) The state resorting to war must have a *fair hope of success*. Here again, however, the doctrine is not entirely clear, since it recognizes that there are times when men are so pressed—or oppressed—that resistance, even hopeless resistance, is the only means by which men can preserve their common dignity. By signing history with their heroism, as the Hungarians did yesterday and the Tibetans are doing today, noble men not only go to God but remind other men everywhere of what it means to be a man. To die on the streets of Budapest, a machine-gun in hand, is not only to save one's dignity and therefore one's soul; it is to offer an example to a timid and even cowardly world, and such a death, the tradition recognizes, may express a love that passes all understanding. "Greater love hath no man," it says than "that he lay down his life for his friend." The Hungarian freedom fighters, I like to think, died not only to save themselves, but to save us; their names should pass into the speech of all whose tongues still utter decency in a disintegrating world. The doctrine teaches, finally, that 5) even a punitive war, a war undertaken to punish a guilty nation, may be a just war. Right order and the future peace of the world may well demand, for example, that gangster nations not be permitted to commit mass-murder with impunity —that, rather they be taught a lesson in morals here and now. (There is, however, no blanket authorization in this regard: the right to wage a punitive war may well be counterbalanced by other considerations. The remitting of punishment, for instance, which is an act of mercy, might in certain circumstances be the higher duty.)

This traditional Christian doctrine, which I repeat, is that of the whole Western heritage, has both restrained the arrogant and given spirit to the timid. It has been articulated step by step, *within* the Christian West and *nowhere else*—which suggests, if it does not prove, that its roots are in the Christian experience itself. It owes as much to philosophic reason as to Revelation, and thus illustrates the Christian baptism of the Greek philosophical experience. It is of crucial importance for the preservation of Western civilization, and only a man weary of both the burdens and the glory of the heritage of that Civilization would seek to undermine it or call it into question. And that is the point about the pacifist; he *is* weary, and weary of both the burdens and the glory; and the consequences of his abdication of responsibility are visited not so much on *him* as on his society or civilization.

Let me make that clear: If the Christian pacifist were an isolated Ebenezer in a frontier society, we could let Bill take care of him—as Bill does in Hilaire Belloc's delightful refrain:

> Pale Ebenezer thought it wrong
> to fight;
> But roaring Bill who killed him
> Thought it right.

But the Christian pacifist is *not* a pale Ebenezer, who seraphically turns his face towards a lonely aggressor. He is a heretic within a society that his actions weaken and, were they to be multiplied, would destroy. The only thing to do with him is to unmask his pretentions, if only to be done with his constant moralizing. Unmask them how? One possibility would be for us to imitate Hilaire Belloc's delightful Bishop of old Auxerre, who:

> . . . With his stout Episcopal staff
> So thoroughly thwacked and
> banged
> The heretics all, both short
> and tall,
> They rather had been hanged.
> Oh, he thwacked them hard,
> and he banged them long.
> Upon each and all occasions,
> Till they bellowed in chorus,
> long and strong,
> Their orthodox persuasions!

But however we unmask him, unmask him we must, and soon. Appealing as he does from the doctrine of brotherly love and Christ's injunction to "turn the other cheek," he has confused them both and confused them badly.

Let us think together for a moment about that injunction to "turn the other cheek," and let us go again for assistance to Thomas Aquinas—not of course because of his supposed authority, but because his teaching on the matter appears to have imbedded itself deep in the conscience of Western civilization, to have entered into and become part of the Western way of life, and to have determined the behavior of countless millions of Westerners—countless millions who certainly could not have put the teaching into words, but have not, for that reason, acted upon it any the less surely or any the less confidently.Who, asks Thomas Aquinas, has the *right* to turn the other cheek?—not, mind you, the duty, but the *right*, since unless we have the right we clearly cannot have the duty. Who has the *right* to submit to unjust aggression? And Aquinas answers: "Only the man upon whom no higher responsibility falls; only the man who owes no other duty, in justice or in charity, to a friend or a wife or a child

or a society that would be adversely affected by the aggression."
Now: let us *arguendo*, grant that such an isolated man, a man
liberated from the responsibilities that normally attach to the
Christian way of life in society, might exist; Thomas wishes us
to ask further: "Does even he have the right to turn the other
cheek?" And we get not a "Yes" answer but a "Yes, but" answer:
Yes, but not always, not in all circumstances: such a man has
the right to turn the other cheek *only if his act of submitting to
the aggressor will, or possibly could, deter the aggressor from
his evil act;* only if his act of bearing injustice for the sake of
Christ may become a symbol of righteousness that might sign
itself within the conscience of the aggressor. Then, and then
only, says Aquinas, ought the Christian to refrain from resistance.
If non-resistance clearly cannot affect this end—as who but the
pacifist supposes it could against a Hitler, or against the disciplined hordes of World Communism—if non-resistance cannot
effect this end, then resistance becomes a duty—not primarily as
a means by which the man unjustly attacked may save himself,
but as a means of preventing the aggressor from carrying out his
act and, by striking back, teach the bully a lesson. Given the circumstances, resistance would be demanded by the *law of Christian love itself.* In a word: I ought to be concerned enough about
the moral and spiritual health of my enemy *to fight him for his
own good!* And the principle is, I repeat, important for "we" not
because it is Aquinas', but because it is and will continue to be
the rule of action of that Western Civilization on which, as I
began by saying, *"we"* place inestimable value. It is, for example,
the rule of action that sent us out to destroy the abomination
known as Nazism; and, as *we* know, it has much further work
to do.

The issue of pacifism, let me repeat, is less important for us
. . . than the locus in which it is argued. And the point to grasp
becomes this: the reasoning on which the doctrine just summarized rests itself moves from a spiritual emphasis that is
unknown to and unknowable by the pacifist. It originates in what
Sombert and Weber and Dawson call the "ec-static" structure of
Christian Love, which is a love that seeks not the *self* but the

perfection of the other; a love so strong that, as we have just seen, it will strike a man down in order that he may rise up the better for the blow! And we cannot, I think, overemphasize the fact that modern Christian pacifism grew up within the climate of that Christian individualism which is an utter distortion of the meaning of Christian love. Should we seek its origins, or at least its earliest full expression, we might well look to that same Rhine Valley gnosticism that produced both Mennonite pacifism and Thomas à Kempis, whose *Imitation of Christ* preaches, as "we" know, a strange new doctrine of Christian perfection. It holds that I am called to love my neighbor because God has thrown him my way as an occasion, as an instrument, for *my own perfection.* Its emphasis is, clearly, upon the self. It teaches a *self-centered Christianity,* the essence of which is that it would sacrifice society, even the life of one's own sons and daughters, on the altar of personal perfection, and this for the sake of personal identification with a misunderstood ideal of the Christian life. Such a Christianity inverts not only the psychological and theological but also the ethical dimension of the human spirit. And the ideal that it distorts, the true ideal of Christian love and thus of Christianity itself, is that caught up in St. John's magnificent injunction: "As the Father so loved you that He gave you His only Begotten Son, so do you love the world." The orthodox Christian loves the other—including his enemy—not because *he* will thereby be perfected, but because the other so needs his love; and in the background of this ec-static doctrine of love, Christ's injunctions to bear suffering and to turn the other cheek take on a transcendent meaning that is one with the sacrifice, even unto death, demanded by the Christian life. When resistance to aggression is the only means whereby I can cure a man of evil, then the love I owe him *demands* that I resist him. The sword ought to be taken up in love; and Chesterton is there to remind us that the cross and the sword are, paradoxically, the same symbol, pointing to the same Reality.

Another point or two, and I shall have done. The pacifist insists that Christian history fails to reveal any instance of a war's having achieved the ends for which it was waged. The assertion is altogether false, of course, in its understanding of the history of the West. To take the simplest and most obvious cases: Had Charles Martel—the *malleus hereticorum*—not taken up the sword against the Mohammedan barbarians, the crescent and not the cross would surely be planted where today there stands Notre Dame de Paris. Had Charlemagne not hurled back the Germanic pagans to the East, we might well be worshipping Odin and Thor and living in a forest of barbarism and blood. Had Don Juan of Austria not turned back the Turks at Lepanto, and had not John Sobieskie halted the Turks at Vienna, our civilization would have gone down in a twilight of the gods that would have left the world empty of decency and bereft of law. These men are the heroes of our cradles; tales of their valour have always been the substance of the childhood dreams of Christian men everywhere. And "we" of the West value our Marlboroughs and George Washingtons—value them, and revere their memories, as we value and revere the memories of our Beethovens and our Shakespeares; each has contributed a kind of knowledge and a kind of devotion without which the West could not have become the West as we know it.

It is objected that the medieval Church forbade the taking up of arms by clerks regular and secular, and on the ground that hands that consecrate at the altar ought not to be stained by blood. Indeed it did; but let no one try to transform this into a leg for pacifism to stand on. The leading theologians of the period are at one in justifying and praising (as well they may!) those religious orders whose mission was the defence of the Holy Places against the Barbarians. The position is crystal-clear: for the "defence of religion and public safety" and out of love for "the poor and the oppressed," men of God were raised up who carried shields and lances; and the tradition approved—as approve it must in view of the leading of Ambrose, who praised those who would defend the fatherland against barbarians; those who would shield the hearth against thieves; those who would stand as living swords between murderers and persons who are sick and infirm. And Ambrose praised them precisely because of their love of *justice*.

Christian love—it is this which is the strength of pacifism, and it is this which makes pacifism a peculiarly hideous heresy. For its love is a pale and fraudulent imitation of the real thing. It loves neither its enemy nor its friend, neither society nor home. To its claim that peace is its end, we answer with Augustine that with Christ "I bring you not peace, but a sword." Peace is something waged for, fought for; and the reason our world today may well find itself forced to wage war again is not that it cannot rise to the pacifist love of peace, but that it loves peace really, and knows it to be inseparable from the obligation to maintain order. To the pacifist charge that war today may well bring total destruction, orthodoxy answers that the decision as to whether the planet and human existence are to be destroyed is God's affairs, not ours; He has made it *our* business not to make policy for the universe but to protect justice and law and liberty, and this out of love for our neighbor. Again a teaching of Aquinas that has entered into the conscience of the West drives the point home: Even if I knew infallibly, Aquinas argues, even if I knew by a Revelation of God that my efforts to save my dying father were doomed to failure, that God Himself had willed my father's death, it would not affect my obligation to try to keep him alive. In a word: God's will for me would remain what it was before the Revelation, namely, that I live up to my obligations. God may have willed the destruction of the planet in an atomic *Gotterdämmerung* (I do not know, of course, and can never know); but "we" are still obligated to use the means at our disposal in order to preserve justice in the situations in which "we" are involved, *to fulfill our duties in all their concreteness and detail.* That preserving, that fulfilling, is God's will for us, and whatever else He may have willed as a consequence of what we do is, I repeat, *God's* business and not *ours.* In acting accordingly we would have behind us the full weight of the only tradition—the Christian tradition—that has made life bearable for man within time.

The temptation to give way to the pacifists—who have now added to their other skills a mastery of what let's call the art of nuclear-weapons blackmail—is very great, and great especially in those quarters where the Scripture the pacifist diabolically cites is held in contempt—except, of course, as a stick with which to beat non-pacifist Christians over the head. . . . The temptation, I say, is very great; it will become greater as time passes; it will be at its greatest on that future day when the Soviet Union delivers to *us* the ultimatum that, back in 1946, we should have delivered to *it*. The thought of surrender on that day—not, I repeat, on Christian pacifist grounds, but out of sheer funk—is indeed present in the atmosphere, is already sapping our national will to resist the Communist enemy, is already pushing further and further into the future the moment when we shall discover, not too late, I hope, that our duty to strike down the Soviet aggressor, our duty to prevent him from doing the wrong he is doing, is not different from but identical to the duty we shouldered a few years ago with respect to the Nazis; and not less urgent, but infinitely more urgent.

Christians themselves may come to feel the temptation—not, as today, in small numbers, but in the large numbers that are the stuff of the so-called Christian pacifist's dreams. And "we" must say to them: you must *resist* the temptation. Let me, this once more, fall back on Chesterton: "It is easy to be a madman; it is easy to be a heretic. It is always easy to let the age have its head; the difficult thing is to keep one's own. . . . To have fallen into any of those open traps of error and exaggeration which fashion after fashion set along the historic path of Christendom —that would indeed have been simple. It is always simple to fall; there are an infinity of angles at which one falls, only one at which one stands. To have fallen into any one of the fads . . . would indeed have been obvious and tame. But to have avoided them all has been one whirling adventure; and in my vision the heavenly chariot flies thundering through the ages, the dull heresies sprawling and prostrate, the wild truth reeling but erect."

V THE LIMITATION OF FORCE: LIMITED WAR

War as an Instrument of Policy

KARL VON CLAUSEWITZ

. . . War is only a part of political intercourse, therefore
by no means an independent thing in itself.

We know, certainly, that War is only called forth through the
political intercourse of Governments and Nations; but in general
it is supposed that such intercourse is broken off by War, and
that a totally different state of things ensues, subject to no laws
but its own.

We maintain, on the contrary, that War is nothing but a continuation of political intercourse, with a mixture of other means.
We say mixed with other means in order thereby to maintain
at the same time that this political intercourse does not cease
by the War itself, is not changed into something quite different,
but that, in its essence, it continues to exist, whatever may be
the form of the means which it uses, and that the chief lines on
which the events of the War progress, and to which they are attached, are only the general features of policy which run all

From *On War*. Routledge & Kegan Paul Ltd., 1908. Reprinted by permission.

through the War until peace takes place. And how can we conceive it to be otherwise? Does the cessation of diplomatic notes stop the political relations between different Nations and Governments? Is not War merely another kind of writing and language for political thoughts? It has certainly a grammar of its own, but its logic is not peculiar to itself.

Accordingly, War can never be separated from political intercourse, and if, in the consideration of the matter, this is done in any way, all the threads of the different relations are, to a certain extent, broken, and we have before us a senseless thing without an object.

This kind of idea would be indispensable even if War was perfect War, the perfectly unbridled element of hostility, for all the circumstances on which it rests, and which determine its leading features, *viz.*, our own power, the enemy's power, Allies on both sides, the characteristics of the people and their Governments respectively, . . . are they not of a political nature, and are they not so intimately connected with the whole political intercourse that it is impossible to separate them? But this view is doubly indispensable if we reflect that real War is no such consistent effort tending to an extreme, as it should be according to the abstract idea but a half-and-half thing, a contradiction in itself; that as such, it cannot follow its own laws, but must be looked upon as a part of another whole—and this whole is policy.

Policy in making use of War avoids all those rigorous conclusions which proceed from its nature; it troubles itself little about final possibilities, confining its attention to immediate probabilities. If such uncertainty in the whole action ensues therefrom, if it thereby becomes a sort of game, the policy of each Cabinet places its confidence in the belief that in this game it will surpass its neighbour in skill and sharpsightedness.

Thus policy makes out of the all-overpowering element of War a mere instrument, changes the tremendous battlesword, which should be lifted with both hands and the whole power of the body to strike once for all, into a light handy weapon, which is even sometimes nothing more than a rapier to exchange thrusts and feints and parries.

Thus the contradictions in which man, naturally timid, becomes involved by War may be solved, if we choose to accept this as a solution.

If War belongs to policy, it will naturally take its character from thence. If policy is grand and powerful, so also will be the War, and this may be carried to the point at which War attains to *its absolute form.*

In this way of viewing the subject, therefore, we need not shut out of sight the absolute form of War, we rather keep it continually in view in the background.

Only through this kind of view War recovers unity; only by it can we see all Wars as things of *one* kind; and it is only through it that the judgment can obtain the true and perfect basis and point of view from which great plans may be traced out and determined upon.

It is true the political element does not sink deep into the details of War. Vedettes are not planted, patrols do not make their rounds from political considerations; but small as is its influence in this respect, it is great in the formation of a plan for a whole War, or a campaign, and often even for a battle.

* * *

There is, upon the whole, nothing more important in life than to find out the right point of view from which things should be looked at and judged of, and then to keep to that point; for we can only apprehend the mass of events in their unity from *one* standpoint; and it is only the keeping to one point of view that guards us from inconsistency.

If, therefore, in drawing up a plan of a War, it is not allowable to have a two-fold or three-fold point of view, from which things may be looked at, now with the eye of a soldier, then with that of an administrator, and then again with that of a politician, etc., then the next question is, whether *policy* is necessarily paramount and everything else subordinate to it.

That policy unites in itself, and reconciles all the interests of internal administrations, even those of humanity, and whatever else are rational subjects of consideration is presupposed, for it is nothing in itself, except a mere representative and exponent of all these interests towards other States. That policy may take a false direction, and may promote unfairly the ambitious ends, the private interests, the vanity of rulers, does not concern us here; for, under no circumstances can the Art of War be regarded as its preceptor, and we can only look at policy here as the representative of the interests generally of the whole community.

The only question, therefore, is whether in framing plans for a War the political point of view should give way to the purely military (if such a point is conceivable), that is to say, should disappear altogether, or subordinate itself to it, or whether the political is to remain the ruling point of view and the military to be considered subordinate to it.

That the political point of view should end completely when War begins is only conceivable in contests which are Wars of life and death, from pure hatred: as Wars are in reality, they are, as we before said, only the expressions or manifestations of policy itself. The subordination of the political point of view to the military would be contrary to common sense, for policy has declared the War; it is the intelligent faculty, War only the instrument and not the reverse. The subordination of the military point of view to the political is, therefore, the only thing which is possible.

If we reflect on the nature of real War, and call to mind . . . *that every War should be viewed above all things according to the probability of its character, and its leading features as they are to be deduced from the political forces and proportions,* and that often—indeed we may safely affirm, in our days, *almost* always—War is to be regarded as an organic whole, from which the single branches are not to be separated, in which therefore every individual actively flows into the whole, and also has its origin in the idea of this whole, then it becomes certain and palpable to us that the superior standpoint for the conduct of the War, from which its leading lines must proceed, can be no other than that of policy.

From this point of view the plans come, as it were, out of a cast; the apprehension of them and the judgment upon them become easier and more natural, our convictions respecting them gain in force, motives are more satisfying, and history more intelligible.

At all events from this point of view there is no longer in the nature of things a necessary conflict between the political and military interests, and where it appears it is therefore to be regarded as imperfect knowledge only. That policy makes demands on the War which it cannot respond to, would be contrary to the supposition that it knows the instrument which it is going to use, therefore, contrary to a natural and indispensable supposition. But if policy judges correctly of the march of military events, it is entirely its affair to determine what are the events and what the direction of events most favourable to the ultimate and great end of the War.

In one word, the Art of War in its highest point of view is policy, but, no doubt, a policy which fights battles instead of writing notes.

According to this view, to leave a great military enterprise, or the plan for one, to a *purely military judgment and decision* is a distinction which cannot be allowed, and is even prejudicial; indeed, it is an irrational proceeding to consult professional soldiers on the plan of a War, that they may give a *purely military opinion* upon what the Cabinet ought to do; but still more absurd is the demand of Theorists that a statement of the available means of War should be laid before the General, that he may draw out a purely military plan for the War or for a campaign in accordance with those means. Experience in general also teaches us that notwithstanding the multifarious branches and scientific character of military art in the present day, still the leading outlines of a War are always determined by the Cabinet, that is, if we would use technical language, by a political not a military organ.

This is perfectly natural. None of the principal plans which are required for a War can be made without an insight into the political relations; and, in reality, when people speak, as they often do, of the prejudicial influence of policy on the conduct of a War, they say in reality something very different to what they intend. It is not this influence but the policy itself which should be found fault with. If policy is right, that is, if it succeeds in hitting the object, then it can only act with advantage on the War. If this influence of policy causes a divergence from the object, the cause is only to be looked for in a mistaken policy.

It is only when policy promises itself a wrong effect from certain military means and measures, an effect opposed to their nature, that it can exercise a prejudicial effect on War by the course it prescribes. Just as a person in a language with which he is not conversant sometimes says what he does not intend, so policy, when intending right, may often order things which do not tally with its own views.

This has happened times without end, and it shows that a certain knowledge of the nature of War is essential to the management of political intercourse.

* * *

Therefore, . . . War is an instrument of policy; it must necessarily bear its character, it must measure with its scale: the conduct of War, in its great features, is therefore policy itself, which takes up the sword in place of the pen, but does not on that account cease to think according to its own laws.

The Economy of Force and the Primacy of Politics

ROBERT E. OSGOOD

The Principle of Political Primacy

In practice, the limitation of war is morally and emotionally repugnant to the American people. Yet it is in accord with America's own best principles. The explanation of this paradox lies partly in the fact that Americans have not understood the relation between military force and national policy, and so they have misconceived the real moral and practical implications of national conduct. Therefore, it is imperative . . . to develop a sound conception of the relation between force and policy as the first step in examining the requirements of an American strategy of limited war.

The justification of limited war arises, in the most fundamental sense, from the principle that military power should be subordinate to national policy, that the only legitimate purpose of military force is to serve the nation's political objectives. This principle of political primacy is basic to all forms and all uses of military power, whether employed overtly, covertly, or only tacitly. It is as applicable to the formulation of military policies and military strategy as to the actual waging of war. In this principle morality and expediency are joined.

The principle of political primacy is essential to the nation's self-interest because military power is of no practical use as a thing in itself but is useful only insofar as it serves some national purpose. It is useful because it is a prerequisite of national security and because upon security all other national goals depend. Coercion is an indispensable feature of all human relations in which basic security and order cannot be guaranteed by the innate sympathy, reasonableness, and morality of men. The essential role of coercion is especially large in international relations, where institutional organization is anarchical or rudimentary and the bonds of law, custom, and sentiment are relatively impotent as against the intense ties of loyalty binding men to their separate and sovereign national groups.

The practical necessity of military power is obvious to Americans today, but it is not always so obvious that military power does not automatically translate itself into national security. Military power may actually be translated into national insecurity when it is employed without a proper regard for its non-military objectives and consequences. Without intelligent and vigilant political control even the most effective use of military force, by purely military standards, will not necessarily bring comparably satisfactory political results. A capricious, impulsive, or irresponsible use of military power cannot be expedient; for when military policy and strategy lack the guideposts of limited and attainable objectives and become, in effect, ends in themselves, they cease to be controllable and predictable instruments of national policy.

The individual soldier, even the commander of a battle, may sometimes promote the national interest by the kind of boldness that does not calculate the results of military action too closely, but it would be a dangerous error to apply to the whole complex problem of harmonizing military policy with national policy in accordance with an over-all strategic plan the far simpler imperatives of the battlefield. In the field of national strategy, uncalculating heroism is mere self-indulgence at the expense of national survival.

In order that military power may serve as a controllable and predictable instrument of national policy, it must be subjected to an exacting political discipline. This discipline depends upon the existence of controlling political objectives that bear a practical and discernible relation to specific policy goals. These kinds of objectives are, preeminently, those that envision specific configurations of power supporting the nation's security. A treaty recognizing specific international relationships; the control or protection of a certain geographical area; the establishment, recognition, or security of a particular regime; access to certain material resources—these are the kinds of objectives that must form the hard core of politically disciplined power.

One must add, because the rule is so frequently violated in practice, that the controlling political objectives in the use of military power must be not merely desirable but also attainable. Otherwise, there will be no practical and discernible relationship between ends and means. Of course, there are an indefinite number of possible objectives toward which nations may direct military power. One can easily establish a whole hierarchy of interdependent objectives, leading from the most insignificant to the most desirable objective imaginable. However, only a very limited number of these objectives will ever be closely enough related to available national power to serve as a controlling political discipline. Unless the nation's objectives pertain to specific and attainable situations of fact, they will remain in the realm of aspiration, not in the realm of policy; and, consequently, the essential condition for the primacy of politics over force will not exist. Therefore, one can describe the principle of political primacy in terms of the following rule: In the nation's utilization of military power, military means should be subordinated to the ends of national policy through an objective calculation of the most effective methods of attaining concrete, limited, and attainable security objectives.

The principle of political primacy described in this rule is as cogent on moral grounds as on grounds of national self-interest. At the outset, before examining the moral basis of the principle, one must recognize that the primacy of policy over power can be moral only if the political ends toward which military power is directed are themselves moral—or, at least, as consistent with universal principles as the ambiguities of international relations permit. But even if one assumes that this is the case . . . one can hardly judge the moral validity of either political ends or military means aside from their interrelationship. The following discussion focuses upon this interrelationship, which is only one aspect of the broader problem of reconciling national policy with liberal, humane ideals that transcend purely national purposes. The principle of political primacy does not embrace all the moral problems that arise in the use of military power. It does not, for example, deal with the question of when or under what circumstances a nation should employ force. However, it is of vital relevance to the question of how and for what purpose a nation should employ force.

The moral basis of political primacy is also its practical basis: the principle that armed force ought to be treated as a means and not an end. Force gains moral justification only by virtue of its relation to some valid purpose beyond its own immediate effect. Furthermore, even when it is a means to a worthy end, armed force must be morally suspect—not only because it is inhumane but because, like all forms of coercion, it is subject to the corruption that accompanies man's exercise of power over man. In Lord Acton's words, "Among all the causes which degrade and demoralize man, power is the most constant and the most active." Certainly, the exercise of military power holds extraordinary opportunities for the degradation of its user and the abuse of those against whom it is used.

But the problem of force is not so easily dismissed. Once we admit that it is morally suspect, we are involved in a moral dilemma. On the one hand, in an ideal world men would dispense with all forms of coercion and settle their conflicts by impartial reference to reason and morality; or, at least, they would channel coercion in social directions by legal controls, which receive the consent of the community. Yet, on the other hand, we know that in the real world men are not sufficiently unselfish or rational to make this ideal practicable. The abolition of force in society would lead either to the anarchy of unrestrained egoism or else to the tyranny of unrestrained despotism. Because of the imperfection of man, force is a moral necessity, an indispensable instrument of justice. Therefore, men are confronted with the fact that their own imperfection makes both force and restraint of force equally imperative from a moral standpoint. There is no way to escape this dilemma. Men can only mitigate its effects. The aim should be, not to abolish force in society, but to moderate it and control it so as to promote social purposes in a manner most compatible with ideal standards of human conduct. How can we translate this principle into the use of military power?

We commonly assume that force is least objectionable morally, as well as most effective practically, when it is exercised with a minimum of violence—preferably, as in the case of police power, when it is implied rather than directly exercised—and when it is exercised legitimately, that is, in accordance with the general consent and approval of society. This assumption suffices for the conduct of everyday affairs within the national community, because the conditions which make it practicable are present— primarily, the conditions that permit force to be exercised in accordance with the orderly procedures of law and government. These legitimate restraints not only moderate force and channel it in social directions; they also provide the individual members of a nation with the basic security they need in order to feel safe in voluntarily subordinating their self-interest to the general welfare.

However, the same procedures for moderating, controlling, and channeling force in socially sanctioned directions do not exist among nations, where the bonds of law, custom, and sympathy are frail and rudimentary. In this age national egoism has such a compelling hold over men's minds that each nation must look to its own independent exercise of power merely in order to survive. The exercise of military power among nations is subject to few of the formal and informal restraints that permit altruism to operate among individuals and groups within nations.

This situation makes a vast difference between what is justifiable in the exercise of force in national society and what is justifiable in international society. It means that among nations military force becomes an indispensable means for promoting national self-interest but a thoroughly ineffective means for attaining the great universal moral goals that transcend national self-interest. This is true, in the first place, because every exercise of military power must be tainted with self-interest and, secondly, because the imperatives of national power and security do not closely conform to the dictates of universal morality.

But military force is not only ineffective as an instrument for attaining transcendent moral goals; it is morally dangerous as well. It is dangerous because the exercise of force for such grandiose goals tends to become an end in itself, subject neither to moral nor practical restraints but only to the intoxication of abstract ideals. The explanation for this tendency lies in the nature of supranational goals. Aside from the powerful tendency of national egoism to corrupt idealistic pretensions, supranational goals are too remote and too nebulous to discipline a nation's use of force. When the determining objective of force is an ideological goal, there is no way of knowing precisely when force has achieved its purpose, since the tangible results of force have no clear relation to the intangible tests by which the attainment of such goals must be measured. When a conflict of wills is put to the test of force, the final restraint and control of force must be the resolution of the conflict by accommodation, unless it is to continue until one party obtains complete acquiescence or both parties become impotent. But difference of principle, unlike conflicts of interest by their very nature resist accommodation. Rather, they tend to arouse passions that can be satisfied only by the unconditional surrender of the adversary. Therefore, in effect, the great idealistic goals, once put to the test of force, become the rationalization of purely military objectives, governed only by the blind impulse of destruction.

That is not to say that moral principles are unjustifiable or irrelevant in a nation's use of military power or that the exercise of force, either overtly or tacitly, cannot indirectly promote ideal ends. The point is simply that universal principles must be translated into practical courses of action, directed toward achieving specific situations of fact appropriate to the nature of force, in order to constitute truly moral and rational guides for the exercise of military power. Only if the realization of these principles is conceived as the by-product of attaining concrete limited objectives can they exert a civilizing influence upon national egoism. The great idealistic goals that have traditionally provided the dynamism and inspiration of American foreign policy, insofar as they can be attained at all by military means, must be attained through a series of moderate steps toward intermediate objectives, defined in terms of national power and interest.

An important corollary of the principle of political primacy may be called the economy of force. It prescribes that in the use of armed force as an instrument of national policy no greater force should be employed than is necessary to achieve the objectives toward which it is directed; or, stated another way, the dimensions of military force should be proportionate to the value of the objectives at stake.

Clearly, this is an expedient rule; for unless a nation has a large surplus of available military power in relation to its policy objectives, one can hardly conceive of the effective use of power without the efficient use as well. Moreover, as an examination of the interaction between military mans and political ends will show, the proportionate use of force is a necessary condition for the limitation and effective control of war.

The moral implications of an economy of force are no less significant. For, as we have acknowledged, the violence and destruction that accompany the use of force are an obvious, though sometimes necessary, evil. Therefore, it is morally incumbent to use force deliberately and scrupulously and as sparingly as is consistent with the attainment of the national objectives at stake.

In applying the principle of political primacy we must make allowances for the legitimate claims of military considerations upon national policy as well as the other way around. The relationship between military means and political ends should be understood as a two-way relationship, such that the ends are kept within range of the means as well as the means made adequate to attain the ends. Common sense tells us that a nation must decide what it ought to do in light of what it is able to do; that it should establish policy objectives in the light of military capabilities. Otherwise, military power will be no more effective or politically responsible than if it were employed as an end in itself.

Moreover, we must recognize the fact that, however scrupulously we may seek to impose political discipline upon military power, military power will remain an imperfect instrument of politics. To a disturbing extent it bears its own unpredictable effects, which create, alter, or preclude the objectives for which it can feasibly be employed.

However, this does not obviate the necessity of determining the claims of military means upon political ends—so far as conscious control permits—within the general framework of national strategy; for in the absence of such a framework there can be no clear criterion for judging the validity of any claims. In other words, if military power is to serve as a rational instrument of policy, the entire process of balancing ends and means, coordinating military with non-military means, must be subordinated to the controlling purpose of pursuing national policy objectives according to the most effective strategic plan.

War as an Instrument of National Policy

The principles of political primacy and the economy of force apply to the whole spectrum of military power in its various uses, not just to its active use in warfare; but this [essay] is concerned primarily with their application to war itself. There is a good reason for stressing this aspect of military power: In all uses of military power, whether overt, covert, or tacit; in all accumulation, allocation, and distribution of military power; and in all military planning there is at least an implicit assumption that the basic measure of a nation's power is its ability to wage war in defense of its interests. In the struggle for power among nations, the ability to wage war has something of the status of a common currency by which nations can roughly measure their capacity to achieve certain basic needs and desires—ultimately, if necessary, by violence.

However, the ability to wage war cannot be measured in

purely quantitative terms of military power. A nation can be adequately prepared to wage one kind of war under one set of circumstances and inadequately prepared to wage another kind of war under a different set of circumstances. The utility of a nation's military power, either in diplomacy or in war itself, will depend not merely upon the size and firepower of the military establishment but also upon its suitability for countering the specific kinds of military threats impinging upon the nation's interests and objectives. Thus the effectiveness of military power depends upon the nature of the military threat, the nation's estimate of that threat, and its ability to fight the kind of war that will successfully meet the threat. It depends, equally, upon the nation's will to wage war; the way in which it combines force with diplomacy; how it enters war, how it terminates war, and how it conducts policy after a war. In other words, the effectiveness of military power depends not only upon a nation's physical and technical command of the means of warfare but, as much, upon its whole conception of war—especially, the relation of war to international politics. And this conception of war is reflected throughout the whole spectrum of military power—in defense policies and the formulation of military strategy as well as in the actual conduct of war. Therefore, since a nation's military power depends upon its conception of war, it behooves us to act upon a conception of war that is compatible with the use of military power as a rational instrument of national policy. That conception must be based upon the principle of political primacy.

But, first, let us be clear what we mean by "war." War can be defined most simply as an organized clash of arms between sovereign states seeking to assert their wills against one another. However, it would be a mistake to regard war as a single, simple, uniform entity or as an independent thing in itself, to which one applies a wholly different set of rules and considerations than properly apply to other forms of international conflict. It is more realistic in the light of the complex and multifarious nature of international conflict to regard war as the upper extremity of a whole scale of international conflict of ascending intensity and scope. All along this scale one may think of sovereign nations asserting their wills in conflict with other nations by a variety of military and non-military means of coercion, but no definition can determine precisely at what point on the scale conflict becomes "war." In this sense, war is a matter of degree, which itself contains different degrees of intensity and scope.

Accepting this description of war, we must see how the principle of political primacy applies to the conduct of war. The primacy of politics in war means, simply, that military operations should be conducted so as to achieve concrete, limited, and attainable security objectives, in order that war's destruction and violence may be rationally directed toward legitimate ends of national policy.

On the face of it, the validity of this principle seems clear enough; and yet in its practical implications it does not meet with ready or universal acceptance. In fact, quite contrary principles of war have commonly received the applause of democratic peoples. For example, in the Kellogg-Briand Pact of 1928 the United States and fourteen other nations promised to "renounce war as an instrument of national policy in their relations with one another," thereby expressing in treaty form a widespread conviction that is still congenial to the American outlook. The principle is valid, of course, if it is interpreted merely as a proscription against unprovoked aggression; but insofar as it implies the divorce of war from the ends of national interest, it is valid neither practically nor ideally. In this sense, nations might better renounce the use of war as an instrument of *anything but* national policy.

Karl von Clausewitz, the famous German military theorist of the nineteenth century, expounded the principle of political primacy with an unsurpassed cogency. In his famous work *On War* he concluded his comprehensive analysis of the mass of factors comprising war by singling out their unifying characteristics. This, he believed, was the essential basis for apprehending all war's complexities and contradictions from a single standpoint, without which one could not form consistent judgments. He described that characteristic in the following words:

Now this unity is the conception that war is only a part of political intercourse, therefore by no means an independent thing in itself. We know, of course, that war is only caused through the political intercourse of governments and nations; but in general it is supposed that such intercourse is broken off by war and that a totally different state of things ensues, subject to no laws but its own. We maintain, on the contrary, that war is nothing but a continuation of political intercourse with an admixture of other means. . . . Accordingly, war can never be separated from political intercourse, and if, in the consideration of the matter, this occurs anywhere, all the threads of the different relations are, in a certain sense, broken, and we have before us a senseless thing without an object.

As a description of the actual nature of war, Clausewitz' dictum that war continues political intercourse is by no means universally true; but as a statement of what war should be, it is the only view in accord with universal moral principles and national self-interest, for it is the only view consistent with the use of force as a means rather than an end. If we find this view as repugnant as the sentiment of the Kellogg-Briand Pact is congenial, then we have not fully grasped the practical and moral necessity of disciplining mass violence. On the other hand, many who can agree with Clausewitz' dictum in the abstract find it difficult in practice to accept the corollary that victory is not an end in itself. Nevertheless, the corollary is logically inseparable from the principle of political primacy. For if war is not an end in itself, but only a means to some political objective, then military victory cannot rightly be a self-sufficient end. If war is a continuation of political intercourse, then success in war can be properly measured only in political terms and not purely in terms of crushing the enemy. To be sure, a measure of military success is the necessary condition for achieving the political objectives of war; but the most effective military measures for overcoming the enemy's resistance are not necessarily the most effective measures for securing the continuing ends of national policy in the aftermath of war.

Therefore, one of the most important practical implications of the principle of political primacy is this: The whole conduct of warfare—its strategy, its tactics, its termination—must be governed by the nature of a nation's political objectives and not by independent standards of military success or glory. Statesmen, far from suspending diplomacy during war, must make every effort to keep diplomacy alive throughout the hostilities, to the end that war may be as nearly a continuation of political intercourse as possible rather than "a senseless thing without an object."

The Dimensions of War

The practical requirements of maintaining the primacy of politics in the conduct of war are not so clear as the general principle, for the general principle must be qualified in the light of the actual conditions of war. The most serious qualification results from the difficulty of controlling the consequences of war as the dimensions of violence and destruction increase. This difficulty emphasizes the importance of striving for an economy of force.

Despite the theoretical validity of the principle of political primacy, in practice we must recognize that war is not a delicate instrument for achieving precise politicals ends. It is a crude instrument of coercion and persuasion. The violence and destruction of war set off a chain of consequences that can be neither perfectly controlled nor perfectly anticipated and that may, therefore, contravene the best laid plans for achieving specific configurations of power and particular political relations among nations.

At the same time, the legitimate claims of military means upon political ends are particularly strong when national conflict reaches the extremity of war. The sheer physical circumstances of the military struggle may narrowly restrict the choice of military means that nations can safely employ. To subordinate military operations to political considerations might mean sacrificing the military success indispensable for the attainment of any worthwhile national purpose at all. Therefore, in practice, military necessities and the fortunes of war may determine the nature of the feasible political choices, and the subordination of certain political considerations to military requirements may be the necessary condition for avoiding defeat.

However, the need for compromising political objectives in the light of immediate military necessities only qualifies, it does not negate, the applicability of the principle of political primacy; because the wisdom of such compromise must still be judged by their relation to some superior political objective if purely military objectives are not to become ends in themselves. Clausewitz acknowledged this very qualification and reconciled it with his view of war as a continuation of political intercourse in words that are compelling today. While recognizing that the political object of war could not regulate every aspect of war, he nevertheless maintained that war would be sheer uncontrolled violence without this unifying factor.

> Now if we reflect that war has its origin in a political object, we see that this first motive, which called it into existence, naturally remains the first and highest consideration to be regarded in its conduct. But the political object is not on that account a despotic lawgiver; it must adapt itself to the nature of the means at its disposal and is often thereby completely changed, but it must always be the first thing to be considered. Policy, therefore, will permeate the whole action of war and exercise a continual influence upon it, so far as the nature of the explosive forces in it allow . . . . What now still remains peculiar to war relates merely to the peculiar character of the means it uses. The art of war in general and the commander in each particular case can demand that the tendencies and designs of policy shall be not incompatible with these means, and the claim is certainly no trifling one. But however powerfully it may react on political designs in particular cases, still it must always be regarded only as a modification of them; for the political design is the object, while war is the means, and the means can never be thought of apart from the object.

If, then, the principle of political primacy holds good despite the considerable claims of military necessity, the task of statesmen is to minimize the difficulties and maximize the potentialities of political control. There are three closely related rules of general application that would greatly facilitate this purpose:

1. Statesmen should scrupulously limit the controlling political objectives of war and clearly communicate the limited nature of these objectives to the enemy. The reason for this is that nations tend to observe a rough proportion between the scope of their objectives and the scale of their military effort; that is, they tend to exert a degree of force proportionate to the value they ascribe to the objectives at stake. Therefore, the more ambitious the objectives of one belligerent, the more important it is to the other belligerent to deny those objectives and the greater the scale of force both belligerents will undertake in order to gain their own objectives and frustrate the enemy's. In this manner a spiral of expanding objectives and mounting force may drive warfare beyond the bounds of political control.

2. Statesmen should make every effort to maintain an active diplomatic intercourse toward the end of terminating the war by a negotiated settlement on the basis of limited objectives. This rule rests on the following considerations. War is a contest between national wills. The final resolution of this contest must be some sort of political settlement, or war will lack any object except the purely military object of overcoming the enemy. To the extent that statesmen keep political intercourse active during hostilities, war becomes a political contest rather than a purely military contest. The immediate object of political intercourse must be a negotiated settlement, but a negotiated settlement is impossible among belligerents of roughly equal power unless their political objectives are limited. This consideration becomes especially important in the light of the fact that even a small nation that possessed an arsenal of nuclear weapons might, in desperation, inflict devastating destruction upon a larger power rather than accept humiliating terms.

3. Statesmen should try to restrict the physical dimensions of war as stringently as compatible with the attainment of the objectives at stake, since the opportunities for the political con-

trol of war—especially under the conditions of modern war, with its tremendous potentialities of destruction—tend to decrease as the dimensions of war increase and tend to increase as the dimensions of war decrease. This proportion between the dimensions of war and its susceptibility to political control is neither universally true nor mathematically exact; but as a rough generalization it finds important verification in the history of war. Three underlying reasons for this fact are especially germane to the warfare of this century:

a) The greater the scale and scope of war, the more likely the war will result in extreme changes in the configurations of national power. These extreme changes are not amenable to control; they result more from the internal logic of the military operations than from the designs of statesmen. At the same time, they tend to create vast new political problems which confound the expectations and plans of the victor and the vanquished alike. Moreover, modern war can change the configurations of power not only through the massive destruction of material and human resources but also by disrupting the whole social, economic, and political fabric of existence. On the other hand, when the destructiveness and the resulting disturbance of the configurations of power are moderate, the chances of anticipating and controlling its political effects are proportionately greater; and the whole character of warfare, in proportion as it is removed from the domination of military events, becomes more nearly a continuation of political intercourse.

b) The magnitude of a war's threat to national survival is likely to be proportionate to the scale and the scope of hostilities. But in proportion as the belligerents' very survival is threatened, they must logically place a higher priority upon immediate military considerations as compared to political considerations. For when war reaches extremities, a belligerent must calculate that even the slightest interference with the destruction of the enemy in the most effective manner possible for the sake of some uncertain political maneuver will involve an exorbitant risk of the enemy destroying that belligerent first. Military victory, no matter how it comes about, at least provides a nation with the opportunity to solve its political problems later; whereas the dubious attempt to manipulate the vast and unpredictable forces of war in precise political ways may end by placing this postwar opportunity at the disposal of the enemy. When immediate military considerations are at such a premium, political control must obviously suffer accordingly; but, by the same reasoning, when the scale and scope of a war impose no such immediate threat of total defeat, the primacy of politics can more readily be asserted.

c) As the dimensions of violence and destruction increase, war tends to arouse passionate fears and hatreds, which, regardless of the dictates of cold reason, become the determining motives in the conduct of war. These passions find their outlet in the blind, unreasoning destruction of the enemy. They are antithetical to the political control of war, because political control would restrict the use of force. Thus the greater the scale of violence, the greater the suffering and sacrifice; and the greater the suffering and sacrifice, the less the inclination either to fight or to make peace for limited, prosaic ends. Instead, nations will seek compensation in extreme demands upon the enemy or in elevating the war into an ideological crusade. Unlimited aims will, in turn, demand unlimited force. Thus, in effect, the scale of war and the passions of war, interacting, will create a purely military phenomenon beyond effective political guidance.

In the light of this proportion between the dimensions of warfare and its susceptibility to political control, the importance of preserving an economy of force is apparent. For if modern warfare tends to exceed the bounds of political control as it increases in magnitude, then it is essential to limit force to a scale that is no greater than necessary to achieve the objectives at stake. By the same token, if war becomes more susceptible to political control in proportion as its dimensions are moderated, then the economy of force is an essential condition of the primacy of politics in war.

The Rationale of Limited War

If this analysis is sound, the principal justification of limited war lies in the fact that it maximizes the opportunities for the effective use of military force as a rational instrument of national policy. In accordance with this rationale, limited war would be equally desirable if nuclear weapons had never been invented. However, the existence of these and other weapons of mass destruction clearly adds great urgency to limitation. Before nations possessed nuclear weapons, they might gain worthwhile objectives consonant with the sacrifices of war even in a war fought with their total resources. But now the stupendous destruction accompanying all-out nuclear war makes it hard to conceive of such a war serving any rational purpose except the continued existence of the nation as a political unit—and, perhaps, the salvage of the remnants of civilization—in the midst of the wreckage. Only by carefully limiting the dimensions of warfare can nations minimize the risk of war becoming an intolerable disaster.

Beyond this general reason for limiting war, which applies to all nations equally, there are special reasons why democratic nations should prefer limited war. Obviously, limited war is more compatible with a respect for human life and an aversion to violence. But apart from humanitarian considerations, we should recognize that liberal institutions and values do not thrive amid the social, economic, and political dislocations that inevitably follow in the wake of unlimited war. The liberal and humane spirit needs an environment conducive to compromise and moderation. Only tyranny is likely to profit from the festering hatreds and resentments that accompany sudden and violent upheavals in the relations among governments and peoples. The aftermath of the two total wars of this century amply demonstrate this fact.

The external interests of democratic powers are not necessarily identified with the status quo in all respects, nor do they require that the rest of the world be democratic. Clearly, neither condition is feasible. However, they do require that the inevitable adjustments and accommodations among governments and peoples should be sufficiently moderate and gradual to permit orderly change. Long-run interests as well as immediate interests of democratic nations lie in preserving an external environment conducive to relative stability and security in the world.

The mitigation of sudden and violent change becomes all the more important in a period like the present, when the most resourceful tyranny in the modern world strives to capture an indigenous revolution among colonial and formerly colonial peoples who yearn to acquire the Western blessings of national independence and economic power but who are fearfully impatient with the evolutionary processes by which the West acquired them. In these areas peace may be too much to expect, but we can anticipate revolutionary chaos or Communist domination if the world is seized by the convulsions of unlimited war.

Finally, we must add to these considerations one of even broader significance. As long as the necessary international political conditions for the limitation of armaments do not exist, the best assurance that armaments will not destroy civilization lies in the limitation of their use.

Nuclear Blackmail and Limited War

ROBERT STRAUSZ-HUPÉ

HANDLED WITH CARE, CLICHÉS HAVE THEIR USES. Without them public discussion of almost any issue would turn into an inter-

From *The Yale Review*, Winter, 1959. Copyright 1958 by Yale University Press. Reprinted by permission.

minable wrangling over definitions. Such terms as "limited war," "unlimited war," "conventional armaments," "graduated deterrence," and "massive retaliation" can be employed profitably in talking about certain hypothetical aspects of war. Yet these abstract terms should not be mistaken for designations of realities. Military theory, like all theory, proceeds by abstraction and simplification. But in real life, as distinct from strategic and tactical models, war, the most unpredictable of all human activities, has the annoying habit of standing theory on its head.

In his largely unread and widely misquoted book *On War*, General von Clausewitz wrote: "War is to be regarded as an organic whole, from which the single branches are not to be separated and in which, therefore, every individual activity flows into the whole." Or as we would say nowadays: hot or cold, nuclear or "conventional," war is still war. In his annotated copy of *On War*, which still exists, Lenin underscored the sentence just quoted—a fact that assumes some significance when it is recalled that Lenin's unique contribution to Communist doctrine is to have expanded Karl Marx's open-ended and fuzzy doctrine of class struggle into a tight doctrine of international conflict. Soviet Communism, as Lenin left it and as it operates today, is a system set up to carry on world-wide conflict, and its astonishing success is due, more than to anything else, to the fact that the Communists have always considered conflict (war) as an "organic whole"—and the Western democracies have not.

The Communist doctrine of conflict combines a clear view of the total objective with great flexibility in the choice of battlegrounds, weapons, and operational tactics. Such flexibility, by confusing the opponent, keeping him off balance, forcing upon him the wrong choices at the wrong times and the wrong places, wears down his resistance. Although it is a strategy for annihilating the opponent over a period of time by limited operations, by feints and maneuvers, psychological manipulations, and diverse forms of violence, it does not rule out the final and total knock-out blow, and the Communists' current strategy of massive nuclear blackmail cannot be written off as a mere psychological bluff that they expect never to be called.

The various techniques of political warfare and graduated violence envisioned by Communist theory range all the way from "peace" propaganda and cultural exchange to an annihilating blow delivered with every suitable weapon available. Plans for protracted conflict include every possible relationship between peoples and groups, not only military, political, economic, and cultural, but also others that in the West's prevailing liberal philosophies seem the exact opposite of conflict. It is this comprehensiveness of view that has permitted the Communists to integrate the nuclear bomb into their strategy. In contrast, the West, psychologically incapable of bridging the dialectic gap between peace and war and between one form of conflict and another, failed to exploit the incalculable advantage it enjoyed when it had an atomic monopoly and later when its weapons systems were more sophisticated and differentiated than those of the Soviets.

As Raymond L. Garthoff has shown in his important book, *Soviet Strategy in the Nuclear Age,* the Communists are confident that they have developed a military strategy that can defeat the West in any kind of war, although they prefer to obtain their ends short of nuclear war. The Communists have accepted atomic weapons, including the H-Bomb, as an integral part of both military and political technology. They have an overall objective—the Communization of the globe—and in pursuit of that objective any and all kinds of weapons may have to be used. But, unlike the democracies who so exuberantly embrace total war whenever their own vacillations and the overreaching arrogance of the aggressor have pushed them into war, the Communists are guided by the oldest maxim of warfare: the economy of force. They propose to use force in carefully measured dosages, no bigger and no smaller than attainment of the political objective requires. Like the old-fashioned "colonialists" and "imperialists," whom they denounce and from whom they have learned so much, they would like to complete the conquest of the globe without destroying the productive capacity of the conquered, for they intend to harness the resources of the conquered as quickly and as completely as possible to their own economy. They have convinced themselves, however, that if in the process some crockery has to be broken, it might as well be broken atomically, and that a vigorous social system like theirs can survive even thermonuclear punishment, whereas the rotten capitalist system cannot. To this extent, Soviet strategy is "positive" and "constructive," for it implements a political doctrine which envisages the creation of a new global order. But Western strategic thought is defensive. It does not propose to wrest the lands under Communism from their rulers. It envisages its weapons systems, including the nuclear, as means of retaliation against attack and not as instruments of a dynamic, "forward" policy designed to bring about a fundamental change in the *status quo*.

Since the West has neither an agreed political objective nor a clear notion of the nature of protracted conflict, it lacks a doctrine for coping with the Communist challenge. It has not been able either to integrate nuclear weapons into its strategy effectively or to make full use of the politcal leverage afforded by either its nuclear or its "conventional" capabilities. The West abhors war, seeks to prevent it, and, if it cannot be prevented, "limit" it. All-out war is the final, the unspeakable alternative when all else has failed. For the Communists, war is just one mode of protracted conflict, and the objective determines the scope of military violence or of any other technique of conflict. Atomic weapons, including thermonuclear bombs, are integral parts of the Soviet conflict machine, preferably to be used as psychological and diplomatic instruments, but ready to be used, if need be, as fire power. The Communists are as well aware as we are that they will suffer terrible losses in a thermonuclear duel. But they do not surrender to the "conventional obsession." Nuclear weapons of all sizes are here to stay, and wishing will not put them back into Pandora's box.

Perhaps nothing is more revealing of the West's defensive and negative mentality than the widely publicized and earnestly debated proposals for the bisection of war. For one half of war, it is argued, nuclear weapons (the "great deterrent") must be kept at hand; for the other half—"limited war" —"conventional" forces must take the field. The West's massive atomic retaliatory power—mostly American—is expected to keep on deterring the Soviets from using theirs. Ready and highly mobile forces armed with conventional weapons will have the task of coping with peripheral challenges, such as border raids by the Communists or their proxies, revolts engineered by Communists in friendly countries, and other "nibbling" tactics. The real problem of the Cold War, as the advocates of "conventional" and "limited" preparedness see it, is to prevent the Communists from scoring gains that would be decisive *cumulatively* but not great enough *singly* to call for the West's all-out retaliation against centers of Communist power.

Advocates of the fashionable bisection of war are fond of invoking an interesting analogy: the "conventional" forces will function as a "fire brigade" ready to snuff out "brush-fire" wars. Like most analogies, this one breaks down if applied in any detail. After all, a fire brigade uses dynamite when circumstances demand it, without worrying very much about whether dynamite is more or less "conventional" than a hose or ladder. In modern war, nuclear weapons are as "conventional" as any other lethal weapon. Muzzle-loaders and halberds are much more unconventional.

There is not the slightest indication that the West is prepared to bear the financial burden of a strategy based on maintaining both a separate "conventional" military establishment and a nuclear "grand deterrent." It would probably mean doubling the defense budgets of the Western Powers. Obviously the nuclear component of Western strategy would have to be maintained at the present rate, for its deterrent power-in-being would have to furnish the umbrella for the conventional forces. At the same time the West's "conventional" forces would have to be armed with weapons at least as modern as those of the Communists' "conventional" forces, and they would have to be about as large. In short, the West would have to return to the concept of large standing ground armies that prevailed before the Second World War. There is no indication that politicians and people will support such a policy anywhere in the West.

The idea that conventional forces can persuade the Communists to desist from starting small wars for fear of landing in unprofitable stalemates or of "tripping off" a nuclear holocaust is based on the assumption that they will and can confine their operations to "conventional" weapons. Now, in fact, nuclear weapons are already an integral part of the Communists' war machine, and it is highly unlikely that they could fight a "limited" war of, say, the dimensions of the Korean War without the use of tactical nuclear weapons even if they wanted to. It is true that they maintain large standing forces that are not equipped with nuclear warheads. But the principal mission of such forces is to keep down rebellious peoples in the satellite countries and at home than to fight foreign wars. The Soviet forces trained for war against the West are schooled in the use of nuclear weapons. They will use them as the exigencies of the tactical situation demand.

The tactics of "conventional" war in the style of the Second World War or the war in Korea differ enormously from the tactics of nuclear war. The former relied upon mass formations and a relatively static system of supplies; the latter must rely upon maximum dispersion and the maximum logistical autonomy of the combat forces. For an attacking force armed with nuclear weapons, "conventional" forces would be so many sitting ducks. Conceivably, were the West to station "conventional" forces along the Oder-Neisse Line, the Russians might do likewise and might even sign a treaty for the denuclearization of continental Europe. It is equally conceivable that they might not read the West's "signal" aright (they might not believe that the Western contingents really were "conventional" and that they really would stop at extinguishing "brush-fire" wars), or might break the agreement for the denuclearization of Europe, a kind of nuclear Kellogg pact and probably even less effective than the original. Then the result would be the total massacre of hundreds of thousands of men who, though armed with the best of non-nuclear weapons, might just as well have been armed with bows and arrows. The proposal has been made to restrict forces of the West German Republic to nonnuclear arms. By assuring the

Russians of the nonaggressive intentions of the West, this muzzling of the Germans is supposed to make easier the unification and ultimate neutralization of Germany. It can be readily seen why the German generals have no stomach for such a proposal. They do not cherish the idea of a "conventional" experiment in which the poor guinea pig might turn out to be the entire German Army. Proponents in the United States and Great Britain of "conventional" and "limited" war might contemplate such an experiment with enquanimity, for if it succeeded their case would have been proved and if it failed there would always be the "great deterrent" to dissuade the Communists from expanding their operations across the ocean or across the Channel. But the Germans cannot be expected to see matters with the same detachment.

In Europe, the defense of any kind and all of the West's positions can be assured only by the most highly integrated forces with a wide variety of weapons, including nuclear warheads, at their disposal. The kind of "conventional" forces to whom exponents of the doctrine of "limited war" would like to confide the security of Europe cannot defend anything worth keeping because they cannot defend themselves. Obvious as this should be, it does not follow that forces armed with nuclear weapons—low-yield nuclear explosives suitable for tactical employment—can keep a war "limited." Even the lowest-yield nuclear weapons would wreak havoc on the densely populated countryside of Europe. If war breaks out in Europe, it will be impossible to circumscribe it geographically, for the logistical lifelines of Western European defense run all the way across the Atlantic to the United States. Any Soviet attempt at interdiction—and such an attempt must suggest itself to any Soviet strategist worth his salt—would threaten the combined military power of NATO at its source. The extension of hostilities to the Atlantic would sooner or later—and probably sooner—give rise to nuclear exchanges from ship to ship, from surface to air, from air to surface, and from mobile launching platforms to outlying bases. Sooner or later—and probably sooner—the commander of one side or the commanders of both sides would feel compelled to order intercontinental nuclear attacks.

But, for the sake of argument, let us assume that a strategy employing tactical atomic weapons in Europe would *not* degenerate into an all-out intercontinental nuclear slug fest. Then, since neither side could afford to lose, both sides would be forced to feed manpower and supplies into the theatre of war either until one side had achieved its military objective or until both sides were ready to settle for a draw. In brief, The Korean experience would be repeated on a larger scale—and with more deadly results, for both sides would now be armed with nuclear weapons. Had the Korean War been fought on the model of "graduated nuclear deterrence" and had the Russians armed the Chinese "volunteers" with tactical atomic weapons, American losses would have been counted not in the thousands but probably in the millions. But we need not consider this hypothetical war seriously. A war of attrition of such magnitude would inevitably lead to a wider conflict and thus a global thermonuclear war.

Nothing is more difficult for the military theorist than to reconcile theory with the reality under his nose. Various theories of limited war that still agitate Western public opinion died an unsung death on the beaches of Lebanon. In the teeth of dire Soviet threats of nuclear attacks against all and everybody, the Sixth Fleet steamed into the Eastern Mediterranean and the United States Marines swarmed ashore at Beirut. They did not encounter Soviet "volunteers." The Soviets did not follow up their impetuous pronouncements; they confined their military operations to troop maneuvers north of the Caucasus. The decisive factor was the United States' capability of massive retaliation. The Soviets were not prepared to test their particular brand of brinkmanship on this particular demonstration of American brinkmanship. The United States was able to make its local intervention stick because its very real threat of massive retaliation impressed upon the Soviets the wisdom of nonintervention. In the light of the United States' outright defiance of Soviet nuclear blackmail it is highly unlikely the Soviets would have intervened even if the United States had cared to extend its intervention from the Lebanon to Iraq. But this is another, a political story which does not bear directly upon the problem of war in our times. The pivot of Western strategy must be the capability of withstanding psychologically the Soviet nuclear threat and to counter it with a superior capability of massive retaliation. This capability in turn must be based on the security of the launching sites of massive retaliation (i.e., their invulnerability to surprise attack) and on adequate military as well as civilian air defense. The conditions of a viable Western strategy are psychological readiness and military technological superiority, the resolution to stand up to the Soviet thermonuclear threat and superior force to counter it. Given the wide spectrum of Soviet challenges, the United States must have the capability of intervening quickly and impressively, as it did in the Lebanon, in "limited" conflict situations. If United States intervention in Lebanon and British intervention in Jordan proved anything, it proved that military intervention in a "limited" conflict is not necessarily fraught with the danger of general war. No doubt, Western military establishments are not too generously endowed with flexibility of doctrine and force levels that the expeditious handling of peripheral crises requires. But it is the capability of massive strategic retaliation which makes United States "limited" intervention feasible and narrows the Soviet choice of conflict techniques.

The West is falling behind in the realm of intercontinental nuclear warfare and its allied techniques. Western budgets for military technology are too small, and the lead times for the production of weapons are too long. Proportionately too much, and not too little, money is still being spent on so-called conventional weapons. As a matter of fact, most of the NATO establishment is still a "conventional" outfit. To be sure, NATO forces require more nonatomic weapons and better ones as well. There is good reason for a better division of labor, and Britain's bid for a place in the hydrogen sun is an unnecessary duplication of effort. But far too few of NATO's divisions are equipped for standing up to a nuclear attack, "limited" or "unlimited."

More important still, the collective Western mind must slough off the pernicious abstraction that war comes in sections. War is an organic whole, and only within this organic whole can any specific action be conceived of as "limited." The West is in mortal danger because, on the one hand, it cannot grasp intellectually the full variety of Communist conflict techniques and, on the other hand, it harbors the illusion that the unlimited aspirations of the Communists can be defeated with cheap gimmicks such as second-best military forces and unilateral declarations of peaceable intentions. The struggle with Communism is an all-out struggle. At its core is the military technological race, a race both immensely expensive and terribly risky. We are given to understand, on the highest authority, that the conflict will continue until the "shrimps have learned to whistle" or until Communists have ceased to be Communists. Until then the West must keep on increasing the power of the "great deterrent" and evolve, under its shield, political and psychological strategies for countering and confounding the Communists. Thus far, Communist strategies have been far more limited than those of "limited war." Without firing a shot of old-fashioned gunpowder, they have penetrated deeply into what is called euphemistically the Free World. There is no reason the West should not be able to counter and turn back their advances, but to do so it must not waste its resources on "limited wars" that will not be fought and on "conventional" forces that cannot be used except to their own detriment.

Controlling Local Conflicts

LINCOLN P. BLOOMFIELD

WE KNOW A GREAT DEAL ABOUT THE THEORY OF SUPERPOWER WARS. Virtually all the literature on the subject of "limited war" has

From *Arms Control for the Late Sixties*, edited by James E. Dougherty and J. F. Lehman, Jr. Copyright © 1967 by Litton Educational Publishing, Inc. Reprinted by permission of Van Nostrand Reinhold Company.

to do with clashes between the U.S. and the Soviet Union in Europe and elsewhere, not using nuclear weapons. There has been quite a lot of experience with individual conflict situations; the postwar history is in many ways one of firefights, brushfires, revolutions, assaults of one kind or another, virtually all outside of Europe and involving the "underdeveloped world." Much has been said about arms control theory, and indeed the most inventive policy literature of our generation has, in my opinion, dealt with the issue of the arms competition and its control. Now we are in the process of trying to educate ourselves about insurgency situations, good and bad, communist or otherwise. Finally, a school of inquiry commonly called "conflict resolution" has been flourishing, often seeming to oscillate between genuine social science and the picket line.

All of these have dealt with parts of the problems of conflict and its control. But there is a dearth of theoretical knowledge tying together these various pieces and yielding up a body of analysis and doctrine on the controllability of less-than-general conflicts outside of Europe. The research I am currently engaged in seeks to bring together the critical masses, so to speak, of our knowledge of local conflict and our growing understanding of arms control, to see what kind of doctrinal detonation they make. At this point I can only throw out a few notions, in a very tentative spirit.

Even the definitions here turn out to be quite inadequate. For among the 52 post-World War II conflicts we are looking at, virtually all are limited not by any natural law but simply because the parties are incapable of making them unlimited. If one recalls that Rome did not need atomic weapons to annihilate Carthage, I think one can get a picture of what some countries and some leaders might do if they had greater capabilities. So "limited" does not necessarily imply deliberate self-denial. In some of the small-bore conflicts we have already witnessed in the postwar years one or another local leader has invoked a threat of bringing on World War III, complete with thermonuclear weapons and the whole apocalyptic package—if he could only do it. A lot of this is of course rhetoric, and we are now consoling ourselves against the further spread of nuclear weapons with the hope that actual possession sobers people up. But I think one wants to be clear that there may not be a qualitative distinction between local wars in Africa, Asia, Latin America, and the Middle East, and what *could* happen if capabilities should increase in various ways.

A related and absolutely crucial point on which we should also be clear is that the physical incapacity of parties to local conflicts to spread the conflicts does not necessarily imply a willingness to reach a settlement. I think this is a very crucial insight, and helps connect up such arms control activity as may be practiced, or contemplated, with respect to India and Pakistan, or between Israel and the United Arab Republic, or in sub-Saharan Africa, with kinds of diplomatic, legal, and other policy activity bearing directly on the resolution of underlying tensions.

As one scans the past, present, and future of our epoch it becomes evident that internal instability is a salient characteristic of the times. This is of course a natural concomitant of the explosive growth of new states often lacking any real attributes of nationhood, with the Congo in 1960 a prime example. And if our topic is local conflict, the most local conflict of all is of course within the boundary of a state. It is precisely these that have turned out to be the hardest of all to control or to stop quickly. We do not often think of these insurrections and rebellions and revolts in the category of "arms control." But there is an excellent reason why great powers, and military staff, and international diplomatic organizations should care at all about these "cats-and-dogs" of the conflict family. The reason is implicit in any discussion of the real-life political security scene in the world. It lies in the ever-present danger of potential involvement. Modern history is replete with civil war situations in which the outside world became enmeshed as a result of the ideological ties between local factions and great external coalitions.

Obvious examples are the Spanish Civil War, the Greek Insurgency, Korea, Cuba, the Congo and now Viet Nam. In our times international security has become indivisible for a great number of reasons, principal among which are the intense ideological warfare being waged, the speed of communications, and the growing mobility of military forces. But in the light of another factor—the excessively destructive nature of nuclear weapons—the effect of making security indivisible is to build in a potential for dangerous escalation in local conflicts virtually anywhere in the world. Of course every local conflict does not escalate, either locally, or in the sense of great power involvement. In fact one highly respected strategic analyst has publicly registered his surprise, looking at Viet Nam, at how hard it is to start a larger war. But again, there is no particular natural law necessarily working itself out here. For all the brickbats thrown at our Department of State and at diplomacy in general, I willingly testify to the continuous, responsible, quiet yet intense processes that have much to do with the fact that many local conflicts do not escalate. In fact, such processes may be as useful, if not more so, than physical controls on weapons, in keeping the peace. Our interest here is to identify, classify, and evaluate *both* as highly relevant to the "controllability" of local conflict. It is evident that the problem is larger than any single category of military or diplomatic or technical activity.

Another interesting issue that arises early in any broad-gauged analysis of conflict control is a fundamental question of value often buried in unspoken assumptions. There is, I find, no real unanimity as to whether it is a good thing or not to control all conflicts. This is one of the most interesting things to ponder while trying to think through these issues in a general sense. I do not mean the lunatics who are spoiling for bloodshed and seek to apply the military virtues to annihilative weapons. Nor can one linger over the total pacifists except to marvel at their freedom from any sense of responsibility to deal with the situations that arise in real life.

But there are responsible people who seriously believe that the world situation would really have been better if Israel had been permitted to fight it out with the Arabs in 1947-8-9; or if the British, the French and the Israelis had been allowed to overthrow Nasser in 1956; or if India and Pakistan had been allowed to see it through to a conclusion in 1965; or if the Cypriots could have settled their differences once and for all.

In each of these cases I found myself, in some instances officially, totally committed to finding pathways to the earliest possible cessation of hostilities, with or without a political solution in sight. Perhaps when the chips are down I am a pacifist too. Or perhaps I believed that in each case our Government was correct in seeking de-escalation as a top priority because of the dangers of spread—and perhaps also because the United States Government, like me, is also fundamentally pacifist, Viet Nam to the contrary notwithstanding. But I do not think one can just dismiss the advice to fight it out in Palestine or Kashmir as wild-eyed raving. It is based on the recurrent nature and durability of the underlying conflict situation in each of those cases. This in turn is related to the vitally important insight that to stop shooting is not necessarily to supply relief to the claims that are in conflict, particularly legitimate pressures. In some cases— Germany in 1918 is of course the prime example—premature cessation of hositilities leaves one party convinced that it was not beaten, that it could have won if the war had lasted longer, and that nothing had really been settled. Much the same attitude can be found among many Arabs who deny they took a licking in 1948–49. The reverse of course is the sense of humiliation and revenge that occurs if one side *is* decisively beaten.

The main operational matter thus brought up is one that may be the most important of all in the control of international conflict. This is the problem of "peaceful change." Our greatest unfulfilled political requirement is a reliable, acceptable, and orderly procedure for change without war, comparable to what a legislature does domestically in enabling conflicting interests to fight it out relatively peacefully and produce a change in the law that no court could have created. This is a complex and perplexing subject, and here one can only flag its prime relevance to the control of local conflicts and indict it as a very underdeveloped topic.

Related to the question of when to stop a fight, and to the larger question of whether the United States has or should have a more general set of principles to follow regarding local conflicts, is a rather painful but inescapable issue. This is whether the United States does in fact have an interest in fomenting rather than suppressing certain kinds of conflict situations, where the alternative is clearly worse, in certain parts of the world. Arguments on both sides of the issue have to be stared at very carefully case by case, and one approaches the matter of a common policy doctrine very cautiously indeed. Elements of the policy problem can be readily discerned for some of the broad propositions assertable on either side: "Since the Communists foment 'wars of national liberation,' the United States must actively oppose them, even when it means escalating a given conflict"; or "Since Communist domination or take-over is intolerable to us, it may be in our interest to foment rather than suppress certain given conflicts." But: "Since escalation is the greatest danger, it is really never in the U.S. interest to foment conflict"; and, finally, "As a relatively fat, happy, status-quo power with no territorial ambitions it is in our interest on grounds of stability to suppress outbreaks of violence that may come to involve us."

Related to this is a very serious argument that certain kinds of local conflict may have the beneficial result of minimizing a larger conflict. A colleague of mine uses as an example the current Yemen conflict that ties up large Egyptian forces and keeps them from greater mischief-making elsewhere.

All one can conclude at this stage is that it clearly is not a black and white set of arguments. If I had to sum up, I have a general intuition that on balance there is a sort of generalized American interest in the minimization of international conflict and the maximization of international procedures for peaceful change and pacific settlement.

I think also that there is a corollary to this in minimum United States involvement. This may make me a "neo-isolationist," although I don't feel like one. But I think this corollary is arguable, if only on the grounds of C. L. Sulzburger's Fourth Cardinal Rule of Diplomacy, which is never to get between a dog and a lamppost.

It is evident that others do not share this general intuition that it is a good thing to suppress conflict and a bad thing to foment it. The Chinese Communists with their extravagant dreams when they are in a doctrinaire mood favoring people's revolutionary wars all over the world, or non-Communists with legitimate claims who have little to lose and do not think terribly much of the established order anyway, certainly do not share this conflict-suppression philosophy. But I think the United States probably has it, and that this represents the basic thrust of our policy in this realm.

The ideal form of conflict control is prevention. The UNESCO constitution is correct when it says that wars begin in the minds of men. The trouble is that of course we are lucky indeed if our own diplomats are able to focus on wars after they have started but before they go along too far. I do not think this is cynicism, and I do not propose to worry about ultimate first causes of conflict so much as about the machinery to abort, suppress, terminate, and hopefully, settle them.

To become concrete, policy measures begin with localizing conflict. This is the primordial meaning of local conflict—to limit its geographical scope. And of course this is one of the few measures open to other people to influence the course of events in a local conflict that does not depend entirely on the intentions, capabilities, or goodwill of the people actually doing the fighting. One looks therefore to external aid, specifically to the arms traffic. The Center for International Studies at M.I.T. has made some interesting recommendations on this subject in connection with a study in 1963–64 on Regional Arms Control Arrangements for Developing Countries under a contract with the U.S. Arms Control and Disarmament Agency. It is a first order of business to get under better control the hardware available to countries to expand local conflicts—whether this is done tacitly, unilaterally, or bilaterally; preferably it should be done multilaterally because all those who have the ability must be brought into cooperation.

A second most important measure of conflict comes under the heading of enforcing the peace. Here one gets into the never-never land of world government. World government just does not seem to me a feasible or perhaps even desirable objective at the present time. And yet a genuine collective security of enforcement must rest on a consensus and a polity and a decision-making apparatus that add up to an agreed political order. One of the fundamental disputes among students of conflict control comes precisely here. Wholly apart from the possible dangers in a world government, one runs into the belief among some of its proponents that enforcement could be agreed to "if only we could all sit down and talk together," which rests on the further belief that "this thing between us and the Russians is really just a misunderstanding," and so on. I do not happen to believe this, or if I came to believe it about the Russians I would find it very hard to fit the Chinese into such a world order, or even that great mass of newly-independent states who don't think much of the White Western Man's version of the "established order." All things considered, I judge us lucky if we can jack up our efforts that focus on aborting conflicts through good offices, mediation and arbitration, the suppression of conflicts through cease-fires, through observation activities, or through peace forces; and sometimes even to resolution of conflicts, although this is very rare and is becoming increasingly rare. More important than anything else may well be the fidelity with which the Western world and specifically the United States genuinely supports these stages of pacification and practices them in its own actions.

One could argue that international organization machinery, being as imperfect as it is, cannot do very many of these things well. I think it *has* been extraordinarily useful to have cease-fires. But as I suggested earlier, when we have cease-fires the next question is how to keep a conflict from getting worse again, or emerging in a worse form if nuclear weapons spread or if the United States gets rid of its B-47s, or whatever the problem might be. The enforcement-of-peace problem again joins up the stage of cease-fire with the problem of ultimate settlement.

Unfortunately, the Western states have themselves been selective in their various policies about cease-fires. Viet Nam is a case where to focus exclusively on getting the guns to stop would not satisfy the political-strategic purpose of communicating a message to Asian Communists that the United States is prepared to fight to discourage take-over attempts. Cease-fires are often unrelated to the merits of the case, particularly when direct military solutions are being attempted, such as in Goa in 1961, or the recent Indonesian "confrontation" with its neighbor Malaysia. Above all, international organizations are proving unable in this age—as are many national organizations—to cope with the new format of conflict within borders—subversion, terror, insurgency, the whole catalogue of conflict types which so far have baffled the international community. I think there is a serious question whether constitutionally or unconstitutionally the United Nations or any international organization is capable of coping with many problems of internal insurgency. This may be our single most unsolvable problem in the field of conflict control.

In speaking of internal conflict control it seems to be obvious that internal reforms are as important as any single factor in the whole spectrum of civil wars. Their absence creates the role of indigenous Communists, who in the still excellent phrase of Walt Rostow are the "scavengers of the process of modernization." The role of external assistance, however, makes the issue internationally ambiguous. Where the issue is primarily colonial it has not been quite so ambiguous; surely there could have been a great deal more conflict control through a more farsighted colonial policy on the part of certain of our friends. One does not have to be Sophocles to predict the nature of the tragedy that is coming in the southern part of Africa and the Portuguese colonies, where the same kind of history is being repeated with the same kind of predictable results.

Even here rigorous candor compels one to point out that in the short term there may be more conflict control if one retains colonial control. To be intellectually rigorous about this problem *no* flat statement based on an ideal seems to stand up without all kinds of scrutiny. But the argument collapses when one looks at the middle range of time, and short-term suppression of conflict through colonial rule turns out to reflect a consistently unsuccessful policy from 1815 and the Holy Alliance through the Indian, Indochinese, and Algerian experiences in modern times.

There are only hints and clues—perhaps banal and obvious—to

a most complex set of issues in the investigation of which all of us are really only at the start. The attempt to find uniformities and regularities that can yield some kind of predictive policy value labors under obvious handicaps. Above all, I think we can be properly cautious of making inferences about the future from the past. Carl Becker once wrote: "In human affairs nothing is predetermined until after it has occurred." But another wise historian of diplomacy also wrote: "I have observed that politicians, unlike diplomats, have no time to learn the lessons of history." This gives us that most valuable thing of all—a place to start.

Foreign Policy and Christian Conscience

GEORGE F. KENNAN

IN THE FABRIC OF INTERNATIONAL LIFE, THERE ARE A GREAT MANY QUESTIONS THAT HAVE NO CERTAIN CHRISTIAN SIGNIFICANCE AT ALL. They represent conflicts between those elements of secular motivation which are themselves without apparent Christian meaning: commercial interests, prestige considerations, fears, and what not. I do not think we can conclude that it matters greatly to God whether the free trade area or the Common Market prevails in Europe, whether the British fish or do not fish in Icelandic territorial waters, or even whether Indians or Pakistani run Kashmir. It might matter, but it is hard for us, with our limited vision, to know.

❋ ❋ ❋

The Moral Implications of War

This brings me now to the questions on which I think a Christian might, with good conscience, really take a stand. They involve not just the national interests of individual governments but rather the interests of civilization: the question of war, and the atom, and the other weapons of mass destruction.

I am aware that the institution of war has always represented dilemmas for Christian thought to which no fully satisfactory answer has ever been offered. I have, in the past, found myself unable to go along with the Quakers in their insistence on a sweeping renunciation of power as a factor in international affairs. I do not see the reality of so clear a distinction as they draw between domestic affairs and international affairs. The Communists have taught us that these two things are intimately connected, that civil wars have international implications and that international wars have domestic implications everywhere. I am unable therefore to accept the view which condemns coercion on the international sphere but tolerates it within the national borders.

But that we cannot rule out force completely in international affairs does not seem to me to constitute a reason for being indifferent to the ways in which force is applied—to the moral implications of weapons and their uses. It is true that all distinctions among weapons from the moral standpoint are relative and arbitrary. Gunpowder was once viewed with a horror not much less, I suppose, than are atomic explosives today. But who is to say that relative distinctions are not meaningful? I cannot help feeling that the weapon of indiscriminate mass destruction goes farther than anything the Christian ethic can properly accept. The older weapons, after all, were discriminate in the sense that they had at least a direct coherent relationship to political aims. They were seen as means of coercing people directly into doing things an enemy government wished them to do: evacuating territory, desisting from given objectives, accepting a given political authority. A distinction was still generally drawn, furthermore, prior to World War I at least, between the armed forces and the civilian population of a hostile country. Efforts were made to see that military action was directed only against those who themselves had weapons in their hands and offered resistance. The law of war did not yet permit the punishment of whole peoples as a means of blackmail against governments.

In all of these respects, the atom offends. So do all the other weapons of mass destruction. So, for that matter, did the conventional bomber of World War II when it was used for area bombing. In taking responsibility for such things as the bombing of Dresden and Hamburg, to say nothing of Nagasaki and Hiroshima, Americans were beyond what it seems to me the dictates of Christian conscience should have allowed (which is not to say that I think their problem was an easy one).

I regret, as an American and as a Christian, that these things were done. I think it should be our aim to do nothing of the sort in any future military encounter. If we must defend our homes, let us defend them as well as we can in the direct sense, but let us have no part in making millions of women and children and noncombatants hostages for the behavior of their own governments.

It will be said to me: This means defeat. To this I can only reply: I am skeptical of the meaning of "victory" and "defeat" in their relation to modern war between great countries. To my mind the defeat is war itself. In any case it seems to me that there are times when we have no choice but to follow the dictates of our conscience, to throw ourselves on God's mercy, and not to ask too many questions.

* * *

We will unavoidably find in the motives and workings of the political process much that is ambiguous in the Christian sense. In approaching the individual conflicts between governments which make up so much of international relations, we must beware of pouring Christian enthusiasm into unsuitable vessels which were at best designed to contain the earthly calculations of the practical politicians. But there are phases of the government's work in which we can look for Christian meaning. We can look for it, first of all, in the methods of our diplomacy, where decency and humanity of spirit can never fail to serve the Christian cause.

Beyond that there loom the truly apocalyptic dangers of our time, the ones that threaten to put an end to the very continuity of history outside which we would have no identity, no face, either in civilization, in culture, or in morals. These dangers represent for us not only political questions but stupendous moral problems, to which we cannot deny the courageous Christian answer. Here our main concern must be to see that man, whose own folly once drove him from the Garden of Eden, does not now commit the blasphemous act of destroying, whether in fear or in anger or in greed, the great and lovely world in which, even in his fallen state, he has been permitted by the grace of God to live.

VI THE UNRESTRICTED
USE OF FORCE:
THERMONUCLEAR WAR

The Balance of Power

HEDLEY BULL

IN INTERNATIONAL SOCIETY AS WE KNOW IT, SECURITY IS NOT PRO-
VIDED BY THE CONCENTRATION OF MILITARY POWER IN AN AU-
THORITY SUPERIOR TO SOVEREIGN STATES, BUT RESTS ON A BALANCE
OF POWER AMONG THEM.

The existence of a military situation in which no one power or
bloc is preponderant is a most precarious and uncertain source of
security. The idea of the balance of power, like that of disarmament, rests on the abstraction of the military factor. If there is a
military balance between opposed powers, such as to leave them
alike without prospect of decisive victory, there is no guarantee
that they will act in accordance with an appreciation of this
balance or even that they will be aware that it exists. The inherent uncertainty that surrounds estimates of military power,
the play of the contingent in military operations themselves, the

inadequacy of intelligence and its frustration by counterintelligence, the willingness of governments to take risks despite unfavorable odds, their frequent failure even to weigh the odds, render peace something precarious even where the balance of power is most stable. Military balances, moreover, do not remain stable for long periods but are inherently temporary. The technological, economic, demographic, political, and other ingredients that go to make up the military strength of each side are subject to constant change, as is the attitude of each side toward the existing balance, which it may find satisfactory and accept, or find unsatisfactory and seek to overthrow.

The unsettling effect of changes on the balance of power is mitigated by the practice of making adjustments in the system of alliances: Changes in the diplomatic combinations of the powers enable the balance among them to accommodate changes in the intrinsic strength of each of them. But the recourse to the adjustment of alliances does not exist for two blocs between whom the world is divided. If, as now, in strictly military terms, neither antagonist can substantially affect the balance by throwing the strength of further powers into the scales, this balance is determined by the efforts of each in the arms race: In the event of the swing of the balance toward one of them, there are no new worlds the other can call into being in order to redress it. Military balances which are unstable and fluctuating are notoriously corrosive of international security: They give rise, in the power with a temporary preponderance, to the counsel of preventive war. . . . Military balances have contributed to the avoidance of particular wars, but they are not a guarantee against war; on the contrary, war is one of the instruments by which the balance is maintained. The chief function of the balance of power in international society has not been to preserve peace, but to preserve the independence of sovereign states from the threat of domination, and to preserve the society of sovereign states from being transformed by conquest into a universal empire; to do these things, if necessary, by war.

Is There Any Acceptable Alternative to a Balance-of-Power Strategy?

Though it is no panacea, the existence of a military balance between politically opposed powers and blocs is one of the chief factors making for peace and order among them. We shall be able to appreciate the importance of the balance of power if we consider carefully what, in the short run, the alternatives to it are. If—like the critics of the balance of power, from Richard Cobden to President Wilson to the present supporters of unilateral disarmament—we contrast the security provided by a military balance with that provided by some imagined political system that might arise in the long run, or with our image of some system that has occurred in the past, we shall be very conscious of its shortcomings. If we examine the present military balance alongside our image of a just and liberal world government, or total disarmament, or free trade and universal brotherhood, or the Roman peace, we must be impressed with its dangers. But if we examine it alongside the alternatives to it that exist now, the alternatives that we by our action or inaction can bring about, we must form a very different impression. The alternative to a stable balance of military power is a preponderance of power, which is very much more dangerous. The choice with which governments are in fact confronted is not that between opting for the present structure of the world, and opting for some other structure, but between attempting to maintain a balance of power, and failing to do so. The balance of power is wrongly regarded as a synonym for international anarchy; rightly regarded as something which mitigates an anarchy which might otherwise be more rampant. It is not a panacea. But it exists now; and among those forces which make for international security and can be built upon by action that can be taken now, it is one of the strongest. To what extent is there a stable balance of military power between the Western and Soviet blocs at the present time?

The Soviet-Western military balance should be considered at

two levels: that of strategic nuclear warfare and that of limited warfare. It is necessary first to establish the distinction between these kinds of warfare and justify their separate treatment.

The varieties of strategic experience do not fall into the neat divisions in which we think about them. Nevertheless, if we are to think about them, distinctions we must have. At the present time, one important contrast is between strategic nuclear war and other kinds of war, which shall be called limited war. Rightly or wrongly, strategic thinking is more concerned with this contrast than with any other. Strategic warfare is warfare directed at the sources of the enemy's power—his cities, population, resources—rather than at his armed forces, and at his opposing strategic forces. Nuclear warfare is warfare involving the use of nuclear explosives. Strategic nuclear warfare is the bombardment of cities, populations, and resources, and of opposed strategic forces, by missiles and bombers carrying nuclear explosives. The distinction between strategic nuclear war and limited war is a crude and inelegant one. In the first place, all wars are limited, more or less—in the objectives for which they are fought, the resources they consume, the combatants that are engaged in them, and the weapons they employ. The notion of "total war," war without any limits, does not bear examination. Strategic nuclear war is only less "limited" than that for which the term has been reserved. In the second place, there are other important distinctions which cut across this one—that between nuclear and non-nuclear war, and that between war which involves the two principal powers in the Soviet and Western alliances, and war which does not. In the third place, each of these kinds of warfare may take a variety of forms. Strategic nuclear warfare may be directed at either cities and resources, or at opposing strategic weapons, or both. It may take the form of an uninhibited and instantaneous exchange of all available weapons in a frenzy of destruction—which is the popular image of strategic nuclear warfare—or it may take the form of bombardments which are closely controlled and limited by specific political objectives, and which do some justice to the principle of the economy of force, the principle of not using disproportionate forces. The nuclear bombardment of a greatly inferior power by a superior power, of a non-nuclear power by a nuclear one, may be leisurely and piecemeal. According to some military theories, strategic nuclear war, even when waged between powers of comparable strength, may take the form of isolated acts of retaliatory bombardment of cities, or the form of a protracted duel in which each seeks out the strategic weapons of the other, while attempting to avert inadvertent destruction to civil society—each power being able to deter the other during the war from increasing the scale of the conflict. Limited war, as here defined, includes a variety of contingencies, from the clash of large-scale forces on the battlefield, perhaps equipped with nuclear weapons limited in range and destructive power to guerrilla operations. For all these reasons, and because it is founded upon a current fashion in strategies and weapons, this distinction is unsatisfactory. But because other distinctions are more unsatisfactory, and because it plays such a prominent part in military thinking, which is important in itself, quite apart from its correspondence to actual military events, it is proposed to employ it.

Strategic Nuclear War and Deterrence

For at least the first decade after World War II, the United States had a preponderance of strength at the level of strategic nuclear warfare. At some point after this, the United States lost this preponderance. There arose a balance of power in respect of strategic nuclear capacity between the U.S. and the Soviet Union.

The coming of this balance had a profound effect upon Western thinking about strategic nuclear warfare and its place in international politics. The effect was that it led to a revision of Western thinking about the relation between American capacity for strategic nuclear warfare and American foreign policy. During the period of her superiority in this field, the United States was able to use her capacity for strategic nuclear warfare as an instrument of policy, and did so by attacking Japan in 1945 and by making the threat of strategic warfare against Russia the basis of her policy of protecting Western Europe. She was also under pressure to employ this form of warfare against China during the Korean War and in the closing stages of the war in Indochina. The more extreme interpretations of the policy of massive retaliation, enunciated by Mr. Dulles in January, 1954, tended to make the capacity for strategic nuclear warfare almost the exclusive military basis of United States foreign policy. The achievement by Russia of a capacity for strategic nuclear warfare against the United States comparable to that by which Russia had been threatened radically altered the position. The American threat, which in the closing years of the American preponderance was being made in relation to a wider and wider range of possible Russian or Communist actions, and in support of a greater and greater number of Western territorial positions, now ceased to carry credibility in relation to many of them. The range of possible Russian or Communist action against which the American capacity for strategic nuclear warfare provided a credible deterrent began to shrink; and American military policy, as it sensed this change, came to rely less exclusively upon this military capacity. . . .

The coming of the balance at the level of strategic nuclear warfare thus led to disillusionment in the West about strategic nuclear warfare as an instrument of Western policy. It came more and more to be held in the United States, and in Britain—where the Defence White Paper of 1957 gave this doctrine its classic statement—that strategic nuclear war was not an instrument of policy, that the catastrophe involved in such a war was such that its occurrence must always represent the breakdown of policy, and that the purpose of possessing this capacity was not to arrest an enemy attack by the waging of strategic nuclear warfare, but (though the threat could in fact be executed) to prevent an attack by the threat to do so: not *defense,* but *deterrence.* Deterrence of the enemy, which has always been among the objects of military policy, thus attained the novel status of the supreme or even the sole object of this particular kind of military preparation. This, at all events, is the idea of deterrent strategy in its purest form. It implies that military policy is concerned not with affecting the outcome of a war, but only with preventing its occurrence, that the outbreak of war is the signal for the abandonment of all policy directed toward the survival of the nation; that the attempt to minimize the effects of the enemy attack by civil defense, by the interception of enemy delivery vehicles in flight, or by the destruction of them before they are launched, is not worth while. It assumes that the only military response to the failure of deterrence is the automatic execution of the retaliatory strike—directed not at the enemy's forces, which is what is required by the logic of a situation in which war has already broken out, but at his centers of population, which is required only by the then outdated logic of the threat that has failed. There are, perhaps, few adherents of the idea of deterrence in this pure form, though in Britain something very close to this is widely believed; and in the United States, where it has never enjoyed the same degree of support, it exerts a profound influence on the shaping of military policy. In the event of the outbreak of war, the failure of deterrence, a situation quite different from that in which the policy of deterrence was implemented, would have arisen. Whether or not, in this situation, military policy will continue to be guided by the outdated logic of deterrence we do not know.

The coming of the strategic nuclear balance did more than affect Western thinking about the place of strategic nuclear warfare in Western policy. If strategic nuclear warfare could not be an instrument of policy for the Western powers, this might also be true of the Soviet Union. If the growth of Soviet strategic power has weakened the West and made the Soviet Union secure from Western attack, it has still left the West fairly secure from Russian attack. In the idea of "deterrence," which was first used to describe a Western strategy designed to preserve the security of the West, there came to be seen a source of security for both sides. The balance of strategic nuclear power was viewed, and sometimes welcomed, as providing *a system of international security*: "the Pax Atomica," "the balance of terror," "the nuclear stalemate," or "the system of mutual deterrence." The powers in the race for military ascendancy had turned a corner and found themselves, to their surprise—and delight or dismay—in Kant's dream and Moltke's nightmare: the condition of perpetual peace.

Has War Abolished Itself?

There can be no question more central to this study than whether or not, and to what extent, the balance of strategic nuclear power provides a source of general security. For if it does, this is something which will greatly affect our attitude to disarmament and arms control. It has been argued above that, in general, a balance of power is an important source of security in a divided and anarchic world, but that the security it provides is something precarious. It is sometimes claimed on behalf of the strategic nuclear balance of power that it provides a source of security qualitatively different from, and superior to, that provided by previous military balances. In my view, the uniqueness of nuclear weapons—their cataclysmic effect on the course of politics—is exaggerated as much by those who welcome this development as leading to peace through terror as by those who deplore it as entailing an inevitable holocaust. Both views arise from what is the bane of much thinking about politics—the conviction of the uniqueness of present problems. The strategic nuclear balance is a source of security in a world which remains as anarchic and divided as ours, but, like other kinds of military balance, a precarious one.

The idea of the strategic nuclear balance as the grand panacea commonly directs attention to two of its features which appear to make of it a firmer guarantee than previous military balances have been. One is that while it lasts it renders strategic nuclear warfare a catastrophe to both sides, and the deliberate choice of it an "irrational" act for both sides (this is what is conveyed by the expression "mutual deterrence"). The other is that it is bound to last: It is an inherently stable balance of power (a "nuclear stalemate"). It is convenient to discuss these two ideas separately.

The idea that while the strategic nuclear balance lasts—so long, that is, as each side is able to threaten the other with a strategic nuclear assault—"war has abolished itself" or is quite unlikely to occur takes a number of forms. The most common view is that the kind of war which as "abolished itself" is only strategic nuclear war, or, at all events, only nuclear war; and this, only between the present nuclear powers. However, sometimes more radical claims are made for "mutual deterrence." It is sometimes held that all kinds of wars among the present nuclear powers are unlikely, not only strategic nuclear war, but also more limited kinds of war. And it is sometimes held that war is a remote contingency not only among the present nuclear powers, but also among future nuclear powers. Consequently, the spread of nuclear weapons is to be welcomed as strengthening international security, not feared as undermining it.

The view that strategic nuclear war will not occur sometimes has no firmer support than an appeal to metaphysics: a claim that such a war is an unimaginable catastrophe which will not occur because it must not. This is a view which is not often made explicit, but which lurks unstated in much of our thinking, and provides even the least metaphysically minded of us with a furtive source of comfort. However, history is littered with catastrophes unthinkable and unimaginable to their victims, who placed their trust in a logic of history which deserted them in their hour of need.

Another view appeals not to metaphysics, but to the essential nature of political man. The catastrophe of strategic nuclear war, on this view, may in principle occur, but it will not, at all events, be deliberately brought about: No "rational" government or person will choose such a catastrophe. Where this argument is used to support the idea of the improbability of strategic nuclear war, it contains three important assumptions: that governments act "rationally"; that the choice of strategic nuclear war is demonstrably "irrational"; and that war is unlikely to occur unless it is deliberately chosen. All of these assumptions are erroneous.

In general, there is no such thing as "rational action." The notice that there is a distinction between rational action and other kinds of action, or between reason and the passions, is indefensible in philosophy and psychology, but it has somehow survived in political theory. The notion of "rational action" is useful only when it is defined in a particular way, for the purposes of a particular body of theory. A great deal of economic theory proceeds upon some such notion of what is "rational action" for "economic man." A great deal of argument about military strategy similarly postulates the "rational action" of a kind of "strategic man," a man who on further acquaintance reveals himself as a university professor of unusual intellectual subtlety. In my view, this kind of formal theorizing is of great value in the discussion of strategic matters when it represents not a prediction of what will happen in the world but a deliberate and conscious abstraction from it, which must later be related again to the world. It is no disparagement of this kind of theorizing—for those who engage in it fully recognize this point—to complain that where "rational action" is defined to exclude the deliberate choice of military catastrophe, this is not a concept in terms of which it is possible to account for any great part of the history of international politics, or to base any confident prediction about its future. The idea that war is a catastrophe which no government will choose to bring about has been a commonplace of writing about international relations since the turn of the century. The decisions of governments on matters of peace and war, like those taken by the European powers in July and August, 1914, do not always reflect a careful weighing of long-range considerations, or a mastery of the course of events. The questions which strike the analyst of these decisions a generation afterward as important appear crudely answered or, more often, not even asked. The governments appear to him to stumble about, groping and half-blind, too preoccupied with surviving from day to day even to perceive the direction in which they are heading, let alone steer away from it.

Can Nuclear Warfare Be "Rational"?

Whatever confidence we may or may not have that governments in the future will not choose catastrophe, we should not assume that the choice of strategic nuclear warfare is always the choice of catastrophe. There are situations which we can readily imagine —and which, though perhaps they do not exist, are not remote from present circumstances—in which "strategic man" himself would choose the initiation of strategic nuclear warfare. There are a number of examples which might be explored, but the most important is the deliberate choice of a surprise attack which promises to destroy or to cripple the strategic nuclear forces of the enemy. In the context of the great offensive power of present-day strategic weapons, and the relative ineffectiveness of defensive measures against them, each side's prospects of victory lie in destroying the weapons of the other before they can be brought into action. There have probably been periods during the confrontation of Russia and America as strategic nuclear powers in which such a strategy has been feasible for the United States. Some writers believe that the "missile lead" and "intelligence lead" of Russia, in a period in which most American strategic weapons remain vulnerable to such attack, may make such a strategy feasible for Russia. It is true that a surprise assault of this kind appears an enterprise of immense risk, even under the most favorable military conditions. The power embarking upon it would require great confidence about many things. He would need to be very sure that his weapons were accurate enough, his intelligence about the enemy's weapons reliable enough, their vulnerability proved enough, to ensure that the retaliation visited upon him would be slight enough to make the enterprise worth while. Yet it is not enough to show that the launching of a strategic surprise attack would be always a risky enterprise. Whether or not it would be embarked upon would depend on what the alternative to it was. There are a variety of circumstances in which an act of desperation might appear the most "rational" solution. The receipt of information, perhaps false information, that the nation concerned was about to be attacked would be one such circumstance. Another would be the imminence of an intolerable political defeat, suggesting that if there is no resort to war, defeat by other means is inevitable; the belief that the balance of power was certain to become unstable and swing in favor of the opponent. These are circumstances which, when combined with military circumstances favorable to a surprise attack, might well suggest that the initiation of war is the least unfavorable outcome, when there is nothing to choose from but disaster, or great risk of disaster, of one kind or another.

Finally, the idea that strategic nuclear war between the present nuclear powers is made quite improbable by the "irrationality" of choosing it, overlooks the possibility of war by accident. Even if we were to assume that "strategic men" are kings, and that situations do not arise in which it is "rational" for them to choose war, there are a variety of other ways in which war might begin, which may be grouped under the heading of "accidental war," in the most general sense of that term. War may be brought about:

    (i)   by technical accident, such as the explosion of a bomb, the misreading of a warning system, the misfiring of a missile;

   (ii)   by the choice of persons not in supreme authority, arising from the breakdown of the system of command and control;

 (iii)   by the "catalytic" action of some third power hoping to provoke a war;

 (iv)   by the decision of a nuclear power to attack a non-nuclear one, leading to the involvement of other nuclear powers;

  (v)   by the "escalation" of a limited war, especially of one involving the use of tactical nuclear weapons, to which the forces of both sides in Europe are increasingly committed.

How Stable Is the Nuclar Balance?

The second feature of the strategic nuclear balance of power which is held to distinguish it from other kinds of military balance, and to make of it a firmer source of international security than these other kinds of balance have been, is that it is an inherently stable balance or "stalemate," and has, in consequence, a tendency to perpetuity which the delicate and fluctuating military balances of the past have not had.

Our knowledge of this history of past arms races and military balances should make us skeptical of this notion of the stalemate or inherently stable balance in strategic nuclear capacity. This skepticism can be supported by analysis of the present military balance. In the United States, Mr. Albert Wohlstetter of The RAND Corporation, in an article which has had a great influence upon thinking about strategic matters, has advanced powerful arguments suggesting that the balance of terror is not something automatic or something flowing from the mere existence of nuclear weapons, but that even for the United States the deterrence of Russia is a most difficult enterprise requiring sustained efforts. He states that the ability of the United States to retaliate in the event of a Russian attack is something which is continually called in question by the measures taken by Russia, and which can be placed beyond question only by measures taken continuously in the United States. If the continued deterrence of Russia by America is to this extent uncertain, so also is the deterrence of America by Russia, and how much more so the deterrence of major powers undertaken by minor nuclear powers.

If the persistence of the strategic nuclear balance is therefore uncertain in the short run, in the long run it is much more uncertain. Both the United States and the Soviet Union are actively engaged in the attempt to break through the stalemate. They are seeking to improve defenses against bomber and missile attacks. They are studying the problems of civil defense. They are gathering information about the whereabouts of opposing retaliatory forces, hiding that of their own, and they are pouring vast resources of skilled manpower into technological innovations of all kinds. There are serious obstacles in the path of the attempt to break through the stalemate—the increasing diversity of weapons systems on each side, which facilitates the rendering of bases invulnerable, and the immense cost of this enterprise. But however skeptical experts who take a short-range view of this problem may be, we cannot, bearing in mind the extraordinary rate of technological innovation in the military art in recent years, and the near certainty that it will continue to accelerate, be confident that over a long period one nation will not place itself in a position of not being deterred by the others.

Has Atomic War Really Become Impossible?

HANS J. MORGENTHAU

ALL-OUT ATOMIC WAR HAS NOT BECOME UNTHINKABLE. Nor has it been agreed upon . . . that it would not be resorted to as an instrument of national policy. Rather, the certainty that under present conditions neither the United States nor the Soviet Union can win such a war has also made it certain that neither side will deliberately start such a war. The "present conditions" from which these two certainties derive are the atomic stalemate which, for all practical purposes, equalizes the power of destruction of the United States and the Soviet Union. It is to this atomic stalemate . . . that the credit must go for the certainty that neither the United States nor the Soviet Union will deliberately start an all-out atomic war.

It will be noted that, when speaking of this certainty, we have made two qualifications, the importance of which it is the purpose of this paper to elucidate. We have spoken of the "present conditions" of the atomic stalemate, implying that there might be conditions under which there would be no atomic stalemate,

From *The Bulletin of the Atomic Scientists*, January, 1956. Copyright 1956 by the Educational Foundation for Nuclear Science, Inc. Reprinted by permission.

and we have referred to the "deliberate" starting of an all-out atomic war, implying that there might be other ways for an all-out atomic war to begin than by deliberate action by either the United States or the Soviet Union.

The present atomic stalemate is composed of four main factors: the for all practical purposes evenly matched atomic capabilities; the similarly matched capabilities for defense; the similarly matched availability of vital targets; and the monopoly, vested in the United States and the Soviet Union, of the capability to wage all-out atomic war. Only as long as these four factors persist together will the atomic stalemate itself persist and continue to assert its restraining influence upon the United States and the Soviet Union. Yet as the present atomic stalemate is the result of the dynamics of modern technology, so is its permanence threatened by the very same dynamics. While some of the four factors of which it is composed appear to be more permanent than others, the permanence of none can be taken for granted.

It is certainly possible from the technological point of view for one or the other side to gain—however temporary—superiority in aggressive or defensive capabilities, which it might be tempted to use in order to remove the threat of atomic destruction once and for all. One can also imagine an accentuation of the already existing discrepancy in the availability of vital targets to such a point as to present to one or the other side the apparent opportunity for a decisive blow without incurring the risk of receiving one. It must also be borne in mind, in view both of the dynamics of technological developments and the uncertainty of their actual effects, that either side's subjective estimate—however erroneous the test of actual performance may reveal it to be—of a decisive advantage in the atomic race may be as instrumental for the deliberate starting of an all-out atomic war as the actual demonstrable advantage itself. In other words, a nation may be tempted to launch such a war because it is convinced that it has broken the atomic stalemate, and in view of the prospect of the outbreak of such a war, it does not matter whether or not this conviction is unfounded.

While thus far we have engaged in a kind of speculation which may well have but a very remote relation to the actual developments of the future, we turn now to a much less speculative development: the forthcoming disappearance of the American and Russian monopoly of the ability to wage all-out atomic war. When atomic power was first used for purposes of destruction, its potentialities for evil were considered to be so great as to warrant a government monopoly of the production and possession of fissionable material. In the meantime, impressed with the opportunities for the peaceful use of atomic energy, the government has moved toward relinquishing its monopoly both with regard to its own citizens and other nations. Yet the same atomic technology which has made feasible the peaceful uses of atomic energy has thereby also opened the door for its destructive uses. The same fissionable material may be used for driving a power plant and for triggering an H-bomb. Technologically speaking, fissionable material is neutral as to the uses to which it may be put.

It is this technological neutrality of atomic energy, no longer monopolistically controlled by two frightened and, hence, responsible governments, which opens political vistas, appalling in their revolutionary implications. For what will be left of the atomic stalemate between the United States and the Soviet Union if a number of other nations should have the capability perhaps not of waging all-out atomic war, but at least of blowing up some of the industrial and population centers of their neighbors and, for that matter, of the two superpowers themselves. Atomic power, monopolistically controlled by the United States and the Soviet Union and keeping each other's destructive capability in check, is a force for peace, however precarious. Atomic power, haphazardly distributed among a number of nations, is bound to be a source of unprecedented insecurity, if not of panic.

It is certainly not necessary here to dwell upon all the possible contingencies which one can visualize. It will be sufficient to point out that any nation, not operating under the restraint of certain destruction through atomic retaliation, is likely to use atomic weapons in pursuit of its national interests, either openly or surreptitiously. To illustrate the latter possibility: under the condition of the existing bipolarity of atomic capabilities, an anonymous atomic explosion in the United States would necessarily be attributed to the Soviet Union, calling forth atomic retribution. Under the condition of dispersion of atomic capabilities among, say, six or ten different nations, such an anonymous explosion could with certainty be attributed to nobody, however much suspicion might point to a particular nation. The constant threat of at least partial atomic destruction, under which all nations will then live, will put a premium on preventive and retaliatory action, and never mind which suspect it will hit. Compared with the anarchy and limitless violence which then will reign, the first decade of the atomic era might well appear in retrospect as a kind of golden age in which the atomic stalemate between two nations guaranteed an uneasy atomic peace. Yet perhaps even more disquieting than these dire prospects of dispersion of atomic power is the apparent unconcern with them on the part of a government and public alike, both of which seem to be satisfied that all-out atomic war has become impossible.

The atomic statelmate is a function of the two-nation monopoly of atomic power; the former cannot survive with the disappearance of the latter. Yet even under the assumption that it will survive for the immediate future, a threat to atomic peace is likely to arise from two interconnected quarters: the new cold war [of] maneuver, the really important change which the Geneva Conference of July 1955 has brought to the international scene, and the possibility of limited atomic war. We are here in the presence of the other qualification we made at the outset about the impossibility of all-out atomic war when we referred to an all-out atomic war being started through other than the deliberate action on the part of either the United States or the Soviet Union.

It is trivial but not superfluous to point out that the atomic stalemate has not altered the intrinsic nature of the political interests with which the great powers are identified, and of the political problems to which the antagonism of those interests gives rise. It has only modified, as long as it lasts, the means by which they pursue these interests and try to solve these problems. In the shadow of the threat of all-out atomic war and of the universal destruction it would bring in its wake, the age-old problems of foreign policy still occupy the chanceries of the great powers, which, however, shy away from any step which might bring the materialization of this threat measurably closer. And what is true of the chanceries applies to the general staffs: they, too, plan for military support of national policies in the conventional strategic framework and with the conventional tactical means, to which atomic weapons have been added.

The period of the cold war which the Geneva Conference of July 1955 seems to have brought to a close offered little opportunity for using either the traditional methods of diplomacy or of warfare. During that period, the main task of the political and military policies of both sides was to hold the line of military demarcation established at the end of the Second World War. Policy consisted, in the main, in the warning, supported by actual preparedness, that a step taken by the other side beyond that line would necessarily lead to all-out atomic war. In one word, a general political and military stalemate corresponded to the stalemate with respect to all-out atomic war.

If indications do not deceive, the Geneva Conference of July 1955 marks the end of the political stalemate of the first postwar decade. The new era in international relations is likely to be characterized by greater flexibility within the two power blocs, tending toward a loosening of their inner coherence if not their dissolution, and, consequently, by greater flexibility between the two power blocs as well. Four facts are in the main responsible for this fundamental change in international relations: the decrease in the dependence of the great powers of second rank upon the superpowers; the impending rise of Germany and Japan to great power status; the impending dispersion of atomic power among a multitude of nations, some of which, by virtue of their possession of atomic power, will gain or regain the status of great powers; and finally, the spread and sharpening of the colonial revolutions in Asia, Africa, and Latin America. These new developments will force the United States and the Soviet Union to embark upon policies of vigorous competition. The problem which their foreign policies must solve is no longer to hold a certain predetermined line, but to establish a new line by gaining the allegiance of powerful uncommitted nations and by weaning committed nations away from the other camp.

It would be surprising if the diplomacy of maneuver which this new situation calls for did not find its counterpart in a new military policy of maneuver, thus ending the military stalemate as well. How will the United States and the Soviet Union meet the military challenge of the new political situation? Committed as they are to foregoing the deliberate resort to all-out atomic war, they must limit themselves to the use of conventional forces and tactical atomic weapons. Yet these two types of weapons are unequally distributed between them. The Soviet Union can rely upon its superiority in conventional forces, unchallengeable in their own terms and restrained only by the threat of all-out atomic retaliation. The United States, on the other hand, must counter this Russian superiority with tactical atomic weapons, sufficient for this purpose but falling far short of all-out atomic retaliation. It is this misproportion of military means and its inner logic which for the immediate future constitutes perhaps the greatest risk of an unintended all-out atomic war.

The United States cannot afford to wage an all-out atomic war because it cannot win such a war. Nor can it afford to wage a conventional war; for, in view of its weakness in conventional forces, it cannot win such a war either. Rather, the United States must prepare for, and fight if necessary, a limited atomic war, with the atomic ingredient carefully adapted to the challenge to be met; strong enough, at the very least, to avoid defeat but not so strong as to provoke all-out atomic retaliation. It must be willing to defend its vital interests to the very limits where the risk of all-out atomic war becomes acute, yet it must forego pushing its advantage if victory can be had only at such a risk.

The very idea of such a war—ever precariously balanced between defeat and suicide—poses two grave and interrelated questions: Can it be controlled, and will it deter?

The successful conduct of such a graduated atomic war, a war with just the right atomic dosage, depends upon the continuous presence of two indispensable factors. On the one hand, the political and military leaders of the United States must bring to their tasks a blend of self-restraint and daring, which very few leaders in history have proven themselves to be capable of for any length of time. Similarly, these leaders must apply to the problem of limited atomic war good political and military judgment to such an extraordinary degree of excellence as to border on the unfailing. On the other hand, the Soviet Union must match these qualities of will and mind.

If one side were to push the other into defeat, in reliance upon the latter's resolution not to start an all-out atomic war, it might provoke that very war. If one side were to declare that under no circumstances would it resort to all-out atomic war it would condemn itself to a policy of appeasement, inviting defeat after defeat and issuing either in impotence or an all-out atomic war fought in desperation under the most unfavorable conditions. The United States and the Soviet Union must face the paradox that their chance to avoid all-out atomic war resides in their willingness and ability to fight it. They can master this dilemma only if they deprive each other of the incentive to resort to all-out atomic war, by creating and preserving political and military conditions which do not call for such a war. Yet what, if one or the other side loosens the reins of self-restraint, taking a risk or an advantage which should not have been taken, or commits an error of judgment, overestimating or underrating intentions and capabilities? These are ominous questions to which there is no good answer.

In any event, the assumption that all-out atomic war has become impossible is not the answer. Nothing in the actual facts warrants this assumption. Quite to the contrary, it is the very essence of the paradox to which we have referred that to the extent that we assume the impossibility of all-out atomic war and act on the assumption, we increase the very possibility of such a war.

The Rungs of
the Escalation Ladder

HERMAN KAHN

AN ESCALATION LADDER
A Generalized (or Abstract) Scenario

AFTERMATHS

CIVILIAN
CENTRAL
WARS

- 44. Spasm or Insensate War
- 43. Some Other Kinds of Controlled General War
- 42. Civilian Devastation Attack
- 41. Augmented Disarming Attack
- 40. Countervalue Salvo
- 39. Slow-Motion Countercity War

(CITY TARGETING THRESHOLD)

MILITARY
CENTRAL
WARS

- 38. Unmodified Counterforce Attack
- 37. Counterforce-with-Avoidance Attack
- 36. Constrained Disarming Attack
- 35. Constrained Force-Reduction Salvo
- 34. Slow-Motion Counterforce War
- 33. Slow-Motion Counter-"Property" War
- 32. Formal Declaration of "General" War

(CENTRAL WAR THRESHOLD)

EXEMPLARY
CENTRAL
ATTACKS

- 31. Reciprocal Reprisals
- 30. Complete Evacuation (Approximately 95 per cent)
- 29. Exemplary Attacks on Population
- 28. Exemplary Attacks Against Property
- 27. Exemplary Attack on Military
- 26. Demonstration Attack on Zone of Interior

From *On Escalation: Metaphors and Scenarios* by Herman Kahn. Penguin Books Inc., 1968.

(CENTRAL SANCTUARY THRESHOLD)

BIZARRE
CRISES

- 25. Evacuation (Approximately 70 per cent)
- 24. Unusual, Provocative, and Significant Countermeasures
- 23. Local Nuclear War—Military
- 22. Declaration of Limited Nuclear War
- 21. Local Nuclear War—Exemplary

(NO NUCLEAR USE THRESHOLD)

INTENSE
CRISES

- 20. "Peaceful" World-Wide Embargo or Blockade
- 19. "Justifiable" Counterforce Attack
- 18. Spectacular Show or Demonstration of Force
- 17. Limited Evacuation (Approximately 20 per cent)
- 16. Nuclear "Ultimatums"
- 15. Barely Nuclear War
- 14. Declaration of Limited Conventional War
- 13. Large Compound Escalation
- 12. Large Conventional War (or Actions)
- 11. Super-Ready Status
- 10. Provocative Breaking Off of Diplomatic Relations

(NUCLEAR WAR IS UNTHINKABLE THRESHOLD)

TRADITIONAL
CRISES

- 9. Dramatic Military Confrontations
- 8. Harassing Acts of Violence
- 7. "Legal" Harassment—Retortions
- 6. Significant Mobilization
- 5. Show of Force
- 4. Hardening of Positions—Confrontation of Wills

(DON'T ROCK THE BOAT THRESHOLD)

SUBCRISIS
MANEUVERING

- 3. Solemn and Formal Declarations
- 2. Political, Economic, and Diplomatic Gestures
- 1. Ostensible Crisis

DISAGREEMENT—COLD WAR

Description of the Rungs and Thresholds

SUBCRISIS MANEUVERING: We are interested here not in day-to-day maneuvers that do not raise the possibility of escalation, but only in the ones that manipulate, either deliberately or otherwise, the fear of escalation or eruption. It will be one of my theses that remote as the middle and upper rungs of the escalation ladder may seem, they often cast a long shadow before them and can greatly influence events well below the violence threshold, or even below that point in a conflict when the explicit threat of violence is voiced.

Rung 1. Ostensible crisis. At this stage, the language of crisis is used, but with some degree of pretense. Either one or both sides assert, more or less openly and explicitly but not quite believably, that unless the dispute is quickly resolved, rungs of the escalation ladder will be climbed.

Rung 2. Political, economic, and diplomatic gestures. Legal but inconveniencing, unfair, unfriendly, discourteous, inequitable, or threatening acts are carried out against the opponent to punish, apply pressure, or convey messages. If this becomes very hostile, these acts are called "retortions" (see Rung 7).

Rung 3. Solemn and formal declarations. These are purely verbal but explicitly solemn and formal actions intended to demonstrate resolve and committal. They may be in the form of legislative resolutions, formal executive announcements, diplomatic notes, or other very explicit and obviously serious declarations. Such a resolution or proclamation may be a simple notice to other nations of one's policy in a certain geographical or other area, or it may address a conflict or dispute more directly. It may often be thought of as a pre-emptive or preventive escalation that tries to forestall escalation by the opponent.

TRADITIONAL CRISES (THE BOAT IS ROCKED): In a thermonuclear balance of terror, both nations will be reluctant to start a crisis that could escalate, perhaps inadvertently, possibly even going beyond control and erupting into an all-out war. There is, therefore, a tendency not to let even a low-level crisis start—a constraint not to rock the nuclear boat.

Rung 4. Hardening of positions—Confrontation of wills. When the situation becomes coercive rather than contractual, the antagonists often attempt to increase the credibility of their commitments by "bridge-burning" acts, a deliberate increasing of the stakes, perhaps a joining together of several issues with the deliberate purpose of making it harder for the other side to believe that one can be made to back down.

Rung 5. Show of force. One side or the other may hint, or even make clear, that violence is "thinkable." If it does this by acts rather than words, we call it a "show of force."

Rung 6. Significant mobilization. The accompaniment of a show of force by a modest mobilization that not only increases one's strength but also indicates a willingness to call on more force or to accelerate the arms race if necessary.

Rung 7. "Legal" harassment—Retortions. One can harass the opponent's prestige, property, or people legally. That is to say, one may act in a very hostile and provocative manner, but within the limits of international law.

Rung 8. Harassing acts of violence. If the crisis is still not resolved, more or less illegal acts of violence or other incidents designed to harass, confuse, exhaust, violate, discredit, frighten, and otherwise harm, weaken, or demoralize the opponent or his allies and friends may be carried out through clandestine or unattributed channels, or through limited paramilitary or other overt agencies.

Rung 9. Dramatic military confrontations. If there is a direct ("eyeball to eyeball") confrontation that appears to be a stark test of nerves, committal, resolve, or recklessness, all participants and observers will take an intense interest in the proceedings. INTENSE CRISES (THE UNTHINKABLE NUCLEAR WAR BECOMES CREDIBLE): Exactly where this threshold occurs is variable and very dependent on a specific course of events, but at some point the "nuclear incredibility"[1] that all of us share may be sharply decreased, if not eliminated. The popular sense of security ends or is shaken, and the "unreal" and "hypothetical" nuclear stockpiles may suddenly be perceived as real threats. This change will not come all at once, and may not be extreme, but it may occur to a large enough degree that a percentage of the population and a majority of decision-makers seriously envisage the possibility of a nuclear war actually occurring.

[1] Raymond Aron's phrase.

Rung 10. Provocative diplomatic break. This act would be intended to communicate to the opponent that one's reliance on the traditional peaceful measures of persuasion or coercion is at an end and that acts of force may now be resorted to.

Rung 11. Super-ready status. Placing military forces on super-ready status automatically involves dangerous or costly actions. If it did not, we would be doing these things normally.

Rung 12. Large conventional war (or actions). Casualties may occur in these acts—a significant deepening of the crisis. But even should these contests reach the level of open and continued fighting, neither side will use its more "efficient" or "quality" weapons —the nuclear, bacteriological, or chemical weapons—unless it wishes to escalate much farther up the ladder.

Rung 13. Large compound escalation. One side may demonstrate its resolve by reacting to an opponent's escalation with actions that raise issues not involved in the original conflict— the posing of a threat in a new area.

Rung 14. Declaration of limited conventional war. A declaration of limited conventional war would be an attempt to achieve one or both of the following objectives: to give the enemy an incentive to reciprocate by making a clear-cut, unilateral announcement of "no nuclear first use"; to limit the conventional war geographically or otherwise in a manner considered most favorable or stable by the side making the declaration. In addition, such a declaration would have grave symbolic, political, and moral effects upon one's own country and the opponent.

Rung 15. Barely nuclear war. During a conventional warlike act (Rung 12) or the super-ready status (Rung 11), one or more nuclear weapons may be used unintentionally (accidentally or unauthorizedly). Or one of the antagonists may make military or political use of a nuclear weapon but try to give the impression that the use was unintentional.

Rung 16. Nuclear "ultimatums." Whether or not there is a conventional or barely nuclear war, the crisis could enter a stage of such increased intensity that the state of nuclear incredulity would not merely be weakened but would vanish. This could occur when one side or the other seriously considered the possibility of a central war and communicated this fact convincingly to its opponent.

Rung 17. Limited evacuation (approximately 20 per cent). This would most likely be at least a quasi-official move ordered by a government for either bargaining or prudential reasons, or both. The difficulties, and possible public and political reactions, make such an evacuation a momentous decision, and one whose consequences could not reliably be predicted. I would also include at this rung serious efforts by one or both sides to prepare for both large-scale evacuation and improvised protection.

Rung 18. Spectacular show or demonstration of force. A spectacular show or demonstration of force would involve using major weapons in a way that did no obvious damage, but appeared determined, menacing, or reckless. The purpose would be to punish the enemy for a previous act, or pre-emptively to punish him for an anticipated one (with the intention of establishing a precedent to deter later provocations), or to intensify the fear of war in the hope of frightening the enemy into backing down.

Rung 19. "Justifiable" counterforce attack. A "justifiable" attack would be sufficiently specialized and limited to seem a reasonable response to provocation, and yet it might significantly, or even decisively, degrade the military capability, prestige, or morale of the opponent.

Rung 20. "Peaceful" world-wide embargo or blockade. This would be an extreme measure of nonviolent coercion brought to bear against an opponent. It is more escalatory than the previous rungs because of its continuing nature.

BIZARRE CRISES (NUCLEAR WEAPONS ARE USED): Up to this point, while nuclear incredulity would have been shattered, nuclear weapons would not have been used extensively. Even if the barely nuclear war had occurred, it presumably would have been accepted as an accident or limited episode, and even a nuclear show of force or "justifiable" counterforce attack might have been understood as a limited action rather than serious nuclear warfare. Now we move wholly into what many consider an entire bizarre range of possibilities, the very limited and restrained use of nuclear weapons.

Rung 21. Local nuclear war—exemplary. Almost every analyst now agrees that, with the possible exception of Rung 19–type tactics, the first use of nuclear weapons—even against military targets—is likely to be less for the purpose of destroying the other side's military forces or of handicapping its operations than for redressive, warning, bargaining, punitive, fining, or deterrence purposes. As this would be the first unmistakably deliberate use of these weapons since World War II, it would be a profoundly consequential act, even if very limited and specialized.

Rung 22. Declaration of limited nuclear war. At this point, it might be judged desirable to make a formal declaration of limited nuclear war—perhaps in hope of setting out relatively exact limits and establishing expectations about the types of nuclear action that the declarer intends to initiate and that he is prepared to countenance from the enemy without escalating further himself.

Rung 23. Local nuclear war—military. It is also possible that nuclear weapons could be used in a local situation for traditional military purposes such as defense, denial, destruction, or degradation of the opponent's capability, and so on, and that, within the established limits, the scale and targeting would be, and would be acknowledged to be, dictated by wholly military and "tactical" considerations.

Rung 24. Unusual, provocative, and significant countermeasures. One side might carry out redeployments or maneuvers that would have the effect of shifting the balance of power by increasing an opponent's vulnerability to attack or otherwise degrading its capability, morale, or will.

Rung 25. Evacuation (approximately 70 per cent). At this point, the situation may be very close to large-scale war. It may now seem advisable to evacuate a large number of people from cities. The total would probably amount to between two-thirds and three-fourths of the population—women and children and those men who are not essential to the functioning of the cities. I would judge that all important industries, communications, transportation facilities, etc., could be operated by about a quarter of the population or less.

EXEMPLARY CENTRAL ATTACKS (VIOLATING THE CENTRAL SANC-

TUARY—NUCLEAR GUNBOAT DIPLOMACY): Attacks that avoid the zone of interior of the enemy observe a salient threshold: the one dividing the categories of "homeland" and "not-homeland." To cross this threshold would open the way to large-scale violence.

Rung 26. Demonstration attack on zone of interior. A "harmless" attack (perhaps on an isolated mountain top or empty desert) which does dramatic and unmistable physical damage, if only to the topography.

Rung 27. Exemplary attack on military. One side might begin destroying portions of the other side's weapons systems, but in a relatively careful way so as not to cause much collateral damage. These attacks could be launched primarily to exert psychological pressure or to reduce the defender's military capability significantly by finding leverage targets.

Rung 28. Exemplary attacks against property. The next step would obviously be to increase the level of these limited strategic attacks. One possibility would be attacks on such expensive installations as bridges, dams, or gaseous diffusion plants. More damaging and dangerous would be limited attacks on cities, presumably after warning had been delivered and the cities evacuated; the purpose would be to destroy property, not people.

Rung 29. Exemplary attacks on population. In any crisis of the mid-1960's, this attack would probably be much higher on the ladder than I put it here, but if the balance of terror becomes sufficiently stable, and governments are believed to be under intense and graduated mutual deterrents, even this attack could occur without an eruption to spasm or other central war.

Rung 30. Complete evacuation (approximately 95 per cent). But at this point, large-scale warfare has either begun or is imminent. If at all possible, each side is likely to evacuate its cities almost completely, leaving 5–10 per cent of the population behind for essential activities.

Rung 31. Reciprocal reprisals. This is a war of almost pure resolve, with more or less continual tit-for-tat exchanges, whether limited to purely symbolic attacks or more destructive exemplary attacks. Many strategists believe that reciprocal reprisal wars—"resolve against resolve"—might be a standard tactic of the future when the balance of terror is judged, whether correctly or not, to be almost absolute or when, because of strategic invulnerability, no other choices are available to desperate or gambling decision-makers.

MILITARY CENTRAL WARS (THE "NEW" KIND OF ALL-OUT WAR): Two groups of central-war rungs lie above the traditional threshold between war and peace (a distinction that has not been obliterated by new developments). In military central wars, the military authorities, or commanders in chief, have access to all the resources of the nation, although their intention is to utilize tactics that avoid or limit damage to an opponent's civilians.

Rung 32. Formal declaration of "general" war. An esoteric possibility, almost completely overlooked in modern defense planning, is that one side will respond to provocation with a formal declaration of war but without immediate acts of large-scale violence. An ultimatum or declaration of war might, as in World War II, be followed by a "phony war" period, in which there was some limited tactical or strategic harassment but no large attacks.

Rung 33. Slow-motion counter-"property" war. In this attack, each side destroys the other's property in tit-for-tat fashion. We sometimes refer to this as a "war of resolve," since each side is attempting to force the other side to back down and there is a naked matching of resolve against resolve. If the exchanges are few in number, and for limited purposes, we call them "reciprocal reprisals" (see Rung 31).

Rung 34. Slow-motion counterforce war. This is a campaign (which could either precede or follow a large counterforce attack) in which each side attempts attrition of the other side's weapons systems over time. One can conceive of a slow-motion counterforce war lasting for weeks or months during which Polaris submarines are hunted down, hidden missiles found, land bases dug up, and so on.

Rung 35. Constrained force-reduction salvo. The attacker here attempts to destroy a significant but small portion of the defender's force in a single strike while avoiding undesired collateral damage. It is especially likely to be used against weak links or high-leverage targets at the outbreak of a war.

Rung 36. Constrained disarming attack. One of the major arguments for the counterforce-with-avoidance attack (see Rung 37) is that not much is lost by narrow military calculations, and with populations spared, the possibility that post-attack blackmail would work is increased enormously. In the constrained disarming attack, one may follow the same logic further. Tremendous military disadvantages might be accepted in order to spare people and improve the possibilities of successful negotiation to determine the war on an acceptable basis. In this attack, the attacker tries to destroy a significant portion of the defender's first-strike forces and even some of his second-strike forces, but avoids civilians targets as much as possible. This might make it disadvantageous for the defender to launch a counterstrike, since his damaged forces might be only partially effective, even in countervalue targeting, while his attacker might be able to deliver an annihilating second blow against the enemy population with his withheld and regrouped forces.

Rung 37. Counterforce-with-avoidance attack. This attack differs from a constrained disarming attack in that it is less scrupulous about avoiding collateral damage to cities and does not deliberately spare much, if any, of the enemy's second-strike forces. This counterforce attack targets everything that does not involve major collateral damage to civilians. In the case of a Soviet strike against the United States, such an attack probably would include hitting Tucson (a city of 250,000 population, completely ringed with Titans), but probably would avoid the San Diego Naval Base, the Norfolk Navy Yard, and the Pentagon in Washington. If it did hit these targets, or the SAC bases near very large cities, 20-kiloton rather than 20-megaton weapons might be used in order to limit the collateral destruction. After such an attack, one must assume a counterattack, but one may still try to use counter-counterthreats of further escalation into countervalue war to limit the defender's response.

Rung 38. Unmodified counterforce attack. Here, no degradation of the counterforce attack is accepted to spare civilians, but there is no deliberate attempt to enlarge such collateral damage as a "bonus."

CIVILIAN CENTRAL WARS (VIOLATION OF THE "NO-CITY" THRESHOLD): The example of strategic city bombing in World War II is so firmly held in many people's minds as "proper" action that they cannot visualize a large strategic war in which cities are not priority objectives. Yet thermonuclear wars are likely to be short, lasting from a few hours to, at most, a couple of months. In such a war, it is unlikely that cities would in themselves be of any great military consequence: factories would not have time to turn out weapons; millions of men would not be drafted and trained; there probably would not even be elections in which the fears or suffering of the civilian population could generate direct pressures to change established national policies. Thus, cities are no longer urgent military targets; they may be destroyed in a strategic war, but there is no military reason to do so, or to do so quickly. Populations, of course, may be evacuated, but buildings cannot be, and it is unlikely that one side or the other would feel so strongly motivated to destroy civilians early in a war that they would attack to pre-empt such an evacuation.

None of the above is necessarily clearly understood by the governments and war planners of either side. If one side or the other decided to go to war, it might, simply because of this lack of thought, attack cities. Of course, the United States has more or less formally enunciated a strategy of "no cities except in reprisal," but this strategy is neither widely understood nor very firmly held even here. And it remains true that if intrawar deterrence were to break down, or "bargaining" seemed to require it, cities might get hit anyway.

Rung 39. Slow-motion countercity war. A war of resolve (see Rung 33) carried to an ultimate form—"city trading."

Rung 40. Countervalue salvo. It is, of course, always possible in fighting a slow-motion counterforce, slow-motion countervalue, or other kind of war, that one side will fire a large number of missiles at civilian targets, in either inadvertent or deliberate eruption.

Rung 41. Augmented disarming attack. This would be a counterforce attack deliberately modified to obtain as a "bonus" as much collateral countervalue damage as could be achieved without diverting significant resources from the military targets.

Rung 42. Civilian devastation attack. An effort to destroy or gravely damage the enemy's society, distinguished from spasm war only by its element of calculation and the fact that there may be some withholding or control.

Rung 43. Some other kinds of controlled general war. It is possible to have many kinds of "all-out" but controlled, as well as "all-out" uncontrolled, wars. (The term "all-out" is enclosed in quotation marks to emphasize again that this is not necessarily a spasm war in which each side strikes indiscriminately against the other's cities and military bases; "all-out" refers to a level of effort, not to whether there is or is not discrimination in targeting, or negotiation.) In a "rational," "all-out," but controlled war, military action would be accompanied by threats and promises, and military operations themselves would be restricted to those which contributed to the achievement of victory (an acceptable or desirable peace treaty), to the limiting of the damage the enemy could do, to the improvement of the nation's postwar prospects (perhaps by worsening the enemy's prospects), or to the gaining of a measured amount of revenge or punishment.

Rung 44. Spasm or insensate war. The figurative word "spasm" is chosen because it describes the usual image of central war in which there is only a "go-ahead" order; all the buttons are pressed, and the decision-makers and their staffs go home—if they still have homes; they have done their job. A spasm war may occur, of course, but to the extent that there is any art of war possible in the thermonuclear age, the attempt must be made to prevent it, to try to get the losing side to cease fire before he has used up his weapons. In a "moment of truth," and particularly if there has been a preliminary crisis that has educated the leaders, all decision-makers are likely to understand at least to some degree that there need be no compulsion to wreak useless and contraproductive destruction just because one has weapons that can be used.

* * *

The Effects
of Nuclear Weapons

HARRISON BROWN and JAMES REAL

THERMONUCLEAR WEAPONS RANGE IN EXPLOSIVE FORCE UP TO SOME-
WHAT MORE THAN TWENTY MEGATONS, CORRESPONDING TO 20 MILLION
TONS OF TNT. These heavy bombs can be carried by B-52 bombers. The sizes of bombs that can be carried by missiles are at
present smaller. Minuteman and Polaris will probably be able
to carry one-megaton warheads by the mid-60's. Soviet ICBM
warheads and Atlas and Titan will probably be able to carry warheads ranging from five to ten megatons.

When a ten-megaton warhead is detonated, roughly a third
of its total energy is released in the form of heat and light. The
bomb material and surrounding air are heated to extremely
high temperatures, and the resultant fireball grows quickly to a
diameter of about three and a half miles. The heat flash persists
for about twenty seconds and on a clear day can produce third-
degree burns out to about twenty miles and second-degree
burns out to a distance of twenty-five miles from the explosion.
A ten-megaton burst in the atmosphere thirty miles above the
earth could set fire to combustibles over 5,000 square miles on a
clear day.

A surface burst of a ten-megaton bomb would produce a
crater about 250 feet deep and a half mile wide. The zone of
complete demolition would be about three miles in diameter.
Severe blast damage would extend to about nine miles from
the center of the explosion, and moderate to major damage

would extend out to twelves miles, or over an area of 450 square miles.

It is likely that firestorms will result from a thermonuclear burst over a large city. A firestorm is a huge fire in which cooled air is drawn to the center of the burning area, elevating the temperature and perpetuating the conflagration. Winds reach hurricane velocities. The holocaust consumes the available oxygen in the air with the result that persons not burned to death may die of suffocation or of carbon monoxide poisoning.

The explosion results in the instantaneous emission of nuclear radiation in quantities that can be lethal at distances up to two miles, but since persons in that area would be killed anyway by the blast and thermal effects, this is not an important factor. Far more dangerous is the radiation from radioactive products which are produced in the explosion and which are scattered over the countryside as "fallout."

More than 200 different radioactive species are formed in the explosion of a thermonuclear weapon. These attach themselves to the inert debris which is swept into the air by the explosion and which forms the familiar mushroom cloud. The heavier particles of debris fall back to earth within the first hour or so. The lighter particles are carried downward and, depending upon the wind conditions, will be deposited over an area fifteen to thirty miles wide and 100 to 500 miles long. A thermonuclear bomb exploded at low altitude deposits about 80 per cent of its fallout locally in this manner. The balance is injected into the stratosphere and is distributed globally. About one-half of the fission debris carried into the stratosphere of the Northern Hemisphere falls to earth within a year.

The local fallout from a ten-megaton explosion could, if spread uniformly, produce lethal levels of radioactivity over about 5,000 square miles of land. Thus, in the absence of some protection from radiation, there could be many deaths far from the center of the explosion. Indeed, in the event of a large-scale thermonuclear attack and in the absence of radiation protection, far more deaths would result from radiation effects than from heat or blast.

Ten Megatons on Los Angeles

In an attempt to comprehend the order of magnitude of the effect of a thermonuclear explosion over a major metropolitan area, let us imagine that a ten-megaton warhead is exploded in the civic area of downtown Los Angeles. The bomb hits during the working hours of a weekday and the attack occurs sometime in the fall—this last in deference to the strategic supposition that a nuclear war will be launched only after the crops are harvested and put underground by the attacker.

The blast effects would exterminate virtually all but the most deeply sheltered living things within a radius of five miles. Blast casualties would be severe up to a distance of ten miles. But the phenomenon that would complete the devastation of life in the entire area would be fire. The area would be one great sea of fire, which would burn until there was nothing more to consume. A good proportion of the metropolitan area's three-and-a-half million cars and trucks would be lifted and thrown like grotesque Molotov cocktails, to spew flaming gasoline, oil, and automotive shrapnel onto and into everything in their paths. In an instant most underground gasoline and oil tanks would rupture and explode within the blast area, and a large proportion of the remainder within the firestorm radius would follow, each in its own particular manner—pumps and pipes sheered and, finally, higher and higher ambient temperatures which would soon expand, rupture, and explode the remainder.

Beyond the blast radius, the remaining area of Los Angeles is occupied by relatively few first-class concrete and steel buildings; a much greater proportion is the debris of an industrial society: auto junk yards, lumberyards, row upon row of cheap flammable commercial structures. But most important, this remaining area is comprised of over 50 per cent brush-covered hills and scrub forest. Anyone who has participated in the fighting of a California brush fire and who is acquainted with the remarkable explosive nature of the oil-carrying greasewood, sumac, and scrub pine is surprised and frightened by the volatility of the material even when it is wet. The novel aspect of a thermonuclear conflagration, however, is that most of these highly flammable materials would break into intense flame simultaneously —a phenomenon never before achieved either by man or by natural causes.

There are relatively few facts about large fires. Several firestorms were produced by the incendiary bombing of German cities, and one such storm occurred after a fire raid on Tokyo. An atomic bomb created a firestorm at Hiroshima, but not at Nagasaki. It seems safe to speculate that in Los Angeles at least a twenty-five-mile radius and an unknown distance beyond it would be, within minutes, engulfed in a suffocating firestorm that would persist for a long time. It seems unlikely that there would be appreciable rainfall for weeks or even months; thus, the basin fire would proceed in all directions with no interference from man or nature.

It seems clear that in the event of such an attack there would be virtually no survivors of the blast and thermal effects, with the possible exception of a few persons who had made elaborate preparations for surviving the catastrophe. Their shelters would have to be very deep and provided with a built-in oxygen supply and cooling system. Unless they were able to maintain themselves in such a shelter for many weeks, their chances of making their way to relative safety would be slim.

A major problem would be trying to get through ankle-high to knee-high ash containing numerous hidden pitfalls; clambering for dozens of miles over huge, smoking piles of radioactive rubble, burned-out timber, wire, and steel. If the survivor made it to the edge of the devasted area, he in all probability would have accumulated by that time a fatal dose of radiation which would shortly claim what was left of his life.

Although the Los Angeles situation is an extreme one, the vulnerability of other major metropolitan areas differs only in degree. If firestorms are indeed the rule rather than the exception, as seems likely in view of the huge quantities of flammable material that exist in all cities, we can expect the survivors of a direct hit by a thermonuclear bomb to be few in number. Civil defense preparations in our major metropolitan areas would appear, under the circumstances, to make sense only if we were willing to rebuild those areas to provide for deep, extensive, and sealed underground quarters. An alternative would be to provide for rapid mass evacuation to the countryside, where shelters need only protect against the fallout. But the time for such evacuation following warning of an impending attack by missiles would be so short that the technological problems involved in moving the people would appear to be considerably greater than those involved in providing deep underground shelters.

In any event, it is evident that individual metropolitan areas are extremely vulnerable to thermonuclear attack. It is also clear that any program designed to decrease the vulnerability of these areas would be difficult to put into effect and extremely expensive. Rationally, were we to make vigorous efforts to survive a large-scale nuclear war, we would forget about our existing cities, reconcile ourselves to the loss of their inhabitants, and concentrate our efforts in other areas.

Twenty Thousand Megatons on the United States

It is not possible to predict with any accuracy what the physical and biological effects of an all-out nuclear war upon the United States would be. At one extreme it could result in the total annihilation of our people and our cities. At the other extreme our cities might be spared, and deaths might be relatively few. All gradations in between are possible. The actual effects would depend upon a multiplicity of factors including the time at which the war starts, the nature of the weapons systems then in effect, and the nature of defenses.

Were the United States to become involved in a thermonuclear war today, the primary targets would probably be the Air Force bases from which we might retaliate, together with certain other military installations. Assuming that the Soviet missiles were guided with reasonable accuracy, these bases could be destroyed quickly with a relatively small number of bombs. Under the circumstances, threats of massive retaliation could be carried out only by those of our planes and missiles that were in the air at the time of attack—conceivably a very small number. With our bases destroyed we would be helpless. The Soviet Union could threaten to destroy our cities unless we capitulated. Thus, the war would be over without the loss of any of our major cities. The lives lost would be those involved with our military installations here and abroad and in adjacent cities and towns where fallout could claim many victims.

In the continental United States about 130 Air Force and other military installations might be the targets of such an attack, and perhaps 500 to 1000 metagons would be dropped. Optimistically, as few as 10 million deaths would result were the attack to take place today. More likely, there would be about 20 million deaths, largely because of the proximity of many important Air Force and other military installations to population centers.

Thus, any thermonuclear attack upon the United States that would make sense from a military point of view would involve a minimum of something over 100 delivered bombs totaling about 500 or more megatons in energy. There are good reasons to suppose that an actual attack would be considerably larger than this. It is difficult to imagine the emergence of a situation other than accident that would result in a smaller attack. A major decrease in the number of key military installations in the continental United States could bring about such a situation, but in spite of the development of the Polaris submarine there is little evidence that this will happen. Let us focus our attention, then, upon attacks larger than 500 megatons.

In 1959 the Special Subcommittee on Radiation of the Joint Congressional Committee on Atomic Energy attempted to provide a picture of the effect upon the United States of a 1500-megaton attack—about three times larger than the "minimum" attack described above. The Committee took testimony from a number of experts concerning the effects of a simultaneous attack upon 224 centers, about half of them military. The data presented indicated that were the attack to take place today nearly

25 million deaths could be expected the first day and an additional 25 million persons would be fatally injured. An additional 20 million persons would be injured, but not fatally. Nearly 75 per cent of the deaths would have resulted from the immediate effects of the explosions and 25 per cent would have resulted from fallout. More than half of the surviving injured would have suffered radiation injuries.

It should be emphasized, however, that these estimates of casualties are minimal, for they include only the estimates of casualties resulting from blast, direct thermal effects, and radiation. The estimates do not include casualties resulting from such secondary effects as the disorganization of society, a disruption of communications, massive fires, extinction of livestock, spread of disease, genetic damage, or the ingestion of radioactive materials.

In the attack visualized, about 12 million dwellings would have suffered blast damage to the extent that they would not be salvageable. An additional 9 million dwellings would have suffered some blast damage. Almost half the dwellings in the United States would have been either severely damaged or contaminated by fallout to the extent that they would not be usable for at least several months after the attack. Estimates were not given for secondary fire damage to structures. This could exceed by a considerable margin the damage resulting from blast.

Thus we could expect that a 1500-megaton attack, were it to take place today, would result in the death or injury of at least one-third of our population. It has been pointed out that with the provision of appropriate shelter protection the number of casualties could be greatly reduced. At the same time we must recognize that attacks considerably larger than 1500 megatons are technically feasible. Indeed, in our present state of unpreparedness for a thermonuclear war, it is possible, in principle, for an enemy virtually to annihilate our population. One may argue legitimately whether the annihilation of our population would serve any useful purpose to any enemy. But the fact that it is possible in principle for another power to achieve such a result warrants a discussion of the possibility.

Were it not for the fact that a substantial fraction of our

country is, at all times, covered with clouds, an enemy could completely scorch our earth by exploding about 600 ten-megaton bombs, evenly spaced, at an altitude of about thirty miles. On a clear day forests, grasslands, and crops would ignite or wither, as would the flammable structure of the cities, towns, and villages. All exposed living creatures, except those living in the water, would perish. A substantial fraction of the human beings who were protected from the initial thermal flash would perish in the resultant thermal holocaust. Others would perish as the result of such secondary effects of the catastrophe as lack of food and adequate medical care.

Fortunately at any one time clouds protect about 50 per cent of the nation, but such a technique could readily be applied to the clear areas. The cloud situation at any given time could be determined by observation from satellites of the Tiros type. Missile guidance could be relatively crude—errors of ten miles could be easily tolerated.

An attempt to annihilate the population with fallout would require more explosive per unit area than would the thermal approach, but in the absence of protective shelters the quantities involved would by no means be prohibitive. In our present unprepared state a 20,000-megaton attack using bombs with a two-thirds fission yield designed to maximize deaths would result in the death from fallout within sixty days after the attack of virtually everyone who had survived the initial effects of blast and heat.

It seems likely that in our present state we could be destroyed as a nation, unable to recover, by an attack considerably less than 20,000 megatons. We do not know the maximum damage that could be tolerated by the United States and that would permit the survivors to rebuild the economy. However, one can conceive of an attack, considering all major direct and indirect effects, which would result in virtual annihilation of our people, cities, villages, forests, and farmlands. Such an attack would consist of a suitable mixture of bombs exploded at high altitude to make maximum use of thermal effects (2,000 to 3,000 mt), of surface bursts designed to destroy military bases and the major urban centers (1,500 to 3,000 mt), and bombs exploded to maximize the effect of fallout in areas which are not damaged by the explosions of the first two categories (1,500 to 4,000 mt).

It seems likely that we have reached, or will soon reach, the point where an attack of this size could be mounted against us from the point of view of the nuclear explosives required. It is improbable that systems for the efficient delivery of such quantities of explosives will be available in the very near future, but the revolution in delivery systems may well bring the Soviet Union to that point in a few years.

Deterrence and Stability

The United States is at present apparently committed to a policy of not striking the first blow in an all-out nuclear war. Even were this not our strong moral position, in the situation toward which we are heading it would be a strong practical position. It is doubtful that we will know accurately the geographic locations of most Soviet ICBM sites. Were the United States, in a first strike, to destroy only a fraction of the Soviet missile bases, those remaining could be launched to create a devastating retaliatory attack.

It is widely recognized that the Soviet Union could have an enormous advantage in launching a first strike against the United States. Committed as she is to a policy of not striking first, the United States has attempted to build up a deterrent force, or second-strike capability, which is aimed primarily at the large cities and industrial complexes of the Soviet Union. In theory, so long as the Soviet leaders believe that the major Russian cities would be utterly destroyed in the event of a strike against the United States, they would not dare launch the attack.

In the days when both the U.S. and the U.S.S.R. relied upon delivery by airplanes, when warning times were relatively long, threats of massive retaliation from our SAC bases could be believable to the Russians and, depending upon the amount of damage the Soviet leaders were willing to sustain, could be effective. But the rapid upsurge in Soviet missile capabilities is creating a situation in which the threat of massive reprisal by the U.S. is rapidly losing credence.

The mainstay of our retaliatory force has consisted of strategic bombers located at SAC bases in various parts of the world. With the arrival of the missile age, in which warning times are short, those bases are quickly becoming extremely vulnerable to attack. The United States is being forced to consider extreme stop-gap measures, such as the airborne alert, to protect its manned bomber capability. It is also engaging in crash programs designed to narrow the deterrent gap. Atlas and Titan intercontinental ballistic missiles are being built to be fired from hardened bases within our borders. The Polaris system, in which missiles are fired from long-range nuclear-powered submarines, is being urgently developed.

It would appear that the United States is entering a period of several years during which our strategic force will not in itself be the primary deterrent to a first strike by the Soviet Union. During this period, if war does not break out, factors other than relative deterrence capabilities will have played major roles in its prevention. These factors may range from the strong desires of the leaders of both East and West for peace to a conviction on the part of Soviet leaders that the U.S.S.R. can attain its political and economic objectives without recourse to violence.

If we pass through the current critical period without war, then the fulfillment of our current major goals, coupled with Soviet reactions to our actions, will probably give rise to a situation in which both the Soviet Union and the United States possess powerful and invulnerable retaliatory missile forces. Some of these will be of the Polaris type. Others will be mobile and land-based. Still others will be underground in fixed locations.

A number of knowledgeable persons are looking forward to the establishment of such systems. When neither nation can destroy the other's retaliatory force in a first strike, it is believed that there will be no first strike. Such a system is often looked upon as being a "stable" one—as distinct from the situation in which we are now involved.

In view of the fact that the combination of technology and international politics is leading us rapidly to the development of relatively invulnerable retaliatory systems, it is important that we examine factors which affect their stability. Can they really be stable? If they can, then in effect technology will have eliminated large-scale war from the world scene. Or is such a system basically unstable? If it is, and if we follow this path to its end, it is likely that we will perish.

* * *

Defense and Recovery in a Thermonuclear War

. . . If war indeed approaches the inevitable, we should inquire into means for minimizing its impact upon us. Can we defend ourselves? Can we recover?

In connection with our military position, it is clear that an offense has enormous advantage over even the most active defense. Undoubtedly in the years ahead there will be considerable progress in the development of anti-missile missiles. But it is doubtful that we will ever be able to destroy more than a small fraction of the missiles headed toward our military installations and cities.

An obvious defense measure would be to attempt to protect the people and their cities from the effects of nuclear weapons. Relatively simple shelters, it is alleged, can protect people outside the areas of blast from the effects of fallout. Very deep and elaborate underground shelters can protect people from the primary and secondary thermal effects. Relatively primitive underground storage shelters can protect stocks of food, equipment, and raw materials.

We saw in an earlier section that a 1,500-megaton attack upon the United States today would result in about 60 million casualties. The installation of fallout shelters in the areas outside the major cities would decrease the number of immediate casualties considerably. Installation of shelters to protect against blast and thermal effects might decrease the casualties to about 5 million.

Were all business activities (except farming) and all residences moved very deeply underground, casualties could be reduced dramatically.

It is difficult to estimate the extent of the damage and the number of casualties which we could support in the United States and still recover from the effects of the blow. A great deal would depend upon the extent of the preparations which had been made. A great deal would depend upon the true vulnerability of modern industrial society to disruption.

The Soviet Union lost about 20 million persons (about 10 per cent of her population) during World War II and recovered rapidly—but the losses were sustained over a period of several years. Kahn has estimated that with rather modest preparations we could sustain a sudden loss of at least 20 million persons and rebuild our economy in about ten years. This estimate makes some assumptions concerning the vulnerability of the industrial-economic organism which may not be true. It assumes, for example, that the major metropolitan areas and the areas of lower population density are relatively independent of each other and that the economy could be rebuilt by the latter were the former totally destroyed. It assumes that people will behave rationally following the attack. It ignores the effect of shock. It minimizes the sensitivity to disruption of the complex network of mines, farms, factories, distribution centers, transportation facilities, and communication systems.

The question of whether or not a nation can recover from a nuclear attack of a given magnitude cannot be answered easily, for it involves a multiplicity of interlocking factors, some physical and others human. One can debate the question endlessly, and in the long run one would not know for certain until the great test was made.

In the light of our best estimates of current Soviet offensive capabilities, were an all-out attack to be made upon us today, recovery *might* be possible. Again, this question is debatable. Were the attack to take place in another five years, and were we to make no preparations, recovery would be extremely dubious. Presumably preparation could expedite recovery from such an attack. For this reason we can expect great emphasis to be placed during the next few years on programs aimed at decreasing the vulnerability of our population and expediting post-attack recovery. The next phase of the "arms race" will almost certainly involve great emphasis upon the area of civilian defense.

How To Survive a Nuclear Attack

EDWARD TELLER and ALLEN BROWN

THE UNITED STATES TODAY IS NOT PROPERLY DEFENDED. We literally invite attack because our potential enemies know that the United States today could not survive a big thermonuclear attack. We have not made a serious attempt to save ourselves. We have spent less than one tenth of one cent from each tax dollar for civilian defense. Our danger is real, but we refuse to do much about it. We adopt the same fatalistic outlook as the last survivors in Nevil Shute's book [On the Beach].

The irrational refusal of the majority of our people to plan and act for their own survival is due to their unwillingness to face the terrifying prospect of an all-out nuclear war. They would rather not think about it. They have, in fact, declared that such a holocaust is "unthinkable." Quite the opposite is true. If the United States remains undefended and incapable of surviving a sudden attack, the prospect of an all-out nuclear attack not only is thinkable, it is more than possible.

Two defeatist arguments have convinced the majority of Americans that civilian defense is futile. Even if some of our people managed to survive a sudden attack, according to one argument, the world after a nuclear war would not be fit for humans: The atmosphere would be poisoned for years; food could not be eaten safely; our factories would be destroyed; there would be no creature comforts; unlucky survivors of a nuclear attack would die of starvation, loneliness, or sorrow. Another argument, because of its simplicity and frequent and skillful repetition, has been accepted widely. This argument holds that survival simply is impossible, that rapid development of nuclear weapons will make today's civilian defense preparations inadequate for tomorrow, that our adversaries can and will devise bombs to destroy any civilian defense shelters we can build.

No prophecy about a future war can be completely reliable. But this much is certain: Properly defended, we can survive a nuclear attack; we can dig out of the ruins; we can recover from the catastrophe. The shelters we need for our defense, properly constructed, will not be made obsolete by the development of new weapons. The strength of nuclear weapons since Hiroshima has increased a thousandfold. The increase of shelter depth required to withstand a direct hit by these bigger weapons has been less than tenfold.

As a nation, we shall survive, and our democratic ideals and institutions will survive with us, if we make adequate preparations for survival now—and adequate preparations are within our reach and our capabilities.

Mere survival, however, is not the only compelling reason for civilian defense. There is another reason that is even more important: Peace. If we are adequately prepared, if we cannot be defeated even by the most sudden and savage attack, then the main motivation for a nuclear attack upon our nation will have vanished.

Our Communist enemies are determined and dangerous. But they are not irrational nor foolish nor inclined to adventure. They are dedicated to the single goal of world domination. They certainly would prefer to achieve this goal without the horrors of an all-out thermonuclear war. There are, I believe, only two circumstances at all likely to prompt the Communists to mount an all-out nuclear attack against the United States. They will do it in self-defense, and they might do it if they were firmly convinced that only with these terrible means could they achieve their end-goal of world domination.

The policy of the United States, established and frequently alluded to, is that we never will deliberately provoke a nuclear world war by striking the first blow. Because of this policy, the Communists know they never will need to strike us in self-defense. But as long as the United States is unprepared to absorb and survive an all-out attack, the Communists have a temptation that might prove irresistible: A quick and easy nuclear victory over the nation most effectively thwarting their aspirations for world domination. If we are prepared for an all-out nuclear war, if we know we can survive the most vicious and widespread nuclear attack, if we guarantee our ability to rebuild our industrial complex after an attack, then the only valid reasons for a Communist attack upon our nation will have been removed. If we prepare, this disaster will never come.

A civilian defense system protecting people all across our nation obviously will be a tremendous undertaking, but it must be undertaken. The task looms larger because so little has been done. We literally must start from scratch, because this peaceful, nonaggressive guarantor of peace has been neglected for so long. The United States today has no comprehensive plan for civil defense, let alone adequate structures for civil defense. But at least the general outlines are clear, and we know that a plan can be written and a civilian defense complex can be built.

What must be done?

An adequate defense demands that we have early warning of attack, shelters, organization, clean-up equipment, and a plan for reconstruction.

Before we can begin to save ourselves from attack, we must know that an attack is coming. We must have as much warning as possible because our chances of survival would be measured in minutes. A rocket's travel time from a launching pad in Russia to a target in the United States would be only about twenty minutes. Fired from a Russian submarine, a rocket could strike a target in the United States in even less time. Without a fast and accurate warning system, an enemy rocket could obliterate a large American city and its unsuspecting residents even before we knew we were being attacked.

The United States, fortunately, has established a complex and effective warning system. We have developed and are refining ways of detecting launchings from any part of the world as soon as the rockets rise into the air. Even more warning of an attack would save millions of lives, and more warning might be possible. The urgent need for the earliest possible warning of attack is one reason why observations of the whole world and all of the earth's activities—an "Open Sky" inspection from airplanes or satellites—have become so vital to our security. We have not yet attained an "Open Sky" inspection, but we have achieved a warning system that will tell us we are being attacked the moment rockets start to fly. So we can depend upon at least a little warning, and the short time we might have to save ourselves probably will not be shortened appreciably in the future because it would be exceedingly expensive to make rockets fly faster.

One of the most essential steps we must take is the establishment of reliable communications that would survive any attack. These communications should be used to warn our people of impending danger and to direct our essential post-attack efforts to save human lives and to recover from the blow.

In a sudden nuclear attack upon our nation, there can be no doubt that millions of Americans would die. But even the brief warning we would have if such an attack came tomorrow would be enough to save perhaps ninety per cent of our people—if they knew what to do in case of attack and had the means to protect themselves. The present warning system would alert our military establishment, but it would not save the majority of our people because they are uninformed about civilian defense methods and unprepared for survival. If we continue to neglect civilian defense, a nuclear attack on the United States could kill well over

100 million people. And the fate of the survivors would be no better than that of those who had perished.

In order to ensure ourselves against the horrors of such an attack by being thoroughly prepared for it, our people must be sheltered, organized, and educated.

Our most urgent need is a nationwide system of public and private shelters. To protect people in all sections of our nation from the expected and probable, a national program of shelter construction should be given at least as high a priority as any other project in our over-all defense effort. Detailed studies and plans are necessary. People in various sections of our nation will require different degrees of shelter protection.

Perhaps two thirds of our people live in the uncongested areas of our nation. Far from prime targets, people in these areas can be protected more easily. They probably would not be subjected to the blast of a direct nuclear attack. They might, however, be endangered by radioactive fallout of a very great intensity; after an attack, clouds of radioactive poisons could be expected to sweep over large portions of our country. They might also be exposed to conflagrations due to high-altitude explosions of the biggest nuclear weapons or carried to their neighborhoods by the winds.

Survival of people outside our cities would be favored by some circumstances: Time would be required for fallout to float downwind from the actual point of attack. In addition to the initial twenty-minute warning of an impending attack, these people could count on another half-hour, one hour, or even more time after attack before they would be endangered by fallout. This would give most residents time to protect themselves.

Effects of fallout often can be decreased simply by going indoors or taking shelter in a conventional basement. Protection almost always is sufficient in a fallout shelter built with thick but not necessarily strong walls and equipped with a filtered air system or properly designed ventilation. A reasonable measure of protection, in some rural areas, can be offered by simple shelters for individual families. These might resemble the storm cellars already built as tornado protection by many families in our Central Plains states. Or rural families could build simple and adequate shelters by piling sandbags around the walls of a small building. The best protection, however, would be in community shelters. All the people in a small town probably would have time to reach a community shelter specifically designed to protect against fallout. Community shelters would offer greater protection at a lower total cost than a number of individual family shelters. And, because fallout might continue to be dangerous for some time, it would be best for entire communities to plan together.

Even though blast would not be a danger in these areas, fire damage is a real threat. This argues for construction of shelters that could survive a conflagration. It would be a further advantage if the shelters contained their own air supply. In many cases, it would be simpler to build the shelter in a location that would not easily be reached by fire.

In cities and prime target areas, the problem of providing adequate protection is much more difficult. People in our urban and suburban areas, like those in our rural sections, must be protected against fallout and radiation. But the people in and near our cities also require protection against nuclear blast and the even greater danger following the blast: Fire.

Civilian defense shelters in metropolitan areas and near important targets must be shock resistant. They should be surrounded with loose material that would dissipate the shock of a nuclear blast, and the shelters themselves should be rigid enough to withstand the shock penetrating the surrounding cushion. Dirt is an excellent shock cushion, and the most effective shelters will be built underground. These need not be deep. People in well-constructed shelters only ten to twenty feet below ground would have reasonable protection from a thermonuclear bomb exploding only one mile away. In shelters 100 to 200 feet below the ground's surface, there would be greater safety. In a thermonuclear attack we cannot ask for complete assurances. But we can and should save most people.

Effective protection against fallout, shock waves, and fire produced by a nuclear attack upon a metropolitan area also can be provided above ground. Our skyscrapers could be built around a windowless, rigid core of concrete made sturdy enough to withstand a blast's shock after it had been dissipated by the offices and corridors in the building's outer structure. These concrete cores would offer substantial protection. And they would be readily accessible to people in the most congested parts of our metropolitan areas.

People in cities will have only a brief warning of an impending attack. Therefore, every worker and every resident of every large city in our nation should be able to reach protection in a five-minute walk. Sturdy shelters should be built to accommodate everyone living or working within a quarter-mile radius of the shelter site.

It is important to realize that not all of the dangerous effects would be generated by each exploding nuclear bomb. Conflagrations over the widest areas could be kindled by very high altitude explosions which create no fallout hazard and which may not cause great shock damage. Air bursts of moderate height produce the widest damage through air shock, but would not damage well-constructed underground shelters and would not be likely to create concentrated fallout. The explosion producing really dangerous fallout would be a ground burst. This explosion also would cause ground shock and could damage underground shelters in the vicinity. But the air blast and the fires resulting from such explosions would cover smaller areas. In constructing shelters, it is important to assess which of these possibilities is the most likely.

Even in target areas, mass shelters can be built offering a real chance of survival for $200 a person. On a national scale, an adequate shelter construction program would cost about twenty billion dollars. This sounds prohibitive. It is not. It is about half of our annual defense budget, and as a necessary insurance against nuclear attack, the cost of adequate shelter protection is cheap.

The price of survival actually might be considerably less than twenty billion dollars because there is no reason for shelters to remain unused except in case of attack. Shelters can be built for more than one purpose. They can be designed and equipped to provide protection if protection is needed, but they also can have other functions.

It would be particularly important to build adequate shelters in our schools. It might even be advisable to contemplate building the schools themselves, with modern lighting and air conditioning, underground. On the surface above the underground school, children could have a really adequate outdoor playground. The underground school, of course, would be constructed and equipped as a mass shelter. There would be no problem of getting the children from classroom to shelter after an alert, and we would be reassured by the fact that our children were given the greatest safety. The cost of this shelter would be reduced by the amount of money that would have been spent on a conventional school.

Dozens of other kinds of buildings, similarly, could be constructed underground and serve dual purposes as housing for normal functions and as community shelters. We could make mass shelters of underground theaters and auditoriums, supermarkets, parking garages, warehouses, hospitals, or any other kind of structure that will accommodate many people. Concrete cores of office buildings, likewise, could be more than shelters. They could be garages, easing congestion in the hearts of our large cities. Garage cores have been built in office buildings in our country, and they have been found to be practical and convenient. Office tenants of the Redick Tower in Omaha, Nebraska, and the Cafritz Building in Washington, D. C., can drive into their buildings and park on the same floor occupied by their offices. These are examples of garage cores; to be shelter cores as well, they need only more sturdy construction. Our cities are the great American repositories of culture. In our cities are the large museums, the most valuable collections of paintings and sculptures, the great libraries of books, the best examples of our cultural heritage. Many of these same cities would be targets for a nuclear attack, and such an attack probably would destroy these cultural achievements of man. I would propose that our museums and libraries be built underground and equipped as community shelters. In case of attack, such shelters would save many lives while preserving some of the chief reasons for living.

Multipurpose shelters may reduce the cost of this phase of civilian defense. But even at a reduced cost, the question must be asked: Who will pay for it?

I don't know the answer to this question. The main concern is that an answer be found soon. The full bill, certainly, would not come due in any one year. Three to four years probably would be required to build the kind of national shelter network we so urgently need. The costs might be paid by the federal, state, or local governments—or shared by all three. It surely would be improper for any new federal or local government buildings—post offices, schools, courthouses, office buildings—to be built without shelters. Much can be done to encourage private individuals and businesses to build shelters. The builders of new warehouses, bowling alleys, theaters, parking garages, or supermarkets might find it to their advantage to build underground if the government offered appropriate subsidies. Real-estate tax exemptions might prove strong incentives for shelter construction. Shelter needs differ from place to place; so while all shelters should be a part of a national plan, details could be settled advantageously on local levels—by states, counties, cities, private individuals, and companies.

If we are attacked, heavy radioactive contamination of the ground and atmosphere may force people to remain in their shelters for days and possibly for weeks. Each shelter should be stocked with enough food, water, and medical supplies to meet the needs of the shelter's occupants for two weeks. It should be a very great help to have a filter system to remove radioactivity from air brought in from the outside, to have enough oxygen to provide an independent air supply for several hours—long enough to last through the fire storm—and to have chemicals which absorb the carbon dioxide exhaled by the occupants. Each shelter should also be equipped with an independent source of power to operate the air filter and to maintain radio communications with other shelters and with civilian defense headquarters. And, finally, each shelter should have a store of water and chemicals for hygiene; urban shelters should be constructed with several exits and stocked with dig-out equipment so their occupants would not be trapped by an explosion's debris.

A few days after an attack, people as a rule will be able to emerge from their shelters for limited times in limited places. Or they may have to remain in their shelters as long as two weeks. Shelters may have to serve as living quarters for months after an attack. Most buildings would be destroyed by an attack, and in many regions of our nation some radiation would remain, and time spent in these areas would have to be limited.

Shelters and equipment will not be enough for survival. We must have organization. All of our people should participate in a civilian defense training program. This is of the greatest importance. Every citizen must understand and practice civilian defense.

Either a limited or an all-out nuclear war would require the services of only highly trained, professional soldiers. General mobilization of manpower would be ineffective, unnecessary, and impossible. Instead of being available for conscription into the Armed Forces, our people should be drafted into civilian defense organizations. All should be trained in civilian defense fundamentals: All must know how and where to seek shelter. Once inside a shelter, our people must know how to organize for the safety of the group. They must be trained to follow the directions of a shelter leader and a shelter doctor. They must be trained to operate communications and air-filtering equipment. Before they can hope to emerge safely from the shelter, they must know how to measure radioactive contamination, and they must know how to wash it away.

An all-out nuclear attack upon our country would be terrible indeed. I do not believe it will come. But if it should come—and if we are prepared to shelter ourselves from its effects, if we are equipped and organized for survival—even an all-out nuclear attack would be no worse than some of the terrible events of past wars.

Radioactive contamination does not stay in the air over the target of a nuclear attack. It is blown away by the wind. It will pass over a given place in half an hour. Within three days of a nuclear attack upon the United States, airborne radioactivity would be blown away from our entire nation. But this is of little comfort because radioactive poisons, in addition to being blown away, can settle onto the ground.

The amount of radioactivity on the ground after an attack would depend upon the altitude at which the bombs were exploded and upon other factors. The post-attack fire storm, by creating an ascending air mass of considerable velocity, might help to keep the ground surface of a target area relatively clean of radioactivity.

But in planning our defense, we must assume that a nuclear attack would leave a good deal of radioactivity on the ground. A thermonuclear explosion would leave a city in rubble, and all or much of that rubble might be radioactive.

In urban areas this radioactive rubble could pose an additional threat to the survival of people who had been sheltered against the initial blast and the terrifying fire storm. In two weeks the radioactivity would have decayed to a level low enough to allow people to come out of their shelters and, in appropriate locations, resume work above ground. In the exceptional cases of very high radioactivity, bulldozers could be brought in and used to clean up essential areas or escape routes by pushing debris and topsoil aside. Radiation, in any case, will decay a little faster than the inverse proportion to the time passed. After one day, only three per cent as much radiation will remain on the ground as was there an hour after the explosion. After a week, the amount of radiation on the ground will be ten times less. After two months, the activity will be ten times less again.

We can save most of our people, and the survivors soon could turn to the problems of the new days to come. They must know what to do and how to do it.

While the majority of our people can be saved from an all-out nuclear assault, we cannot hope to save most of our goods or the factories that manufacture our goods. In an all-out attack, our industrial complex probably would be effectively destroyed. It can be rebuilt if we provide for its reconstruction. But it cannot be rebuilt and survivors of a nuclear attack will be without support and may face starvation if they have to start the task of reconstruction from scratch with no better tools than their bare fingers.

Much of the strength of our industrial society, fortunately, is not in our industrial plant. Our factories are expendable. Our strength is in our know-how and in our organization. Our gross national product, the value of everything manufactured or mined or produced in the United States, now is more than 500 billion dollars a year. But the total value of everything that exists in the country—all the houses, clothes, food, factories, minerals, farms, services, cars, everything that can be bought or sold—is only about 1500 billion dollars. Everything we have, in other words, could be produced by our present industrial complex in only about three years. This means our present standard of living is extremely high and our rate of consumption is prodigious. This also means that survivors of an all-out nuclear attack, given food and a bare minimum of essential tools, could rebuild our industrial complex in a very short time. Even if our industrial plant were totally destroyed in an all-out attack, properly fed and equipped survivors living in austerity and working with complete dedication could rebuild our industrial plant to its pre-attack productive capacity within five years.

Just as we need to plan the construction of shelters to protect our people, we should begin a searching and exhaustive study of the things those people would need to survive after an attack and to rebuild our economy. We should plan and provide for our economic survival as well as for our personal survival. A thorough study must precede a complete plan for economic survival, but some potential needs already are obvious.

Survivors would need food. Shelters, hopefully, would be stocked with enough food to sustain people for two weeks after an all-out attack. This would feed them during their confinement in the shelters, but more food must be easily available after they emerge. Fortunately, we have a solution at hand. We have a national treasure that is considered an embarrassing pol-

bleak and cheerless, and life's prospect would be the necessity of rebuilding our productive capacity before stored supplies of food were dissipated.

In such a world, people would have to live and work according to a plan. Teamwork would be essential. The pressing goal and aim of our people would be group effort and survival.

If we wait until we are attacked to plan our postwar organization, there is a very real danger that we might lose our individual liberties and freedoms permanently. The postwar society will need rigid organization for its own survival, and rigid organization usually leads to tyranny.

If, on the other hand, we plan a postwar organization before we are attacked, our liberties can survive.

When young men and women join the Armed Forces today, they lose many of their rights as individuals. They must subject themselves to a rigid discipline. But they know that this discipline is only temporary. They know that when they leave the Armed Forces, their full rights will be restored.

It is this kind of postwar organization we must plan now. We must anticipate a strict state of emergency, but we must limit it to the time of the emergency. We must understand that during the critical five years after attack, when the needs of the group and of the nation are paramount, the individual will have to make great sacrifices. But we must guarantee that after the emergency has passed, after our economy has been rebuilt, our way of life, our right to the pursuit of happiness, will be restored.

We should define the necessary emergency measures while we can do so rationally and in freedom. In this way, we can be sure that the emergency measures will be properly limited.

Our almost total lack of civil defense is the weakest link in our national security, and so it is the greatest danger to peace. In an area where so much needs to be done and so much should be done, we have done practically nothing. Russia, on the other hand, has done much.

Our Office of Civil and Defense Mobilization says: "Official Soviet interest in new shelter construction has been apparent since about 1950. New building construction in some Soviet cities is known to include shelter as a matter of routine. . . . The impression is gathered that the inclusion of protective construction features in new buildings is a standard practice in many centers of population and industry, and that basement shelter of some kind already is available to an important segment of the population of urban areas of the USSR." The average adult Russian is given about sixty-four hours of civil defense training each year. The Soviet government has distributed plans for "hasty shelters" that can be erected to protect Russian families against fallout within twenty-four hours after warning of an attack. An estimated fifty million Russians participate in some phase of the Soviet Union's civil defense program; the United States has only 2000 professional civilian defense workers, and private citizens now are given almost no training.

Even though Russia is struggling to build her economy, even though it is more painful for the Soviet Union to spend money for civilian defense, Russia has spent much more than the United States on shelters and on an effective civilian defense organization. Unless we change, unless we spend vastly greater amounts, it is likely that Russia would survive an all-out nuclear war and we would not.

It is useful to compare the economies of Russia and the United States. We are fat and Russia is lean. In a conflict, to be lean is an advantage. But our wealth can enable us to put things aside for a dreadful rainy day, helping to ensure that we will never meet the lean ones in conflict. To stockpile food and machinery for survival is incomparably easier for us than it is for Russia. We have surpluses. Russia does not.

Judicious stockpiling in the United States during the next few years would make it completely clear to the Communist nations that we could recover faster and more effectively after an all-out nuclear war than could Russia.

I believe that the Soviet Union is not anxious to participate in an all-out nuclear war for an important economic reason. The Russian people have made tremendous sacrifices to build up the Soviet industrial plant. Russians are proud of their new factories and of their new products, and they do not want to lose them. Those factories and those products are important Russian assets in their fight for world domination. With adequate civil defense preparation and organization, we can assure ourselves and the world that after an all-out war the United States would be able to re-establish economic strength sooner than Russia— and so the United States would remain by far the strongest nation in the world. Thus every trace of motivation for Communist attack upon our nation would vanish. . . .

Even in case we are attacked, we can survive if we are determined and translate our determination into action. The first and basic objective of any defense is survival. If our individual and national survival is assured, we can proceed with confidence to build all the other bulwarks that are needed to maintain peace.

VII THE CONTROL OF FORCE: ARMS CONTROL

The Nth Country Problem and Arms Control

ACUTE FEARS HAVE BESET US SINCE THE INTRODUCTION OF NUCLEAR WEAPONS OF MASS DESTRUCTION. But we have occasionally found some comfort in the thought that peace might be assured by a "balance of terror": that, while nuclear weapons are confined to just a few great nations with an enormous stake in the planet's land and people, an all-out nuclear war is unlikely. This balance is an uneasy one, involving many complicated factors and it impels a continuing race for new offensive and defensive armaments.

Equilibrium and Nuclear Weapons Distribution

. . . The production of both atomic and hydrogen weapons by Great Britain, the more recent development by France of atomic weaponry (which will soon be demonstrated by a test explosion), and the rumors of nuclear weapons research in Communist China raise disquieting doubts about the validity of the "balance of terror" formula. Atomic weapons may eventually become so widely diffused that there will be no equilibrium or symmetry in their distribution. Among their owners may someday be rulers —and perhaps even ex-rulers—who have no major stake in world stability. Indeed, it has even been suggested that eventually atomic weapons, like other powerful armaments, might find their way into the international open market, or that they might fall into the hands of outlaws and revolutionaries.

This is a problem which has caused considerable concern for some time. It was referred to in our earlier report, *1970 Without Arms Control,* and in recent months it has been the subject of considerable discussion in the United States and abroad.

* * *

. . . many nations are capable of creating an atomic weapon without outside assistance. But . . . no encouragement [is offered] to those who think that such a program can be undertaken without facing difficult obstacles and high costs. And the cost of the warhead represents only a small part of the cost of maintaining the deterrent.

It is as easy to overestimate the rapidity of the spread of nuclear weapons as it is to underestimate it. The difficulties and delays faced in the French atomic weapons program demonstrate concretely that a nuclear weapons capability is not easily arrived at. After the first working models have been produced, many hurdles remain. Even the testing of weapons presents problems: France has received strong protests from nations neighboring her test site and from the United Nations General Assembly, which called on France, by a vote of 51 to 16, to cancel her proposed tests in the Sahara.

Deep fear of the imminent spread of independent nuclear capability has on some occasions been accompanied by an emotional zeal to wash the problem away by dramatic gestures. Perhaps as a reaction to the seeming complacency of statesmen, individuals in Britain and elsewhere have urged such desperate measures as unilateral nuclear disarmament. Those who view the problems of mankind in a context larger than their own immediate time and place are entitled to great respect. Their contribution to public discussion of security problems is a valuable counterbalance to an all too prevalent tendency unthinkingly to accept outworn concepts. However, the lessons of recent history warn that, within the realities of the moment, it is possible that such counsels may lead, not toward peace, but toward war. It is arguable that World War I, would not have been started if the attitude of the allied powers, particularly America, had been clear from the outset; that Hitler would never have embarked on his infamous adventures if he had been aware of America's deep commitment to European security; and that the North Koreans would not have invaded South Korea if they had correctly understood the concern of the United States with the integrity of the Republic of Korea. Further, it is the nature of world politics today that those urging unilateral disarmament can speak freely on one side of the world but not on the other. Their right to speak openly is essential to the maintenance of free government. However, in foreign countries which are not accustomed to free and vocal public discussion, reports of these activities might create an impression of division and irresolution, which might well tempt an act of aggression.

But while the immediacy of the dangers of nuclear diffusion is often overestimated, it is obvious that four nuclear powers present different problems than do two nuclear powers. If France could independently produce an atomic bomb at a time when her military and economic power were being subjected to heavy strain, still more countries might also produce one at some time in the future. It is by no means clear how fast events are moving, but it is certain that they inevitably move only in one direction —toward the greater spread of nuclear weapons capability.

Dangers of Diffusion

This committee feels that the prospect of widely scattered nuclear weapons presents a very serious threat to world stability. This scattering was called the "third country problem" in the days before Britain had nuclear power; it was called the "fourth country problem" before France had the bomb within her reach; and it is now safer to call it the "Nth Country problem." It is a challenge which is not receiving the very serious attention it deserves at home or abroad. It is also a possible opportunity—an opportunity to find at least one common concern which might move the nuclear powers of both the East and of the West to achieve some limited agreements for joint action.

Proliferation of nuclear weapons will inject incalculable factors into the equation of international politics. Some countries, under economic or other pressures, may eventually sell atomic weapons. Governments under fanatics or dictators may act rashly. The possibility of accidental or of unauthorized use of atomic weapons will increase. Irresponsible "mischief-making" by one small nation could catalyze a nuclear conflict between larger powers, or might cause pre-existing nonnuclear hostilities to escalate into nuclear hostilities.

The risk of accidental war by the mischievous action of a third party or by the possible mismanagement of tests, war exercises, strategic miscalculation, and the like is further enhanced by the rapid introduction of "quick reaction" systems. These tend to be inflexible, so that full-scale war may grow out of inadvertencies or deliberate mischief. It will become even more difficult to achieve and enforce arms control agreements, and much harder to inspire confidence in their effectiveness.

Since it is hardly reasonable to expect a nation developing nuclear weapons to refrain from testing them, world-wide radio-active contamination is likely to exceed predictions based on projected tests by the present nuclear powers only.

The Nth Country problem derives urgency from the fact that we are approaching the point where it will no longer be possible for the present nuclear powers to control the spread of nuclear weapons. Once a nation has successfully completed an atomic weapons program, it will have nuclear stockpiles which can be stored without appreciable deterioration, which can survive changes of government, and which can be sold, exchanged, or given away.

The period, then, in which the major power blocs have a common opportunity to limit membership in the "atomic club" is, in the long view of history, a very brief one. We are now living in that period, and ten years of it have gone by.

The question of whether to invest or not to invest in nuclear armaments will be debated in many capitals during the years ahead. No aspirant can afford to ignore the grave difficulties and heavy expenses which confront a would be atomic power, nor ignore the fact that a profuse capacity for destruction is not necessarily a source of security. It is certainly clear that atomic weapons projects are not, in the present state of the art, easy for a middle-sized nation to undertake. But standards of rational priorities of economic effort are not always observed, and from the days of the pyramids of Egypt, human needs have been sacrificed to concepts of glory. We cannot predict with assurance what nations will have, and what nations will not have, independent atomic capabilities in the years ahead. . . .

Suggested Solutions to Problems

This committee is agreed that it would be desirable to prevent the wider diffusion of nuclear weapons capability. However, it finds that the problem is an extremely complicated one, since the basic requirements—scientific knowledge, industrial and material resources, as well as technological skills—are already being distributed around the world at a rapid rate. It has considered many possible solutions.

TREATY LIMITATIONS: Some have suggested an international treaty which would limit nuclear weapons to the present "have" nations without embracing other aspects of arms control and international security. This idea was rejected because it was felt that it could easily be evaded and that it would be meaningless in the event of war. Its enforcement would require a high degree of inspection in the nonnuclear countries. Those who are innocent of any nuclear power would naturally resent being inspected more than those who possess atomic weapons.

VOLUNTARY LIMITATION: A suggestion advanced by Ireland's Minister for External Affairs, adopted by the United Nations

Political Committee on November 16, 1959, calls for voluntary measures: Nuclear powers should undertake to refrain from supplying nuclear weapons to states which do not possess them, and nonnuclear nations should undertake to refrain from manufacturing or acquiring such weapons. This, like all pronouncements which are merely declaratory, would operate effectively against open societies but would not operate against closed societies.

INTERNATIONAL CONTROL OF NUCLEAR TESTING: In our Statement, "International Control of Nuclear Testing" (July, 1958), we pointed out that one of the primary values of an agreement to discontinue nuclear tests would be its tendency to curb independent nuclear development by new powers. We stated:

> A prohibition on nuclear tests by itself cannot prove a completely effective control on the spread of nuclear bombs among many nations. . . . A relatively crude bomb could be developed by a determined nation without testing, although it is not likely that any nation would even commit a weapon to use without some testing and/or practice firing by its nationals. Also, certain countries, such as Britain, France, and Sweden, might test at least until agreement is negotiated, although we doubt that they would block agreement.
>
> Thus, other control measures, particularly a control on the production of nuclear materials, will be necessary adequately to prevent the spread of nuclear weapons. Nonetheless, a test prohibition can be one helpful measure, and it is clearly the simplest and most feasible step that can be taken now.

Although not a guarantee of complete certainty, we believe that a test discontinuance agreement would effectively limit the membership of the so-called "atomic club."

AGREEMENT TO CEASE PRODUCTION OF NUCLEAR MATERIALS: International arms control agreement to cease production of nuclear materials would, of course, make possible a far more effective method of preventing the development of nuclear weapons by the nuclear "have nots," because it would install a more thorough type of inspection machinery, which would enable the detection of preparations for weapons manufacture at early stages.

Up to the present time, negotiations for both a production cutoff and a test agreement have been stalled, because of the Soviet Union's refusal to accept the inspection machinery which is required to check on compliance. But it is difficult to conceive that the nonnuclear nations will accept a nuclear inspection system which does not also apply to the nuclear nations.

LIMITATION IN EXCHANGE FOR PROTECTION: It has also been suggested that the have-not nations could be dissuaded from independent development of atomic weapons if the have nations would give them a firm assurance to protect them by the use of their own nuclear weapons. However, a have-not nation may find it difficult to believe that its ally would risk nuclear destruction in its behalf.

LIMITATION OF INDEPENDENT CAPABILITY BY FREER DISTRIBUTION OF WEAPONS: Another suggestion has been that the have nations freely offer nuclear assistance to their allies, under conditions which restrict the availability and use of these weapons. This suggestion is of some value if the problem is to prevent the immediate commencement of research and development programs; however, it obviously is not a bar to the ultimate diffusion of independent weapons capability. It spreads derivative nuclear capability in order to prevent the spread of independent nuclear capability. The reasoning behind the proposal is: They are going to get it anyway, so why not share it in a way that retains some military and legal control in the center of the power bloc?

LIMITATION ENFORCED BY HAVES: Finally, it has been urged that the have nations agree to impose their will by force on the have-not nations, and to introduce a rigid inspection system which would also be imposed by force.

It has also suggested that the three nuclear powers, in giving economic assistance in nuclear power production, should supply reactors on a lease system only, and should reserve to themselves the processing of reactor fuel elements. This would satisfy a demand for electrical power without giving control of fissionable material. A simple inspection process would prevent fuel reprocessing. The penalty for violation would be a joint withdrawal of economic aid by the nuclear powers.

This proposal did not recommend itself to the committee because it was felt that so high-handed a procedure would hardly be an acceptable method of enforcing the peace. It was also felt that since the have powers have had so much difficulty in reaching agreement on far less controversial matters, it was very unlikely that they would work together in so unconventional a project and at the expense of their allies.

Furthermore, with respect to this and other limitation proposals, this committee feels that unless a have-not country is presented with an alternative which will guarantee its security, it cannot be expected to renounce its aspirations to achieve weapons which the have nations already possess. The basic problem is to achieve some method of offering security to a nation which is asked to forego its nuclear potentiality.

Findings and Conclusions

In conclusion the Committee finds:

1) That if present national policies continue, independent nuclear military power will be spread widely among many countries within the next 30 years.

2) That the diffusion of independent nuclear weapons among many countries will, over the years, upset international stability and increase the danger of war.

3) That the spread of nuclear know-how and equipment through international assistance in peaceful economic uses of nuclear power, although useful and praiseworthy, might tend eventually to contribute to the diffusion of military nuclear power.

4) That nuclear military assistance programs providing for the gift and loan of warheads do not directly create independent

nuclear power, but are factors which will tend over the years to contribute to the growth of such independent nuclear power.

The Committee concludes:

1) That the dangers of the wide diffusion of nuclear weapons within the next 30 years are real. Such diffusion may very well vitiate the stability which could conceivably otherwise arise in an era of balanced nuclear forces. These dangers must be considered by both the United States and the Soviet Union in all their negotiations on arms control. Neither side wishes to take substantial risks, but both sides must consider the heavy risks involved in continued inaction.

2) That the nuclear powers could curtail the dangers of perversion of economic aid programs for peaceful uses of nuclear power if they would make greater use of international agencies which impose stringent controls. Both the East and the West could operate through the IAEA without loss of national advantage. This would require no further treaties. If one side embarked upon such a policy and the other did not follow, there would be no loss greater than a slight loss of operating efficiency and of influence on the commercial aspects of reactor operation.

3) That direct control of the spread of independent military nuclear power is possible only in terms of larger disarmament arrangements. The promulgation and enforcement of an effective international accord to cease nuclear tests will tend to prevent the development of nuclear weapons by new countries. More comprehensive agreements—particularly those looking toward controls on production—will provide a more potent inspection system, which could enable control authority to detect evasions with certainty and accuracy.

Summary and Conclusion

The physics of the pure fission bomb is today widely understood by scientists. The legend of the "secret" is totally obsolete. Except for the details of detonation design and isotope separation, scientists may freely obtain all the basic facts they need. For example, most of the physical properties of plutonium—including critical size, and the various fission and neutron capture probabilities—can be derived from the open literature.

The remaining problem for the potential manufacturer of nuclear weapons consists of (1) finding enough skilled scientists and engineers to transform basic physical knowledge into design, and (2) providing the necessary economic and industrial base, as well as the necessary special materials.

Upon detailed consideration of requirements, together with a rough estimate of existing conditions in the major countries of the world, the authors have concluded that the manufacture of a few nominal atomic devices is within the reach of some 10 or more countries. The time required for such an achievement would be on the order of five years. The total capital cost is estimated at about $50 million, and the total yearly operating cost at about $10 to $20 million, so that an expenditure of about $100 million would be required before a single bomb could be produced.

Many countries are developing or purchasing reactors today for the purpose of physical research and the production of electrical power. There is activity in 42 countries, excluding the nuclear weapons powers. In traveling the road to an operational power reactor, a country is simultaneously traveling well over half-way toward an operational plutonium bomb. The only process which separates the reactor stage from plutonium is cooling, followed by chemical processing for the extraction of the plutonium.

Thus, while chemical processing is a tough job, and of no small expense, the general statement that independent development would require five years is certainly quite conservative, since it is based on the assumption that a country would begin with virtually nothing. As a matter of fact, however, Sweden could, by operating her power reactors for plutonium production, produce by 1962 enough unprocessed plutonium for 15 nominal bombs per year. As another example, France, though already committed to a weapons program could increase her yearly plutonium production from 90 kg per year to 300 kg per year in 1962, if she chose to use her electrical power reactors for plutonium production.

Therefore, a more correct description of present capabilities would not only include the fact that 10 or more countries can achieve bomb production within five years, but that operation of existing (or soon to be functioning) electrical power reactors for weapons purposes could make the time of success considerably shorter.

Because the process of independent development is complex and time-consuming, there is little question that a fool-proof system of controls could easily be designed. There are many ways, furthermore, by which this could be done. The general idea is that there exist numerous special "handles" to the problem of control, which make possible the establishment of critical checkpoints. For example, close surveillance of the times of fuel rod removal from reactors will insure that weapons-grade material is not produced—for beyond a certain maximum period in the reactor, the plutonium 239 that is collecting in the fuel elements becomes "poisoned" and hence more difficult to use for weapons purposes. Universal nuclear test cessation would make considerably more difficult the development of reliable nuclear weapons. Controlling the operation of chemical processing plants would be a third way which could insure that weapons are not produced; since chemical processing plants are large and conspicuous, both by virtue of their size and their radioactive waste products, detecting such plants is easy.

Briefly, the big difference between Nth County controls and controls for the present nuclear powers is that in case of the nuclear powers the problem is one of finding existing weapons which are generally small and concealable objects, while in the case of the Nth Countries, the chief problem is one of keeping a check on readily identified industrial programs.

Whether this study may have contributed to the understanding of suggested and possible solutions to the Nth Country problem, it surely has pointed out that the emergence of new nuclear weapons countries is more imminent than would have been supposed; that a minimal weapons program is within reach of more countries than one would expect from the legend of the "great secret"; and finally, that controls of a weapons production program should be a much simpler technical problem compared to the difficulties that exist in controlling stockpiles.

The Technical Requirements

LEONARD BEATON

ANY GOVERNMENT INTENT ON FURNISHING ITS ARMED FORCES WITH NUCLEAR WEAPONS FACES TWO DIFFERENT PROBLEMS: the first is to acquire nuclear bombs or warheads in a form which is light enough, small enough and reliable enough to do the job which might be required of them; and the second is to acquire an effective means of delivering them against the targets which have been chosen for them. The original nuclear programme in the United States in the Second World War was entirely concentrated on the problem of producing explosives. The B–29 bombers then in existence (and the British Lancasters as well) were capable of carrying the proposed bombs if only they could be constructed. On the other hand, American, Soviet and British concern in recent years has been almost entirely directed to delivery problems. It is true that bombs and warheads have been made consistently lighter and smaller; but this has usually been done to allow delivery systems to be made less vulnerable, more accurate and cheaper.

Although the question of delivery systems is, of course, important, the first problem is obviously the diffusion of the capacity to manufacture nuclear explosives themselves. The ability of a country to reach a certain number of targets with a certain weight of weapons will always depend on unknowns like reliabil-

From *Must the Bomb Spread?* Penguin Books, Inc., 1966. Reprinted by permission of Chatto & Windus, Ltd., London. The English edition of this book is entitled *The Spread of Nuclear Weapons*.

ity, previous enemy attack, weather and luck. But to possess fabricated nuclear explosives is a fact which a government can be certain about; and the carrying out of nuclear tests is something which the whole world can observe and from which enemies and friends alike are bound to draw conclusions.

In theory there are several ways of acquiring nuclear explosives. In time, new nuclear powers may use methods which were not understood in the early 1940s. It is already well over a generation since the Americans and British chose their road to nuclear explosives and began to design the necessary industries. It would be surprising if nothing had changed. But this seems to be the case. The French nuclear programme which was laid down between 1954 and 1962 was a repetition without observable change of the steps taken by the original nuclear powers. Costs, too, seem to be at very much the same level and, if anything, French costs were higher than British costs. This situation could change gradually over a period of years, but at present there is no evidence that it will.

The basic problem of nuclear explosives is to acquire a quantity of fissile material of sufficient purity to sustain a chain reaction long enough to produce large quantities of heat. Only one such material exists in nature: the seven parts in a thousand of all natural uranium which is Uranium 235 (the rest is Uranium 238 in which fission is much more difficult to achieve). This U–235 is itself a very important nuclear explosive. It can be used, however, to produce two other fissile materials: Plutonium 239 and Uranium 233. Neither of these is found in nature. Both are the products of reactors which achieve a controlled chain reaction in uranium thanks to the U–235. In such a reactor, some of the U–238 will become plutonium; and if another natural metal, thorium, is introduced into the reactor, some of it will become Uranium 233.

There are thus three materials which will produce a fission explosion: Uranium 235, Plutonium 239 and Uranium 233. For reasons which have not been published, Uranium 233 has not made much appeal to the weapons manufacturers of the original nuclear powers. From all published indications, it would seem that its technology is largely unexplored and that it has no particular theoretical appeal. What has not attracted the Americans is unlikely to attract others. India, it is true, has most of the thorium so far discovered in the world, and some thorium has been irradiated in the Indian atomic energy programme. But, for the moment, it seems reasonable to assume that the development of fission weapons will depend either on Uranium 235 or Plutonium 239.

However, military technology makes extensive use of another nuclear phenomenon besides fission; this is fusion. Instead of employing the heaviest element in nature, uranium, this makes use of the lightest, hydrogen. At very high temperatures, certain kinds of hydrogen (deuterium and tritium) fuse into heavier elements, giving off great quantities of heat. This is the basis of the hydrogen bomb which in its Russian 57 megaton form (the largest yet exploded) is nearly 3,000 times as powerful as the atomic bombs dropped on Hiroshima and Nagasaki. Hydrogen bombs are more commonly designed to yield about one megaton, which is 50 times the power of the 1945 bombs.

To explode a hydrogen bomb, heats of several million degrees centigrade must be produced. No power has yet tried to do this with anything but the explosion of a fission bomb using plutonium or Uranium 235. It remains theoretically possible that the necessary heat might be achieved through some other method; but for the foreseeable future it seems reasonable to assume that this will not be possible for military weapons. The road to hydrogen bombs lies for the present therefore through fission weapons. But there is a steady stream of evidence that in practice H-bombs are generally designed around fission weapons using Uranium 235 and not plutonium. Although thermonuclear explosions are certainly possible in a device based entirely on plutonium, and one French plutonium test probably involved fusion, it has been assumed by both the French and Chinese that a full range of thermonuclear explosives will require Uranium 235. This is presumably a question of practicality, weight, and cost. An official British Government description of fusion weapons published in 1959 referred to a core of fissile Uranium 235, making no mention of plutonium. An informed, though un-official American discussion of the problem finds U-235 a "more suitable material for the construction of a fission trigger for an eventual thermonuclear device, thought both Uranium 235 and Plutonium 239 appear to have been used."

It will be seen that this probable, though not definitive, technical conclusion will have an important influence on the whole question of acquiring fissile material. What is certain is that countries wishing to have a range of sophisticated nuclear weapons will require both Uranium 235 and plutonium. Uranium 235 alone will probably make a fairly unsophisticated range of fission weapons and also H-bombs. Plutonium alone will probably produce a somewhat more flexible range of fission weapons. Over a long period of time, the whole array of weapons which the Americans and Russians have developed must be assumed to be eventual thermonuclear device, though both Uranium 235 and plutonium.

This distinction is important because the industries required to produce Uranium 235 for weapons and plutonium for weapons are quite different. A country deciding to acquire both will have a much heavier financial and technical burden to carry than one which decides to settle for one or the other. The industrial circumstances are also very different, because the production of plutonium is based on a major modern industry—nuclear reactors for the generation of electric power or for the production of heat for such purposes as desalination of sea water. Uranium 235, by contrast, has only been produced by exceedingly expensive and specialized methods which have very little industrial value. The difference between these two materials and the known ways of acquiring them therefore plays a major part in decisions about national nuclear weapons programmes. They must be looked at separately.

Uranium 235

Uranium 235 exists in nature in substantial quantities. Nuclear and thermonuclear weapons can be made by those who can extract this metal and purify it. To those, at least, who have substantial deposits of uranium, this might seem to be a fairly conventional process of mining ore and extracting and purifying the mineral. In fact it is not. There is a great barrier across the road from the possession of uranium to the construction of a uranium nuclear explosive. Technology might remove this barrier, but so far it has shown no sign that it will.

The basic difficulty is that only .7 per cent of natural uranium is Uranium 235. The rest is U-238. Conventional methods will extract natural uranium from uranium ore; but to separate the U-235 from the U-238 is a matter of distinguishing between atoms which have a slightly different weight but are in every other way identical. When this problem was first studied in 1940, it was a novel problem which would obviously make immense demands on the industry of even the most advanced countries. Furthermore, it was by no means clear which of several methods would yield the best results. Some people doubted whether any method would get a high enough proportion of U-235 in sufficient quantity.

The four methods considered then were: 1. electromagnetic separation; 2. liquid thermal diffusion; 3. gas centrifuges; 4. gaseous diffusion. A fifth theoretical possibility, chromotography, has emerged since. The first of these was pressed hard by the United States during the Second World War and yielded a small quantity of virtually pure U-235. But as a means of producing large quantities for a weapons programme it was dropped by the Americans and has so far had little attention elsewhere. Although some recent French work has suggested that its possibilities may have been underestimated, it seems safe for the present to ignore it. The same can be said for liquid thermal diffusion and also, for the present, for chromotography. Any country wanting to acquire U-235 for weapons is unlikely to consider any methods besides gas centrifuges and gaseous diffusion. Both of there are based on the same technique of tranforming uranium to a gaseous form (uranium hexafluoride) and then separating the lighter from the heavier molecules. By repeating the separation process many thousands of times, it is possible gradually to concentrate the

U-235. In a gas centrifuge, this is done by rotating the gas at a very high speed. The heavier atoms tend to concentrate around the periphery. In gaseous diffusion, the gas is pumped up against a wall containing billions of microscopic holes through which the lighter molecules tend to pass more easily.

Although the Americans built a centrifuge as part of their wartime effort, they decided eventually that the basic technology was not sufficiently developed to make it effective. Since then, industrial processes have come a long way. By 1961 work had developed to a point where the United States Government decided to subject all its centrifuge work to rules of secrecy: and it persuaded the West German and Netherlands governments to do the same with the centrifuge development which was going on there. (Work in the field has since apparently ceased in West Germany.) The general position is that the necessary very high speeds are being achieved, but great difficulties have developed about regulating the behaviour of the uranium hexafluoride inside the centrifuges. It is obvious that a great deal of work remains to be done—perhaps about five years' development by a nation of good industrial capacity. Even if such a power pushed centrifuge development, it would still be necessary for it to build several thousand centrifuges at very considerable cost.

Gaseous diffusion therefore still holds the field as the classic method. Apart from some small production in the American wartime programme, it has provided all the weapons-grade uranium ever produced. About eighty-five per cent of all the fissile material in the vast American nuclear weapons programme has come from three gaseous diffusion plants (the other fifteen per cent is plutonium from eleven reactors). The Soviets have two such plants, the British one at Capenhurst and the French are completing one at Pierrelatte. The Chinese also probably have one, though it may not be completed.

Although much useful information about gaseous diffusion has been published in the official American histories, important parts of the technology remain secret. In particular, the means of producing the barrier with the billions of holes through which the gas must pass and the means of sealing the pumps (to standards far higher than any required by industry) must still be found by other countries through expensive development work. Even so advanced a power as France has found gaseous diffusion a great deal more difficult than was supposed when the original estimates for the gaseous diffusion plant were made.

The Americans said in 1945 that their first uranium bomb (the one used on Hiroshima) had cost "about a billion dollars" (£350m.)* The French figures for their gaseous diffusion plant show about the same result, of which more than 40 per cent was apparently research and development costs. Neither the United Kingdom nor the Soviet Union have published figures. It is likely that an inferior industrial power would spend even more and would have to put even larger resources into the effort. Gaseous diffusion remains undoubtedly the most difficult and most demanding industrial process there is. Apart from the heavy first cost, the operation of a plant involves very large quantities of electric power. At their peak, the American gaseous diffusion plants absorbed up to a tenth of all the power being used in the country.

There is no sign of any decrease in the cost of gaseous diffusion. A number of difficulties have been removed by the American decision to publish certain information; but a gaseous diffusion plant remains an exceedingly ambitious project. It is also one which would be very difficult to conceal. The installation must be very large and has a specialized character which would be difficult to hide. The fact that a large supply of electric power must be available is also inclined to draw attention to it.

Any prospect of an easier road to uranium weapons must depend on centrifuges. On the whole they are not particularly promising. Though there is little doubt that the technology could

* The figure used by the United States Atomic Energy Commission in 1957 for the cost of the three American diffusion plants was $2,300,000,000. Careful estimates have concluded that it cost $205,000,000 a year to provide them with power, and $116,000,000 a year for personnel and maintenance. (See M. Kalkstein and W. Smith "An Estimate of the Nuclear Stockpile from Unclassified Sources" in D. H. Frisch (ed.), *Arms Reduction: Program and Issues,* The Twentieth Century Fund, New York, 1961.)

be mastered, there is very little prospect that this will involve an important reduction in cost. The first cost of a centrifuge plant adequate to produce uranium suitable for weapons would probably be similar to that for a gaseous diffusion plant. What can be said for centrifuges is that they would probably be simpler to conceal and that the power consumption might well be lower. It would be rash to suggest that they will not be developed; but there is no evidence to suggest that they are going to make the acquisition of U-235 either cheap or easy. Sorting out chemically identical atoms on an industrial scale is always likely to be an expensive business.

Plutonium

Plutonium production has had a justifiable reputation for being simpler than U-235 production. It has had much more appeal to powers which did not feel that they had huge resources to expend on a nuclear weapons programme. Britain and France, in particular, both devoted the first five or six years of their nuclear programmes almost entirely to creating the facilities for plutonium production. This was cheaper and easier to do than building a gaseous diffusion plant; and what was even more important was the fact that it created an industry of great potential value to the civil economy.

To produce plutonium for weapons, a country must acquire substantial quantities of natural uranium, it must operate one or more large nuclear reactors, and it must separate the resulting plutonium in a chemical separation plant. There is no shortage of uranium in the world and the major uranium producing countries are very anxious to find markets for the output which they developed (largely for the American and British markets) in the 1950s. Indeed, the surplus is so serious that production may well contract, producing a serious shortage when major reactor programmes become widespread in the middle and late 1970s.

Uranium is available in some quantities in most parts of the world. At a very high price, it could even be extracted from sea water. But no government has shown any sign of being prepared to extract uranium at heavy cost from inferior deposits. Those sources with low uranium content which are being exploited are usually ones which yield some other important substance—gold in South Africa, for example, or fertilizers in Israel. Appendix I gives the Euratom estimates of the world reserves of economical uranium and the richness of the ores in which they are to be found. This table shows how completely the Canadians, Americans and South Africans dominate the world uranium supply at present. This could be upset by major discoveries, but the falling off in the uranium market has discouraged prospecting. The fact that no other non-Communist producer could support a major atomic energy programme is best illustrated by the recent efforts of the fourth largest producer, France, to negotiate a major twenty-year contract with Canadian producers.

The availability of large quantities of uranium free of controls will depend mainly on the attitudes of these three countries. The position of the United States cannot be in doubt: from the beginning, it has had a strong and determined non-dissemination policy. This is steadily becoming even stronger as the scale of the problem of the nuclear spread becomes clearer. There have been doubts about the Canadian position, particularly because of the importance of the Canadian uranium industry to whole areas of the country. Canada provided uranium free of controls to the British and American atomic weapons programmes from the earliest days of the allied project; and the very large and tempting French offer placed the Canadian Government in a difficult position. Many millions of Canadians are of French extraction and it would be difficult and invidious to provide licences for sale to the British or Americans where these were not applied to the French. On the other hand, an open sale of this kind to France would go a long way to breaking down all controls over world uranium supplies.

In the circumstances, the Canadian Government decided to adopt a firm and universal anti-proliferation policy. In a formal statement to the House of Commons, the Prime Minister, Mr. Pearson, said:

> Export permits will be granted, or commitments to issue
> export permits will be given, with respect to sales of uranium
> covered by contracts entered into from now on, only if the
> uranium is to be used for peaceful purposes. Before such
> sales to any destination are authorized, the Government will
> require an agreement with the government of the importing
> country to ensure, with appropriate verification and control,
> that the uranium is to be used for peaceful purposes only.

It remains to be seen how "appropriate verification and control"
will be defined. Certainly a decision to insist on Canadian or
I.A.E.A. inspection over any Canadian uranium bought by the
United States or Britain will be an interesting and unprecedented
innovation.

There has been some suspicion of the intentions of the South
African Government where the export of uranium is concerned.
It is likely, however, that it is no more willing than the Canadian
Government to become the agent of a vast and uncontrolled nuclear proliferation. It might also choose to use its uranium
resources as a bargaining weapon if, as is likely, it finds it needs
outside support in an increasingly hostile world.

From the earliest post-war days, the original Manhattan Project partners (the U.S., Britain, Canada) have made a major
effort to see that an open market did not develop in uranium.
Except where the customers were the United States or Britain
(and with an important exception in the case of India), the sale
of uranium has always been covered by an agreement to impose
safeguards against the diversion of the resulting plutonium to
military purposes. In the early years, these agreements were bilateral: they were laid down as part of the contract of sale. The
earliest Western attempt to control the spread of nuclear weapons, the Baruch Plan of 1946, was based on the idea of controlling the sources of fissile material: and this concept was
continued in the Anglo-American-Canadian control system.

Following the first "atoms for peace" conference in Geneva
in 1955 and the subsequent foundation (after long negotiations
and delays) of the International Atomic Energy Agency, a major
effort was made to broaden this control into an international ar-

rangement which would allow a wide expansion of atomic energy without a spread of plutonium. The agency has largely adopted the control methods worked out by the Americans and imposes these on materials supplied through it. Thus, instead of Japan receiving uranium under a bilateral agreement which gives the Canadian Government rights of inspection, it is bought from the Canadian Government by the Agency and sold by it to Japan, subject to Agency safeguards. Some of the uranium now being sold is subject to Agency safeguards in this way; some is still sold subject to bilateral safeguards; and any producer can decide at any time to sell free of controls.

The reactors in which plutonium is created are also the subject of important international agreements and a growing body of arrangements of major military importance. Some countries— Canada, Germany, Sweden among the non-nuclear—have the ability to build large reactors of considerable sophistication. Others will steadily achieve this ability as they work up from more modest reactors. These plants are an advanced modern industrial technology and need considerable specialized equipment; but they are well within the grasp of any country with a reasonable scientific and technological base. Because of the emphasis which has been put on nuclear technology through the "atoms for peace" and other programmes, most of the important information about reactors is published and widely known. Many thousands of scientists and technicians from countries which might become nuclear powers have been trained in these techniques. Industrial organizations capable of building these installations are being created. Reactors are increasingly being located on the soil of non-nuclear countries under their own ownership and this process seems virtually certain to go on at an accelerating pace. A number of countries have made an effort to get reactors without controls. The Canadians built one for India but refused to repeat the exercise for Pakistan. The French are generally assumed to be ready and willing to provide reactors without controls, as they have co-operated in the construction of one in Israel. The Spanish Government has been showing interest in such collaboration with France.

Although there is no fundamental distinction between reactors for civil purposes (like power or desalination) and those for military purposes, there is an important distinction between two different kinds of reactor. Some reactors are fuelled with natural uranium while others are designed around enriched uranium—that is to say, uranium which has had its proportion of U-235 increased in a gaseous diffusion plant. The percentages of enrichment in U-235 may vary widely. The Belgian BR-2 reactor uses uranium which is 90 per cent U-235 (and is of weapons grade) while their BR-3 reactor uses uranium which has only about four per cent U-235. Broadly speaking, the United States has tended in its reactor technology to concentrate on enriched uranium while Britain, France, Canada, Sweden, India and Israel have shown a preference for natural uranium. This difference is to some extent a natural reflection of the large capacity for uranium enrichment which the United States possesses in her three gaseous diffusion plants. Whatever the reason, the implications for the spread of plutonium production are very important. It will be recalled that plutonium is produced in a reactor from the non-fissile U-238 present in its natural uranium: and to the extent that this is depleted and U-235 increased there will be less plutonium produced. But the really important consideration is that a reactor built to work with enriched uranium cannot normally be used with natural uranium. Therefore a country which has been equipped with these reactors must depend on a country with a gaseous diffusion plant for its fuel. At present, this means the United States or the Soviet Union. On the other hand, a country with a reactor designed for natural uranium has a plutonium production facility which could be fuelled from many different sources. This somewhat technical consideration suggests that American-built reactors in other countries will be much easier to control over the years than those being built by the British, Canadians, and French for foreign customers.

In these first two stages of plutonium production (the acquisition of uranium and the building of reactors) the needs of power and the needs of weapons run parallel. Canada and Germany have achieved an immense potential for manufacturing weapons without concerning themselves with deliberate military programmes at all. But the third stage, the chemical separation of plutonium, is much more specifically related to weapons. For this reason, the technology has remained largely secret; and there is reason to believe that France ran into difficulties here, as she did with her gaseous diffusion plant. Plutonium is a difficult substance to handle and the plant must do its work automatically and with great reliability because of the radiation levels which will be present in the fuel rods extracted from a reactor. Separating plutonium from uranium is a simpler matter than separating U-235 from U-238, because it is a different metal with different chemical properties and the cost of such a plant will be a few million pounds rather than the few hundred million pounds of a gaseous diffusion plant. Nevertheless, it is an effort and takes time. The significant thing about the Indian atomic energy programme is that a small chemical separation plant has been built and is being put into operation. While such a plant can be justified (as could a gaseous diffusion plant) on the ground that it was producing fuel for new reactors, plutonium separation is not really likely to be considered essential at this stage unless military considerations have played a part in the decision.

Building the Weapons

The country with a growing stock of plutonium or Uranium 235 is in a position to start designing atomic weapons. Published information does not reveal just how much of each is required, but some approximations are available. One of the leading figures in the French atomic energy programme, M. Bertrand Goldschmidt, wrote in 1960 that the minimum critical mass for a U-235 explosion was twenty kilograms and that for a plutonium explosion was seven kilograms. An official British document has said that a sphere of U-235 of four and a half inches diameter weighing sixteen kilograms would be critical if enclosed in a heavy tamper. The amount of plutonium needed is clearly less than this, but it is more difficult to explode and a novel method of encasing it in carefully designed explosives has had to be developed.

There has been some debate in the context of the 1963 partial nuclear test ban about whether testing is really essential to a weapons programme. Several considerations enter into this. Technically and militarily, both governments and military commanders are likely to want to know the effectiveness and reliability of the weapons they possess. On the other hand, the Americans used their uranium bomb against Hiroshima without a test. It was because there were doubts about the plutonium explosive method that a test of the Nagasaki bomb was considered necessary.

Politically, it might be generally assumed that a new nuclear power would be anxious to demonstrate that it had nuclear explosives. This has been true in the past. The Soviet Union felt that it had to challenge the nuclear monopoly of the United States in 1949 and there has been a substantial element of prestige in the British, French and Chinese programmes. Powers wanting a military option and fearing that they might lose prestige by demonstrating nuclear weapons—this might be true of Sweden or Israel—might acquire a stock of weapons with the intention of demonstrating their existence only when they were challenged militarily. A country like Israel might also fear the consequences of an enemy knowing that it possessed these weapons. This raises the possibility of secret tests. These would be difficult. They would obviously have to be underground (atmospheric tests are easily detected); but in the absence of on-site inspections it could not yet be demonstrated with absolute certainty that an underground explosion was not an earthquake.

It is most unlikely, in any case, that any country wanting to conduct nuclear tests would be particularly inhibited by the present partial ban. Any government which has decided on a nuclear programme clearly considers these weapons to be extremely important. In any case, the test ban contains a loophole: "Each party shall (it says), in exercising its national sovereignty, have the right to withdraw from the treaty if it decides that extraordinary events, related to the subject matter of this treaty, have jeopardized the supreme interests of its country." It will be noted that the definition of an extraordinary event is left to the country wanting to test. So what little formal inhibition the treaty might be expected to create is dispelled by the wording of the treaty itself. Underground tests for weapons up to one megaton have also proved to be exceptionally valuable to weapons designers. Their disadvantages are that they are expensive and they do not provide information on the effects of nuclear weapons.

A number of countries would have difficulty in finding a suitable place to test their weapons. Thermonuclear weapons, in particular, would pose serious problems. On the other hand, the Pacific Ocean and Indian Ocean are available to any who are prepared to sacrifice a ship and surround it with instrumentation in other ships. A testing programme of this kind would undoubtedly be very expensive, and countries which can establish regular testing grounds within their own frontiers can probably get better results very much more cheaply. But the British and French programmes have shown that a large number of tests is not necessary to a small nuclear power and the Chinese may be equally economical in destroying their small stocks of fissile material in order to gain more information.

Delivery Systems

The military use of nuclear explosives involves getting them on to a target at the desired time. Something must be able to carry them and to get through. Just what this should be and how it will be acquired will be very different in different countries. The problems of the explosives themselves (uranium and plutonium) are the same for every country. It is unlikely that any weapons programme will be very different in essence from any other. But delivery systems are a different matter. Chiefs of staff ordered to find an effective way of mounting a national nuclear force could take a wide variety of paths. Any government asking itself how it should solve this problem will recognize different potential enemies, different industrial capacity in the country itself, and different relations with the great powers who can supply the elements of a delivery system.

This military problem has proved to be very difficult. Nuclear weapons have a logic which forces them to steadily higher levels of sophistication; and all the nuclear powers have tended to recognize this. The first priority of the United States, Britain, France and no doubt the Soviet Union over a long period of time has been the effectiveness of their nuclear delivery systems. To be truly first class, a power must have a delivery system which is not subject to surprise attack and which can be sure of its capacity to penetrate any foreseeable defence. This will be beyond the hopes of the new nuclear power in the early stages. On the other hand, there has recently been a tendency for innovation in weapons to slow down and there are signs that there may be a considerable period without anything which can really be called a strategic arms race. The United States, which is the world leader in most technologies, is hoping to get a long period of service from its new generation of weapons (*Polaris* and *Minuteman*). If this proves to be true, it will greatly increase the possibility that over a period of time lesser powers might produce delivery systems which could maintain themselves against first-class competition. It is possible, however, that the major powers will obtain the ability to defend their cities or even their whole area against attacks by small nuclear powers. The United States Defense Department has studied the possibility of attack on the U.S. in the 1970s by a primitive nuclear force. According to the Secretary of Defense, Mr. McNamara, "Our preliminary conclusion is that a small balanced defense programme could significantly reduce fatalities from such an attack." The spread of nuclear weapons may re-start the strategic arms race so as to allow the Soviet Union and the United States to maintain a qualitative superiority over others for at least a few years.

If all new nuclear powers were to accept the premise that their system of delivery should be comparable with those of the major powers, there can be no doubt at present of the strong preference for ballistic missiles. As far as the use of weapons against an enemy homeland is concerned, the United States is concentrating virtually entirely on missiles for deployment either in underground bases or in submarines. Less is known about the future plans of the Soviet Union, but it is probable that they too are concentrating on rocket weapons. Britain plans to shift her prime nuclear force into submarines by 1970. The French Government is developing the *Mirage IV* light bomber primarily for strategic delivery, but this is recognized to be an interim weapon and a substantial rocket industry is being developed with the stated intention of achieving a submarine-based weapon by the early 1970s. All the evidence of the Chinese programme is that ballistic missiles rather than bombers are being pushed ahead vigorously.

For the country aspiring to be a strategic nuclear power, however small, the development of bombers would seem to be hard to justify at this stage. They have two important defects: they are vulnerable to modern air defences; and they are difficult to deploy in peacetime in a way which does not expose them to destruction through surprise attack. For missiles, the most secret and impenetrable medium in the world is available in the rocket-firing submarine. Because the earlier nuclear powers have progressed through bombers to missiles, it has generally been assumed that this was a logical sequence. But missiles are to a large extent a new start and an independent industry. This gives the new nuclear powers a certain advantage: they do not have the development of years to catch up. On the other hand, it is difficult to make primitive missiles into nuclear delivery vehicles or to make the fullest use of modern missiles with primitive nuclear warheads. The years between 1947 and 1953 which the American missile programme lost still teach an important lesson. It was in those years that the military planners argued that ballistic missiles could not be used over long ranges with atomic bombs alone because the power of the weapons would not compensate for inaccuracy: and it was not until 1953 that they realized that it would be possible to make a thermonuclear weapon which would be small enough to fit into a rocket. It is possible that this problem will still raise difficulties for the new nuclear power. If it decides to concentrate on what it will ultimately need—that is to say, on ballistic missile development—it may spend many years with weapons which are more or less unusable because their accuracy is so poor as to make their warheads valueless. The obvious thing is to find an interim solution: ideally, to buy out-of-date bombers from a great power and use these to bridge the gap. Whether such bombers will be available will depend on the effect which the national nuclear weapons programme has had on great power friends. The period of Chinese development of nuclear weapons has coincided with a decline of its close relations with the Soviet Union. The political atmosphere has been similar in Franco–American relations, but the United States has been prepared from time to time to make sales of equipment which was of the first importance to General de Gaulle's *force de frappe*.

The cost and time involved in developing a rocket industry and bringing thermonuclear warheads down to an appropriate size will vary from one country to another. Ten years is probably a minimum. If submarines were required, this would be another major development effort; and if their power-plants were to be nuclear (a great advantage in remaining concealed) it would take very much longer and cost very much more. Only an industrial power of some standing—a country like Germany or Japan— could really hope to attack the problem of nuclear power on such a broad front. Even for them, it would be expensive and would take a long time.

Things would be very different, however, if extensive cooperation was available from one or more of the original nuclear powers. Britain has had a number of agreements with the United States which have greatly simplified her problem in remaining a first-class nuclear power. In 1957, the United States made available its designs for marine nuclear power-plants; the British and Americans have always had close collaboration on submarine designs; a few years later, it was agreed to exchange substantial quantities of American enriched uranium for British plutonium; very advanced warhead designs for the *Skybolt* and *Polaris* air-launched and submarine-launched ballistic missiles were released to the British Government when they decided to buy these missiles; and the British submarine-based missile fleet will go to sea in 1968–70 with the *Polaris* missiles and associated equipment all bought direct from their American producers. This is probably an extreme example of sharing. On the other hand, the United States might be expected to show the same intimacy with such countries as Australia and Canada if they chose to become nuclear powers; and they have already offered France the *Polaris* on the same terms as Britain (the offer was refused before it could be established whether warhead designs were included) and have sold twelve air refueling tankers specifically intended for the *force de frappe*. What the American attitude would be to requests for important elements for a delivery system for Swedish, Swiss, Indian, German or other, so to speak, friendly nuclear weapons could only be seen in the political context of the time. Both the French and the Chinese experience suggests that a power embarking on a nuclear weapons programme at this stage worsens its relations with the major powers. But how permanent and how severe this will be can only be worked out in individual cases. If the past teaches any lessons, it is perhaps that political opposition to the spread of nuclear weapons will be decisive until it is clear that a particular country's programme is inevitable. Then commercial interests in exporting expensive items (which normally have no export prospects) can be expected to take precedence.

There is also a sophisticated military argument which may help to sustain the commercial argument. It is that allies, or indeed enemies, are safer and more reliable if they have invulnerable nuclear weapons. Vulnerable weapons force governments to be trigger-happy. The knowledge that at any time their force may be utterly destroyed on the ground makes its commanders ready to fire on the first suggestion that they may be under attack. This makes them prone to accident or to miscalculation. Although the logical conclusion is that they should be sold the least vulnerable weapons, the great powers are unlikely to accept this argument unless political and financial considerations point in the same direction. When they do (as in the case of America's relations with Britain and France), this technical military argument might come to carry weight.

The more nuclear weapons spread, the smaller will be the countries which are acquiring them or are tempted to acquire them. While general industrial strength is rising in many parts of the world, any spread of nuclear weapons is likely to include countries of very limited industrial strength; and it is quite possible that such countries will try to get along for many years without a first-class delivery system. There is as yet no evidence that the Chinese will have a striking force of any quality for many years; nor have the French pretended that the *Mirage IV* force will give them very much more than a general status as a nuclear power. It is difficult to see what kind of striking force India or Israel would create, though India's requirement for ranges of many thousands of miles to reach Chinese cities is in sharp contrast with Israel's very small range requirements. If countries such as Indonesia or the United Arab Republic are going to start thinking about becoming nuclear powers (a distant prospect), the possibility of nuclear stocks without modern means of delivery will have to be taken seriously.

This reopens the question of unorthodox methods for the use of these weapons. This was given extensive study in the early 1950s; but when it became clear that the nuclear powers of the day had no intention of allowing them to be spirited about the world, sailed into harbours in merchant ships, buried in the basements of embassies, or any of the other blackmail possibilities, the subject was allowed to drift into the background. The fact is that the Soviet Union, the United States and Britain all had expensive but successful programmes for bombers or rockets to carry these weapons from the security of national control to a target at what was regarded as the unlikely moment when a government would choose to give the order. What of countries who do not have such programmes? Will they be tempted by blackmail possibilities? No prediction can be made. All that can be said is that the possibilities of various primitive delivery systems (including the somewhat orthodox use of civil jet airliners as bombers) may one day become important once again to world security.

Among all these possibilities, there is wide choice. Although many of the countries which might develop nuclear weapons now—such countries as Germany, Canada and Sweden—would feel obliged to equip themselves with first-class delivery systems, a wide diffusion of nuclear weapons would probably include many countries which would have different requirements. India and Japan would no doubt relate their requirements to the strength of the Chinese air and missile forces in ten or twenty years' time, not to the quality of Soviet and American forces.

New nuclear powers will also no doubt look through the lists of their friends to see which might be able and willing to sell them bombers or missiles. The chances are that in the coming years there will be no new bombers in any of the leading powers able to carry the heavy load of primitive nuclear weapons; but there is a range of heavy air transports available from the United States, the Soviet Union, Britain, France and Canada. Old bombers will be in the hands of the United States, the Soviet Union and Britain in increasingly large numbers and there is already an evident readiness to make these available to allies. (The United States offered the Australians B-47 medium bombers free of charge while they waited for their F-111 light bombers. The R.A.A.F., however, decided that they would be too expensive to operate. The Soviets have also made Badger bombers available to Indonesia.) Ballistic missile production can probably be expected in the United States, the Soviet Union, France and probably China for many years to come.

Uranium Reserves

THE FOLLOWING ARE THE URANIUM RESERVES of non-Communist countries which can be extracted at a price below $10 per lb. of uranium oxide (U_3O_8). They are stated in tonnes (1 tonne = 1000 kilograms).

	RESERVES		
Country	Metal	Ore Content %	Reference Dates
Canada	145,000	0.1	1962
U.S.A.	134,00	0.2	1962
South Africa	115,000	0.017	1962
France	26,000	0.14	1962
Australia	10,000	0.09–0.15	1961
Congo	8,000	0.3	Dec. 1960[1]
Portugal	5,500	0.12	1962
Gabon	5,000	0.45	1962
Argentina	3,800	0.1–0.2	1962
Italy	1,600	0.10	1962
Spain	1,500	0.11	Dec. 1960
India	1,200	0.06	1960
Japan	1,000	0.042	Dec. 1960
Germany	800	0.2–0.5	1962
Miscellaneous	1,000		

Source: *The Problem of Uranium Resources and the Long-Term Supply Position* (Euratom EHR414e 1963).

[1] Most known Congo reserves have been exhausted.

TABLE 1: RESEARCH REACTORS IN NON-NUCLEAR COUNTRIES

	Name	Foreign Patron	Rating (thermal mW)	Uranium Enrichment	In Operation	Possible Bombs Per Year
Australia	HIFAR	U.K.	10	80%	1958	**
Austria	ASTRA	U.S.	12	90%	1960	**
Belgium	BR-2	none	50	90%	1960	**
	BR-3	U.S.	40	4.4%	1962	**
Brazil	IEAR-1	U.S.	5	20%	1957	**
Canada	NRX	none	40	natural	1947	2
	NRU	none	200	natural	1957	10
	NPD	none	80	natural	1962	4
Denmark	DR-2	U.K.	5	90%	1958	**
India	CIR	Canada	40	natural	1960	2
Israel	Dimona	France	24	natural	1964	1
Italy	PRO	none	30	90%	1964	**
	ESSOR	France	38	natural	1967	2
Japan	JRR-2	U.S.	10	90%	1960	**
	JRR-3	none	10	natural	1962	½
	JPDR	U.S.	45	2.6%	1963	2

Norway	HBWR†	none	20	natural	1959	1
Pakistan	PARR	U.S.	5	90%	1965	**
South Africa	Safari-1	U.S.	20	93%	1965	**
Sweden	R-2	U.S.	30	90%	1960	**
	R-3/Adam	none	65 (later 130)	natural	1963	3(6)
Switzerland	Diorit	none	20	natural	1960	1
	Lucens	none	30	0.95%	1965	2
West Germany	FRG	U.S.	5	90%	1958	**
	VAK	U.S.	60	2.6%	1961	3
	FR-2	none	12	natural	1961	½
	FRJ-1	U.K.	5	80%	1962	**
	FRJ-2	U.K.	10	80%	1962	**
	AVR	none	49	20%	1965	**
	MZFR	none	200	natural	1965	10
Yugoslavia	R-A	U.S.S.R.	10	2%	1959	¼

† This is a joint undertaking of the European Nuclear Energy Agency and as such is subject to safeguards to see that it "shall not further any military purpose."

** Plutonium from these reactors would be negligible.

TABLE 2: POWER REACTORS

	Name	Foreign Patron	Rating (electrical mW)	Uranium Enrichment	In Operation	Possible Bombs Per Year
Belgium	SENA	U.S.	280	3.1%	1965	56
Canada	CANDU	none	220	natural	1964	44
	HWR-1800	none	900	natural	1970	180
Czechoslovakia	HWGCR	U.S.S.R	150	natural	1970	30
India	Tarapur	U.S.	380	slightly enriched	1968	76
	Rajasthan	Canada	200	natural	1969	40
	RAP-2	none?	200	natural	1970?	40
	Madras	none?	400	natural	1972	80
Italy	Latina	U.K.	230	natural	1962	46
	SENN	U.S.	160	1.6-2.1%	1963	32
	SELNI	U.S.	270	3%	1964	54
Japan	Tokai-Mura	U.K.	166	natural	1965	32
	Tsuruga	U.S.	300	some enrichment	1968	60

Netherlands	SEP-BWR	U.S.	50	slight enrichment	1967	10
Sweden	R-4/EVA	none	160	natural	1968	32
	KRB	U.S.	250	2.6%	1966	50
	KWL	U.S.	240	some enrichment	1968	50
West Germany	KBWP	none	240	2.5-3%	1968	50
	HDR	none	25	3%	1968	5
	KKN	none	100	natural	1968/9	20

359

The Strategic Consequences of Nuclear Proliferation

JAMES R. SCHLESINGER

* * *

Dimensions and Measurement

Any serious attempt to assess the dimensions of the proliferation threat should begin with some calculations regarding the spectrum of strategic capabilities given varying levels of investment. Further development of the point that proliferation in certain essential respects is a quantitative problem is basic to our understanding. Proliferation is really quite unlike pregnancy, though in the intuition of many something akin to pregnancy is used as a rough analogue. It is frequently observed—usually by way of admonition—that there is no such thing as being a little bit pregnant. But this is because the results and the time involved in the process are pretty well defined. In size and weight full-term babies tend towards a normal distribution; the variance is not a matter of great moment. But suppose that in pregnancy there were no tendency toward a unimodal distribution of the results and that the time involved in gestation were subject to enormous variation. Suppose again that the ultimate progeny could be Lilliputians or Brobdingnagians—or, for that matter, a varied assortment of misshapen dwarfs, possibly lacking essential organs, limbs, or faculties—and that the specific result depended upon not only the intake of the mother but her intel-

From *Arms Control for the Late Sixties*, edited by James E. Dougherty and J. F. Lehman, Jr. Copyright © 1967 by Litton Educational Publishing, Inc. Reprinted by permission of Van Nostrand Reinhold Company.

ligence. This is really a more revealing analogy. It explains why being a *little bit proliferated* may be a meaningful concept, while being a little bit pregnant is not. In this area controlling the ultimate dimensions may be even more important than preventing conception or birth.

The range of possible nuclear capabilities is simply enormous. One must be aware of the importance of the distinctions to be drawn among capabilities—and how these distinctions relate to size and vulnerability. Consider the existing array of nuclear capabilities. The United States, which has invested most heavily, possesses a capability which is not only a solid deterrent, but which is not incredible in terms of a carefully controlled, countermilitary initial strike. The Soviet Union, which has invested less, has an impressive second-strike force, which is an effective deterrent. Britain possesses a much more limited capability, presently dependent for delivery on obsolescent aircraft; both the influence and the credibility of the British "independent contribution to the deterrent" are steadily on the wane. The French capability is even more limited in respect to its potential for inflicting damage upon the Soviet Union, though it promises to exploit more advanced delivery systems indigenously-produced. Finally, the Chinese capability—presently drawing the lion's share of attention—is barely past the embryonic stage. There is some question whether it should even be referred to as a *capability*.

The degree to which a nuclear capability is strategically exploitable—and this is substantially dependent on the credibility of the threat to employ—is determined by its size and sophistication and by the vulnerability of the society it is designed to protect. Strategic posture ultimately depends upon the ability to inflict and to limit damage. All these are roughly correlated with the volume of resources the society has invested or is able to invest in its capability. Happily for the wealthy and powerful, this ability is subject to considerable variance. As someone has astutely observed, there is no cheap substitute for money. It is doubtful whether the inexorable requirement for money is anywhere more decisive than in relation to the development of a nuclear capability. Sophisticated nuclear weapons and sophisticated delivery systems are terribly expensive. The cost of developing a capability which could seriously disturb the superpowers (as opposed to one's unarmed neighbor) is staggering.

Let me indicate roughly what kind of sums are involved. In order to develop a convincing second-strike capability against one of the superpowers, a nation must be prepared to spend billions of dollars annually—and these expenditures would continue for a decade and longer. Estimates differ; five billion dollars a year may be too high and three billion dollars a year might be adequate. These sums, however, run well beyond what most nations have been prepared to spend—including some that are present members of the nuclear club. Resources will be required not only for delivery systems and compatible weapons, but also for certain supplementary capabilities whose costs are rarely reckoned. How often do we remember to include such indispensable items as reconnaissance and intelligence in the list of required outlays? But any nation contemplating a confrontation with a superpower had better learn something about the location of targets and about the location and capabilities of its opponent's air defense and missile systems. The upshot is that only through very heavy outlays can a nation develop more than a very minimal threat against a superpower.

To illustrate the problem, let us consider some historic cost figures. Take the matter of weapons development and stockpiling. Down to early 1966, the United States had invested on the order of eight billion dollars in the development of nuclear weapons. For AEC operations generally, it has now appropriated close to $40 billion. These are substantial amounts. How many nations are in a position to spend even 20 percent or 25 percent of these amounts? Yet, for the creation of a serious capability, requiring deliverable weapons in the megaton range, heavy investment in weapons development is unavoidable.

Though the spread of *missile* capabilities is now a matter of increasing concern, the problem of compatibility implies that development of advanced weapons is preliminary to deployment of an effective missile force. To develop a warhead for an early-generation missile with limited thrust and size (the goal of a development program or the initial goal of a program for an aspiring nuclear power), there must be heavy investment in weapons testing in order to get yield-to-weight ratios to a point where a weapon adequate for target destruction can successfully be delivered in the vehicle. Moreover, there will have to be major investment in guidance technology simply to insure that missiles will be accurate enough to place weapons near the point targeted —whether military bases or cities. In this respect, it is vital to recognize the tradeoff between weapon size and weapon accuracy. With very large yields, considerable inaccuracy may be tolerated. However, with the very low-yield weapons of the sort that can be developed with small amounts of money, yet which must be delivered with limited-payload vehicles, the accuracy requirements become very severe. But missile accuracy is neither cheap nor easy to obtain.

The implication is that no nation is going to be in a position to develop a strategic capability that is both sophisticated and cheap. In the absence of major investments or extraordinary outside assistance the only option open to most nuclear aspirants is the aerial delivery of rather crude nuclear weapons. Though such capabilities can, of course, dramatically transform a regional balance of power (provided that the superpowers remain aloof), the superpowers themselves will remain more or less immune to nuclear threats emanating from countries other than the principal opponent. For the foreseeable future, only the Soviet Union will be able to deliver the requisite megatonnage to threaten major devastation in the United States. Threats from other quarters may be faced down.

The superpowers therefore will remain in a position in which they can dominate any nuclear confrontation. Only a superpower—and in this connection the term applies particularly to the United States—will be able to intervene in such confrontations in third areas. If it desires to pay the costs and is willing to run the risks, other nations, including the present three minor members of the nuclear club, will continually be deterred. Not only will they be precluded from implementing nuclear thrusts, but in the relevant cases, their capabilities will remain vulnerable to a disarming first strike unless they are given protection by an associated superpower. In any showdown with a superpower, a minor nuclear power relying on its own resources will simultaneously be deterred and be subject to disarming.

This asymmetrical relationship between major and lesser nuclear powers brings us back to a point raised earlier: why it may be counter-productive to talk in a panicky way about proliferation's threat to mankind-as-a-whole. If we are to dissuade others from aspiring to nuclear capabilities, what we should stress is that, if weapons spread, they are not likely to be employed against the superpowers. The penalties for proliferation would be paid, not by the United States, or the Soviet Union, but by third countries.

The likelihood that the first nuclear war, if it comes, will originate in and be confined to the underdeveloped world should play a prominent role in any assessment of proliferation's consequences. The tenor of the existing discussion of proliferation has led some people in the underdeveloped countries to conclude that the major powers would be the chief beneficiaries of curtailing the spread. If nuclear spread is to be effectively opposed, it should be made crystal clear just whose security is placed at risk and whose is not.

Countermeasures

The problem of nuclear spread is not exhausted by the attempt at prevention. The effort to dissuade additional states from acquiring nuclear capabilities, while good in itself, is not likely to be wholly successful. Control includes much more than simply preventing nuclear dispersion. Influencing the character and consequences of whatever nuclear spread does take place should not be neglected out of disappointment with the "failure" to prevent proliferation entirely.

We should recognize that the long-run problem is how to live with the spread at minimum risk. This implies a form of control which will require continuing effort over time; it is not an all-or-none problem to be settled in some particular time period. If we adopt the position that the issue is simply one of *counting* those nations claiming nuclear weapons status and setting this number as a ceiling on the assumption that *if this number increases* we are undone, then we will fail to examine the second-stage opportunities for control. Given our policy of trying to minimize the number of nuclear powers, there should be additional strings to the non-proliferation bow, to be employed as the number of nuclear weapons states increases. What are these additional strings? First, if new weapons programs are launched, we may hope to keep the resulting capabilities as limited as possible. (This would reduce the damage potential of any nuclear wars taking place in third areas.) Second, we can take steps to reduce the likelihood that these capabilities, whatever their size, will or could actually be employed by rational political leaders, especially against the United States. Moreover, any actions which sharply reduce the size or the likelihood of employment of additional capabilities may also serve to weaken the motives for acquisition.

Under the heading of limiting the size of additional capabilities, the methods at our disposal are indirect ones. Recognizing the ordinary tradeoff between cost and quantity, our actions should be designed to keep the cost of strategic capabilities at a high level, thereby weakening the temptation to acquire larger capabilities. This implies a policy of withholding direct assistance from the strategic nuclear programs of other nations, save in rare and unusual circumstances. Through rigorous strategic trade controls we may also hope to limit indirect assistance. Above all, we should make every effort to see that international assistance intended for the support of peaceful nuclear programs is not diverted to support of military programs. These are not easily achievable goals, and we ought not pitch our definition of success at too high a level. The instruments for control are imperfect. Moreover, costs of themselves cannot exclude other nations from seeking nuclear capabilities. Given the existing system of national sovereignties, the ability to influence the decisions of other states is quite limited. Nonetheless, something can be achieved.

To whatever extent we can prevent the deflation of costs, we can limit the size and the potential destructiveness of budding nuclear capabilities.

The second heading—reducing the likelihood that new capabilities will be actually employed or, if employed, limiting the potential damage—represents that aspect of living-with-proliferation-at-minimum-risk over which we ourselves have most control. There are certain hardware possibilities and other physical arrangements that can limit the potential for damage. One obvious possibility may be to buttress the air defense capabilities of threatened states. A more controversial possibility is the deployment of new systems that will sharply reduce the damage that Nth countries could inflict on the major nuclear powers.

* * *

My remarks should not be taken as an endorsement of the ABM system, for that decision involves complex arms control, strategic, and cost-effectiveness calculations, which are beyond the scope of this paper. But one factor that is relevant to the final decision deserves stressing here: deployment of an ABM system or other systems that substantially reduce the damage that can be inflicted on the United States may serve to curtail the harmful consequences which might otherwise flow from proliferation. Through such damage-limiting measures, the willingness and ability of the United States to intervene in third areas when the use of nuclear weapons is threatened is enhanced. Consequently the U.S. ability to prevent the misuse of nuclear capabilities will be strengthened. The strongest deterrent to a lesser power's employing its capability is the possibility that a major nuclear power will enter the lists against it.

Given the existing preponderance of U.S. power, the deployment of major new systems may not be essential to achieve this result. Certain types of developments do appear desirable, however, in order to exploit the discrepancy between major and lesser nuclear powers for the purpose of driving home to lesser powers how ill-advised they would be to initiate the use of nuclear weapons. For example, in a world of many nuclear powers in which anonymity is at least a hypothetical possibility, we should invest considerable effort in developing methods for "fingerprinting" nuclear weapons and parallel systems through which we may in a crisis quickly ascribe responsibility for any detonation that occurs. Then, if we wish to offer protection to threatened nations, we could see to it that punishment for any irresponsible nuclear act would be swift and condign.

An approach of this sort, which relies on superpower preponderance to withstand the potentially baleful effects of proliferation, is not one that is universally and automatically appealing. Hedley Bull has characterized this approach as "high posture" and has contrasted it with one that he prefers: the "low posture" in which the differences between the greater and lesser powers are muted. Let me therefore say a few words in defense of the so-called "high posture."

First, phrases like "high posture" and "low posture" have a certain allure, but the question must be raised whether they accurately describe the underlying realities or the true alternatives. The gap in military nuclear power between the superpowers and other nations is enormous and will continue to be so. In fact, it is more likely to increase than diminish. If we accept that the strategic gap will continue to be enormous, what seems desirable is that the character and width of the gap be sufficient to permit the superpowers to exert a stabilizing influence on the restless third areas of the world. Moreover, this stabilizing function needs to be perceived by those who may come to possess a minor nuclear capability. This potential stabilizing function should not lightly be discarded in the quest for a somewhat mythical "low posture."

Second, the spread of nuclear capabilities into third areas will very much intensify the existing elements of instability and magnify the danger of instability beyond what it is today. The new nuclear capabilities will be unsophisticated and vulnerable. Given the existence of vulnerabilities and the temptation to exploit a temporary strategic edge, the likelihood of nuclear initiation through a hair-trigger response seems obvious. Most persons who seek a more peaceful world would find beneficial the ability of the superpowers to forestall the initial use of such capabilities. In seeking arms control arrangements, we must keep in mind the bilateral U.S.-Soviet relationship, but we should also remember that increases in our capabilities, when matched by the Soviet Union, may serve to diminish the risks of dangerous outbreaks in third areas of the world.

Third, most nations, even when they strongly disapprove of specific aspects of U.S. policy, desire that the United States stand ready to counter nuclear threats against nations lacking in the means of self-protection. The United States, in particular, is being called upon to perform functions that other nations are not called upon to perform. If the United States is expected to play the role of a nuclear Galahad, risking nuclear retaliation and loss of population in behalf of others, it does not seem unreasonable for the United States to possess protective measures of a type not universally available. Nor does it seem wholly consistent for those who rely on U.S. protection simultaneously to urge the United States to accept a low posture *and* to stand ready to intervene in the defense of nuclear "abstainers." If a nation is expected to accept losses in behalf of others, it seems reasonable that plans should be laid to hold the potential losses to a minimum. That those on whom the role of nuclear Galahad is thrust should desire thicker armor seems quite understandable.

There has been a tendency to exaggerate the strategic importance of proliferation because the problem has been viewed qualitatively in respect to enumerating those nations that might acquire a small capability rather than quantitatively in respect to the destructive potential of the capability that might be achieved. As far as we can see into the future, the strategic environment will continue to be dominated by the preponderant military power of the United States and the Soviet Union. It is possible that the spread of weapons will increasingly inhibit the use of power by the United States or the Soviet Union in regions of less than vital concern. The degree of inhibition will depend upon the risks that we (or the Soviets) are willing to run. However, if we desire to accept the risks, we could, because of our preponderant power, continue to intervene in unsettled areas to diminish the risk of small-scale nuclear war.

With the spread of weapons there would be a greater likelihood of use or misuse, but the risk of use or misuse will be concentrated primarily in the third areas of the world. Given the current and prospective stable military balance between the United States and the Soviet Union, it is difficult to envisage conflicts in third areas escalating into exchanges between the homelands of the two major powers. This implies, of course, that proliferation would impose enlarged risks primarily on other nations. The superpowers will continue to be relatively immune to strikes from the parvenus; the threat to them will continue to come primarily from each other. In all analyses of proliferation this asymmetrical distribution of the risks should be stressed because of its possible impact on the incentives of aspiring nuclear powers.

A substantial diminution of the strategic gap between the superpowers and others is simply not in the offing. The only way in which reduction of the gap could be influential is if it undermines the credibility of intervention by a superpower to stabilize conditions in third areas being subjected to nuclear threat. This is not necessarily beneficial, and it is doubtful whether those in threatened areas would desire such an outcome, if they were to think seriously about the problem. What may be desirable is to make crystal clear that despite nuclear spread the major powers will retain the ability to intervene to deter nuclear threats or to punish nuclear irresponsibility without risking substantial damage to themselves. This does not necessarily mean that the major powers will be forced to deploy all those systems, like ABM, which hold some promise in this regard; it does mean that they shall be forced to work diligently so as continually to upgrade their ability to detect, deter, disarm, or punish the national source of nuclear irresponsibility.

While nuclear spread is basically destabilizing, its strategic consequences need not be too severe. Simple nuclear capabilities cannot play the role of "equalizers" in international conflict. The strategic position that the United States and the Soviet Union currently enjoy is so unassailable that even continuing action by third parties is unlikely to upset the central strategic balance for the next twenty years. Properly exploited, this central strategic balance could continue to provide some stability in regional conflicts—even in the face of nuclear proliferation.

Basic Requirements of Arms Control

ROBERT R. BOWIE

THE CONCEPT OF "ARMS CONTROL" INCLUDES ANY AGREEMENT AMONG SEVERAL POWERS TO REGULATE SOME ASPECT OF THEIR MILITARY CAPABILITY OR POTENTIAL. The arrangement may apply to the location, amount, readiness, or types of military forces, weapons, or facilities. Whatever their scope or terms, however, all plans for arms control have one common feature: they presuppose some form of cooperation or joint action among the several participants regarding their military programs. Is such cooperation feasible between major powers whose national purposes are in basic conflict? Concretely, is there any basis for such arrangements between the USSR and the United States? If so, what are the conditions and limits of reliable arms control?

Definition of the Problem

Many are convinced that agreements for arms control with the Soviet Union are not possible or in the national interest of the

From *Daedalus*, The Journal of the American Academy of Arts and Sciences, Fall, 1960. Copyright 1960 by The American Academy of Arts and Sciences. Reprinted by permission.

United States. In general their view derives from some or all of the following propositions:

(1) Military forces are only the reflection of political hostility. They are not the source or origin of tensions and conflicts among nations. Consequently, it is futile to try to regulate or reduce military forces separately from their underlying political causes. When basic hostility is resolved, reduction in arms will follow automatically as the nations feel themselves more secure and less threatened. To attempt control of military forces before removing the political sources of friction or threat is to put the cart before the horse.

(2) The purposes of the Sino-Soviet bloc are fundamentally hostile to the non-Communist nations. In the Communist view the conflict between their "system" and any other is irreconcilable and will be resolved only by the ultimate victory of the Communist order. Its leaders believe that Communism is destined to triumph throughout the world, and they intend to advance their cause by the vigorous use of all feasible means. Apparently, the Communist ideology no longer considers a global military showdown inevitable under present conditions. But the Communist leaders still define "wars of liberation" as "progressive," and have not abandoned the use of force (as in Hungary) or threats (as in Berlin) when either serves their interests.

(3) The Communists would not make or carry out any arms agreement in good faith. Any means are legitimate in seeking to promote Communist advance. Treaties are only instruments for pursuing their basic aims and will be violated or evaded as suits their interests. In 1939-1940, the Soviet Union overran and divided Poland and absorbed Esthonia, Lithuania, and Latvia, in flagrant violation of nonaggression treaties with each of these nations. Soviet disregard for commitments regarding Eastern Europe, and of its Potsdam obligations regarding Germany, is too well-known to need laboring.

It would be rash indeed to disregard these lessons in devising and analyzing any arms-control proposals. The grounds for distrusting the Soviet Union and its purposes should make even the optimistic cautious. The record of broken agreements should warn us not to rely on Soviet promises or good faith as the basis for arms-control measures. And the only safe course is to accept at face value the constant Communist assertions of their basic hostility to our social order.

But, this does not dispose of the problem. One could also cite many agreements which the Soviets have carried out. The crucial point is to understand what kinds of arrangements they can be expected to comply with and why. The safest premise is this: in breaking or keeping agreements, the Soviets *can be trusted* to pursue their own interests as they see them. Hence, measures for arms control should be reliable if they can be so devised that compliance will be more in the Soviet interest than evasion or violation.

Distrust is not, of course, limited to one side. The Soviets, reflecting Communist ideology, are deeply suspicious of the "capitalist" nations and of their "ruling circles," which are seen as ruthless and unscrupulous in maintaining and improving their power and position. Within this conception, however, they are expected to pursue their interests.

The remaining discussion will be mainly concerned with how to make compliance conform to self-interest, given the fact of basic antagonism and distrust. It will examine, *inter alia,* how far the first proposition above—the relation of politics and arms control—remains valid under modern conditions.

Basis of Common Interests

At the threshold is the question: How can the Soviet Union and the United States have parallel or common interests in measures to control armaments if their basic purposes are antagonistic?

The answer lies essentially in the changing nature of war, especially general war. Until recently, large-scale military force could be used as an effective instrument for the pursuit of political aims. An aggressor might hope to win and to benefit from his victim's defeat. Conversely, potential victims could normally assure their own security by confronting the possible aggressor with sufficient opposing strength, either alone or with allies, to deter attack or defend themselves if it occurred. The resulting balance might preserve peace for extended periods under favorable conditions.

The development of modern weapons has changed the situation radically. As always, threat has produced deterrent which has largely succeeded thus far in preventing large-scale war. But the military balance remains unstable, entailing substantial risks and burdens. More important, these conditions jeopardize both sides. The loss of one need not be the gain of the other. If large-scale war meant mutual destruction, it would not advance the political interests of either side; both would be better served, *despite basic political hostility*, by preventing its occurrence. Thus, military instruments, while still related to political conflict, have taken on a life of their own and have become a separate source of tension and danger. . . .

One serious factor of instability arises from the disparity between offense and defense. The state of military technology puts a heavy premium on striking the first blow. Surprise attack not only could grievously injure the victim; it might also knock out much of his capacity to retaliate, so long as delivery systems remain relatively vurnerable. Even so, an aggressor would run a serious risk of severe damage from even a limited surviving retaliatory capability. While that situation prevails, an aggressor is not likely to be tempted to initiate an attack unless he believes himself in peril of an attack. The sense of exposure and vulnerability, however, creates strong pressures for rapid reaction to strike in case of threatened or apparent attack, before the means of striking is jeopardized. The necessity for quick decision creates serious dangers of war by accident or premature response, due, perhaps, to the misreading or misjudging of warnings. Progress in reducing vulnerability by hardened, concealed, and mobile weapons may lessen these risks, but may also introduce new instabilities of their own; they may, for instance, complicate communication and central control.

The dynamic character of military technology forces each side to strain constantly to develop new or improved weapons systems in order to better its position or at least maintain the balance. Whenever one or the other achieves an earlier success, it creates tension and uncertainty and the necessity for adjusting on both sides. The rapidity of change entails the risk of rash action prompted either by a fear of imminent inferiority or by a belief, whether correct or mistaken, of overwhelming superiority. The latter could lead to efforts at blackmail which could precipitate unintended large-scale war.

The spread of nuclear weapons into the control of more and more nations seems likely to enhance seriously these risks of instability and to introduce additional ones.

The effort to maintain an effective deterrent and to keep up in the arms race will probably become more burdensome. In any case, the greater part or all of the effort will only serve to neutralize the capability on the other side. Neither alone can safely stop its frantic activity, but the question is certain to arise as to whether mutual deterrence could not be achieved at lower levels of forces and expenditure.

As even so brief a summary indicates, both sides have possible common or parallel interests* in preventing an unintended all-out war and in minimizing the burden of the deterrent. Each side can continue its unilateral efforts to make its deterrent more effective. If these efforts merely produce enhanced or more secure capacity to damage the opponent, the result will still be a system of mutual deterrence, subject to risks of the sort out-

---

* Since these parallel interests result mainly from hazards inherent in major nuclear-weapons systems, they extend to any activities or violence entailing risks of the ultimate use of such weapons. Hence, the desire to mitigate that danger can be the basis for measures to control conventional weapons. If the use of such nuclear-weapons systems were, however, fully neutralized by technology (as might happen) or eliminated by arms-control measures (as seems remote), would this common interest persist for controlling conventional weapons? It might not if a potential aggressor considered that nuclear-weapons systems had been finally removed from the equation; but that condition is hardly likely to be fulfilled, at least by arms-control measures. Moreover, even in that case, there could be a common interest in reducing the burden of conventional forces if both sides concluded that a standoff existed in such forces and could be maintained at lower levels.

lined. Conceivably, one side might achieve a technical break-through, reducing its own vulnerability to an opposing strike so radically as to destroy the "stalemate." But, the chances and value of that possibility must be weighed against the opposite danger and the other risks inherent in an unrestricted arms race. In making that appraisal, both sides could readily conclude that their interests would be better served by measures to stabilize the system or reduce its burden. There are limits, however, to how far this can be achieved by unilateral action. Certain kinds of measures useful for these purposes require joint action or co-operation. This objective fact must be the basis for any progress toward arms control under present conditions.

Criteria of Acceptability

The thesis of this paper is that the validity and stability of any arms-control system will depend ultimately on the same kinds of motives and factors as those which underlie the existing "system"—namely the self-interest of the parties. Arms-control measures broaden the arsenal of instruments available for con-structing and reinforcing a viable deterrent system by means of agreed standards, limitations, or safeguards. They may serve to reduce the likelihood of war, or (possibly) the burden of effec-tive deterrence. But any proposed system of arms control must be judged by whether it makes it more attractive to the parties (in terms of their own interests) to maintain the system and its safeguards than to disrupt it by resorting to violence or evasion.

Constructing an arms-control plan that meets such a test is far from easy and must overcome serious technical and political obstacles. The existence of common interests does not assure that practical methods for working together are attainable. To es-tablish arms control, the parties will have to be in accord on: applicable limitations; methods of verifying compliances; and the consequences of violation. These three aspects, which inter-act as will be discussed later, may affect the several parties dif-ferently. In appraising any plan, each party will compare its benefits and risks under the plan with its prospects without it. Before accepting any plan, each nation will have to be satisfied on two issues:

First, if carried out according to its terms, how will the plan serve its security or other interests compared to the situation without it? Will it lessen the risks of war, whether deliberate or unintended? Will it allow reductions in military expenses without loss of security? These two aims are not necessarily complementary. Some joint actions to stablilize deterrence might even require increasing expenditure. For example, if the all-out nuclear deterrent were virtually neutralized, stability would depend on the balance in other weapons and forces. Unless attained by major reductions in Soviet and Chinese forces, this would probably require increases in those of the West.

And, second, would possible violations of the arrangements entail undue risks to its security compared to the situation in the absence of the arrangements?

In essence, this question breaks down into several parts. What are the chances that another party could evade some or all of the agreed limitations without prompt detection? How seriously might any such violation upset the military balance? Could the victims redress the balance or compensate for the violation if detected, and, if so, how rapidly? What detriment might the violator suffer from detection? Taking all these questions into account, how likely is it that evasion would be attempted? And, how do these risks compare with those without an agreement?

To be acceptable, any arms-control plan must combine its limitations, safeguards, and remedies so as to satisfy both criteria for all parties. In seeking to do so, it is essential to understand how these several elements may reinforce each other or conflict, and what limits they impose on the feasible scope of such a system.

The remainder of this paper attempts to analyze some of these limits and interactions and their implications. Its purpose is not to develop a specific proposal but to examine certain conditions and relations inherent in the situation, which apply to any arms-control measures in existing circumstances.

Balancing of Restrictions

One serious obstacle to arms control arises from the difficulty of equating the impact of specific restrictions or other terms on the several parties. The task of assessing the effect of any acceptable change in military forces or armaments on the absolute and relative capability of the parties is extremely complex.

Since the armed forces of each nation rely on their own special "mix" of armaments and men, any restriction of a particular weapon has different impacts on each of them. In the 1930's enormous amounts of energy and time were devoted without success to efforts to equate different kinds and numbers of conventional weapons. Nuclear weapons and missiles have, if anything, made this task even harder because of the wide range of uncertainty regarding their effects on offense and defense and the relations between nuclear and conventional capabilities. Moreover, with dynamic-weapons technology, each side is likely to be ahead in developing specific fields, and therefore will appraise the prospects and significance of newer weapons in quite different terms. Especially under these conditions, military experts on each side almost inevitably tend to overestimate the harm to their capability from any proposed restriction and to discount its effects on the potential enemy. Hence, the greater the uncertainty regarding the value and equivalence of weapons and forces, the more likely is the conservative bias on both sides to block agreement on any material change.

A second obstacle arises from differing appraisals by the United States and the USSR of the value and costs of inspection inherent in the divergence between a "closed" and an "open" society. Effective inspection is more vital for the United States than for the USSR. The vast range of published data on the United States military programs available to the USSR through the press, Congressional reports and hearings, etc., would greatly reduce its dependence on the inspectorate and provide cross-checks and leads for its operations. Moreover, the very nature of an open, democratic society would make it far more difficult, if not impossible, for the government to carry on any large-scale secret evasion or violation, even if it desired to do so. Conversely, the closed character of the USSR necessitates more intensive inspection to provide data and greater dependence on the data so obtained with fewer chances for cross-checks, etc. Hence, the United States is forced to insist on a degree and reliability of inspection for which the USSR is likely not to feel a corresponding requirement.

In terms of costs or burdens of inspection, the appraisals will also differ. The Soviets undoubtedly look on their secrecy as a military asset. In allowing it to be pierced by inspection, they consider they are making a separate, or additional, sacrifice of their military potential. Hence, they will assess the cost of reciprocal inspection (particularly, if intensive) as high, especially as compared to its value for them. The United States will certainly not estimate the burden as nearly so great, though it might appear more onerous (at least for private activities) if negotiations ever got down to practical details.

The consequence is that, in striking a balance between costs and value of inspection, the United States will inevitably favor more intensive and thorough systems and methods than the USSR. In this respect their interests tend to diverge materially and to obstruct agreement on a common system.

Their interests may diverge in another respect. A system which succeeded in neutralizing the all-out deterrent could have ancillary consequences differing according to the purposes of the two sides. For the Soviets, widespread confidence in the system might make it more difficult to utilize the fear of war for attaining political advantages. For the United States, one result might be to narrow the value of the all-out deterrent in inhibiting aggression in peripheral areas. Today, lack of certainty about its use may deter rash Soviet action, especially where the stakes are small compared to the price of a mistaken judgment. Some forms of arms control, by more effectively neutralizing the strategic capabilities, could erode this effect in the less vital areas. Finally, the prospect of rapid technological change complicates the creation of an acceptable system. Where radical innovation has become usual, a nation may hesitate to tie its hands too tightly when the future is so uncertain.

Limits of Inspection

Inspection (used here to mean any method of obtaining or verifying evidence) has come to be the cornerstone of arms control. Indeed, it is often said that inspection must be "foolproof." If, in fact, 100 percent certainty were required in the inspection system, virtually no arms control would be feasible. In practice, no technique depending on human skills and judgment can be infallible. This truism is especially applicable in a field where actual experience is so lacking. Moreover, the Soviet Union (certainly) and the United States (probably) would not agree to inspection of the scope and intensity which would be necessary to attain the highest feasible reliability.

But infallibility is not the proper criterion. Inspection should be viewed as a technique for reinforcing and maintaining the self-interest of the parties in the continued effective operation of the system. The restrictions and the related inspection should be considered as a system of deterrence. Their combined aim should be to create *risks* of detection which a rational participant would not consider worth running. He need not believe that the inspection techniques are certain to discover the violation: he need only be convinced that the odds of discovery are too high to make the attempt worthwhile in the light of the possible benefits and costs. Of course, the reliability of the inspection process is still a vital factor in determining the extent of feasible arms control. But it can not be judged in isolation. It is intimately related to the nature of the restriction and remedies included in the system, and to the interest of the parties in its continued operation.

This interplay is apparent even when the primary purpose is to provide reciprocal information for reassurance or the avoidance of mistakes, as in some schemes for preventing accidental war or for inhibiting surprise attack. Inspection to prevent mistake or surprise may be greatly facilitated by agreed-upon restrictions concerning readiness or disposition (of strategic air forces or missiles, for example) which would almost surely have to be violated to mount such an attack. Inspection could not prevent such restrictions from being disregarded, but their existence would enable inspectors promptly to interpret as hostile an action which might otherwise be ambiguous.

For any specific restriction, the potential violator will weigh the value of the evasion against the risks and consequences of detection. He will hardly assume the risks of discovery (whatever they may be) unless he can foresee some commensurate advantages. Thus, the crucial question is not whether the inspection system could discover every *technical* evasion, but what prospects it offers for detecting any *significant* one. In assessing this, several factors become relevant.

One is the scope and duration of activity required for a significant violation. If evasion had to be carried out on a large scale or over a long period before yielding benefits, there would appear more chance of its detection by cross-checks or random sampling or other means. Thus, if conventional military equipment had been reduced to a certain level, its replacement in substantial amounts should be reasonably risky with even moderate inspection in operation.

Also, the amount of clandestine production required to be "significant" would also depend on the levels to which agreed reduction had dropped. If other powers had reduced virtually to zero, relatively small violations might give the offender a great advantage. But if they retain major capabilities, much larger evasions would be necessary.

In assessing advantages of evasion, the violator must think in terms of usable weapons systems—fragmentary evasions may not give any real superiority. Thus, if restrictions were applied to existing nuclear material, the fact that it could be secreted in little space without continuing activity would make the prospects of detection very small indeed. The significance of a violation, however, would depend partly on the level to which others had reduced and partly on how much else the violator would have to do to make his secret stock-pile usable. Added safeguards might arise from other reinforcing restrictions which could be inspected more readily—such as limits on delivery vehicles which might involve a much wider range of activities for evasion.

Inspection seems likely to present some of the hardest problems at the start of an arms-control system. Time will be required for it to be organized and installed, to gain experience, and to earn the confidence of the participants. Moreover, at that stage, the degree of intensity of inspection is most likely to seem out of proportion to the modest initial restrictions or reductions: checking on certain kinds of isolated limitations could require nearly as much probing as that for more extensive reductions. For this reason, under a comprehensive system put into effect by successive stages, the inspectorate would hardly need to expand in step with the restrictions. In selecting initial limitations, therefore, one major factor should be to find those which minimize the scope and burden of inspection.

One method for facilitating inspection at all stages is to require the participants to prove their compliance with specific obligations. They may be in a position to produce convincing evidence of their action much more easily than inspectors could establish the facts without assistance. The making of reports of various kinds by the parties can serve a similar purpose of facilitating inspection. The early stages of a system should capitalize on such techniques by beginning with limitations for which they are especially helpful.

The nature of the inspection system and its value are also related to how the data it produces will be used. The deterrent effect will be affected by how violations are established and redressed.

Measures Relating to Violation

Since the purpose of the inspection system is to assure compliance, a central issue involves the treatment of violations. Actually, two factors are involved: the method for determining that a violation has occurred; and the remedies available for redressing it.

DETERMINING VIOLATIONS: In considering procedures for determining violations, two alternatives can be conceived: the inspectorate could be required to produce and submit evidence of any violation to an impartial tribunal which would judge the issue like a court; or the evidence could be furnished to the parties for their information and decision as to how to act on it. Some have taken for granted that the first method was inevitable or desirable.

This is by no means self-evident. In some cases, the state of the evidence may require a court to find that the violation is not proved despite suspicious circumstances. The other parties may still suspect evasion, and be tempted themselves to evade in "self-defense," if the decision of the court leaves no alternative. If the parties have the privilege of deciding how to interpret and act on the suspicious data the deterrent to violation may be enhanced. The practical effect might be that they could then take overt counter-measures. Indeed, they could announce the protective counter-measures, and offer to withdraw or terminate them upon satisfactory proof that the suspicions were unfounded. The suspected party would then have a real interest in establishing innocence. And it will frequently be far simpler for him to offer persuasive proof that he is not in violation than for the inspectorate to prove the real state of facts. Consequently, if the system is designed to serve the continuing interests of both sides, the right of the parties to interpret suspicious evidence may be better calculated to maintain the viability and stability of the system than final authority in a tribunal for this purpose.

There are, however, considerations favoring a tribunal. Any agreement will entail some ambiguous provisions on which there is room for legitimate dispute. Both sides might well be willing to allow a tribunal to resolve the issue. Similarly, it may be useful to have a forum for presenting evidence of violations, especially where clear, in order to exert pressure on the violator or to have the support of a judgment of the tribunal to justify any counter-action the victim might decide to take.

Hence, the best solution may be to seek to combine both methods. To obtain the benefits mentioned, a tribunal could be available for resolving disputes about the terms of the agreement or the evidence of violations; but the parties might still have the right to suspend or cancel the agreement if the result seemed to require it for the protection of their security.

REMEDIES FOR VIOLATION: What remedies are available in case of violation of the arms agreement? The answer to that question sets a basic limit on the kind and extent of restrictions which are feasible.

In their comprehensive plan for world disarmament, Clark and Sohn provide for an international agency with authority to require compliance and adequate power for enforcement. No such agency now exists. Even if the International Court had compulsory jurisdiction to determine a violation, it would lack effective means to enforce its decree or to provide remedies to the other parties. Under existing political conditions, the Soviet Union and the United States could not agree to create an international agency with sufficient power to coerce their compliance with its decrees. The existing distrust and cleavage make joint action for that purpose wholly impracticable.

If that solution is now unfeasible, it is essential to realize that dependence in case of violation must be placed on self-help. Consequently, in making any agreement, the parties must seek to appraise the following: if they fulfill their obligations under the agreement, how will their relative capability compare with that of a violator who has whatever advantage he could reasonably be expected to obtain by evasion before detection? The crucial question is whether or not the honest parties would still be able to assure their security under these conditions. Would the violation be likely to upset or jeopardize the deterrent balance?

The answer to the question depends on a variety of factors involved in any specific plan. Of course, if the plan affects the capabilities of either side only in ways readily rectified or reversed, its cancellation could leave the parties substantially where they had been before its adoption. Some forms of limitation might operate in much this way. For example, the plans for depositing weapons in international stockpiles on the territory of the several members are designed to have this effect. If one party should reclaim his weapons, others might quickly follow suit.

Moreover, the effect of a violation depends on the general level and character of forces retained. Smaller evasions might not be really significant to upset the balance if major deterrent forces were kept in being by all parties; but, as the general levels were reduced more and more, the significance of the same violation could grow.

Violations which do not threaten to upset the military balance might be more difficult to handle. For example, one party may impede the work of the inspectorate in various ways which infringe on their rights under the agreement. The experience under the North Korean Armistice offers many examples of such methods. The other parties might be loath to terminate the agreement with all that would entail, just as was the case in the Korean Armistice. They might, however, be able to resort to lesser pressures to coerce compliance, such as imposing similar restraints on inspection (which might not be adequate) or suspending other provisions or restrictions until the noncompliance was corrected. Of course, this could lead to an ultimate breakdown of the agreement—but it would confront the offender with the necessity of choosing whether to comply or to run that risk.

In deciding whether or not to attempt a major evasion and risk detection, however, a potential violator would have to weigh a wider range of considerations.

An evasion might so shock and solidify world opinion against the violator as to create a stronger coalition against him than would have existed beforehand. It could produce crash programs of rearming such as resulted from Korea. Moreover, the violator might run a serious risk of provoking preventative action based on the conviction that the other parties have no choice in view of his demonstrated perfidy. The uncertainty and unpredictability of these consequences would be likely to exercise very great restraints against major violators.

Conclusion

The basic point should be stressed again: no arms-control plan will remain effective and dependable unless it continues to serve the national interests of each of the parties, as its leaders conceive those interests. In reaching their judgment, however, they will appraise the alternatives. The main function of inspection and of the remedies available to the other parties is to make evasion unattractive as an alternative course. To achieve that result, the inspection system should confront the potential violator with risks of detection and counter-measures outweighing the significance of the violation for the relative capabilities of the participants. The system as a whole must be designed to offer benefits to all participants which they are likely to prefer not to jeopardize.

The analysis leads to one tentative conclusion. It may be wise for the agreement to allow any participant to withdraw at any time (or after relatively brief notice) without cause. Such a privilege has several merits.

First, it emphasizes the fact that the validity and continuance of any plan depends on its *continuing* appeal to the self-interest of the participants. It underscores the fact that their *promise* to comply should not be the basis for reliance.

Second, it resolves the problem of the determination of compliance or violation. If one party becomes suspicious of another's compliance, he can protect himself at once by suspending some or all of his own obligations. The threat to do so, or conditional suspension, could be one means to require the suspected party to provide positive evidence of compliance.

Third, such a provision would underscore the necessity for each party, either alone or with allies, to be able to protect his security at all times if the agreement breaks down. This again is calculated to forestall any false reliance on the agreement which it can not provide, and to confront each participant constantly with the need for realistic appraisal of the operation of the plan.

Fourth, it would meet the problem of revision of the agreement. An arrangement in this field may not operate exactly as anticipated, either with respect to restrictions or safeguards. As a result, they might bear unfairly on one or more parties. Moreover, technological progress could easily skew the initial effects of a plan in favor of one side or the other. It would be extremely difficult, if not impossible, to prescribe detailed procedures for modifying or revising the plan by arbitration or other usual methods for breaking deadlocks. The privilege of withdrawal may be the simplest way to force renegotiation where justified.

It must be recognized, however, that such a privilege has some drawbacks. The fact that ending the agreement would not entail the breaking of a commitment might reduce the pressure to preserve the system under some cases. In practice, however, that pressure could hardly prevail if the continuance were considered to imperil the security of a party for whatever reason. In the case of the democracies, it might delay the decision somewhat more than in the dictatorial regimes.

Even with the privilege, however, there could still be substantial forces inhibiting a participant from withdrawing from or upsetting a working system for light causes. The dangers of reviving an urgent arms race with less likelihood of renewing arms control later would normally gives serious pause. Such action, if taken for arbitrary or narrow reasons, would also involve major political costs all over the world, and, at least in the democracies, at home as well. Consequently, if the system were operating fairly and effectively, it seems reasonable to assume that the privilege of ending it would not be used casually by any major party. So long as they felt the system served their security interests, they should also be able to assure that its continuance would not be jeopardized by the withdrawal of others.

The privilege of canceling or suspending could be used as a very flexible device. The choice need not be all or nothing. A party could suspend specified portions of the restrictions or other provisions commensurate with the violation or evasion, or adequate to adjust to changed conditions. Moreover, any such suspension could be made conditional, or to be effective after a certain interval, in order to induce a negotiation for agreed modifications in the agreement. The experience with the Korean Armistice indicates that changes can be made in this manner without destroying the agreement, even when it contains no such privilege. In that case, the Communists introduced planes into North Korea contrary to the armistice; thereafter, the United States, in compensation, suspended certain restrictions on bringing new weapons into South Korea. Despite these changes, the armistice itself has remained in effect.

Some may feel that the foregoing analysis is unduly pessimistic or that it virtually forecloses any prospect of an extensive arms control. That, in my opinion, is not a proper conclusion. Within the limits discussed, there is room for substantial measures to stabilize the deterrent and to make initial modest reductions. Moreover, experience with inspection, and the application of imagination and invention to developing its techniques, could broaden the area for further measures. In particular, by cooperation through such means, the major opponents might be able to work out ways of maintaining the strategic deterrent at lower levels of resources and expenditures, especially if newer generations of missiles create the possibility of relatively invulnerable defensive capability. If their role comes to be recognized as one of essentially mutual neutralization, more modest levels might be adequate within an operating arms-control system. Moreover, in such a context, a reduction in the levels of conventional forces is within the realm of feasibility and could serve to lower the general level of defense expenditures below what otherwise might prevail.

These prospects fall well short of total disarmament. But realism seems to require recognition of the fact that such a state can be approached, if at all, only under conditions which permit international enforcement to operate effectively. In particular, it appears to call for an international agency with adequate authority and coercive means to punish and constrain a violator of the system. And that presupposes such fundamental changes in the political sphere as would pose a different range of problems within a new context. Such changes, if they occur, will depend on a wide range of policies and actions, involving many fields besides arms control. Limited progress in arms control to stabilize the situation will help in providing the time for such other actions to produce results.

VIII THE ABOLITION OF FORCE: DISARMAMENT

Gentlemen: You Are Mad!

LEWIS MUMFORD

WE IN AMERICA ARE LIVING AMONG MADMEN. Madmen govern our affairs in the name of order and security. The chief madmen claim the titles of general, admiral, senator, scientist, administrator, Secretary of State, even President. And the fatal symptom of their madness is this: they have been carrying through a series of acts which will lead eventually to the destruction of mankind, under the solemn conviction that they are normal responsible people, living sane lives, and working for reasonable ends.

Soberly, day after day, the madmen continue to go through the undeviating motions of madness: motions so stereotyped, so commonplace, that they seem the normal motions of normal men, not the mass compulsions of people bent on total death. Without a public mandate of any kind, the madmen have taken it upon

From *The Saturday Review*, March 2, 1946. Copyright 1946 by The Saturday Review Associates, Inc. Reprinted by permission.

Mr. Mumford's ideas are further developed in "The Morals of Extermination," *Atlantic Monthly*, October, 1968.

themselves to lead us by gradual stages to that final act of madness which will corrupt the face of the earth and blot out the nations of men, possibly put an end to all life on the planet itself.

These madmen have a comet by the tail, but they think to prove their sanity by treating it as if it were a child's skyrocket. They play with it; they experiment with it; they dream of swifter and brighter comets. Their teachers have handed them down no rules for controlling comets; so they take only the usual precautions of children permitted to set off firecrackers. Without asking anyone's permission, they have decided to play a little further with this cosmic force, merely to see what will happen at sea in a war that must never come.

Why do we let the madmen go on with their game without raising our voices? Why do we keep our glassy calm in the face of this danger? There is a reason: we are madmen, too. We view the madness of our leaders as if it expressed a traditional wisdom and a common sense; we view them placidly, as a doped policeman might view with a blank, tolerant leer the robbery of a bank or the barehanded killing of a child or the setting of an infernal machine in a railroad station. Our failure to act is the measure of our madness. We look at the madmen and pass by.

Truly, those are infernal machines that our elected and appointed madmen are setting. When the machines go off, the cities will explode, one after another, like a string of firecrackers, burning and blasting every vestige of life to a crisp. We know that the madmen are still making these machines, and we do not even ask them for what reason, still less do we bring their work to a halt. So we, too, are madmen: madmen living among madmen: unmoved by the horror that moves swiftly toward us. We are thinking only of the next hour, the next day, the next week, and that is further proof that we are mad; for if we go on in this fashion, tomorrow will be more heavy with death than a mortuary. . . .

The madmen act as if nothing were happening, as if nothing were going to happen: they are taking the madmen's usual precautions with the madmen's usual confidence. But the awakened ones, those who are still the madmen's prisoners, know better than this. The pleading words they have guardedly sent us have been lying around for months, and only our paralyzed bodies and our dead minds have kept us from picking the fragments up and piecing them together. Let us read their plain message: it is the only warning we will ever have.

Here is the message of the awakened ones:

"The madmen are planning the end of the world. What they call continued progress in atomic warfare means universal extermination, and what they call national security is organized suicide. There is only one duty for the moment: every other task is a dream and a mockery. Stop the atomic bomb. Stop making the bomb. Abandon the bomb completely. Dismantle every existing bomb. Cancel every plan for the bomb's use; for these clever plans are based on stark madness. Either dethrone the madmen immediately or raise such a shout of protest as will shock them into sanity. We have seen the infernal machine in action, and we hold that this action is not for man to invoke.

"We know there is no quick way out of this madness, for the cooperation of mankind cannot be purchased cheaply by terror; but the first step, the only effective preliminary step, is to put an end to the atomic bomb. You cannot talk like sane men around a peace table while the atomic bomb itself is ticking beneath it. Do not treat the atomic bomb as a weapon of offense: do not treat it as a weapon of retaliation: do not treat it as an instrument of the police. Treat the bomb for what it actually is: the visible insanity of a civilization that has ceased to worship life and obey the laws of life. Say that as men we are too proud to will the rest of mankind's destruction even if that madness could for a few meaningless extra moments save ourselves. Say that we are too wise to imagine that our life would have value or purpose, security or continuity, in a world blasted by terror or paralyzed by the threat of terror."

So reads the message of the awakened ones.

. . . The first move toward sanity lies with us. Abandon the Atomic Bomb! Give it up! Stop it now! That is the only order of the day. When we have performed this duty the next step will be visible, and the next duty will add a new safeguard against the smooth automatism of the madmen. But we must be quick to overcome our own madness. Already the clockwork is ticking faster, and the end—unless we act with the awakened ones—is closer than anyone yet dares to think.

The Case for Graduated Unilateral Action

CHARLES E. OSGOOD

IMAGINE TWO HUSKY MEN STANDING FACING EACH OTHER NEAR THE MIDDLE, BUT ON OPPOSITE SIDES, OF A LONG AND RIGID, NEATLY BALANCED SEESAW. As either man takes a step outward, the other must compensate with a nearly equal step outward on his side or the balance will be destroyed. The farther out they move, the greater the unbalancing effect of each unilateral step and the more agile and quick to react both men must become to maintain the precarious equilibrium. To make the situation even worse, both of these husky men realize that this teetering board has some limit to its tensile strength—at some point it is certain to crack, dropping them both to destruction. So both men are frightened, but neither is willing to admit if for fear the other might take advantage of him. How are these two men to escape from this dangerous situation—a situation in which the fate of each is bound up with that of the other?

One reasonable solution immediately presents itself: let them agree to walk slowly and carefully back toward the center of the teetering board in unison. To do this they must trust each other. But these men distrust each other, and each supposes the other

From "How We Might Win the Hot War and Lose the Cold," *Midway 4, 1960.* Condensed from "Suggestions for Winning the Real War with Communism," *Journal of Conflict Resolution,* III, 4 (Dec. 1959). Copyright 1960 by The University of Chicago. Reprinted by permission.

to be irrational enough to destroy them both unless he (ego) preserves the balance. But now let us suppose that, during a quiet moment in the strife, it occurs to one of these men that perhaps the other really is just as frightened as he is and would also welcome some way of escaping from this intolerable situation. So this man decides to gamble on his new insight and calls out loudly, "I am taking a small step toward you!" The other man, rather than have the precarious balance upset, also takes a step forward, whereupon the first takes yet another, larger step. Thus they work their ways back to safety by a series of unilateral, yet reciprocal, steps—very much as they had originally moved out against each other.

Assumptions underlying this policy. We will talk about graduated unilateral disengagement (rather than disarmament) to emphasize the fact that we are considering a much wider range of acts of a tension-reducing nature than the notion of disarmament includes. This policy is based on the assumption that the Russian people and leaders are sufficiently like us to accept an unambiguous opportunity to reduce the probability of mutual nuclear destruction. It also assumes that the Russian leaders are susceptible to moral pressures, both from without and from within, since such pressures are an index of the success or failure of their system. It assumes that, unlike mutual negotiations which can easily be twisted into cold-war propaganda, unilateral acts of a tension-reducing nature are relatively unambiguous. It assumes that each unilateral act that is reciprocated makes the next such sequence easier to accomplish. Finally, it assumes that the Communists are as convinced that their way of life will win out in non-military competition for men's minds as we are that ours will and that they would be satisfied to compete on those terms. Many statements by Communist leaders in recent years indicate that this is their view.

Nature of this policy. To be maximally effective in inducing the enemy to reciprocate, a unilateral act (1) should, in terms of *military aggression*, be clearly disadvantageous to the side making it, yet not cripplingly so; (2) should be such as to be clearly perceived by the enemy as reducing *his* external threat;

(3) should not increase the enemy's threat to our heartland; (4) should be such that reciprocal action by the enemy is clearly available and clearly indicated; (5) should be announced in advance and widely publicized to ally, neutral, and enemy countries —as regards the nature of the act, its purpose as part of a consistent policy, and the expected reciprocation; (6) but should not demand prior commitment to reciprocation by the enemy as a condition for its commission.

In general, the initial acts of unilateral disengagement would be small in magnitude of potential risk, should they not be reciprocated, but would increase in magnitude of risk potential as reciprocations were obtained. The initial series of unilateral acts would be designed to be cumulative in their tension-reducing effect upon the enemy but non-cumulative in their effect upon our capacity to deliver massive retaliation should this policy fail —that is, the acts would not be such as to weaken us progressively in the same area or in the "survival" area at all. Progressive unilateral disengagement should be viewed as a Phase I "primer," as a means of starting a reversal in the kinds of reciprocal actions now being made (i.e., the arms race); it should not exclude other policies, such as mutual disarmament negotiations, as they become available to us. Above all, it should be a policy entered into sincerely as an attempt to probe the enemy's true intentions, not as merely another weapon in the cold war, and it should be continued consistently until it is entirely clear what the enemy's intentions actually are.

The following is intended solely *as an illustration* of what a sequence of unilateral tension-reducing acts might be like; it is not a proposal of what the specific acts should be. As I tried to make clear in the beginning, I do not have the necessary training or information to make concrete proposals in this area, but I am sure there are people in our government who would be fully capable of doing so.

1. The United States government announces to the world that on a date one month from that time it intends to share with the Russians (and all other nations) the information it has been gathering on the conditions of outer space, on the manufacture

of "clean" nuclear bombs, and on various other developments in science whose main values are peaceful and scientific in nature. We indicate that, whereas our own action is not contingent upon their prior commitment, we expect them to respond in kind by sharing information of a similar nature. We also announce that this is part of our new policy—to reduce world tensions by direct, progressive unilateral steps.

2. On the date set, this action is taken. Our next move depends upon what the Russians have done at this point. (a) If they have reciprocated, we take a larger step: perhaps we announce that one month from that time we intend to deactivate and withdraw from a major military base—one closest and most threatening to the Russian heartland—and we invite them to send observers to check this operation. Again, we assert our general policy and suggest appropriate reciprocation on their part. (It probably should be pointed out that, in an age of nuclear missiles, stable military bases whose locations are well known are "sitting ducks" anyhow, since they would be the first targets in a surprise attack against us; their only value is in terms of threat or in terms of a surprise attack on our own part—which I have argued we would not launch.) (b) If the Russians have failed to reciprocate to our first unilateral act, we take another small step: perhaps we announce that on a date one month from this time we intend to ban for a period of one year all further tests of nuclear weapons, and again we invite their inspection. We restate our general policy and our expectation that they will reciprocate.

3. On the date set, this second unilateral action, (a) or (b), is taken. If the Russians have been reciprocating, we take still larger steps bearing on focal points of tensions. It is quite possible, of course, that by this time the Russians may be trying to outdo us in "walking inward on the seesaw"—they have already made some tentative moves in this direction (e.g., their unilateral decision to ban nuclear-bomb testing for a period). If, on the other hand, the Russians have not reciprocated, I think we should continue our series of tension-reducing but non-crippling acts until either mounting moral pressure forces them to reciprocate or their negative intention becomes completely clear.

I believe that graduated unilateral disengagement can provide the basis for a positive and consistent foreign policy, one that is appropriate to international relations in a nuclear age and one in which we can take the initiative. In recent years our foreign policy has been essentially reactive and opportunistic. This is not only ineffective but downright dangerous, because it allows others to manipulate us by simply applying the right stimuli. We could find many opportunities to apply "psycho-logic pressure" to the Russians, if we were not such blind adherents to our own psycho-logic—that is always taking a posture of opposition to them, regardless of the issue. For example, we should side *with* them on issues where we can do so in good faith— which would put *their* oversimplified picture of the world under stress. Acceptance of China into the UN may be a case in point. It seems to me that we have accepted too readily the role of defending the status quo, and, in doing so, we have forgotten that our own way of life is itself a major revolution in men's minds that is just getting under way.

A Foreign Policy for Survival

SIDNEY HOOK

No one knows whether the use of tactical atomic weapons can be limited and the use of the ultimate weapons with thermonuclear warheads avoided. During the last war, despite all the prewar Cassandras, poison gas was not used because of the certainty that it would be employed by the other side in retaliation. The same might be true for hydrogen bombs in the next war. Nonetheless, it seems to me to be true that the ultimate weapon can be a deterrent only if the Kremlin believes it will

From *The New Leader,* April 7, 1958. Reprinted by permission.

be used. *This means that the ultimate weapon of the West is not the hydrogen bomb or any other super-weapon but the passion for freedom and the willingness to die for it if necessary.* Once the Kremlin is convinced that we will use this weapon to prevent it from subjugating the world to its will, we will have the best assurance of peace. Once the Kremlin believes that this willingness to fight for freedom at all costs is absent, that it has been eroded by neutralist fear and pacifist wishful thinking, it will blackmail the free countries of the world into capitulation and succeed where Hitler failed.

. . . It is possible to panic the West by a picture of the universal holocaust a nuclear world war would bring, to panic the West to a point where survival on any terms seems preferable to the risks of resistance. The pages of history show that moral integrity in extreme situations is often the highest political wisdom. The struggle against totalitarianism is not only a political struggle but also a moral one, which limits the extent to which we can carry appeasement. If Hitler had commanded the weapon resources of the Soviet Union, would we have yielded to one Munich after another until the world was one vast concentration camp? I hardly think so. Those who are prepared to sacrifice freedom for peace and for mere life will find after such sacrifice no genuine peace and a life unfit for man. Paradoxical as it may sound, life itself is not a value. What gives life value is not its mere existence but its quality. Whoever proclaims that life is worth living under any circumstances has already written for himself an epitaph of infamy. For there is no principle or human being he will not betray; there is no indignity he will not suffer or compound.

* * *

. . . After all, we cannot be certain that, if we have to defend ourselves by nuclear weapons, they will inevitably destroy the entire human race; nor can we be certain that the terror of Communism will not endure or be followed by something worse.

* * *

We do not, however, need to strike an heroic stance in shaping a viable foreign policy. Intelligence must be our guide. If we can keep the free world from falling into the trap set by the Kremlin and preserve peace by increasing the power and readiness of the free world, we can then rely upon the processes of education, the force of example, the contagion of free ideas, the cultural osmosis of the great traditions of the West gradually to soften, to liberalize, to round off the edges of the totalitarian regimes of the world until their own peoples rally their energies to overthrow their oppressors and establish the democratic governments necessary to establish one free world republic. . . .

The Future Development
of Nuclear Weapons

FREEMAN J. DYSON

A YEAR AND A HALF AGO THE WESTERN POWERS BEGAN NEGOTIA-TIONS WITH THE SOVIET UNION FOR A TREATY TO END THE TESTING OF NUCLEAR WEAPONS. The negotiations were warmly welcomed by the public, and by scientists in particular. It appeared to many people that this was one area of disarmament in which agreement should not be too difficult to reach. The generally optimistic feeling about the negotiations had its origin in three widely held beliefs. It was believed that the development of nuclear weapons had reached a point of technical stagnation; that the military consequences of new inventions in this field would be small; and that a political agreement to cease further development

From *Foreign Affairs*, Vol. 38, No. 3, April, 1960. Copyright 1960 by the Council on Foreign Relations, Inc., New York. Reprinted by special permission.

could be adequately controlled by a system of long-range explosion-detectors. These views have been repeatedly expressed by scientific experts, and many citizens and politicians have come to accept them without serious question.

It is my purpose here to argue the contrary views. I believe that radically new kinds of nuclear weapons are technically possible, that the military and political effects of such weapons would be important, and that the development of such weapons can hardly be arrested by any means less drastic than international control of all nuclear operations.

This by no means implies that negotiations to end weapon-testing should be abandoned. If my views are correct, then to end weapons development becomes vastly more difficult to achieve than had been thought, but it also becomes vastly more rewarding. Any agreement to cease weapon-testing upon a sound and verifiable basis will require an opening of communications and a breaking down of barriers among the nuclear laboratories of the world. The aim of our negotiations will thus be not merely the prohibition of weapon testing, but the establishment of an open world. To many thoughtful people, since the early days of nuclear energy, the great hope has been that nuclear weapons would compel mankind to cooperate not only in nuclear affairs but in other areas too. This dream could well be realized if the negotiations which were begun in order to control weapon tests should end in a system adequate to control more substantial disarmament.

II

Until now we have had two essentially different types of nuclear weapons, the fission bomb and the hydrogen bomb. It is not necessary to discuss in detail how these things work. The essential facts about their performance are the following. A fission bomb cannot explode at all unless it contains a certain quantity (the critical mass) of extremely expensive metal. Thus every fission bomb, regardless of its power, costs a certain fraction of a million dollars and eats up a certain fraction of the available supply of fuel. Every fission bomb using its fuel with reasonable efficiency has an explosive power of the order of kilotons of T.N.T. A hydrogen bomb is able to extract its energy from a much cheaper and more abundant fuel (heavy hydrogen), but it requires at least a moderately efficient fission bomb to ignite it. Thus every hydrogen bomb costs at least as much as a fission bomb. Its cheapness becomes impressive only when its explosive power moves toward the megaton range.

So the basic built-in characteristic of all existing weapons is that it is relatively much cheaper to make a big bang than a small one. Below a certain explosive yield of the order of a kiloton, nuclear weapons are grossly inefficient and extravagant. However, for military purposes other than wholesale annihilation, a kiloton is already an unreasonably big bang. There is a clear and acute military need for an explosive which would fill the gap between a ton and a kiloton of T.N.T. with a cost which is proportional to the yield instead of being independent of it.

There is theoretically a simple way to escape from the tyranny of the critical mass. This is to burn heavy hydrogen without a fission bomb to ignite it. A fission-free bomb, containing a small quantity of heavy hydrogen and no fissionable metal, is logically the third major step in weapon development after the existing fission and hydrogen bombs. Such a bomb has been occasionally mentioned in newspapers and magazines and described as a "100-percent clean bomb." It would not be 100-percent clean. It would contaminate the countryside enormously less than existing fission or hydrogen bombs, but this is not its main advantage. The decisive advantage of a fission-free bomb is that it could be built economically in small sizes. It would have no critical mass. It would provide without gross inefficiency an explosive power adapted to the needs of small-scale and local warfare.

There seems to be no law of nature forbidding the construction of fission-free bombs. The question remains whether this theoretical possibility is likely soon to be realized. In this connection some sentences from a report by L. S. Artsimovitch entitled "Research on Controlled Thermonuclear Reactions in the U.S.S.R." are interesting. The report was published in *Uspekhi Fizicheskikh Nauk* in December 1958 and is now available in translation.

The quotation is condensed and some technical phrases are omitted.

> It may also be possible to realize a pulsed thermonuclear reaction under conditions in which the high temperature is produced by a charge of conventional explosive (such as T.N.T. or something more powerful) which surrounds a capsule containing heavy hydrogen. Without dwelling on the experimental details, we may note that conditions have been found under which the generation of neutrons in hydrogen reactions has been established reliably and reproducibly. In experiments carried out in 1952, there is no doubt that we have observed neutrons which are formed as a result of the heating of matter to extremely high temperatures. This process takes place under conditions in which the density of matter is very high (significantly exceeding the normal density of solids).

Artsimovitch is a well-known and first-rate physicist who played a prominent part in the Soviet weapons program (at the appropriate times he received Stalin and Lenin Prizes). These remarks which he published are an indiscretion, and presumably a calculated indiscretion. It is at least highly interesting for us to know that the Russians were experimenting with fission-free explosive systems in 1952. No doubt somebody on the Russian side hopes by such a minor indiscretion to stimulate a more serious indiscretion on our side. This is the kind of poker game we are playing.

I shall not be so indiscreet as to say anything about the more recent history of fission-free bombs. What I wish to make clear is that these bombs are a theoretical possibility, and that their importance is well understood by at least some individuals on both sides of the iron curtain. Any political arrangement which fails to take these facts into account is doomed to failure.

The future growth of nuclear explosion technology will have military importance in many ways which are hard to foresee now. There are many areas of weaponry in which important problems remain unsolved. The unsolved problems are not, as is often claimed, to make slight or marginal improvement in existing designs. There are several directions in which qualitatively new methods of design may lead to qualitatively superior weapons, or to weapons performing qualitatively new functions. To give only one example, it is possible that a nuclear explosive system designed for the efficient propulsion of a space ship could be the key to long-range and economical space travel. Any country possessing a markedly superior propulsion system in space would reap important advantages, both military and nonmilitary.

To illustrate as forcibly as possible the military importance of new weapons, I return to the example of fission-free systems. Imagine a hypothetical situation in which the United States is armed with its existing weapons, while some adversary (not necessarily the Soviet Union) has a comparable supply of nuclear fuel and has learned how to ignite it fission-free. The adversary's bombs would then outnumber ours ten or a hundred to one, and theirs could be used with far greater versatility in infantry warfare. Suppose that in this situation a local war of the Korean type should begin. God help the American infantryman who is sent in to fight against these odds. Practically speaking, our army would have only two alternatives, either to retreat precipitously or to strike back with our much more limited number of heavier nuclear weapons and thoroughly destroy the whole country. This is not a pleasant situation to contemplate, and yet it is necessary that our people understand that it is a possibility. Any country which renounces for itself the development of nuclear weapons, without certain knowledge that its adversaries have done the same, is likely to find itself in the position of the Polish Army in 1939, fighting tanks with horses.

III

Next let us turn to the stubborn subject of long-range explosion-detectors and their effectiveness for policing an international agreement to halt weapon testing.

A conference was held at Geneva in the summer of 1958 at which scientific experts from East and West met and discussed the problems of long-range detection of explosions. The records of the existing long-range detectors and the responses of these detectors to past weapon tests were examined in detail. After some strenuous argument, the conference agreed upon a statement of conclusions. The statement describes a particular system of detectors which is suggested as a basis for a future international control of weapon-testing. This system, now generally known as the "Geneva system," consists principally of 180 control posts equipped with a variety of scientific instruments and distributed over all parts of the earth. The statement concludes "that it is technically feasible to establish, with the capabilities and limitations indicated below, a workable and effective control system to detect violations of an agreement on the world-wide suspension of nuclear weapons tests."

The agreement of the Geneva "conference of experts" was widely hailed as a shining example of the triumph of scientific objectivity over national and political differences. In many ways it was indeed a triumph. For the first time since the advent of nuclear weapons, men from East and West were sitting together to discuss the nuclear facts of life with some degree of openness. And the speed with which this technical conference could reach an agreement was in startling contrast to the interminable sterility of earlier negotiations with the Soviet Union.

The experts at Geneva in 1958 did not know to what extent artificial concealment of nuclear explosions was technically possible. Probably for this reason they decided to say nothing about it. Scientific objectivity would, however, have required them to report that the concealment problem had not been explored.

Since the summer of 1958, political negotiations between the Soviet Union and the Western powers have been in progress, aiming at an agreement to cease weapon tests. Throughout these negotiations, the Soviet delegates have adamantly held to the line that the Geneva system could effectively police such an agreement. They have refused even to enter into any realistic discussion of the concealment problem. Meanwhile, a small number of Americans have started belatedly to think about concealment, and some small non-nuclear experiments have been carried out. It has gradually become clear to the American experts that a high

degree of concealment is theoretically possible. In a report issued in June 1959 by a panel appointed by the Science Advisory
Committee of the United States Government to study the possible
improvement of the Geneva detection system, it was stated:

> In considering the possibility that the capabilities, now or
> in the future, of the Geneva System might be reduced by
> the intentional concealment of underground tests, the panel
> concluded that decoupling techniques existed which could
> reduce the seismic signal by a factor of ten or more. More-
> over, preliminary theoretical studies have shown that it is
> possible in principle to reduce the seismic signal from an ex-
> plosion by a much greater factor than this.

The technical facts concerning concealment were held secret
until December 1959. It will still be some time before the facts
are published in detail and exposed to the scrutiny of the international community of scientists. Only after such public scrutiny,
and a great deal more experimental work, will it become possible
to make an objective judgment of the effectiveness of concealment. Meanwhile, the limits of uncertainty remain very wide.

My personal opinion is that nuclear explosions in the kiloton
range could be concealed very completely. That is to say, I believe it will be feasible to build a building, looking externally
like a normal industrial structure, within which kiloton explosions can be contained. The cost of such a facility may not be
exorbitant, and the earth tremors which it produces may be no
larger than those produced by ordinary industrial operations.
Giving free rein to the imagination, one may envisage a weapon
testing facility bearing on the outside the inscription "Kazakhstan
Consolidated Steel Mills" and carrying on a legitimate business
of steel fabrication as a side line. Concealment of this sort could
be detected only if the international control authority were em-
powered to travel everywhere and to open all doors.

So long as the concealment problem has not been thoroughly
and openly investigated, the effectiveness of long-range detectors
against concealed explosions will be known only to those governments which conduct their own clandestine experiments. Under

these conditions the idea of international control of explosions by long-range detectors is a dangerous illusion. If, as I suspect, the total concealment of explosions is possible, then a long-range detection system can never guarantee the observance of a test-cessation agreement. No party to the agreement can be sure that his adversaries are not secretly and successfully carrying on the development of new weapons. Especially dangerous is the circumstance that many of the militarily important new weapons will require test explosions only of very low yield.

If we sign an agreement to cease weapon-testing on the basis of a long-range detection system, ignoring the possibilities of concealment, we are trusting to the good faith of all the signatory powers. Now it can be argued that an agreement with the Soviet Union based upon good faith is not worthless. One need not assert that the Soviet Union would feel inclined to violate such an agreement whenever it were technically possible to do so with impunity. It is enough that a world-wide agreement to stop testing, based on good faith alone, would be very unlikely to last forever. Somewhere, sometime, some government would yield to temptation and resume testing in secret.

Public opinion in the West has a terrifying readiness to take refuge in illusions. For some years after 1945 we took refuge in the illusion that our preponderance in nuclear weapons would be more or less permanent. Now many of us are taking refuge in the illusion that the development of nuclear weapons can be stopped all over the world by a painless international agreement and a few hundred seismographs. It is necessary that we face facts resolutely. One fact is that militarily important weapons can be developed in secret by any government keeping a large part of its territory closed to foreigners. Another fact is that, in the absence of an effective international control of armaments, the pressures driving other governments to surpass ours in the technology of nuclear weapons will be almost irresistible.

To ensure that new weapons are not developed, there must exist an international force of detectives with unrestricted rights of travel and inspection. Such an international detective force is at present unacceptable to the Soviet Union. For this reason it seems inevitable that the development of nuclear weapons will continue, either openly or in secret, for many years to come. For the peace of the world, it is far better that the new weapons should be developed openly than in secret. We must forever be thankful that the unconcealed testing of large hydrogen bombs has made the power of these weapons known to everyone.

The only wise policy for the United States at present is to continue the exploration of nuclear weapons technology, including the testing of weapons, until a reliable international control of testing is established. We should not be discouraged by the fact that the Soviet Union will not now accept such a control. In the last ten years the Soviet Union has come a very long way toward accepting the unpleasant facts of life in the nuclear age. It is quite possible that in another ten years the pressure of logic will carry the Soviet leaders a great deal further. In particular, it is possible that the Soviet authorities may in ten years recognize the fact that a rigid international control of all nuclear activities is the only guarantee of their safety as well as of ours.

IV

To many people the continuation of any sort of nuclear weapons development is morally repugnant. To these people my arguments will carry no conviction. They will feel that these arguments merely reveal a moral blindness and an insensitivity to the overwhelming evil of nuclear warfare.

Everyone is agreed that war is evil and that nuclear war is surpassingly evil. And we live in a world where independent sovereign states have undisputed power over stockpiles of nuclear weapons. What then is to be done? I find no escape from the logic which impelled Lilienthal and his colleagues in 1946 when they drew up their plan for the international control of nuclear energy. If nuclear war is to be permanently avoided, it is necessary that somehow, sooner or later, sovereign states voluntarily hand over their nuclear armaments to an international authority. And the international authority must control everything, not only weapon tests but also production facilities, stockpiles and research.

The prospect of an adequate international control of armaments is remote, although possibly not as remote as it seems. Our whole endeavor must now be directed to stay alive somehow and to maintain the stability of the world through the interim period while international anarchy prevails.

During the period of international anarchy, we have a moral choice, either to strive to the utmost to remain in the forefront of nuclear weapons technology or to let the leadership pass into the hands of others. These are the only two alternatives before us. We do not have the power to change the laws of nature so that the possibilities for developing new weapons will disappear. Our moral choice is, either to possess the new weapons ourselves, or to leave it to chance to decide who shall possess them.

The moral dilemma facing the designers of weapons today is not essentially different from that which faced the builders of the fission bomb in 1943 and the builders of the hydrogen bomb in 1951. In each case the choice is the same. You discover that a new and horrible kind of weapon can be made. Either you make it yourself, or you leave it to chance to decide who makes it.

I believe the morally right decisions were made in 1943 and 1951. And I believe the morally right decisions now must be the same. Apart from all considerations of patriotism, it would be wrong for us to leave the future development of nuclear weapons to chance. Our development and possession of these weapons will help to maintain the stability of the world, until in the fullness of time we can hand over all such devilish inventions to an international authority powerful enough to prevent their abuse.

The Balance of Terror

WINSTON CHURCHILL

THESE FEARFUL SCIENTIFIC DISCOVERIES [THE RAPID AND CEASELESS DEVELOPMENTS OF ATOMIC WARFARE AND THE HYDROGEN BOMB] CAST THEIR SHADOW ON EVERY THOUGHTFUL MIND, BUT NEVERTHELESS I BELIEVE THAT WE ARE JUSTIFIED IN FEELING THAT THERE HAS BEEN A DIMINUTION OF TENSION AND THAT THE PROBABILITIES OF ANOTHER WORLD WAR HAVE DIMINISHED, OR AT LEAST HAVE BECOME MORE REMOTE. I say this in spite of the continual growth of weapons of destruction such as have never fallen before into the hands of human beings. Indeed, I have sometimes the odd thought that the annihilating character of these agencies may bring an utterly unforeseeable security to mankind.

When I was a schoolboy I was not good at arithmetic, but I have since heard it said that certain mathematical quantities when they pass through infinity change their signs from plus to minus—or the other way round. I do not venture to plunge too much into detail of what are called the asymptotes of hyperbolae, but any hon. Gentleman who is interested can find an opportunity for an interesting study of these matters. It may be that this rule may have a novel application and that when the advance of destructive weapons enables everyone to kill everybody else nobody will want to kill anyone at all. At any rate, it seems pretty safe to say that a war which begins by both sides suffering what they dread most—and that is undoubtedly the case at present—is less likely to occur than one which dangles the lurid prizes of former ages before ambitious eyes.

I offer this comforting idea to the House, taking care to make

From *The Unwritten Alliance*. Speeches 1953-1959 by Winston Churchill, edited by Randolph Churchill. Copyright 1961. Reprinted by permission of Cassell and Company, Ltd.

it clear at the same time that our only hope can spring from untiring vigilance. There is no doubt that if the human race are to have their dearest wish and be free from the dread of mass destruction, they could have, as an alternative, what many of them might prefer, namely, the swiftest expansion of material well-being that has ever been within their reach, or even within their dreams.

By material well-being I mean not only abundance but a degree of leisure for the masses such as has never before been possible in our mortal struggle for life. These majestic possibilities ought to gleam, and be made to gleam, before the eyes of the toilers in every land, and they ought to inspire the actions of all who bear responsibility for their guidance. We, and all nations, stand, at this hour in human history, before the portals of supreme catastrophe and of measureless reward. My faith is that in God's mercy we shall choose aright.

The Conference of the Animals

WINSTON CHURCHILL

Disarmament

Once upon a time all the animals in the zoos decided that they would disarm, and they arranged to have a conference to arrange the matter. So the Rhinoceros said when he opened the proceedings that the use of teeth was barbarous and horrible and ought to be strictly prohibited by general consent. Horns, which were mainly defensive weapons, would, of course, have to be allowed. The Buffalo, the Stag, the Porcupine, and even the little Hedge-

From *The Eloquence of Churchill* edited by R. B. Czarnomski. Copyright 1957 by The New American Library. Reprinted by The New American Library, Inc., New York.

hog all said they would vote with the Rhino, but the Lion and the Tiger took a different view. They defended teeth and even claws, which they described as honourable weapons of immortal antiquity. The Panther, the Leopard, the Puma, and the whole tribe of small cats all supported the Lion and the Tiger. Then the Bear spoke. He proposed that both teeth and horns should be banned and never used again for fighting by any animal. It would be quite enough if animals were allowed to give each other a good hug when they quarrelled. No one could object to that. It was so fraternal, and that would be a great step towards peace. However, all the other animals were very offended with the Bear, and the Turkey fell into a perfect panic.

The discussion got so hot and angry, and all those animals began thinking so much about horns and teeth and hugging when they argued about the peaceful intentions that had brought them together that they began to look at one another in a very nasty way. Luckily the keepers were able to calm them down and persuade them to go back quietly to their cages, and they began to feel quite friendly with one another again.

Aldersbrook Road, West Essex, October 25, 1928

Living with H-Bombs

EUGENE RABINOWITCH

SHORTLY AFTER THE DISCOVERY OF ATOMIC ENERGY IN 1945, SCI-ENTISTS WERE THE FIRST TO CALL FOR ITS INTERNATIONAL CONTROL, AS A WAY OF PREVENTING THE POSSESSION OF ATOMIC WEAPONS BY INDIVIDUAL NATIONS AND THIS IDEA WAS SOON ACCEPTED, IN PRIN-

From *The Bulletin of the Atomic Scientists*, January, 1955. Copyright 1955 by the Educational Foundation for Nuclear Science, Inc. Reprinted by permission.

CIPLE, BY ALL MAJOR NATIONS, INCLUDING THE USSR. Now, nine years later, controlled atomic disarmament still remains the official aim of all nations, including the United States and the Soviet Union.

In the meantime, however, U.N. negotiations on the practical implementation of international control have been deadlocked since 1948. The Western governments, advised by their technical experts, have maintained that the only effective method of control would be a world-wide *monopoly* of all large-scale atomic industries—from smelting of uranium ore to the generation of electricity in atomic power stations. The USSR has refused to accept this principle, denouncing it as an attempt to dominate socialist industry by an essentially capitalist monopoly. The Soviet speakers insisted that effective control could be achieved by inspection of national and private atomic plants by an international agency; but they never got around to outlining a concrete system of inspection, which could serve as adequate substitute for international ownership (or, at least, international management) of all atomic industries.

Ever since the control negotiations bogged down, prominent individuals and organizations all over the world, from the Pope to the Prime Minister of India, from the International Council of Churches to the Partisans of Peace, from the Parliamentary Union to the Red Cross, have not ceased urging the leaders of the world to search for a compromise solution; and recently, disarmament discussions in the United Nations have raised faint hopes that both sides may now be willing to budge from their previously immovable positions. However, controlled atomic disarmament is not only a matter of political reasonableness, but, above all, one of *technical feasibility;* and this aspect of the problem seems somehow to have slipped out of the public eye.

* * *

The report of September 27, 1946, prepared by the Technical Subcommittee of the U.N. Atomic Energy Commission, with the participation of Russian scientists, asserted the technical feasibility of international control. It was the only unanimously agreed-upon document in the long history of the U.N. control negotiations. However, at the time this report was prepared, the only thing to be controlled was the *production of atomic explosives.* Stockpiles of these materials existed only in the U.S. and were too small to constitute a serious threat, provided further production could be effectively controlled. The situation is different now. According to authoritative statements, American stocks of atomic explosives are approaching a level at which further production, while by no means militarily valueless, will cease to be vital, since the materials on hand will be sufficient to destroy, perhaps several times over, every worthwhile target on the face of the earth. The Soviet stockpile probably is considerably smaller, but it, too, is much too large now to be disregarded in the establishment of controls. Therefore, technical feasibility of atomic disarmament depends now on a reliable *inventory* of existing stocks of fissionable materials. Considering the extremely small bulk of these materials, and the absence of penetrating radiations emanating from them, which could reveal their presence to properly equipped outside inspectors, the only possibility of inventorying them is for the agents of the U.N. control body to be led to the stockpiles by national officials who know where they are located. Neither the West nor the USSR can be expected to base their own atomic disarmament on the faith that the other side has not concealed a substantial part of its stockpile. In the democratic countries, an international control organization could at least hope for a check on governmental compliance through information supplied by citizens; but in totalitarian police states, reliance on such cooperation seems out of the question.

If this conclusion is true, then we may have to add, to the appalling knowledge of the material and biological damage of an atomic war, the recognition that time for an effectively controlled atomic disarmament has irretrievably passed, and that attempts to find a compromise solution leading to such a disarmament, are therefore bound to remain futile. This conclusion is much too serious to be accepted without most conscientious examination. . . . If however, the experts conclude, as I am afraid they will, that controlled abolition of atomic arms is impossible under the conditions of a world-wide abundance of nuclear explosives, this will mean that mankind will have to live, from now on, with unlimited and unchecked stockpiles of atomic and thermonuclear explosives piling up, first in America and the Soviet Union, then in Great Britain, and later in other countries as well. The only realistically possible form of "atomic disarmament" may be, from now on, the *cessation of further bomb tests*. Such an agreement could perhaps be effectively controlled by an international monitoring agency from neutral territory, but it could not produce more than a standstill, or at best a very slight relaxation of international tension (and is likely to prove unacceptable to the Soviet Union, because of America's present lead in weapon development). It is hardly necessary to mention that President Eisenhower's "atomic pool" plan, however desirable it may be for various other reasons, is not likely to lead to any significant atomic disarmament.

One could suggest that an indirect way to atomic disarmament could be found through the abolition of the *means of delivery* of atomic explosives—bomber planes, rocket launching devices, guided missiles, atomic cannons. It is, however, doubtful whether even a very elaborate control over such means of transporting atomic explosives could have the same effect in lessening the danger of war as would an actual elimination of atomic stockpiles.

* * *

Altogether, it seems that the chance to stop the march of history at the threshold of the atomic age, and to give mankind time to adjust its political habits to a changed technological habitat before entering it, has been lost. The technological clock has been inexorably advanced, and we are now deep in the age of atomic plenty, from which atomic explosives cannot be banished by any ingenious political compromise. Having failed to slow down technical progress to permit the survival of our international way of life, mankind is now facing the task of adjusting this way of life to the inexorable technological facts.

* * *

Human Nature
and the Dominion of Fear

HERBERT BUTTERFIELD

THE SITUATION IS STILL FURTHER COMPLICATED BY CERTAIN HUMAN PREDICAMENTS WHICH WE ARE TOO SELDOM CONSCIOUS OF, AND WHICH I CAN ONLY CALL THE PREDICAMENT OF HOBBESIAN FEAR— HOBBESIAN BECAUSE IT WAS SUBJECTED TO PARTICULAR ANALYSIS BY THE SEVENTEENTH-CENTURY PHILOSOPHER, THOMAS HOBBES. If you imagine yourself locked in a room with another person with whom you have often been on the most bitterly hostile terms in the past, and suppose that each of you has a pistol, you may find yourself in a predicament in which both of you would like to throw the pistols out of the window, yet it defeats the intelligence to find a way of doing it. If you throw yours out the first you rob the other man of the only reason he had for getting rid of his own, and for anything you know he may break the bargain. If both of you swear to throw the pistols out together, you may feel that he may make the gesture of hurling his away, but in reality hold tight to it, while you, if you have done the honest thing, would then be at his mercy. You may even have an *arrière-pensée* that he may possibly be concealing a second pistol somewhere about his person. Both of you in fact may have an equal justification for suspecting one another, and both of you may be men who in all predicaments save this had appeared reasonably well-behaved and well-intentioned. You may both of you be utterly honest in your desire to be at peace and to put an end to the predicament, if only in order to enable you to get on with your business. If some great bully were to come into the room and try to take your pistols from you, then as likely as not you would both combine against him, you would find yourselves cherished allies, find yourselves for the time being as thick as thieves. Only, after you had eliminated this intruder, you would discover to your horrible surprise that you were back in the original predicament again.

In international affairs it is this situation of Hobbesian fear which, so far as I can see, has hitherto defeated all the endeavour of the human intellect. Not only may both sides feel utterly self-righteous, but where a great obstruction occurs—as over the question of toleration in the sixteenth century, and that of disarmament in the twentieth—both may feel utterly baffled and frustrated; and sometimes even allies fall to blaming one another, as on one occasion papers of all complexions in England, out of pure exasperation, blamed France for the failure of the Disarmament Conference. Though one side may have more justice than another in the particular occasion of a conflict, there is a sense in which war as such is in reality a judgment on all of us. The fundamental predicament would not exist if men in general were as righteous as the situation requires, and of course the fundamental predicament is itself so maddening and exasperating that men sometimes resort to desperate measures with an idea of cutting the Gordian knot.

Does Disarmament Mean Peace?

HANS J. MORGENTHAU

DISARMAMENT HAS BEEN CAPABLE OF REALIZATION ONLY UNDER EXTRAORDINARY CONDITIONS. Even when it seemed to have been

Fom *Politics Among Nations,* 3rd ed. Copyright 1948, 1954 © 1960 by Alfred A. Knopf, Inc. Reprinted by permission of the publisher.

realized, more often than not disarmament meant increase in armaments rather than reduction. These considerations, however, are but preliminary to the question which is decisive in the context of our discussion. What is the bearing of disarmament upon the issues of international order and peace? Provided the nations of the earth could agree upon quantitative or qualitative disarmament and would actually disarm in accordance with the agreement, how would such reduction of all, or elimination of certain, armaments affect international order and peace?

At the foundation of the modern philosophy of disarmament there is the assumption that men fight because they have arms. From this assumption the conclusion follows logically that if men would give up all arms all fighting would become impossible. In international politics only the Soviet Union has actually taken this conclusion seriously—and it is questionable whether it was very serious after all—by submitting to the World Disarmament Conference of 1932 proposals for complete, universal disarmament (with the exception of light arms for police functions). The contemporary Russian attitude with respect to atomic disarmament is somewhat in keeping with that position. But even where less extreme conclusions are drawn, the proposition is tacitly admitted that there exists a direct relation between the possession of arms, or at least of certain kinds and quantities of arms, and the issue of war and peace.

Such a relation does indeed exist, but it is the reverse from that which the advocates of disarmament assume it to be. Men do not fight because they have arms. They have arms because they deem it necessary to fight. Take away their arms, and they will either fight with their bare fists or get themselves new arms with which to fight. What makes for war are the conditions in the minds of men which make war appear the lesser of two evils. In those conditions must be sought the disease of which the desire for, and possession of, arms is but a symptom. So long as men seek to dominate each other, to take away each other's possessions, fear and hate each other, they will try to satisfy their desires and to put their emotions to rest. Where an authority exists strong enough to direct the manifestations of those desires

and emotions into nonviolent channels, men will seek only non-
violent instruments for the achievement of their ends. In a
society of sovereign nations, however, which by definition constitute the highest authority within the respective national territories, the satisfaction of those desires and the release of those
emotions will be sought by all the means which the technology
of the moment provides and the prevailing rules of conduct
permit. These means may be arrows and swords, guns and
bombs, gas and directed missiles, bacteria and atomic weapons.

To reduce the quantity of weapons actually or potentially available at any particular time could have no influence upon the
incidence of war; it could conceivably affect its conduct. Nations
limited in the quantity of arms and men would concentrate all
their energies upon the improvement of the quality of such arms
and men as they possess. They would, furthermore, search for
new weapons which might compensate them for the loss in
quantity and assure them an advantage over their competitors.

To eliminate certain types of weapons altogether would have a
bearing upon the technology of warfare and through it upon the
conduct of hostilities. It is hard to see how it could influence
the frequency of war or do away with war altogether. Let us
suppose that it were possible, for instance, to outlaw the manufacture and the use of atomic bombs. What would be the effect
of such a prohibition, provided it were universally observed? It
would simply reduce the technology of war to the level of the
morning of July 16, 1945, before the first atomic bomb was exploded in New Mexico. The nations adhering to the prohibition
would employ their human and material resources for the development and discovery of weapons other than atomic bombs. The
technology of warfare would change, but not the incidence of
war.

The abortive attempts of Great Britain to have the World Disarmament Conference outlaw aggressive, in contrast to defensive, weapons illustrate the impossibility of solving the problem
by way of qualitative disarmament. Great Britain started with the
assumption that the ability to wage aggressive war was the
result of the possession of aggressive weapons. The conclusion

followed that without aggressive weapons there could be no aggressive war. However, the conclusion falls with the assumption. Weapons are not aggressive or defensive by nature, but are made so by the purpose they serve. A sword, no less than a machine gun or a tank, is an instrument of attack or defense according to the intentions of its user. A knife can be used for carving meat, for performing a surgical operation, for holding an attacker at bay, or for stabbing somebody in the back. An airplane can serve the purpose of carrying passengers and freight, of reconnoitering enemy positions, of attacking undefended cities, of dispersing enemy concentrations poised for attack.

The British proposals really amounted to an attempt to make the status quo secure from attack by outlawing the weapons most likely to be used for overthrowing it. They tried to solve the political problem by manipulating some of the instruments which might serve its solution by violent means. Even if it should have been possible to agree on the characteristics of aggressive weapons, the political problem would have reasserted itself in the use of whatever weapons remained available. Actually, however, agreement on that point was out of the question. For the weapons which Great Britain deemed to be aggressive happened to be identical with those upon which the anti-status quo nations placed their main reliance for achieving their political ends. For instance, Great Britain thought that battleships were defensive and submarines were offensive weapons, while nations with small navies put it the other way around. As part of an enterprise generally beset by contradictions and doomed to futility, the British proposals for qualitative disarmament bear to a peculiar degree that lack of political insight which brought the World Disarmament Conference to an inglorious end.

Let us finally assume that standing armies and their weapons were completely outlawed and would in consequence disappear. The only probable effect of such a prohibition on war would be the limited and primitive character of its beginning. The armaments race among hostile nations would simply be postponed to the beginning of hostilities instead of preceding and culminating in it. The declaration of war would then be the signal for the warring nations to marshal their human and material resources and, more particularly, their technological skills for the speedy manufacture of all the implements of war which the technological development makes feasible. It is indeed possible to outlaw the atomic bomb; but it is not possible to outlaw the technological knowledge and ability to create atomic bombs. It is for this obvious reason that the prohibition of particular weapons has generally not been effective in war. This has been true, for instance, of the use of light-weight projectiles charged with explosives or inflammable substances, of the bombing of civilians from airplanes, and of unlimited submarine warfare.

Victory is the paramount concern of warring nations. They may observe certain rules of conduct with regard to the victims of warfare; they will not forego the use of all the weapons which their technology is able to produce. The observance of the prohibition of the use of poison gas in the Second World War is but an apparent exception. All the major belligerents manufactured poison gas; they trained troops in its use and in defenses against it and were prepared to use it if such use would seem to be advantageous. Only considerations of military expediency deterred all belligerents from making use of a weapon of which they had all availed themselves with the intention to use it if necessary.

That quantitative and qualitative disarmament affects the technology and strategy, but not the incidence of war, is clearly demonstrated by the results of the disarmament which was imposed upon Germany by the Treaty of Versailles. This disarmament was quantitative as well as qualitative and so thorough as to make it impossible for Germany to wage again a war similar in kind to the First World War. If this had been the purpose it was fully realized. If the purpose, however, was to incapacitate Germany forever to wage war of any kind—and this was the actual purpose—the disarmament provisions of the Treaty of Versailles were a spectacular failure. They forced the German General Staff to part with the methods of warfare prevalent in the First World War and to turn their ingenuity to new methods not prohibited by the Treaty of Versailles because they were not widely used at all during the First World War. Thus the Treaty of Versailles—far from depriving Germany of the ability to wage war again—virtually compelled Germany to prepare for the Second World War instead of, like France, for a repetition of the First World War. Disarmament in terms of the technology and strategy of the First World War, then, was for Germany actually a blessing in disguise. Disarmament made it virtually inevitable for Germany to refashion its military policy along the lines of the future rather than of the past.

It has, however, been suggested that, while disarmament could not by itself abolish war, it could to a great degree lessen the political tensions which might easily lead to war. More particularly, the unregulated armaments race with the fears it causes and the ever increasing financial burdens it imposes is apt to lead to such an intolerable situation that all or some parties to the race will prefer its termination by whatever means, even at the risk of war, to its definite continuation.

Disarmament or at least regulation of armaments is an indispensable step in a general settlement of international conflicts. It can, however, not be the first step. Competition for armaments reflects, and is an instrument of, competition for power. So long as nations advance contradictory claims in the contest for power, they are forced by the very logic of the power contest to advance contradictory claims for armaments. Therefore, a mutually satisfactory settlement of the power contest is a precondition for disarmament. Once the nations concerned have agreed upon a mutually satisfactory distribution of power among themselves, they can then afford to reduce and limit their armaments. Disarmament, in turn, will contribute greatly to the general pacification. For the degree to which the nations can come to terms upon disarmament will be the measure of the political understanding which they were able to achieve.

Disarmament, no less than the armaments race, is the reflection of the power relations among the nations concerned. Disarmament, no less than the armaments race, reacts upon the power relations from which it arose. As the armaments race aggravates the struggle for power through the fear it generates and the burdens it imposes, so disarmament contributes to the improvement of the political situation by lessening political tensions and by creating confidence in the purposes of the respective nations. Such is the contribution which disarmament can make to the establishment of international order and the preservation of international peace. It is an important contribution, but it is obviously not the solution of the problems of international order and peace.

Preparations for Progress

RICHARD J. BARNET

DISARMAMENT HAS SEEMED SO FUNDAMENTALLY AT ODDS WITH THE HARD FACTS OF A DIVIDED WORLD THAT IT IS WIDELY REGARDED AS A UTOPIAN SOLUTION. The question is, however, whether disarmament is any more utopian a means of preserving peace than the mechanism of deterrence on which we have put such great reliance. The success of each appears to require a basic change in existing patterns of behavior. Peace through disarmament would demand a willingness to look for security through means other than military power; peace through deterrence, a willingness to accept permanently a threatening status quo. Historical support for each alternative is pessimistic, although perhaps less conclusive in regard to disarmament since so little has been tried. Deterrence by threat of violence—our historical legacy—has never prevented war. Unilateral disarmament and the few cautious steps towards mutual disarmament that have been taken have never prevented war either.

To be "for" or "against" disarmament in our world, therefore, seems a singularly unrealistic approach. Neither the military planner who sees no end to the arms spiral nor the pacifist who calls upon the world to make itself over by a sheer act of will offers any practical basis for progress towards peace. To tell the world to go on making and testing nuclear weapons is like telling a drunk to go on drinking. To say "there has *got* to be progress on disarmament" is as fruitful as telling the drunk to pull himself together.

It is difficult to envisage much progress on disarmament until we stop treating it as a theoretical problem and recognize that it is an approach to salvation that is peculiarly appropriate to our own world. This does not mean that disarmament will necessarily work, but it does mean that it is worth the kind of research we are quite willing to devote to marketing techniques, satellite construction, or refinements of the atomic bomb. Valuable research has always been completed on aspects of inspection, but the mechanics of the disarmament treaty represent only one phase of the problem and by no means the most important or difficult one.

There is, for example, a series of questions waiting to be faced concerning the achievement of security in a disarmed but still divided world. Where can we put our trust in a world where we have abandoned our trust in arms? If an international authority with police power over the major nations is impractical, what alternative stabilizing mechanisms would be available? How much (or, more realistically, how little) would Russia have to change its approach to international relations before the United States should take the risks of substantial disarmament? And what would be the effect of disarmament on our national goals? In a disarmed world would we retain the capacity to guarantee the security of our allies against Communist infiltration? Against spontaneous revolution? Would it be crucial for us to be able to guarantee their security in either such case? Would retention of our system of alliances be desirable? Are we irrevocably committed to the prevention of Communist expansion merely by military means, or must we for our security resist all Communist encroachments by whatever means effected? Would we dare to contend with Russia in a world without arms for the friendship and loyalty of the emerging underdeveloped peoples, or would any competition bound to become so threatening to one side or the other that the use of force would be resumed? In a world disarmed would a revolutionary power be more likely to moderate its ambitions, or would it exploit the physical defenselessness of its neighbors to work their destruction through the treacherous use of force? Would we be willing to see the balance of power shift decisively to the other side as a result of peaceful competition without lifting a hand in anger to stop this course? Would the Soviet Union? What kind of assurance would we want from Russia that it would not try to destroy us whenever it acquired sufficient relative power to justify the attempt? What kind could it give and what would the assurance be worth? What kind of guarantees could we in turn give the Soviet Union?

Then there are questions concerning the conditions under which disarmament might prove acceptable. It has become quite clear by now that neither the Soviet Union nor the United States is willing to make gratuitous contributions to an "atmosphere of mutual trust." Each concession for the relaxation of tensions, quite properly, has a price tag. Arriving at the right price while the arms race continues is particularly difficult because the subjects of possible concessions are themselves intimately involved in the military competition. For example, the reunification of Germany is as much a military as it is a political problem. In a disarmed but still divided world Germany would continue to be the subject of competition, but its overriding importance would be diminished because it would not represent a military threat to either side. Today, however, any solution of the German problem would vitally affect the military balance of power in Europe. In the context of an arms race each side, therefore, has been reluctant to offer real concessions for fear of appearing weak and encouraging the other to make further demands. Concessions have been in such short supply that prices have remained inflationary.

One of the most difficult problems of a disarmament agreement is caused by the natural desire of the signatories to hedge against disaster in case the system should fail. Keeping bombs in reserve for such an eventuality is unsatisfactory because their very existence poses a threat. Is there any other way of providing each signatory an escape in the event of the treachery of its rival without thereby wrecking the treaty? Is there a mechanism for restoring the innocent power to a relative position equivalent to, or at least not much worse than, the relative position he was in with respect to his rival before each of them agreed to disarm? Or must we in order to give disarmament any chance of success burn our bridges behind us?

A related problem involves the integration of arms reduction and arms control. The French delegate to the U.N. Disarmament Commission described the goal in this area in these words: "Neither control without disarmament; neither disarmament without control; but progressively all the disarmament that can be controlled." Implementing this program has proved extraordinarily difficult because the equation in any particular situation is uncertain. To put the question from the Russian viewpoint, how much of a weakening of American military power should be required to offset the disadvantage incurred in exposing such Soviet military secrets as the location of missile launching sites? Or, to put the same question from the American point of view, how much of a guarantee of Soviet compliance should we require before we reduce our strength? Technical studies of the mechanics of control indicate that the more comprehensive the system of inspection the greater the guarantee of compliance. Since comprehensive inspection will only be acceptable in the present world if accompanied by comprehensive disarmament, which involves serious risks in the event of noncompliance, we are in a paradoxical situation in which the disarmament treaty offering the greatest security against evasion also presents the greatest risks if in fact it is evaded. Is there a point at which we would assume those risks short of a millennial change in the Communist world? If so, what is the point and how do we arrive at it?

What about the impact of disarmament on the domestic economy? The Russians are undoubtedly convinced that American business leaders, fulfilling the prophecies of Lenin, are conspiring to keep America armed. Lenin believed that the "crisis of capitalism" could be postponed only by massive military expenditures. Communist propaganda repeats this theme today. And it is undeniable that military expenditures play an important role in our economy. Each year some $25 billion is spent for weapons and military facilities. Conceivably, there might be more general interest in disarmament if the demands of defense production resulted in a shortage of the consumer luxuries to which we are all accustomed. But, unlike the economy of the Soviet Union, where production of consumer goods has been sacrificed in favor of military requirements, the American civilian economy may have benefited from the stimulus of military expenditure.

We have boldly answered the Communists that the American economy can take substantial disarmament in its stride and still produce prosperity. But we have yet to start the necessary planning to make good on our claim. Whatever the ultimate effect of disarmament on the American economy, such a step will require a number of important decisions which must be made well in advance of actual reconversion. Indeed, they ought to be made before serious negotiation begins. We must face such questions as these: How much of the capital presently devoted to weapons production and research should go to support machinery? What program should be adopted to soften the effects of the unemployment that will result during the transition of the economy from military to nonmilitary production? How should America spend its surplus when disarmament does begin to release resources for other purposes? What kind of additional foreign aid programs would we feel a need to promote for our security in a disarmed world? What domestic projects would deserve our attention?

Answers to these questions are as vital to an approach to disarmament as they are to life in a disarmed world. Yet we do little to answer them.

The investigations of the Senate Subcommittee on Disarmament reveal that as of September 1957, after eleven years of disarmament negotiations, "no agency of the executive branch has made efforts to ascertain the economic consequences of a reduction in armaments." And over a year later, in October 1958, in its Final Report the same Senate Subcommittee made this observation:

> There are only some 6 or 7 persons who work full time on disarmament in the State Department. The subcommittee is struck by the disparity in the effort the world is putting into thought and action for controlling and reducing armaments and the effort going into the development, fabrication and build up of armaments.

And outside of the State Department in the other executive agencies there is little sustained and intensive attention to disarmament. From time to time, the Administration has called upon distinguished private citizens to review our policy, make recommendations, and even negotiate agreements with the Russians. The contributions of these individuals have been important, but it is unquestionably true that no one can acquire the background essential to deal with these stubborn problems in a few months of service. There is no more reason to put the responsibility for formulating disarmament policy and negotiating disarmament agreements in the hands of conscientious, but inexperienced, amateurs than there is to put the Pentagon under the control of *ad hoc* committees or part-time generals.

Moreover, the only agencies in the government that do have a continuing interest in disarmament are those which have a primary responsibility for and hence a commitment to military defense. Since bureaucracies are notoriously inefficient at seeking their own dissolution, it is too much to ask those to whom our defense effort and atomic energy program are entrusted to prepare for disarmament as well. . . . Clearly what is needed is a permanent agency with responsibility for conducting research in disarmament and advising the President in the formulation of disarmament policy.

But this is not enough.

Not only the government but the American public must prepare ourselves if there is to be any hope of achieving the breakthrough to peace we are all seeking. While many aspects of disarmament are highly technical and are perhaps completely comprehensible only to experts, the ultimate decisions, whether to take one kind of risk or another, are appropriate to the democratic decision-making process. Indeed, no statesman—of whatever stature—could make the kind of commitment which disarmament requires unless he had the public with him. In the final analysis, the public must sit as a jury to weigh the options and recommendations with which we are confronted, as best we can, and then decide. And the decision cannot be delayed. The longer the arms race continues, the more difficult a solution becomes and the greater the risks of war. It is, therefore, more urgent than ever to face the challenge of disarmament and decide whether we *want* disarmament, for upon our decision may well depend the future of civilization on this planet.

Four Who Made a Lion

A SANSKRIT TALE

THEN THEY SAID TO ONE ANOTHER, "Let us search the earth and learn a special science."

So they decided, and after they had agreed on a place where they would meet again, the four brothers started off, each in a different direction.

Time went by, and the brothers met again at the appointed

From *Tales of Ancient India* by J. A. B. Van Buitenen. Copyright 1959 by the University of Chicago Press. Reprinted by permission.

meeting place; and they asked one another what they had learned.

"I have mastered a science," said the first, "which makes it possible for me, if I have nothing but a piece of bone of some creature, to create straightaway the flesh that goes with it."

"I," said the second, "know how to grow that creature's skin and hair if there is flesh on its bones."

The third said, "I am to create its limbs if I have the flesh, the skin, and the hair."

"And I," concluded the fourth, "know how to give life to that creature if its form is complete with limbs."

Thereupon the four brothers went into the jungle to find a piece of bone so that they could demonstrate their specialties. As fate would have it, the bone they found was a lion's but they did not know and picked up the bone. One added flesh to the bone, the second grew hide and hair, the third completed it with matching limbs, and the fourth gave the lion life. Shaking its heavy mane the ferocious beast arose with its menacing mouth, sharp teeth, and merciless claws and jumped on his creators. He killed them all and vanished contentedly into the jungle.

Thus the four brahmins perished because of their unfortunate creation of a lion. For who can stay happy if he raises something evil? In this manner it may happen that a specialty which one has been at pains to acquire may not at all work out to his profit, if fate is hostile, but to his doom. Only if its roots are firm and watered with intelligence and encircled with trenches of worldly wisdom will the tree of human effort bear fruit.

After telling this tale . . . the Vampire asked King Trivikramasena, . . . "Sire, which one of the fourth brothers carries the blame of creating the lion that killed them?" . . .

. . ."The only one to blame is the one who gave life to the lion. The others are innocent because they were ignorant; they could not know what kind of creature it would prove to be when each practiced his skill and fashioned its flesh, skin, hair, and limbs. But the last one saw the finished form of a lion and he gave it life only to show off his science. He stands guilty of four brahmin murders."

IX THE PROSPECTS BEFORE US

Chemical and
Thermonuclear Expolsives

AT THE PRESENT MOMENT THE ARMAMENTS OF THE GREAT POWERS
ARE ENORMOUSLY EXPENSIVE, AND, BY ATOMIC AGE STANDARDS, NOT
VERY POWERFUL. Calculations indicate that millions of Americans
would probably survive a heavy salvo of nuclear rockets. From
this it is sometimes deduced that the Nth power problem is
unimportant. If one great power finds it difficult to destroy the
other, surely France and other countries with a few nuclear
weapons cannot do any serious harm. There is a flaw in this
argument. The inefficiency of armaments of the great powers is
the result of deliberate choice. It is quite feasible to construct
devices for indiscriminate destruction which are both much
cheaper and much more deadly than the present rocket warheads.
These are referred to by Herman Kahn in *On Thermonuclear
War* as Doomsday machines. The current absence of such de-

From *The Bulletin of the Atomic Scientists*, November, 1961. Copyright
1961 by the Educational Foundation for Nuclear Science, Inc. Reprinted by
permission.

vices is not due to any physical limitation; rather it is an indication that the leaders of the great powers have more sense than they are often credited with. Such devices would be very useful to several second-class powers as a means of deterring great power interference, and the self-restraint of these minor states is doubtful.

The cost of the Manhattan Project was two billion dollars. At a reasonable estimate, this is about the current cost of getting H-bombs into production, considering that the new atomic power would have the benefit of our experience, as well as more time. France is planning to spend four times this amount on a strategic striking force. Any country which can build a nuclear detonator can produce a billion dollars worth of heavy water, 10 thousand tons, with the additional effort half of that used to get into the nuclear weapons business in the first place.

Suppose the People's Republic of China desires a minimum thermonuclear capability, including 10 thousand tons of heavy water, a dozen detonators, and accessories. This program should cost under five billion dollars, compared to a total present Chinese industrial production of around 20 billion dollars a year. According to U.S. and Soviet experience, the program should be completed about 10 years after major resources are devoted to the program. The Chinese are secretive about their nuclear operations. We do not know when or if they have started, and the program may be finished any day from now on.

Quite accurate design calculations can be made by amateurs for an important class of Doomsday machines if one assumes that certain features of the technology of chemical high explosives carry over to thermonuclear explosives. It can be shown that this assumption is plausible. The neutron chain reaction is a unique phenomenon, but chemical and thermonuclear explosives have a close resemblance in principle. In either case, the explosive is a mass of metastable material. A small part of the mass is suddenly heated. It then goes over to a more stable compound or nuclear arrangement, releasing enough energy to heat up the next part of the explosive to the reaction temperature, and so on until all the explosive is consumed.

A stick of high explosive is commonly detonated by applying a sudden increase in pressure at one end. This heats the explosive near the end sufficiently for the chemical reaction in it to occur, releasing enough energy to heat and compress the next disk of explosive, and so on. The detonation wave proceeds along the stick of explosive at up to a few miles a second. There is no doubt that a pipe filled with heavy water or any deuterium-rich compound will detonate in the same way. The temperature of the water must be raised to a thousand times the detonation temperature of the chemical explosive, but the nuclear reaction releases twenty million times the energy of the chemical reaction.

For any explosive, there is a minimum charge diameter for detonation. In a thinner stick of explosive, the rate at which energy is lost through the sides of the stick is too great, and not enough energy is transferred along the stick to maintain the detonation wave. The minimum charge diameter is an issue of considerable commercial importance in the case of chemical explosives. It is possible to calculate the minimum diameter for detonation of a pipe full of heavy water from basic physical constants. The rate at which energy is generated by the deuteron-deuteron reaction as a function of temperature and density has been carefully calculated in connection with the attempt to produce hydrogen power reactors, and the results published. The rate at which heat is converted to kinetic energy by the expansion of the charge may be calculated in the same way as for chemical explosives. The rate at which energy is carried away by radiation can be calculated by the methods of astrophysics, since the temperature and density conditions in an exploding heavy water charge are quite similar to those in stellar interiors.

An exact calculation of the critical diameter would be difficult, but is not necessary for present purposes. After making sweeping approximations, I arrive at the conclusion that a pipe with thick uranium walls will detonate if it has an inside diameter larger than two or three feet. A pipe with low density walls would have to be 5 or 10 feet in diameter. This is to be taken as merely an indication that the minimum size is not unreasonably large as compared with the available supply of heavy water.

When a ton of either heavy water or uranium is consumed, the energy released is equivalent to 20 megatons of TNT. H-bomb tests have been conducted in which the energy released was much less than this, and consequently the bomb must have been much smaller than the above estimate. This is reasonable, since several obvious refinements and no doubt some subtle ones can be made on the plain water pipe design. If a large enough fusion explosion is wanted, the plain water pipe design is a good as any. The large charge will stay hot long enough to consume all the deuterium, and deuterium is a very cheap and effective fuel. The charge which is large enough is probably not much larger than the smallest charge which will detonate at all.

Given a charge capable of detonation, it is necessary to provide enough energy to set up a detonation wave at one end. It is possible to detonate an extremely sensitive chemical explosive by hitting one end of the charge with a hammer. The primer in a rifle cartridge is designed to operate in this way. If a large charge is to be detonated, it is usual to use a booster made up of blocks of explosive of progressively increasing diameter and decreasing sensitivity.

The very expensive substances such as plutonium and tritium play much the same role in nuclear explosives as does mercury fulminate in chemical explosives. They are useful for making small, expensive explosions as boosters to set off large, insensitive charges. There is a minimum size at which any particular explosive can be detonated, but no maximum. If one stick of dynamite will detonate, then any larger stick, of the same chemical composition, will detonate. In the thermonuclear field this means that the size of explosions is limited only by the amount of explosive material the designer wishes to collect in one place. One may picture a large thermonuclear bomb as a detonator set at one end of a pipe of heavy water, the deuterium in the heavy water being almost completely consumed during the explosion. This picture fits the few scraps of official information on H-bombs which have been published, notably the cost estimates above.

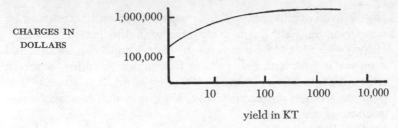

COST OF NUCLEAR EXPLOSIVES vs. YIELD

The graph is easily interpreted in terms of a rather expensive detonator which is used to explode a main charge. The main charge gets progressively cheaper as the energy release increases, reaching the price of heavy water—$5000 per megaton—at about a 10 megaton energy release.

Many chemical explosives will burn slowly at atmospheric pressure. Crews handling waste TNT sometimes build a bonfire of TNT blocks in order to warm their hands, though the practice is discouraged by safety officers. Heavy hydrogen nuclei are an abundant fuel, and people are trying now to design a reactor which will burn them slowly. The problem is almost hopelessly difficult because cooling by conduction and radiation is very rapid at nuclear fusion temperatures. The enormous rate of heat leakage from a fusion reactor can be tolerated if the "reactor" is a bomb, burning tons of fuel in a few microseconds, but a power reactor consuming a few pounds of fuel yearly must have fantastically good insulation to keep the reacting gas hot.

Heavy water occurs mixed with ordinary water in the proportion one part in 6700. To separate the heavy water, one requires mainly a lot of steam or a lot of electric power. Any nation can therefore go into heavy water production immediately, since most of the equipment required is commonly used in the power industry, as it would be to produce plutonium or tritium. Since any reasonable fraction of a nation's resources can be quickly diverted to heavy water production, the amount of nuclear explosive available to that nation is most conveniently estimated by comparing the cost of heavy water with the national budget. Heavy water is used by the ton in several types of reactors, and it moves in international trade in fairly large amounts. A recent estimate of its cost is only $20-$30 per pound. If a country is to produce a large quantity quickly, $50 per pound is a reasonable estimate of the cost.

After the necessary materials have been manufactured, the actual design of an H-bomb detonator is still a difficult problem. Most atomic secrets are greatly over-valued, but in this particular case one old blueprint would save a great deal of trouble. The Chinese could probably steal one in Moscow. As the U.S. noticed in 1940-45, it is difficult to keep important information from the agents of an ally. After the program is finished one bomb test would demonstrate that everything is working properly.

If a nuclear weapons program is designed to produce a maximum of indiscriminate destruction with the available resources, a few very large bombs would be built. Then few expensive detonators would be required and the main efforts would be devoted to making powerful explosives. The submarine, preferably atomic powered, appears to be the best device for the transport of such weapons. Submersible barges could be towed to the general vicinity of the enemy, anchored, and eventually exploded by time fuse or code signal. It is fairly easy to construct a device with any radius of destruction up to a few thousand miles, so exact delivery on target is unnecessary.

In 1945 the American Navy would have had substantially no chance of intercepting a submarine towing a nuclear mine to the American coast. The present situation is obscured by secrecy, but judging from the popular press, the improvements in submarines since that time have more than balanced the improvements in antisubmarine weapons. This view is supported by the construction of the Polaris force. The well informed persons responsible seem to feel that submarines hiding in the open sea are nearly invulnerable. Submarine transport is cheaper than rockets by several orders of magnitude. Intercontinental rockets cost more than their warheads, and many times more than the deuterium in the warheads. Rockets are useful because they are capable of destroying quickly a small specific target with little extended damage. They have political uses, as they can be tested and brandished. They cannot compete with mines as an instrument of complete destruction.

Effects of Nuclear Mines

A heavy water bomb could be made with a boron blanket, in which case the only radioactivity produced in the explosion would be the small amount due to the detonator. A comparatively innocuous bomb of this type might be used to raise a tidal wave. Assuming that the scale factors derived from explosions equivalent to a few thousand tons of TNT apply to a large mine containing a thousand tons of heavy water, the mine could be placed in water two miles deep. The wave would be 100 feet high at 200 miles from the center. Such waves may rise to an elevation either much higher or much lower than the crest height in the open sea as they move onto a coast, depending on its configuration. A more damaging bomb would have a blanket of sodium oxide. Sodium is a rather poor neutron absorber, so a thick blanket would be required. This is of little consequence because sodium is very cheap. When one gram of neutrons had been absorbed in sodium the resulting sodium–24 would, if distributed over one square mile, deliver nearly a hundred thousand roentgens to a man in the open. The lethal radiation dose is 500 roentgens.

A bomb containing 1000 tons of heavy water will yield about 20 tons of neutrons. Applying the usual scaling laws, the area actually heavily contaminated may be estimated at 200,000 square miles. Assuming one-tenth of the radioactive sodium formed actually reached the ground in this area, the average radiation dose would be a million roentgens. This would destroy all animal life including people in an average basement bomb shelter, all active vegetation, and nearly all seeds. The landscape would be temporarily transformed to lunar desolation. One feature of the sodium bomb is its lack of backlash. The half life of sodium–24 is 15 hours. By the time the winds carry the bomb products to the next continent, it will have decayed almost completely. A blanket of cobalt around heavy water is the famous cobalt bomb. This will produce nearly as much fallout radiation as the sodium bomb, but the half-life of cobalt 60 is five years. Since the total radiation dose to be delivered is spread over a longer time, it follows that the initial radiation level for cobalt–60 is about 3000 times less than for sodium 24. A man in an area contaminated with enough sodium to give a million roentgens total dose would collapse in 10 minutes. After coalt fallout yielding the same infinite time dose, the initial radiation level would be only 20 roentgens per hour. It would take a man a day to accumulate a lethal dose, and a week to die. For the present, cobalt bombs have no value. Killing the enemy by inches is not only inhumane but while dying he may do unpleasant things to whoever caused the fallout.

The effects of sodium fallout can however be nullified. If one could reach a highly effective bomb shelter before the fallout reached the ground, it would only be necessary to lie low for a week until the sodium had decayed. If the fallout were cobalt-60, it would be necessary to lie low for some years. The construction of bomb shelters in which most of the U.S. population could stand a siege of a year or two has been advocated. This is a fine idea unless it provokes the enemy into building cobalt bombs. If they should adopt this very cheap and obvious countermeasure, everyone would be worse off than before the program started, particularly innocent bystanders. Cobalt lasts long enough to drift with the wind to continents not directly involved.

Peacetime fullscale tests of a device intended to depopulate a continent are impractical. The "small" bombs tested to date have needed uranium blankets to detonate properly. Fission products produce about as much radiation, per gram of effective neutrons, as cobalt. The distribution over time of the resulting gamma radiation is probably not attractive from the designers' standpoint.

Cobalt Fallout

Anyone with an atomic weapons program will have some uranium-238 lying around. In the current year the U.S. AEC is expending six billion dollars for 30,000 tons of uranium. It will consume about one per cent of this, the rest being waste U-238. By proper design it is probably possible to put a lot of U-238 into a cobalt bomb without affecting the yield of cobalt-60 much. The fast neutrons intercepted by the U-238 could be balanced or exceeded by the slow neutrons emitted. The extra energy released by uranium fission would cause the local fallout to cover a larger area. The designer would probably find this desirable, because the fallout directly downwind from a cobalt bomb would be unnecessarily heavy. The above calculations indicate that any nuclear power can easily destroy the U.S. with the close range fallout effect. The extermination of the human race is a much more difficult task. One might consider effecting this with remote fallout.

About five tons of uranium fissioned in tests have resulted in a gamma radiation dose of 50 milliroentgens plus a strontium 90 bone marrow dose of 10 milliroentgens per year, in well watered countries near 40 degrees north latitude. Dosage is less by a factor of 50 in dry countries on the equator. A large mine containing 1000 tons of heavy water would fission 5000 tons of uranium. Fifty such mines would be required to produce any lethal remote fallout. Cobalt bombs are much more effective because the half-life of cobalt is well matched to the residence time of bomb debris in the stratosphere.

Long ago Leo Szilard pointed out that only 50 tons of neutrons, obtainable from 2500 tons of heavy water, would produce enough cobalt-60 to give a dose of 10,000 roentgens over the whole earth. The lethal dose in man, for radiation distributed over a long period of time, is thought to be 5000 roentgens, but it is not certain that a 10,000 roentgen dose in the open would kill the entire population. Not everyone will react to fallout with the serene fatalism of the characters in *On the Beach*. Some people would decontaminate their living quarters or even go live in a cave during most of the year. Such measures would reduce exposure by an unknown but large factor, especially for children. The dose required to reliably exterminate the population may be several tens of thousands of roentgens.

The test fallout was distributed with extreme non-uniformity, though we had no way of knowing in advance that this would happen. If cobalt-60 fallout should distribute itself in the same way, large favored areas would have a radiation level 300 times less than the world average. Various steps could be taken to cause a more uniform distribution of fallout if this is deliberately desired. Even the designers will not know in advance how well such measures will work. Taking into account the effects of improvised shelter and the remaining nonuniformity of fallout distribution, cobalt bombs designed to exterminate the human race will require a few hundred thousand tons of heavy water and an equal amount of cobalt.

The indications are that the human race will survive the H-bomb, though it will be a close thing. Until some more efficient process is discovered, extermination will require a major effort by one or both great powers, which hopefully will not be forthcoming. Lesser states will have to be content with destroying most people and making the rest miserable.

A deterrent against great power interference is useful to any second-class power which desires to change the status quo. As an example it may be assumed that the Chinese have the minimum Doomsday machine capability already described—10 thousand tons of heavy water, a dozen detonators, and accessories. The Chinese can then proceed to invade any neighboring country which they feel like annexing, with little fear of U.S. interference. Consider for instance the extreme case of direct nuclear blackmail. The Communists may demand that Formosa surrender, *or else*. If Chiang and Company refuse to comply, a medium size bomb would be brought up and the population of Formosa exterminated. This is unnecessary ruthlessness, but it might actually be done in order to make a profound impression on the Japanese and the other islanders in the neighborhood. One may then consider how various policy slogans could be applied to the situation.

The Chinese leaders did not scare well even in the John Foster Dulles period when the threat of massive retaliation was plausible. If they have a Doomsday machine they will never believe the U.S. would commit suicide over anything which happens in Asia, no matter what it may promise in advance. Neither do I.

The U.S. might exact compensation (measured retaliation) for the loss of its ally by atomizing Shanghai. The Chinese would respond to this unjustified (in their opinion) interference in their private civil war with a moderately destructive tidal wave or fall-out cloud. The Chinese authorities give the impression that they would cheerfully have a few cities vaporized, with their inhabitants, in exchange for a free hand in Asia. The annual increase of the Chinese population exceeds 10 million, so the cities could be quickly rebuilt and repopulated. It seems likely that the U.S. public would tire of this game, and make its decision clear to its government, before the mutual destruction goes far enough to make any impression on the Chinese rulers. The U.S. could then decide that the Asians are able to settle their own affairs without our assistance, and retire to Hawaii. It might leave the Japanese or Indians a few H-bombs on the way out, with a view to keeping the Chinese too busy to assist us in solving the problems of the Western hemisphere. The treaty commitments of the U.S. in East Asia are either shallow or temporary or both. The SEATO treaty commits the U.S. to consult about Chinese agression, not to do anything. The defense treaty with Chiang has an article providing for cancellation of the treaty on a year's notice by either party.

Usually it is futile to yield to blackmail, because one can confidently predict that the blackmailer will merely produce another demand. In the present case several events may prevent the Chinese from carrying their demands beyond Asia. They may be destroyed in some quarrel with their fellow Asians. Such a

Editor's Note: First steps toward the Doomsday machine are the 50 and 100 megaton bombs that Premier Khrushchev has described. President Kennedy appealed to the USSR not to test such weapons "as they have no military value."

course of events would be dangerous and unpleasant to us, but it is better than destroying the Chinese ourselves. If they do get Asia reorganized to their satisfaction, they may become rich and complacent like Americans and Russians. The USSR is not an ideal neighbor, but another like it would not make the situation much worse. Altogether it seems likely that a Chinese Doomsday machine would force the U.S. to adopt an Asia for the Asians policy. The Chinese therefore have a very powerful incentive to build one.

China has been used as an example to illustrate the value of a Doomsday machine. Numerous other countries are only slightly less menacing. If the Boers should decide to exterminate the black Africans (or vice versa) they will need a Doomsday machine to deter the great powers from interfering with this program. In Europe, France is already pursuing grandeur via hydrogen bombs. The West German government has refused to recognize the present frontiers of Germany, and has passed a resolution in favor of acquiring nuclear weapons with which to change them. No action has been taken on these intentions yet, but Germany has a significant peacetime nuclear industry and can move quickly when the time comes.

A nuclear test suspension is a start toward controlling the Nth power problem, though a very small one. Full control would require something like the Baruch plan. Suppose, for instance, that it is agreed that the U.S., USSR, and the U.N. may own and operate nuclear reactors, uranium mines, etc. Anyone else requiring a nuclear power plant would contract for its construction with whichever authority offers the best terms. The Baruch plan specifies swift and condign punishment for anyone violating the rules. It does not seem likely that the U.N. or any such group is capable of sufficiently drastic action. One alternative is to enforce the agreement by extralegal action. A hint might be dropped that any forbidden nuclear works, or any secret facility which might be one, may be vaporized without warning by a rocket salvo fired by an unidentified submarine. No one fears the U.N. but everyone fears at least one of the great powers, so this threat might be effective.

The common citizen divides the human race into good guys and bad guys. Action against Nth powers involves moving against our heroic anti-Communist friends in alliance with the archfiends. Plans for this will be received about as sympathetically as a proposal for taking precautions against our heroic anti-Nazi allies in 1945. The prospect that any plan harsh enough to be effective will be adopted is dim, but perhaps worth talking about.

* * *

DOOMSDAY MACHINE:

A reliable and securely protected device that is capable of destroying almost all human life and that would be automatically triggered if any enemy committed any one of a designated class of violations.

"Glossary of Terms on National Security,"
S. M. Genensky and Olaf Helmer,
The RAND Corporation

Must the Bomb Spread?

LEONARD BEATON

AS LONG AS THERE ARE SOVEREIGN STATES RESPONSIBLE FOR THEIR OWN DEFENCE, THERE WILL BE A STRONG INTEREST IN ACQUIRING NUCLEAR WEAPONS. To that extent, the problem of nuclear proliferation is basic and not subject to definite solutions. Equally, however, it is becoming clearer all the time that many powers do not want to produce them if they can find a reasonable alternative. The necessary facilities remain expensive and they amount to a

From *Must the Bomb Spread?* Penguin Books, Inc., 1966. Reprinted by permission of Chatto & Windus Ltd., London. The English edition of this book is entitled *The Spread of Nuclear Weapons*.

large specialized industry. Most strategic thinkers and chiefs of staff regard nuclear weapons as unusable in the kind of military situations they regard as most probable though they will continue to play an important part in shaping general world power relationships.

The greatest incentive to a wide spread of these weapons is the conviction that it is inevitable. For several years in the late 1950s this was the attitude of much informed opinion and it made it difficult to get governments to take an anti-proliferation strategy seriously. This has now changed. There is no question of a dozen or two dozen nuclear weapons programmes in the next few years. We are dealing with a definable group of countries: and in each case the men who must decide genuinely want to do what is best for their own security and that of the world. If they accept without question the notion that they should not acquire these weapons, they can foresee dangerous uncertainties. Looking around them, they can see these weapons becoming more important in war plans in the great powers; they can see their possible enemies building up plutonium production capacity; in many cases they have no assurances that anyone will come to their defence and they shrink from the political implications of seeking such assurances; they have growing wealth, which all experience tells them must be applied in reasonable amounts to their physical defence if they are to survive; and they can see other powers claiming special privileges because they have these weapons.

Unless this situation can be changed, the present strong inhibitions to national nuclear weapons programmes will slowly disappear. Inducing the main non-nuclear powers to sign a non-dissemination agreement in 1965 or 1966 may delay things; but it will not lift the real pressures. In the meantime only a cut-off can prevent plutonium from becoming the possession of many governments and accumulating in stocks all around the world. How and when it might be fabricated into military explosives cannot be foreseen; but it is difficult to envisage any real distinction between a world in which plutonium is widely owned and one in which there are many nuclear powers. Nothing would be more spurious than to buy peace of mind with some nominal non-dissemination arrangement under which the production of fissile material in many countries goes steadily ahead.

Any arrangements which genuinely discourage the spread of nuclear weapons must involve one of two policies by the nuclear powers: a threat of force which is genuine enough to frighten new nuclear powers; or an acceptance of a new range of obligations. The first of these is most unlikely. There is therefore little alternative to an arrangement which recognizes that the present stocks of nuclear weapons are, in effect, held on trust. To claim a monopoly in these weapons, the nuclear powers will find they must undertake heavy obligations. To some extent, the United States has already shown that it is prepared to accept this burden where its allies are concerned; but it has not managed to put this on to anything which looks like a permanent basis. Germany or Japan cannot count on their alliance relationships for 1975 or 1985; yet a nuclear weapons development programme begun now would only become really effective in that period. Only a sense of long-term commitment can affect such a long-term problem.

This case must be recognized and argued by the members of the non-nuclear club. The group of countries which have deliberately held back on the development of these weapons should become self-conscious and force the pace in broad international arrangements as the price of their continued non-nuclear status. To the original members of this club—Canada, Germany, Japan, India and Sweden—might be added Belgium, the Netherlands, Czechoslovakia, Switzerland and Italy if these countries get to the point where they can choose and they take the decision to hold back. This is a formidable list of countries. It can be expected to grow if the group of non-nuclear middle powers becomes strong and influential. These countries are not without bargaining power: for if reasonable provision is not made for their security and general influence they will have no alternative to developing their own nuclear weapons. A policy of this kind would undoubtedly gain wide acceptance in the first five non-nuclear powers. Domestically, all five governments would find it a convenience in the coming years to have a solid political alternative to national nuclear weapons. A Canadian Government would not easily persuade parliament that the expenditure involved in producing these weapons was justified; a Swedish Government would encounter strong opposition among socialists; a German Government would expose the country to serious dangers; an Indian Government would have to reduce the national standard of living and also hold back on conventional rearmament; and Japan would face a deep division which could be politically very damaging.

In converting their domestic difficulties into world initiatives, these powers would be taking the lead in what are likely to be the decisive diplomatic negotiations of the coming years. If means are not found to contain proliferation, the whole structure of world security is going to become very difficult to sustain. The course of proliferation itself will contain many perils, especially in those situations in which one side of a local rivalry is well ahead of the other. Though this might be said to apply to India, in relation to Pakistan, the more dangerous example is Israel. Other equally disturbing cases will probably emerge. In the Israeli case, as in others, the major powers will have to face the dilemma of becoming militarily and politically involved to try to balance a coming imbalance, or of withdrawing into isolation, leaving the possibility of a terrible local conflict. If the Americans and Russians were to take joint action there might be no difficulty. But there is still no sign that they either could or would put their common interest ahead of their traditional rivalries and loyalties.

The financial implications of nuclear weapons programmes will be very serious for many of those countries who may feel compelled to try to construct the necessary industry. If plutonium-producing reactors can be obtained from others, the cost of a small-scale programme may be as little as a few hundred million dollars, but even this would be a heavy price to pay. In many cases, high cost uranium extraction and home-built reactors may be necessary, as well as a chemical separation plant and a testing programme. Delivery systems will have to be found or the necessary industries developed. In the end there will be a steady pressure towards enriched uranium and hydrogen bombs. If a large number of countries were to develop such programmes unilaterally, the burden on world economic development would be very heavy. Major powers with aid programmes are unlikely to be ready to give substantial amounts of aid to those who are spending so much of their own resources in this way.

When we start to contemplate a world of twenty, thirty or forty nuclear powers, the part which these weapons will play both in diplomacy and in disputes becomes very difficult to predict. No doubt international relations would go through phases. A doctrine of non-intervention might be developed and then be exploited by some bold empire-builder. The major powers would then be compelled to show their determination and would find themselves drawn into increasingly dangerous commitments. With an increase in the number of nuclear powers going on all the time, it may be doubted if any viable system of international security could be successfully sustained. The best that could be hoped for would be a situation so intolerable to everyone that an organized world security system would become unavoidable.

It is difficult to avoid the conclusion that the development of arrangements which will make new nuclear weapons programmes difficult or impossible will become the main preoccupation of the coming years. Those elements of the Geneva disarmament proposals which have most prospered have been those which made some contribution to this object. The partial nuclear test ban is the leading case, but there are others coming after it.

In the overwhelming majority of governments, great forces are working against a decision to spend heavily on national nuclear weapons and their delivery systems. These will grow stronger or weaker as the major powers become more or less committed and as nuclear strategies are emphasized or played down. The future is therefore one of political choice, not of technical capacity. If the major powers choose to create a structure which will effectively prevent proliferation over a long period of time, they must in the process change the facts of power. Weapons of mass destruction which seem to give their sovereign independence a secure future will force them to sink that independence in wider arrangements. If they choose to do nothing and leave others to take what decisions they must, the world around them will steadily become much less tolerable. Those who control the decisive weapons would obviously like to go on as we now are; but that is the one choice which is not open to them.

How Israel Won
World Sympathy A FANTASY

EPHRIAM KISHON

On that memorable evening, Prime Minister Ben-Gurion sat all by himself in his office, staring rather dejectedly into the air.

"O Lord"—he whispered—"upon my word I am at a loss what to do. Days and nights we keep arguing, trying to prove to the world that all we want is peace, that our only aims are that the Israel farmer should be able to return safely from his fields, that our highways should be safe at night, too, and that our ships should not be sunk. Everybody knows that right is on our side and yet, the whole world votes against us. How can that be? Does virtue no longer mean anything nowadays? For months we have been pleading for justice—and retreating into the teeth of an ominous future. We are at the end of our tether. O Lord, do something for Thy people . . ."

The terrible explosion which rocked the whole area knocked the Ministry building awry and smashed most of its window

From *The Carpenter,* January, 1958, official publication of the United Brotherhood of Carpenters and Joiners of America. Reprinted by permission.

panes. The blast hurled the Prime Minister out of his chair and onto the big world map hanging on the wall opposite him.

On that evening, Moscow's seismographs were all wrecked. The Russian technicians stood awed round the sensitive instruments and concluded that an explosion whose force surpassed the measuring capacity of the seismographs had occurred in the Middle East. Scientists all over the world confirmed the Russians' finding. In Italy and Greece, the inhabitants of the coastal belt panicked.

Next day the Pentagon issued a reassuring communique to the effect that "an earthquake of unprecedented force had apparently swept over the southern part of the Negev desert." The Israel Foreign Ministry on that very day published a laconic denial, saying that "no earthquake of any kind had struck the Middle East region." World public opinion received the contradictory announcement with understandable alarm. As usual, there was no leakage from official Israel sources.

The awed silence was broken by the London Observer's Middle East correspondent: "Let's face it" he wrote from Beirut— "Israel possesses an atomic bomb of stupendous power."

The report confirmed rumors which had been rife in diplomatic circles, but the first reliable information was given by Abba Eban before the U.N. Plenary, on the day the Afro-Asian ultimatum over the complete and unconditional evacuation of the Sinai Peninsula expired. In an extremely tense atmosphere, the Israel delegate rose to speak:

"Gentlemen"—he said. "I have the honour to inform the Plenary session that the Israel government possesses a most up-to-date atomic device, the so-called 'phosphate bomb,' whose destructive power is 190 times of the atomic devices hitherto known. The phosphate bomb can be delivered by guided missile or other means to any point on the globe. Thank you for your kind attention."

After this, the Israel Ambassador left the speaker's rostrum, without wasting so much as a single word and the delegates were thunderstruck by the announcement and at least a minute passed in utter silence, until finally the French delegate rose and broke into stormy applause. After a while, the Australian and New Zealand delegates joined the manifestation of sympathy, then the diplomats of Latin American and small European states broke into spontaneous cheering.

The British delegate did not applaud, but turned towards the Israel delegation, an ingratiating smile on his face. The Plenary Chairman asked the leaders of the Asian bloc for their comments on the Israel announcement, whereupon these requested a *sine die* postponement of the meeting.

It took the world a few days to recover from its stupefaction. The Soviet Union, which up to then had not reacted in any way to the unexpected turn of events, now decreed partial mobilization and concentrated large numbers of troops along the Persian border. Then Ben-Gurion sent his famous letter to Mr. N. Bulganin, warning the Soviet government that Israel would not tolerate a violation of the neighbouring small nations' sovereignty.

"What would the Soviet Government say"—thus the note—"if Russia were to be attacked by a power possessing atomic weapons superior to her own?" The Soviet authorities did not publish the text of the note but called off the troop concentrations.

The President of the U.S. sent a long congratulatory telegram to its friend the Israel government "for the brilliant results achieved in the field of scientific research," and expressed the hope that phosphate energy would be used for peaceful purposes. The President at the same time invited the Israel government to participate in a "fruitful exchange of information between the two friendly great powers, with a view of furthering their scientific research work."

The President's proposal was coolly received. According to the brief communique of the Foreign Ministry, "the proposal is being considered on its merits, but for the time being is unlikely to be accepted."

India was the first to sound the voice of morality.

"No atomic weapons of any kind will change our conviction" Nehru declared before the National Assembly—"that Egypt is entitled to guarantees for the security of her borders, and that the Arab States are within their right when they demand a final settlement of the Middle East conflict through direct negotiations."

At the same time, Nehru announced that Saudi Arabia was initiating diplomatic relations with Israel.

Simultaneously with Dag Hammarskjöld's arrival in Cairo to review the UNEF's terms of reference, the first unbridled anti-Arab attack was launched in "Izvestia" under the headline "Progressive Israel Breaks Through Feudal Arab Ring." The unusually sharp-voiced editorial unmasked the Western Imperialist-sponsored Arab dictators, who for years have been endangering the region's peace. President Nasser was rumored to have informed the U.N. Secretary General that he would agree to the clearing of the Suez Canal only if UNEF were permanently stationed in the Sinai Peninsula.

The U.N. Plenary reconvened only after three weeks. Dag Hammarskjöld, who before the session had walked up and down for two and a half hours with Foreign Minister Golda Meir, submitted an extremely favorable report. The Secretary-General enthusiastically praised the extensive administrative and social improvements carried out by Israel in the Gaza Strip, mentioning the extremely humane treatment of the PoW's and the contentment of the Arab civilian population. The report finally noted that small but progressive Israel had created conditions in Gaza and the Gulf of Eilat which put to shame anything achieved by the Egyptian authorities.

Dag Hammarskjöld's report was received most favorably, especially by the 17 nations of the Israel bloc, which comprised, in addition to the smaller European and Latin American States, France, Burma and Ceylon. The new draft resolution of the Asiatic Bloc "on the discussion in a friendly atmosphere of the theoretical aspects of withdrawal," was put on the agenda purely as a matter of form, and rejected—as foreseen—by 59 votes against nine. Eight states, including Britain, Iraq, Lebanon and Venezuela, abstained. The British delegate announced that he opposed on principle any further U.N. intervention in Israel's "regional development policy," and only abstained from voting in view of HM Government's traditional friendship for the Jordan people.

The Yugoslav chief delegate's speech was most remarkable: "We always opposed the principle of artificial withdrawal," he said. "Israel proved that the small states, too, are morally entitled to fight for their historic rights. . . ."

The Syrian delegate requested permission to report on certain Israel troop concentrations, but the chairman refused him permission to speak, and at the suggestion of the Soviet delegate expelled him from the hall.

On the day after the session, the final draft of the Eisenhower plan was made public, and it transpired that the President had secretly earmarked not less than $750m. for economic aid to Israel, justifying this with the fact that "Israel was the Mid-Eastern bastion of democracy, freedom and progress."

Pakistan was the first to moot a meeting of the Big Three, with the participation of Eisenhower, Khrushchev and Ben-Gurion. Israel's PM gave his consent to the meeting, stipulating, however, that it take place at a somewhat later date, and that its venue be nearby Cyprus. At the time of Golda Meir's visit at the White House, the world press was campaigning for a prompt signing of peace treaties between the interested Middle Eastern states.

Lebanon's Malik pointed out that in fact there were no obstacles in the way of regular relations with dynamic Israel. The Soviet Encyclopaedia sent out to Encyclopaedia owners an appendix containing a reappraisal of Israel, and asked them to paste it over the former analysis of Israel, which must be considered a "criminal vestige of the Beria era." In a radio speech, Nuri Said stressed that Iraq had in fact never been in a state of war with Israel, and announced that the Haifa pipeline was intact.

At a GOP caucus, Secretary of State Dulles called the Suez operation one of history's most brilliant campaigns, through which Israel won the moral position it deserved in the western family of free nations. Dulles, by the way, accompanied Eisenhower to Cyprus, and can be seen in the historical picture in which the Big Three toast regional peace and Khrushchev raises his glass shouting "Lehayim."

Thus faith, hope and justice triumphed, and since then none doubts Israel's moral right to exist as a state. There remained only two unanswered questions: who was the blundering fool at the Israel GHQ who had stacked up all the ammunition and explosives captured in the Sinai campaign in one point of the southern Negev desert, and why did it blow up?

Abraham '59 –
A Nuclear Fantasy

F. B. AIKEN

July 14, 1959

NOW THAT IT IS ALL OVER IT IS EASY TO THINK BACK AND REALIZE THAT TODAY'S EVENTS HAD BEEN WELL PREFIGURED, EVEN BEFORE THE SOVIET LAUNCHING OF SPUTNIK I IN OCTOBER OF 1957. I remember having read what was at the time a strange-seeming article. It was just at the beginning of 1958. The author was one of that new breed of military "hardware" experts. He understood about nuclear blast effects, logistical problems, missile capabilities, and the paramount struggle between Russia and America to reduce their comparative "lead-times" between the development of a new weapon and its production for tactical use. This was called the Research and Development lead-time war. We had already lost, he said, the "lead-time" war. From then on out, the rest of the Cold War moves and counter-moves would merely be a series of demonstrations of America's inferiority as she was forced to back down in area after area.

Of course, such writing was not even dignified by ridicule,

From *Dissent*, Winter, 1959. Reprinted by permission.

those few short months ago. When other new-model theorists of Cold War strategy claimed to have developed a series of mathematical formulas whereby electronic computers could be used to project the outcome of possible military conflicts, everybody found the notion of war as extrapolations from a series of mathematical formulas impossible to assimilate. The historical reminder that General Lee had "proved" to himself the South was defeated before the Civil War began, failed to alert even those of us relatively close to the President to the implications of new methods of analysis which could definitively "prove" in advance the outcome of a hypothetical conflict.

I remember actually laughing when I read one of those futuristic-seeming projection papers which concluded a series of proofs with the proposal that we immediately dismantle the Strategic Air Command, our only defense against Russia, and try to bargain with them for anything we could get in return! "Sell out SAC now," wrote the author, "while it is still worth something. The Russians have indicated that above all they want to be recognized by the West as a mature culture. We can give them that for comparatively little and in addition trade SAC for a number of stabilizing concessions which then may allow us five years of relative freedom to prepare for a potent reentry into the R and D lead-time war."

This conclusion, which seemed ludicrous to me at the time, followed from an analysis purporting to prove that the Russians had demonstrated with Sputnik I something like a one-year lead-time drop on us. During that interval, which was estimated to go into effect toward the end of 1958, SAC would have become worthless and we would still be over a year away from operational countervailing ICBMs. Should we merely sit by and idly watch the approaching obsolescence of SAC and our ensuing international helplessness? Or should we not instead bargain SAC when it was still a danger to the Russians, trading them a year of greater security now for a preserved American capability to overreach them at some point in the future? "Paper logic" I remember thinking to myself. It was neat, but really kind of insane. But this was by no means all.

"Our policy of massive retaliation" read the analysis produced by the electronic calculators at the Ranard Military Policy Center, "is so ill-founded as to amount to a potentially catastrophic self-delusion. Break down the massive retaliation policy into a series of war game moves and counter moves. Suppose the Russians devastated the United States with nuclear weapons, literally burning off the country. Should the United States then, with its dying gasp, activate SAC units in other parts of the world to burn off Russia as well? To what end? How would this help us or anyone else? We can hope that this threat will deter them from starting anything, but what if it actually does not deter them? Would we actually carry out our own threatened retaliation? Should we? It is clear that there could be no possible gain in so doing. If that is clear, then the policy itself is devoid of the deterrence feature we attribute to it."

"Suppose alternatively," continued the analysis, "that the Russians did not burn off the entire United States, but only the Eastern seacoast industrial area: the New England-Middle Atlantic area, leaving the rest of the country largely intact physically if not genetically. Should we then retaliate 'massively,' burning off part or all of Russia? What good would *that* do? With the destruction of American industrial capacity the world would be converted instantly into a Russian hegemony, for the Russians would then control all sources for reindustrialization aid. Would the remaining American population be better off by our going through with nuclear devastation? Or would we not be better off by just calling off the entire conflict at that point? What would be the best strategy for minimizing our maximum losses at the second phase which would have been introduced by partial devastation? On any view, massive retaliation cannot be in the American interest and must be abandoned as an unrealistic foundation for American policy."

But who could at that time give credence to such a strangely detached point of view? No even I, proud though I was of what I had always regarded as a superior cold bloodedness in evaluating political forces. All this was to be given a hideously ironic twist before the end of spring.

Because of the blanket of secrecy which had long clouded security questions from the public it is still not widely understood how matters came to take their tragic turn. The conception with which the Strategic Air Command had been developed was the key to all the happenings of that fateful spring.

We had always understood the dangers of a potential human failure if it should ever become necessary to send another bomber squadron manned by normal American boys on a mission of nuclear genocide. Every danger that they might for some reason become incapable of delivering their bombs on the selected targets had to be foreseen and counteracted or the whole policy of massive retaliation would stand for naught in the showdown it had to envision. For that reason extremely elaborate psychological tests and indoctrination methods had to be devised for selecting and training the crews to man our SAC bombers. The crew members had to be converted into almost the opposite of what we had always conceived of as "normal" American boys. They had to be made capable of fanatic devotion to their superiors, regardless of what spot *in the entire world* they might be ordered to bomb. Absolute and unquestioning obedience, though the order might seem cruel, inhuman, or even "unAmerican" by normal standards, had to be drilled into those crews. In this way they became inured against normal reactions to authority and the typical American feeling that any order should be explained to its executor. Since it was necessary to have crews in the air at all moments ready and able to deliver bombs on enemy targets, an unceasing indoctrination effort had to be a permanent feature of the lives of these dedicated crews, so that each day at the moment they rose into the air with their "pistols cocked" they were in effect demoniac anti-Communist janisaries, straining to unleash a patriotic cataclysm and fulfill the mission for which they had been created. It is necessary to keep in mind this feature of the recent past in order to appreciate the inevitability of the succession of events of the spring of 1959.

It was a pleasant April day—April is about the only civilized month in Washington's climate, and I had felt a pent-up spring exhilaration all day. I had taken the late lunch hour at the White

House mess, for that was the time those closest to the President usually ate. It was wise, I thought, to be seen by them often, and though never more than brief friendly nods were passed my way, it always made my blood run a little faster to be in the presence of these great ones who exuded power and who seemed to hold the destiny of the world in their hands. As White House Russian translator my position was strange. For months on end I was little more than a clerk, translating Russian documents or perhaps some of the passages the President might want especially included in a State Department communication to the Russians. However, at very rare intervals all this might change and I would get an emergency call to provide the President with a concurrent translation in a transatlantic telephone communication with Khrushchev. At these times, and for just a few hours afterward, I talked intimately with the mighty ones around the President. I was then of great importance to them, for until the transcriptions were ready I was the only one aside from the President who knew what had taken place.

I had not been back at my desk thirty minutes when the emergency call came through to proceed instantly to the President's office. The urgency of the command and the excitement with which I looked forward to these tasks led me to run down the stairs from my second floor East Wing office to the ground floor and then down the long corridor under the White House proper to the President's office in the West Wing. I remember now that everything seemed entirely normal. The relays of guards were at special alert, as they always are when the President is in the White House, but nothing unusual at any point prepared me for what was to come.

The President's secretary met me at the door to his office. "They are waiting below," she said, and led me to an elevator. So this was it. I had heard about the White House bomb shelter and now either a grisly drill was under way or I was going to experience the mixed blessing of finding out whether the President's bomb shelter would serve the purpose for which it was designed.

As the elevator came to a stop its automatic door opened onto a hall like that in any normal office building. I was led past a series of doors to the end of the corridor. The room we entered contained about fifteen men. Some were in clumps around the edges. At the far end the President sat at a desk, surrounded by five others. As I glanced around I recognized most of them as the great ones I had seen often at lunch. I remember that the atmosphere in the room was strangely subdued. It was as if everyone was straining so hard to keep down tension that the strength of their effort became quickly oppressive.

The President looked up as I approached. His face was calm but his eyes dominated everything. I'd always found those eyes disconcerting, but that day they seemed to have been drained of color.

The President's armor-piercing eyes rested on me briefly and then, glancing quickly about the room, he said: "Now I'd like for all the rest of you to leave for a little while."

Quietly the room emptied. Still the President remained silent. Finally he motioned me to a chair: "Sit here please by this extension telephone. I've got a little thinking to do before we get to work. Maybe it would help a little if I run over the situation once more out loud. We've all thought it out as far as we can and everyone comes to the same conclusion. But perhaps one more time would be helpful and in any case you should be briefed on what's coming off for otherwise you would almost certainly make a dangerous translation error at the crucial spot."

There was nothing for me to say. The President was obviously talking to himself—perhaps a little anxious to postpone action a while longer.

"The situation is as follows," he began. "Early this morning we received word that one of our SAC squadrons had not returned to its home base from a routine flight. An emergency search failed to turn it up. Finally about two hours after it was first missed the squadron itself opened radio communications with its base. It had waited until it had gotten far enough toward Moscow that our own planes could not intercept it in time to prevent its reaching the target. It then radioed back the code signal for an attack on Moscow.

"We cannot stop it. The staging of these SAC attacks is such that we are relatively certain the Russians have no equipment, either ground to air or air to air, capable of stopping it. We must assume that in just about four hours Moscow will be obliterated because one of our bomber crews decided to take it upon themselves to save the world from the Russian threat.

"What can we do? What would you do? We have spent two hours trying to figure every angle of the situation. We could throw in enough additional SAC units to put all Russia out of commission. What would Russia be likely to do in either case?

"We know that she has bomber groups like our own Strategic Air Command and that she could devastate the United States even if we delivered the full force of an attack throughout Russia. We might think that it would not be in her interest to retaliate, but what would her Communist leaders think? If we leave the bombing of Moscow as it is with this one mutinous squadron the Russians are almost certain to throw everything they have at us. If we levy everything we can against her, there is still a strong likelihood that she will retaliate with everything. As near as we can figure it the odds are not favorable in either case; not enough so as to defend *either* standing pat on this one berserk squadron, or adding everything we've got to it. The danger of our own obliteration is a little less great in one case than the other, but in both cases that real danger is real enough that our assured preservation requires a better strategy than either of these two."

It was absolutely unreal. I sat there quietly and politely listening to the President of the United States discuss the pros and cons of the nuclear obliteration of American and Soviet civilizations. He continued thinking out loud, for the moment oblivious to my presence—

"Now the situation would be somewhat different if it were possible to really convince the Russians that this is an accident. But how would you convince them of that? Suppose I were to call Khrushchev via transatlantic telephone and tell him of this accident through you on the extension phone beside you. He could then try to intercept the squadron. We have a strong conviction that this could not succeed.

"How would he react to the warning? Would he take it at face value for a mutinous accident? Even if he did, what difference would this make? Would he not feel required to inflict at least as great a damage on us? What would be a comparable loss for us? New York?

"But would he stop at New York? How could we be certain he would stop with New York, even if we make him believe it was an error? How could we do that, I ask you?"

With a start I realized that he really was asking me, peering at me intensely, leaning forward taut, now in his desk chair.

"How could we do that, I ask you! How could we convince the Russians that this is an accident and be confident of limiting their retaliation? That is the problem. Is there *any* strategy which will ensure it?"

There were literally no thoughts in my head. I prepared to make some lame response, but before I could it was clear he had forgotten about me again and was racing on with his thoughts.

"Suppose," he mused, "I were to set up a four-way telephone connection. Suppose I were to call Khrushchev, the American Embassy in Moscow and the Soviet Consulate in New York City. The American Embassy in Moscow would be necessary to report to me whether our squadron actually delivered their bombs. We would pray with them at our Moscow Embassy that it would not be their dying report, but it would be necessary for us to have the report in either case.

"With you continuing as translator I would then tell Khrushchev of the accident, describe for him my plan to convince him that it *is* an accident and that there is no reason for retaliatory action on his part.

"He could then retire to the Kremlin bomb shelter or get far enough from Moscow for safety and reopen telephonic communications with my four-way network. Then we would maintain constant contact, hoping that our squadron fails, but at least assured of limiting the mutual devastation—perhaps even providing a sure, though ghastly foundation for future peaceful relationships. . . ."

"But Mr. President!" I had half risen in bewilderment. "This doesn't make sense. You proved just before that we would *not* be sure of convincing him it was an accident, and that we could *not* be certain of limiting the counter attack!"

"Quite so," he replied gently, "because I have not yet told you of the plan we are about to describe to Mr. Khrushchev."

He looked at his watch for a moment and then resumed. "It is absolutely necessary that you make no mistake in translation, for now, the only place where an error might bring total American-Soviet devastation is in the translation. I must be certain of your ability to translate precisely the message I give you. That is why I have taken so much of the little valuable time remaining to go over this thoroughly with you."

"At two hours from now, under my personal order, a second SAC squadron will arrive over New York City. If our report from the American Embassy in Moscow tells us that they have been bombed, the squadron over New York will be immediately directed to devastate that city. Mr. Khrushchev will have instantaneous confirmation from his own Consulate speaking directly to him over our telephone network.

"Nothing short of this could prove to him our sincerity. Nothing short of this could insure our getting out of this mess with a minimum of two cities gone. Only this could convince him he has nothing to lose by waiting to see whether we go through with it because if we were to fail to take out New York ourselves, he could still give the orders for our total devastation.

"If the plan I have described is carried out precisely each country will lose her brightest jewel, but everything else will be saved. However this could not be assured short of our arranging it ourselves, since we caused the initial accident. Do you think you are up to it? If the plan goes according to this schedule, two stations in our telephonic network will drop off dead before we are through."

I looked up. The President's eyes were boring through me, trying to read my every reaction.

"I am ready, Mr. President, whenever you are," I said.

He turned and reached for his telephone.

Nightmare for Future Reference

STEPHEN VINCENT BENÉT

That was the second year of the Third World War,
The one between Us and Them.
                              Well, we've gotten used.
We don't talk much about it, queerly enough.
There was all sorts of talk the first years after the Peace,
A million theories, a million wild suppositions,
A million hopeful explanations and plans,
But we don't talk about it now. We don't even ask.
We might do the wrong thing. I don't guess you'd understand
    that.
But you're eighteen now. You can take it. You'd better know.

You see, you were born just before the war broke out.
Who started it? Oh, they said it was Us or Them
and it looked like it at the time. You don't know what's that's like.
But anyhow, it started and there it was,
Just a little worse, of course, than the one before,
But mankind was used to that. We didn't take notice.
They bombed our capital and we bombed theirs.
You've been to the Broken Towns? Yes, they take you there
They show you the look of the tormented earth.

But they can't show the smell or the gas or the death
Or how it felt to be there, and a part of it.
But we didn't know. I swear that we didn't know.
I remember the first faint hint there was something wrong
Something beyond all wars and bigger and strange,
Something you couldn't explain.
                                    I was back on leave—
Strange, as you felt on leave, as you always felt—
But I went to see the Chief at the hospital,
And there he was, in the same old laboratory,
A little older, with some white in his hair,
But the same eyes that went through you and the same tongue
They hadn't been able to touch him—not the bombs
Nor the ruin of his life's work nor anything.
He blinked at me from behind his spectacles
And said, "Huh. It's you. They won't let me have guinea pigs
Except for the war work, but I steal a few.
And they've made me a colonel—expect me to salute.
Damn fools. A damn-fool business. I don't know how.
Have you heard what Erickson's done with the ductless glands?
The journals are four months late. Sit down and smoke."
And I did and it was like home.
                                    He was a great man.
You might remember that—and I'd worked with him.
Well, finally he said to me, "How's your boy?

"Oh—healthy," I said. "We're lucky."
                                    "Yes," he said.
And a frown went over his face. "He might even grow up,
Though the intervals between wars are getting shorter.
I wonder if it wouldn't simplify things
To declare mankind in a permanent state of seige.
It might knock some sense in their heads."
                                    "You're cheerful," I said.
"Oh, I'm always cheerful," he said. "Seen these, by the way?"
He tapped some charts on a table.
                                    "Seen what?" I said.

"Oh," he said, with that devilish, sidelong grin of his,
"Just the normal city statistics—death and birth.
You're a soldier now. You wouldn't be interested.
But the birth rate's dropping."
                                    "Well, really, sir," I said,
"We know that it's always dropped, in every war."

"Not like this," he said. "I can show you the curve.
It looks like the side of a mountain, going down.
And faster, the last three months—yes, a good deal faster.
I showed it to Lobenheim and he was puzzled.
It makes a neat problem—yes?" He looked at me.

"They'd better make peace," he said. "They'd better make
      peace."

"Well, sir," I said, "if we break through, in the spring . . ."

"Break through?" he said. "What's that? They'd better make
      peace.
The stars may be tired of us. No, I'm not a mystic.
I leave that to the big scientists in bad novels.
But I never saw such a queer maternity curve.
I wish I could get to Ehrens, on their side.
He'd tell me the truth. But the fools won't let me do it."

His eyes looked tired as he stared at the careful charts.
"Suppose there are no more babies?" he said. "What then?
It's one way of solving the problem."
                                    "But, sir—"I said.
"But, sir!" he said. "Will you tell me, please, what is life?
Why it's given, why it's taken away?
Oh, I know—we make a jelly inside a test tube,
We keep a cock's heart living inside a jar.
We know a great many things, and what do we know?
We think we know what finished the dinosaurs,
But do we? Maybe they were given a chance
And then it was taken back. There are other beasts
That only kill for their food. No, I'm not a mystic,

But there's a certain pattern in nature, you know,
And we're upsetting it daily. Eat and mate
And go back to the earth after that, and that's all right.
But now we're blasting and sickening earth itself.
She's been very patient with us. I wonder how long."

Well, I thought the Chief had gone crazy, just at first,
And then I remembered the look of no man's land,
That bitter landscape, pockmarked like the moon,
Lifeless as the moon's face and horrible,
The thing we'd made with the guns.
                              If it were earth,
It looked as though it hated.
                        "Well?" I said,
And my voice was a little thin. He looked hard at me.
"Oh—ask the women," he grunted. "Don't ask me.
Ask them what they think about it."
                              I didn't ask them,
Not even your mother—she was strange, those days—
But, two weeks later, I was back in the lines
And somebody sent me a paper—
Encouragement for the troops and all of that—
All about the fall of Their birth rate on Their side.

I guess you know now. There was still a day when we fought,
And the next day the women knew. I don't know how they knew,
But they smashed every government in the world
Like a heap of broken china, within two days,
And we'd stopped firing by then. And we looked at each other.

We didn't talk much, those first weeks. You couldn't talk.
We started in rebuilding and that was all,
And at first nobody would even touch the guns,
Not even to melt them up. They just stood there, silent,
Pointing the way they had and nobody there.
And there was a kind of madness in the air,
A quiet, bewildered madness, strange and shy.
You'd pass a man who was muttering to himself

And you'd know what he was muttering, and why.
I remember coming home and your mother there.
She looked at me, at first didn't speak at all,
And then she said, "Burn those clothes. Take them off and burn
        them
Or I'll never touch you or speak to you again."
And then I knew I was still in my uniform.

Well, I've told you now. They tell you now at eighteen.
There's no use telling before.
                            Do you understand?
That's why we have the Ritual of the Earth,
The Day of Sorrow, the other ceremonies.
Oh, yes, at first people hated the animals
Because they still bred, but we've gotten over that.
Perhaps they can work it better, when it's their turn,
If it's their turn—I don't know. I don't know at all.
You can call it a virus, of course, if you like the word,
But we haven't been able to find it. Not yet. No.
It isn't as if it had happened all at once.
There were a few children born in the last six months
Before the end of the war, so there's still some hope.
But they're almost grown. That's the trouble. They're almost
        grown.

Well, we had a long run. That's something. At first they thought
There might be a nation somewhere—a savage tribe.
But we were all in it, even the Eskimos,
And we keep the toys in the stores, and the colored books,
And people marry and plan and the rest of it,
But, you see, there aren't any children. They aren't born.

                                                [1938]

On the Beach

NEVIL SHUTE

THEY HAD LEFT PORT DARWIN AS THEY HAD LEFT CAIRNS AND PORT
MORESBY; THEY HAD GONE BACK THROUGH THE TORRES STRAIT AND
HEADED SOUTHWARD DOWN THE QUEENSLAND COAST, SUBMERGED. By
that time the strain of the cruise was telling on them; they talked
little among themselves till they surfaced three days after leaving Darwin. Refreshed by a spell on deck, they now had time
to think about what story they could tell about their cruise when
they got back to Melbourne.

They talked of it after lunch, smoking at the ward-room table.
"It's what *Swordfish* found, of course," Dwight said. "She saw
practically nothing either in the States or in Europe."

Peter reached out for the well-thumbed report that lay behind
him on the cupboard top. He leafed it through again, though it
had been his constant reading on the cruise. "I never thought of
that," he said slowly. "I missed that angle on it, but now that
you mention it, it's true. There's practically nothing here about
conditions on shore."

"They couldn't look on shore, any more than we could," the
captain said. "Nobody will ever really know what a hot place
looks like. And that goes for the whole of the Northern Hemisphere."

Peter said, "That's probably as well."

"I think that's right," said the commander. "There's some
things that a person shouldn't want to go and see."

John Osborne said, "I was thinking about that last night. Did it ever strike you that nobody will ever—*ever*—see Cairns again? Or Moresby, or Darwin?"

They stared at him while they turned over the new idea. "Nobody could see more than we've seen," the captain said.

"Who else can go there, except us? And we shan't go again. Not in the time. "

"That's so," Dwight said thoughtfully. "I wouldn't think they'd send us back there again. I never thought of it that way, but I'd say you're right. We're the last living people that will ever see those places." He paused. "And we saw practically nothing. Well, I think that's right."

Peter stirred uneasily. "That's historical," he said. "It ought to go on record somewhere, oughtn't it? Is anybody writing any kind of history about these times?"

John Osborne said, "I haven't heard of one. I'll find out about that. After all, there doesn't seem to be much point in writing stuff that nobody will read."

"There should be something written, all the same," said the American. "Even if it's only going to be read in the next few months." He paused. "I'd like to read a history of this last war," he said. "I was in it for a little while, but I don't know a thing about it. Hasn't anybody written anything?"

"Not as history," John Osborne said. "Not that I know of, anyway. The information that we've got is all available, of course, but not as a coherent story. I think there'd be too many gaps— the things we just don't know."

"I'd settle for the things we *do* know," the captain remarked.

"What sort of things, sir?"

"Well, as a start, how many bombs were dropped? Nuclear bombs, I mean."

"The seismic records show about four thousand seven hundred. Some of the records were pretty weak, so there were probably more than that."

"How many of those were big one—fusion bombs, hydrogen bombs, or whatever you call them?"

"I couldn't tell you. Probably most of them. All the bombs

dropped in the Russian-Chinese war were hydrogen bombs, I think—most of them with a cobalt element."

"Why did they do that? Use cobalt, I mean?" Peter asked.

The scientist shrugged his shoulders. "Radiological warfare. I can't tell you any more than that."

"I think I can," said the American. "I attended a commanding officers' course at Yerba Buena, San Francisco, the month before the war. They told us what they thought might happen between Russia and China. Whether they told us what *did* happen six weeks later—well, your guess is as good as mine."

John Osborne asked quietly, "What did they tell you?"

The captain considered for a minute. Then he said, "It was all tied up with the warm water ports. Russia hasn't got a port that doesn't freeze up in the winter except Odessa, and that's on the Black Sea. To get out of Odessa on to the high seas the traffic has to pass two narrow straits both commanded by NATO in time of war—the Bosporus and Gibraltar. Murmansk and Vladivostok can be kept open by icebreakers in the winter, but they're a mighty long way from any place in Russia that makes things to export." He paused. "This guy from Intelligence said that what Russia really wanted was Shanghai."

The scientist asked, "Is that handy for their Siberian industries?"

The captain nodded. "That's exactly it. During the Second War they moved a great many industries way back along the Trans-Siberian railway east of the Urals, back as far as Lake Baikal. They built new towns and everything. Well, it's a long, long way from those places to a port like Odessa. It's only about half the distance to Shanghai."

He paused. "There was another thing he told us," he said thoughtfully. "China had three times the population of Russia, all desperately overcrowded in their country. Russia, next door to the north of them, had millions and millions of square miles of land she didn't use at all because she didn't have the people to populate it. This guy said that as the Chinese industries increased over the last twenty years, Russia got to be afraid of an attack by China. She'd have been a great deal happier if there had been two hundred million fewer Chinese, and she wanted Shanghai. And that adds up to radiological warfare. . . ."

Peter said, "But using cobalt, she couldn't follow up and take Shanghai."

"That's true. But she could make North China uninhabitable for quite a number of years by spacing the bombs right. If they put them down in the right places the fall-out would cover China to the sea. Any left over would go around the world eastwards across the Pacific; if a little got to the United States I don't suppose the Russians would have wept salt tears. If they planned it right, there would be very little left when it got around the world again to Europe and to western Russia. Certainly she couldn't follow up and take Shanghai for quite a number of years, but she'd get it in the end."

Peter turned to the scientist. "How long would it be before people could work in Shanghai?"

"With cobalt fall-out? I wouldn't even guess. It depends on so many things. You'd have to send in exploratory teams. More than five years, I should think—that's the half-life. Less than twenty. But you just can't say."

Dwight nodded. "By the time anyone could get there, Chinese or anyone else, they'd find the Russians there already."

John Osborne turned to him. "What did the Chinese think about all this?"

"Oh, they had another angle altogether. They didn't specially want to kill Russians. What they wanted to do was to turn the Russians back into an agricultural people that wouldn't want Shanghai or any other port. The Chinese aimed to blanket the Russian industrial regions with a cobalt fall-out, city by city, put there with their inter-continental rockets. What they wanted was to stop any Russian from using a machine tool for the next ten years or so. They planned a limited fall-out of heavy particles, not going very far around the world. They probably didn't plan to hit the city, even—just to burst maybe ten miles west of it, and let the wind do the rest." He paused. "With no Russian industry left, the Chinese could have walked in any time they liked and occupied the safe parts of the country, any that they fancied. Then, as the radiation eased, they'd occupy the towns."

"Find the lathes a bit rusty," Peter said.

"I'd say they might be. But they'd have had an easy war."

John Osborne asked, "Do you think that's what happened?"

"I wouldn't know," said the American. "Maybe no one knows. That's just what this officer from the Pentagon told us at the commanding officers' course." He paused. "One thing was in Russia's favour," he said thoughtfully. "China hadn't any friends or allies, except Russia. When Russia went for China, nobody else would make much trouble—start war on another front, or anything like that."

They sat smoking in silence for a few minutes. "You think that's what flared up finally?" Peter said at last. "I mean, after the original attacks the Russians made on Washington and London?"

John Osborne and the captain stared at him. "The Russians never_bombed Washington," Dwight said. "They proved that in the end."

He stared back at them. "I mean, the very first attack of all."

"That's right. The very first attack. They were Russian long-range bombers, II 626's, but they were Egyptian manned. They flew from Cairo."

"Are you sure that's true?"

"It's true enough. They got the one that landed at Puerto Rico on the way home. They only found out it was Egyptian after we'd bombed Leningrad and Odessa and the nuclear establishments at Kharkov, Kuibyshev, and Molotov. Things must have happened kind of quick that day."

"Do you mean to say, we bombed Russia by mistake?" It was so horrible a thought as to be incredible.

John Osborne said, "That's true, Peter. It's never been admitted publicly, but it's quite true. The first one was the bomb on Naples. That was the Albanians, of course. Then there was the bomb on Tel Aviv. Nobody knows who dropped that one, not that I've heard, anyway. Then the British and Americans intervened and made that demonstration flight over Cairo. Next day the Egyptians sent out all the serviceable bombers that they'd got, six to Washington and seven to London. One got through to

Washington, and two to London. After that there weren't many American or British statesmen left alive."

Dwight nodded. "The bombers were Russian, and I've heard it said that they had Russian markings. It's quite possible."

"Good God!" said the Australian. "So we bombed Russia?"

"That's what happened," said the captain heavily.

John Osborne said, "It's understandable. London and Washington were out—right out. Decisions had to be made by the military commanders at dispersal in the field, and they had to be made quick before another lot of bombs arrived. Things were very strained with Russia, after the Albanian bomb, and these aircraft were identified as Russian." He paused. "Somebody had to make a decision, of course, and make it in a matter of minutes. Up at Canberra they think now that he made it wrong."

"But if it was a mistake, why didn't they get together and stop it? Why did they go on?"

The captain said, "It's mighty difficult to stop a war when all the statesmen have been killed."

The scientist said, "The trouble is, the damn things got too cheap. The original uranium bomb only cost about fifty thousand quid towards the end. Every little pipsqueak country like Albania could have a stockpile of them, and every little country that had that, thought it could defeat the major countries in a surprise attack. That was the real trouble."

"Another was the aeroplanes," the captain said. "The Russians had been giving the Egyptians aeroplanes for years. So had Britain for that matter, and to Israel, and to Jordan. The big mistake was ever to have given them a long-range aeroplane."

Peter said quietly, "Well, after that the war was on between Russia and the Western powers. When did China come in?"

The captain said, "I don't think anybody knows exactly. But I'd say that probably China came in right there with her rockets and her radiological warfare against Russia, taking advantage of the opportunity. Probably they didn't know how ready Russia was with radiological warfare against China." He paused. "But that's all surmise," he said. "Most of the communications went out pretty soon, and what were left didn't have much time to talk to us down here, or to South Africa. All we know is that the command came down to quite junior officers, in most countries."

John Osborne smiled wryly. "Major Chan Sze Lin."

Peter asked, "What *was* Chan Sze Lin, anyway?"

The scientist said, "I don't think anybody really knows, except that he was an officer in the Chinese Air Force, and towards the end he seems to have been in command. The Prime Minister was in touch with him, trying to intervene to stop it all. He seems to have had a lot of rockets in various parts of China, and a lot of bombs to drop. His opposite number in Russia may have been someone equally insignificant. But I don't think the Prime Minister ever succeeded in making contact with the Russians. I never heard a name, anyway."

There was a pause. "It must have been a difficult situation," Dwight said at last. "I mean, what could the guy do? He had a war on his hands and plenty of weapons left to fight it with. I'd say it was the same in all the countries, after the statesmen got killed. It makes a war very difficult to stop."

"It certainly made this one. It just didn't stop, till all the bombs were gone and all the aircraft were unserviceable. And by that time, of course, they'd gone too far."

"Christ," said the American softly, "I don't know what I'd have done in their shoes. I'm glad I wasn't."

The scientist said, "I should think you'd have tried to negotiate."

"With an enemy knocking hell out of the United States and killing all our people? When I still had weapons in my hands? Just stop fighting and give in? I'd like to think that I was so high-minded but—well, I don't know." He raised his head. "I was never trained for diplomacy," he said. "If that situation had devolved on me, I wouldn't have known how to handle it."

"They didn't, either," said the scientist. He stretched himself, and yawned. "Just too bad. But don't go blaming the Russians. It wasn't the big countries that set off this thing. It was the little ones, the irresponsibles."

Peter Holmes grinned, and said, "It's a bit hard on all the rest of us."

"You've got six months more," remarked John Osborne. "Plus or minus something. Be satisfied with that. You've always known that you were going to die sometimes. Well, now you know when. That's all." He laughed. "Just make the most of what you've got left."

"I know that," said Peter. "The trouble is I can't think of anything that I want to do more than what I'm doing now."

"Cooped up in bloody *Scorpion*?"

"Well—yes. It's our job. I really meant, at home."

"No imagination. You want to turn Mohammedan and start a harem."

The submarine commander laughed. "Maybe he's got something there."

The liaison officer shook his head. "It's a nice idea, but it wouldn't be practical. Mary wouldn't like it." He stopped smiling. "The trouble is, I can't really believe it's going to happen. Can you?"

"Not after what you've seen?"

Peter shook his head. "No. If we'd seen any *damage* . . ."

"No imagination whatsoever," remarked the scientist. "It's the same with all you service people. That can't happen to *me*." He paused. "But it can. And it certainly will."

"I suppose I haven't got any imagination," said Peter thoughtfully. "It's—it's the end of the world. I've never had to imagine anything like that before."

John Osborne laughed. "It's not the end of the world at all," he said. "It's only the end of us. The world will go on just the same, only we shan't be in it. I dare say it will get along all right without us."

Dwight Towers raised his head. "I suppose that's right. There didn't seem to be much wrong with Cairns, or Port Moresby either." He paused, thinking of the flowering trees that he had seen on shore through the periscope, cascaras the flame trees, the palms standing in the sunlight. "Maybe we've been too silly to deserve a world like this," he said.

The scientist said, "That's absolutely and precisely right."

There didn't seem to be much more to say upon that subject, so they went up on to the bridge for a smoke, in the sunlight and fresh air.

Off the Beach

EDWARD TELLER and ALLEN BROWN

* * *

NEVIL SHUTE'S BOOK IS A PROPHECY. Some prophecies are misleading. They may come true, but not in the way that is expected. *On the Beach* may be correct in prophesying an end, but it will not be the end of the human race. It may be the end of our Western civilization, of our society with its ideals of human dignity and freedom.

Humans are tough and ingenious. The race certainly will survive. Our age of science and of scientific miracles is not headed for extinction. In our world, which is such a strange combination of the real and the fantastic, this one fact should stand out clearly: Man is here to stay.

It is repulsive to make calculations about millions of human deaths, but to conjure up nightmares about a radioactive doomsday is certainly worse. These nightmares have little to do with reality. If some maniac wanted to put enough radioactivity into the atmosphere to endanger all human life, he would have to explode the equivalent of at least 1000 tons of our present bombs for each and every human being on the earth. He would have to explode a bomb of more than Hiroshima strength on each square mile of the globe. This would not be impossible, but it would be exceedingly difficult and it would serve no military purpose. The aim of even the most savage wars is not completely indiscriminate and total destruction. What man, what organization, what nation would carry out a gigantic plan which has for its aim not defense, not victory, not power, but universal suicide?

From *The Legacy of Hiroshima*. Copyright © 1962 by Edward Teller and Allen Brown. Reprinted by permission of the authors and Doubleday & Company, Inc.

We can safely ignore the modern heralds of the Apocalypse. But we cannot disregard the possibilities of war. Even though we can forget about a Doomsday War, we cannot discount the possibility of a nuclear war. We should realize, however, that even if the attempt were made during such a war to kill all people, the human race would not be wiped out. Some would have a place to hide, because there is a defense against nuclear bombs: shelters. Civilian defense methods can help people survive nuclear wars of almost any scale. The biggest nuclear conflict would be a catastrophe beyond imagination. But it will not be the end.

From the Cradle to the Cave

HARRISON BROWN and JAMES REAL

IF THE ARMS RACE CONTINUES, AS IT PROBABLY WILL, ITS FUTURE PATTERN SEEMS CLEAR IN BROAD OUTLINE. As a result of the emergence of the current tremendous capabilities for killing and destroying, programs will be started aimed at the evacuation of cities, the construction of fallout shelters in regions outside the major metropolitan areas, and the construction of limited underground shelters. Increased offensive capabilities will then emerge which will to some extent neutralize these efforts. Larger bombs will be compressed into sufficiently small packages to be carried by ICBM's. Very large bombs (about 1,000 megatons) will be built which, when exploded at an altitude of about 300 miles, could sear six Western states.

The new developments will cause people to burrow more

From *Community of Fear,* a pamphlet published by the Center for the Study of Democratic Institutions, Santa Barbara, California, copyright 1960. Reprinted by permission.

deeply into the ground. Factories will be built in caves, as will apartment houses and stores. Eventually most human life will be underground, confronted by arsenals capable of destroying all life over the land areas of the earth. Deep under the ground people will be relatively safe—at least until such time as we learn how to make explosives capable of pulverizing the earth to great depths.

The arms race and the associated uprooting of established institutions will outstrip by far the spiral of upheaval described by Wang Chi during the War which preceded the T'ang dynasty:

> These days, continually fuddled with drink
> I fail to satisfy the appetites of the soul.
> But seeing men all behaving like drunkards,
> How can I alone remain sober?

The Soviet Union has apparently, in the last few years, instituted a civilian defense program of substantial magnitude. It is probable that within the next two or three years the United States will embark on a crash shelter program for a large proportion of its citizens and some of its industry. Once the shelter program is underway, it will constitute a significant retreat from the idea of the obsolescence of war.

Once the people are convinced that they can survive the present state of the art of killing, a broad and significant new habit pattern will have been introduced and accepted, one grotesquely different from any we have known for thousands of years—that of adjusting ourselves to the idea of living in holes. From that time onward it will be simple to adjust ourselves to living in *deeper* holes.

Tens of thousands of years ago our Mousterian and Aurignacian ancestors lived in caves. The vast knowledge which we have accumulated during the intervening millennia will have brought us full cycle. The epic of man's journey upward into the light will have ended.

The Future of Mankind

KARL JASPERS

Atomic doom is not a necessary process that comes over us and has to be accepted. Every step depends on men who take it on the road to disaster: the discovery of natural phenonmena as well as their translation into technology, the order to make the bombs as well as the order to drop them and its execution. We must recognize the difference between man's work, which is up to us, and the work of nature, which we can master only to a degree. We must not fail in what is up to us, by submitting to fate from the outset. To fulfil the obligation of our freedom, we must not renounce it by a premature surrender.

Our great "successes"—triumphantly achieved, jubilantly enjoyed, and blind to the consequences—have plunged us into the great guilt of being content with them as sources of material power. But to know this, and to say so, is not enough, either. No amount of realism and disclosure, no perception or expectation or hope will help if man himself does not come to a decision.

The task of our thinking is to visualize the crucial situation. It should illuminate whatever evasions obscure it. But the decision itself should also be thought through: what it consists in and what the results can be. Such thinking is not yet the act itself, but it may be preparatory to inner action.

But, some will object, what fantastic expectations! Think of the reality of armaments! Are these huge efforts, consuming half the labor of the nations, to have been "in vain"? Are their products never to be used? Surely this whole vast output of energy rests on a serious purpose to resort to these weapons.

And yet—if at first only under the growing stress of the fear that grips all men in view of its reality—this very purpose may change direction. From the possession of the most destructive weapons ever known, on the ground of a boundless courage of sacrifice, of daring destruction by these weapons, there may arise a high resolve to discard them and mutually to give peace to mankind. It would mean that the courage of sacrifice itself had turned into a will to make sacrifices—not only to let such enormous works vanish unused but to submit to a transformation of life as a whole, with all the renunciations this involves, but also with new vistas of immeasurable possibilities.

No one can say that man is up to such a transformation. But we may remember our guideposts, both in Asia and in the West, and we may hope that man might be as such vistas would presuppose. There is no other way out, and to call the step impossible is to pronounce a death sentence upon mankind, to be carried out within the next hundred years.

The political condition, the rational ethos, in which abolition of the atom bomb would be possible requires all political decisions to be examined and ranked as to importance in the light of the extremity of doom. This extremity must not be obscured for one moment. It should help us prevent selfish, indolent, and wishful obfuscation. Even seemingly trivial decisions are to be weighed in the balance of extremity. The freedom that brings reason to the fore in politics is true and real only if it stands the test in all stages and in all spheres of human activity.

There is a radical difference between particular problems and a change in man. The former can be solved in the annex of the planning human intellect, leaving man himself untouched. The latter demands the commitment of all of man. The change cannot be sought as a purpose. It cannot be planned; the very act of planning would, in our situation, be a choice of the road to perdition. Something else is needed, coming—or failing to come— from the depths of the free human person, from the resolve in which he finds himself changed to a new kind of preparedness that will let him plan but cannot be planned itself.

We hear the objection that a change in man, who is always an individual, is not a change in politics at large. Great powers that have no common ground as forms of political life, not even in language, are facing each other in the present state of the world with the irreconcilability of mutually exclusive faiths. Even if a change occurred in the politics of one circle, it would still be impossible in the world as a whole; because the others are always there too, and vastly powerful, we cannot do without the old kind of politics that gets its bearings from force as a last resort. The reform of politics, this argument concludes, has always been an infinite and hence insoluble task; there are no visible indications that the pressure of the new total danger will compel a solution.

We can only answer that if a change in politics should come, it would not come by any objective sociopolitical process. It would come if the individuals were changed. What will happen to mankind depends on the individuals who will be standing at the helm in crucial moments. In the final analysis it depends on all the individuals; what goes on between them, between any two or more, lays the foundations of political realities to come.

The realist who has raised those objections may reply that political guidance cannot be expected from the individuals. In the vastness of human history, the individual sees himself as an infinitesimally minute atom; history at large is bound to strike him as a natural process that he cannot influence and must simply accept as it passes over him.

Against this, we should keep reminding ourselves that history at large is still the result of action by innumerable individuals. From the outset, there are individuals. In everything he does, the individual shares the responsibility for the whole. He has some power, however little, for he has a hand in events by acting—in his domain. By every small act of commission or omission he helps to prepare the ground on which other individuals, in the seats of power, will take the actions that will be decisive for the whole. What is done is done by human beings, and human beings always are individuals. Even when they act in groups, in nations, in masses, their every action is that of individuals— however much they may feel like tools of superior powers or of a common will. The suprapolitical element resides in man himself, because it is a matter of his freedom.

There is a blight on the roots of man. A glance at history shows him struggling upward only to relapse; most of his high points were paid for in the cruelty and misery that made them possible. But the blight on the roots lies in every individual. We experience it in ourselves, as the "radical evil" that overpowers us if we do not fight it constantly and freely. Fundamentally, salvation and damnation both proceed from freedom.

The hardest task to be performed anew by every individual— a task which no man can shift to another, which none can do for another—has always been to come to himself in extremity, to be changed, and then to be guided in life by the impulses springing from the change. At first, the fact of the bomb can shock only individuals into a reflection radical enough to make them live henceforth in an earnestness commensurate with the two present tasks of mankind: salvation from total rule and salvation from total destruction. And nothing short of this earnestness is adequate to our eternal task of growing truly human.

How do we stand today? The individual as such has always been a rarity; does he not now seem all but nonexistent? Is it not an enormous illusion to keep hoping for the individual? Have we not long reached the stage of collective leveling—conformist in America, totalitarian in Russia, technological and functional wherever there is industry and bureaucracy? Have we not long forgotten what it is for man to be himself, to think and live freely, and to realize himself in his world? Has all this not long been said, forecast, and observed? Is it not laughable to try opposing the steam roller of history with things that are gone forever, like selfhood and reason?

No knowledge, no experience, can compel affirmative answers to these questions. They fall upon a willing soil of despair, yet against their persuasive magnetism stands the will to keep the road open where it is not blocked by truly compelling knowledge.

Today, because of the technological situation, the blight on the roots of humanity must lead to total extinction unless extremity induces man to change—freely, but with an "assist from above" that can be neither calculated nor experienced nor expected, that can only be hoped for if we really do our best, if a supreme tension in our innermost being lets us hear and practice what our best can be.

What the individual—and it will always be up to individuals—will do when he holds the engines of destruction in his hand, when he is to give or to carry out orders for their use, depends on himself. Whether and how the engines will be used depends upon the outcome of his inner actions in the course of his life. The process is the same throughout technology: its use is determined by what man becomes when he is himself. The salutary use of technology does not come from continued technological thinking but from a different source.

Outward Bound

FREDERICK L. SCHUMAN

POWER POLITICS IS APPROACHING ITS TWILIGHT. The Great Neighborhood, already made one by scientists and engineers, will find rulers to give it unity and will move forward to a new millennium. This transition is as "inevitable" as any change in human affairs can be. For the alternative to union is the wrecking of the World Society and the descent of modern Man into an endless nightmare of savagery. Man still has a will to live. He will choose the way which offers hope of life.

The human denizens of the turning earth, warmed by a flaming star a hundred million miles away and fed by the lesser forms of life which flourish on the flowering planet, face a change that comes but once in the cycle of every culture. Of the distant origins of this, and of the other man-made mansions of men, little enough is known. Of ultimate destinations no man can speak. From its remote birth out of the loins of ape-like ancestors half a million years ago, and from the dim emergence of literate cultures some ten thousand years in the past, the species moves on toward unseen goals hidden in the dawns and dusks of countless days to come. But the social artifacts of men move now and then through streams of change which lie in charted waters between ports which are clearly seen. And from time to time in mid-passage comes an hour unlike all before when the vessel escapes the fury of storm and strife and enters calm seas between the sunset and the quiet night. Such an hour now draws near for the weary voyagers of our time.

The change that looms ahead is a change from an age of violence and an epoch of warring States to a time of peace under a government of all mankind. Such was the change which came under the law and the legions of Rome to the Mediterranean peoples two thousand years ago. Such is the change now overdue for the peoples of the 20th century, already united in a common civilization and waiting to be united under a government of all the planet. Embattled freemen will win mastery of tomorrow if they will but undertake this task. If they will not, they will fail and fall and yield the future to the hosts of the Caesars. The task of union is reserved for those who see its need and who act courageously to bring the gift of ordered peace to men. Let those most worthy take the helm.